The Rise of Liberal Religion

The Rise of Liberal Religion

Book Culture and American Spirituality in the Twentieth Century

MATTHEW S. HEDSTROM

OXFORD
UNIVERSITY PRESS

OXFORD
UNIVERSITY PRESS

Oxford University Press is a department of the University of Oxford.
It furthers the University's objective of excellence in research,
scholarship, and education by publishing worldwide.

Oxford   New York
Auckland   Cape Town   Dar es Salaam   Hong Kong   Karachi
Kuala Lumpur   Madrid   Melbourne   Mexico City   Nairobi
New Delhi   Shanghai   Taipei   Toronto

With offices in
Argentina   Austria   Brazil   Chile   Czech Republic   France   Greece
Guatemala   Hungary   Italy   Japan   Poland   Portugal   Singapore
South Korea   Switzerland   Thailand   Turkey   Ukraine   Vietnam

Oxford is a registered trademark of Oxford University Press
Press in the UK and certain other countries.

Published in the United States of America by
Oxford University Press
198 Madison Avenue, New York, NY 10016

Hedstrom, Matthew S.
The rise of liberal religion : book culture and American spirituality
in the twentieth century / Matthew S. Hedstrom.
p.   cm.
Includes bibliographical references and index.
ISBN 978-0-19-537449-0 (hardcover); 978-0-19-023123-1 (paperback)
1. United States—Religion—History—20th century.
2. Liberalism (Religion)—United States—History—20th century.
3. Religious literature, American—Publishing—History—20th century.   I. Title.
BL2525.H443 2013   200.973'0904—dc23
2012004647

Each age, it is found, must write its own books; or rather, each generation for the next succeeding. The books of an older period will not fit this.

      —Ralph Waldo Emerson, "The American Scholar," 1837

I am reaching a stage where repeating thoughts from books feels like plagiarism, or even hypocrisy. I need to have LIVED it before I want to say it.

      —Frank C. Laubach, letter, 1930

If it were not for the magic of books, we would be infinitely more limited personalities than we are now.

      —Joshua Loth Liebman, "My Three Favorite Books of the Year," 1946

Have you ever considered what a sacred thing a book is? Have you ever considered what a sacred trust is ours who deal intimately with the circulation of books? Is there one of us but knows of the change made in the life of another because of a good book placed in his ready hands?

      —Eugene Exman, "Summary of Proceedings: Ninth Annual Conference, American Theological Library Association," 1955

For Sarah

CONTENTS

The Rise of Liberal Religion

Introduction

In 1904 the Quaker mystic and philosopher Rufus Jones published *Social Law in the Spiritual World* with a grand ambition. "The cure for skepticism," Jones declared at the outset, "is always deeper knowledge," and with this book he sought to bring deeper knowledge to a new generation of modern skeptics.[1] Like many intellectuals of his day, Jones knew firsthand the struggle of the modern believer, as he had grappled first with Darwinian evolution and then with the even more unsettling theories of modern psychology. "There are few crises to compare," he noted, based on this experience, "with that which appears when the simple, childhood religion, imbibed at mother's knee and absorbed from early home and church environment, comes into collision with a scientific, solidly reasoned system."[2] Yet Jones had emerged from this collision of ideas with a deep sense of divine presence intact. *The Varieties of Religious Experience*, the landmark study from the Harvard psychologist and philosopher William James published two years earlier, had greatly excited Jones—it too had been the product of a profound spiritual crisis engendered by modern thought—yet Jones found James's work too intellectual to inspire or comfort ordinary Americans. He wrote *Social Law* to meet this need. "The trouble with many of the best works on these themes," Jones declared, "is that they are too learned and technical to help the wayfaring man who wants to get the newer insight and who yet cannot find any way to get into the onward moving current. This present book is an attempt to help such persons."[3]

Social Law was both a skillful reinterpretation of James by a practicing mystic and a bridge between James and the popular inspirational writers of the twentieth century. The great preacher and author Harry Emerson Fosdick, for example, later wrote that Jones's *Social Law in the Spiritual World* "opened the door to a new era in my thought and life.... Much of my message has been rooted in the rich soil which that book provided."[4] As Fosdick recognized, Jones's work brilliantly incorporated Jamesian psychology into a living religious system. It stands as an influential first attempt to make the pragmatic openness of James's thought religiously relevant and accessible. Though *Social Law* never reached a wide audience, its grand religious project succeeded better than Rufus Jones could ever have imagined. The liberal approaches to religion found in James and Jones—intellectually engaged, psychologically oriented, and focused on personal experience—characterized large swaths of middle-class spiritual life by the middle of the twentieth century.

In the pages that follow, I argue that this popularization of religious liberalism happened largely in and through books. Jones's understanding in *Social Law* that modern religion required modern books in order to reach "the wayfaring man" was prescient: books and book culture were integral to the rise of liberal religion in the twentieth century. In order to succeed at all, the liberal project of renovating religion in light of modern knowledge had to succeed in the marketplace of print. And, by and large, it did. In the centuries since the Protestant Reformation and the invention of moveable type, print culture and religious culture had grown increasingly intertwined at the popular level. Only in the nineteenth and twentieth centuries, however, did the economic, cultural, social, and religious forces align to make the consumption of mass-market books a part of everyday American spiritual practice. When Jones wrote *Social Law*, he could only begin to glimpse the swirl of religious and commercial interests that would continue to shape this religious and reading revolution in the twentieth century. This book tells that story.

To be clear, what follows is not a work of cultural or theological criticism, but rather a history of popular religion and spirituality. My intention is to identify, describe, and account for significant religious and cultural developments and chart their change over time. In fact an argument (mostly implicit) in what follows is that the theological and cultural commitments of scholars have too often limited their ability to see significant developments in American popular religion, including the spread of liberal religious sensibilities through middlebrow culture as described here. As the sociologist Eva Illouz writes, "A critique of culture cannot be adequately waged before we understand the mechanism of culture: how meanings are produced, how they are woven into the social fabric...and why they come to organize our interpretation of the self and others."[5] This study aims to further our understanding of the mechanisms of popular religion and spirituality in modern America. Though my own leanings undoubtedly color my account in many ways, my aim first and foremost is to document and understand, not critique.

After this introduction, which outlines critical background in the nineteenth century and early twentieth, the ensuing chapters focus on the decades after World War I, when a modernizing book business and a modernizing religious liberalism together facilitated wider spiritual horizons for a great many middle-class Americans. This book tracks those developments through the 1920s, 1930s, and 1940s, pivotal yet underappreciated decades in American religious history. Most important, these decades witnessed the full flowering of American consumer culture, and through it the increasing integration of American religion and the print marketplace. Scholars often speak of American religious life in terms of a "spiritual marketplace," yet the metaphorical marketplace of "seekers" and "church shoppers" rests on the foundation of a very real consumer marketplace.[6] In material ways that go beyond adherence to broad cultural norms, participation in religious and spiritual life *happens* through commodities bought and sold, and for much of the twentieth century the most significant of these religious commodities was the book.

Historians and social critics have long understood media and the consumer marketplace to be defining aspects of modern American culture. Yet my argument about the powerful and enduring cultural influence of religious liberalism may elicit a bit more surprise. After all, for decades now the dominant story in American religion has been the cultural and political mobilization of religious conservatives. The Protestant mainline and the various other institutional forms of religious liberalism garner much less attention, and the attention they do receive generally highlights decline and dysfunction. To some degree the media have rediscovered the Religious Left as a political force in recent years, yet the broad cultural significance of liberal religion in the twentieth century is still poorly understood.[7] Nevertheless liberals coordinated massive, nationwide cultural programs during much of the twentieth century—especially reading programs—that exerted significant religious influence. While many liberal churches and denominations are indeed in significant demographic decline from their midcentury heyday, my examination of religious reading and publishing programs not only demonstrates the powerful cultural force of liberalism in the mid-twentieth century, but also suggests new ways of seeing the cultural imprint of liberal religion in our own times. As the sociologist Christian Smith (echoing Jay Demerath) has observed, "Liberal Protestantism's organizational decline has been accompanied by and is in part arguably the consequence of the fact that liberal Protestantism has won a decisive, larger cultural victory."[8] The legacy of Jones and James lives on in deeply significant ways, and an examination of religion and book culture in the mid-twentieth century helps us see how and why.

Despite this significant insight about the "cultural victory" of liberal Protestantism, scholarly work on religious liberalism has tended to focus, often exclusively, on Protestant churches and seminaries. Generations of scholars have exhaustively chronicled the intellectual history of Protestant liberalism— its Enlightenment roots; its romantic flowering in the transcendental movement; its embrace of history, Darwinian biology, and psychology; its postmillennial faith in progress and human nature; its Social Gospel activism—while failing to see that over the course of the nineteenth and twentieth centuries liberalism's seeds found fertile ground not only in churches but all across the American landscape.[9] The "cultural victory" Smith and others observe happened not because more Americans joined liberal churches, but because liberal religious values and sensibilities became more and more culturally normative. A full account of religious liberalism therefore must encompass its manifestations both in the churches and in the wider culture, yet only recently have historians begun to chart the cultural and spiritual contours of liberal religion farther afield. Some might see "religion farther afield" as a product of secularization, as a symptom only of the decline of churches and orthodoxies. I maintain, in contrast, that religious liberalism flourished beyond the bounds of churches, making this a story of rise rather than of decline.[10] In the 1920s, 1930s, and 1940s we see most clearly the ties between institutional Protestantism and the wider culture of religious liberalism that was then reaching critical mass.

Liberal Protestantism since the nineteenth century had sought to redeem the culture through full participation in it. In contrast to the more familiar evangelical formulation calling believers to remain "*in* but not *of* the world," American religious liberals endeavored to achieve their ends through an empowerment of secular culture.[11] This meant, at times, that liberal Protestants so thoroughly embraced the culture, politics, and intellectual life of the wider society that their own Christian distinctiveness was diminished. But in the first half of the twentieth century, this stance nevertheless bore considerable fruit, especially in the critically important arena of books. Liberal Protestants often occupied key positions as publishers, booksellers, and civic leaders and quite naturally used these positions of influence to advance their cultural and spiritual agendas. Though liberal religious leaders and secular professionals in the book trade shared an initial apprehension about the possible corruptions of the marketplace, each recognized the tremendous commercial and religious opportunities their social influence afforded and eventually embraced the marketplace with enthusiasm.

In spite of this apparent optimism, my tale of religious liberalism and the book business begins in a moment of crisis. World War I dealt a mortal blow to simple notions of progress, especially moral progress, arising from nineteenth-century liberalism. As many Americans learned—including protagonists of this story, such as Harry Emerson Fosdick—one could not look at human societies, or human nature, in the same way after Verdun and the Somme.[12] The crisis of liberalism wrought by the horrors of war in Europe compounded challenges already endemic to American cultural life, especially the rise of vast state and corporate bureaucracies, an increasingly pervasive mass culture and ethos of consumerism, rapid scientific and technological advances, and continuing urbanization and industrialization. The journalist and public intellectual Walter Lippmann best captured the spirit of the times when he wrote of the "acids of modernity"; to many Americans it did indeed appear that the world they knew was rapidly corroding.

The crisis of liberalism forms the essential historical framework for understanding the interplay of the book business and religious culture in the 1920s and 1930s. In religious terms, both modernism and fundamentalism arose in the late nineteenth century and early twentieth in response to these modern

conditions, and the wrenching battles between these camps in many denominations furthered the sense of crisis. Leaders of major Protestant denominations
and the ecumenical Federal Council of Churches responded with a number of
initiatives, including the various book programs described here, designed to
cope with these challenges. Those most afflicted by this post–World War I crisis
were white, educated urbanites, and therefore this study attends most especially
to this group of Americans. Yet the impetus behind the new reading initiatives
was precisely to extend embattled liberal religious sensibilities beyond their
demographic base in the cities and reach into the suburbs and small towns, while
similarly moving beyond the solidly middle class out to those strivers not quite
yet in the middle class. In the process that which was to be defended was transformed, and new forms of liberal spirituality emerged into wider public
consciousness.

These cultural processes unfolded most importantly in the marketplace of
print. In the decade after World War I, liberal Protestant leaders, executives of
the American publishing industry, and other important cultural figures collaborated on a series of new initiatives to promote the buying and reading of religious books in the United States. In response to the moment of crisis, these
cultural leaders sought to guide American moderns by offering their expertise in
the field of religious reading. They believed that a common set of widely accepted
religious ideas, practices, and presuppositions would hold together a fragment-
ing culture, expand existing markets for books, and maintain their privileged
status in American religious discourse. In this last ambition they failed; the core
values they proclaimed in fact undermined the very idea of religious authority.
Nevertheless the reading campaigns that liberal Protestants crafted—Religious
Book Week in the 1920s, the Religious Book Club, founded in 1927, and the
Religious Books Round Table of the American Library Association, among
others—formed the basis of a thriving religious reading culture that remained
central to American cultural and religious life through much of the century. In
addition major New York publishing houses, such as Harper's and Macmillan,
established religion departments for the first time in the late 1920s, a transformation at once rooted in changing economic realities and in religious liberals'
openness to market culture. From these reading and publishing endeavors
emerged new structures for the promotion of reading, but even more significantly a greater entanglement of religious practice with the patterns of consumerism and an enhanced emphasis on spiritual forms emerging from and moving
beyond liberal Protestantism. Chapters 1, 2, and 3 detail these reading and publishing initiatives.

The most important of the new spiritual forms for twentieth-century liberalism were psychology and mysticism. The centrality of mystical and psychological
approaches to religion stemmed from the liberal search for a universal essence of
religious experience. Both the German Friedrich Schleiermacher and the

American Ralph Waldo Emerson had influentially argued in the nineteenth century that individual experience remained the inviolable heart of religion after the assaults of modern thought had stripped away dogma, revelation, and ecclesial authority.[13] James's *The Varieties of Religious Experience*, first published in 1902, was the landmark text along these lines for twentieth-century liberals. It presents obvious shortcomings to readers in religiously diverse twenty-first-century America, since James universalized liberal Protestant assumptions about the nature of religion. The anti-institutional bias inherent in James's privileging of individual religious experience reflected, most especially, the pervasive anti-Catholicism of his cultural milieu, while neglecting the myriad ways those experiences are socially embedded and produced. Yet *Varieties* functioned marvelously as a psychology of religion designed specifically to help twentieth-century Protestant moderns retain spiritual vitality. Later American inspirational writers such as Rufus Jones turned to James's work precisely because of its applicability to those seeking meaning, happiness, and wholeness in a modern, consumerist, psychologically oriented culture.

The Jamesian emphasis on religious experience permeated American religious liberalism in the twentieth century and branched in a variety of directions. Some drew most heavily on James's conception of "the religion of healthy-mindedness" and became what I call laissez-faire liberals.[14] Laissez-faire liberals blended psychology with the mind-cure spiritual tradition (often called New Thought or positive thinking) to argue for the practical, material benefits of religion. These liberals typically eschewed liberalism's mystical spirituality and ethical concerns. Historians, sociologists, and numerous other social critics have extensively described, documented, and generally lamented the rise of a therapeutic culture in the twentieth century, which they have typically connected to the ascendancy of liberal theology and the advancement of consumerism.[15] Therapeutic ideology, these critics contend, provided no resources for social or political criticism. Rather, therapeutically empowered individuals merely adapted as needed to the demands of society, while consumer culture gave them the tools to do so, often in the form of self-help books described by one historian as the "success literature of modern consumer capitalism."[16] The laissez-faire liberalism of popular writers like Henry C. Link, Emmet Fox, Glenn Clark, and Norman Vincent Peale contributed to the conceptual framework of therapeutic culture. This branch of liberalism, according to critics, represented the final stage of the modernization of soul care and the ultimate victory of therapeutic consumerism over redemptive and prophetic religion.

Other twentieth-century religious liberals, however, moved in more mystical and ethical directions. Mystical and ethical liberals, such as Rufus Jones, Harry Emerson Fosdick, and Joshua Loth Liebman, also understood religious experience psychologically but never embraced mind cure's strictly utilitarian philosophy of religion. Their mystical sensibilities and ethical commitments tempered liberalism's inherent individualism with an ever-present attention to realities beyond the self. The political quiescence and consumerist hedonism of laissez-faire liberalism was matched by the social activism and moral sophistication of mystical and ethical liberalism. The distinction, though not hard and fast, is a useful reminder that religious liberalism does not equate neatly with political liberalism. Many laissez-faire liberals in fact were politically conservative—often tending toward libertarianism—while the mystical and ethical liberals typically championed a more progressive politics, including a robust social welfare state and, on occasion, pacifism. Nevertheless the main story of this book is religious and cultural, not political. Through that cultural lens we see that despite their differences, authors from each branch of liberalism, through their popular writings, brought into the American cultural mainstream spiritual vocabularies inflected with the accents of mysticism, mind cure, and psychology.

The most significant force shaping middle-class reading practices in the 1920s, 1930s, and 1940s, and therefore critical to the cultural agenda of religious liberalism, was what scholars of popular literature call "middlebrow" culture.[17] Middlebrow literary culture arose in the early twentieth century as middle-class Americans anxiously engaged with the emerging mass culture, hoping to solidify their tenuous social status with cultural markers acquired by reading the "right" books. But middlebrow culture was not simply "other-directed," to use David Riesman's term. Middlebrow readers also toiled for inner reasons, to use the resources provided by an expanding cultural and intellectual marketplace to better understand themselves and their place in the modern world. Indeed, in addition to devouring the popular novels, outlines of history and philosophy, and Book-of-the-Month Club selections commonly associated with middlebrow reading, vast numbers of American readers participated in a vibrant but little studied *religious* middlebrow culture. Though the academy remains divided between those who embrace the study of popular cultural forms, including middlebrow literature, and those who recoil in horror, I find the category middlebrow useful to highlight questions about expertise, access to books and learning, the organization of knowledge, and reasons for reading. Middlebrow, in this way, refers to a relationship between consumers and producers, between readers and those who tried to shape reading. The cultural process of "middlebrowing" happens in the packaging of a text, especially its presentation by experts to the public, and in the interaction between reader and text, especially through the hopes, desires, and fears a reader brings to the act of reading. Those who read inspirational and religious bestsellers in the decades after World War I read them in the context of middlebrow culture, according to middlebrow rules, and for this reason we must understand the culture of middlebrow reading if we hope to understand the print culture of liberal religion in this period.

World War II brought about a significant new phase in the course of religious middlebrow culture. As political leaders declared books to be "weapons in the war of ideas," an interfaith organization, the National Conference of Christians and Jews, became the central broker of religious reading, coordinating a second, vast Religious Book Week campaign that ran from 1943 to 1948. This reading program built on the foundation of mystical and psychological spirituality formed in the 1920s and 1930s, and changes in American reading and book culture during the war, to advocate interfaith exchange as a cornerstone of modern American spirituality. During World War II spiritual openness was seen not simply as morally desirable for individuals but as essential to national survival. In this context the previously dominant understanding of the United States as a Protestant nation gave way to a new, pluralistic framework that included Jews and Roman Catholics, and the term *Judeo-Christian* entered the national vocabulary. These developments of the 1940s popularized and democratized a cosmopolitan spiritual outlook that had previously been the privileged domain of a cultural elite. The cosmopolitan ambition to be a citizen of the world—to live out the ancient credo "I am human: nothing human is alien to me"—had animated transcendentalists, Theosophists, and even certain supporters of the famed 1893 World's Parliament of Religions.[18] The spiritual cosmopolitanism that emerged in the 1940s typically eschewed this sort of grandiose universalism, favoring what the philosopher Kwame Anthony Appiah calls a benign universalism that acknowledged a shared humanity while celebrating authentic difference.[19] The political drive toward Judeo-Christianity and the religious reading campaigns of the war years together brought this more modest version of spiritual cosmopolitanism to the American middle class. The huge success of Rabbi Joshua Loth Liebman's *Peace of Mind* (1946) and the Trappist monk Thomas Merton's *The Seven Storey Mountain* (1948) testifies to the arrival of postwar popular cosmopolitanism. Chapters 4, 5, and 6 chart these changes in religious middlebrow culture during the war and postwar years.

This remarkable energy in promoting book buying and reading, despite its significant cultural successes, was not enough to maintain the institutional vitality or privileged cultural status of the liberal establishment. In many ways, in fact, liberal elites were the victims of their own success, as their drive for a universal spiritual language and true pluralism—a drive rooted, at its core, in their own sense of Christian ethics as much as in their desire to stay culturally relevant—made their grasp on power, centralized and hierarchical as it was, increasingly untenable. The cultural victory of liberal Protestantism actually contributed to its institutional decline, partly because religious individualism naturally resists institutionalization. But even more, as religious liberals embraced the notion of redeeming the entire culture, they found increasingly meaningful outlets for their religious energies outside the churches, both in social activism and in cultural programs such as reading promotion.[20] The story of Frank Laubach, which I take up in the conclusion, offers the most compelling example of reading promotion as a sublimated form of religious mission. In this way my story tells of men and women seeking a spiritual center for the culture as a whole who inevitably confronted the ultimate reality that, in the modern world, as Yeats observed, "the center cannot hold." The religious leaders, authors, critics, editors, and publishers who sought to define and hold together a common faith for a vast continent of a nation, steeped in consumerism, fractured along fault lines of race and gender, class and region, denomination and religious tradition, swam against the tides of history and their own liberal tradition, and tired short of their goal.[21]

Yet even as liberal Protestant institutions and leaders failed to hold their privileged place in the national discourse, the spiritual vocabularies and sensibilities liberals promoted gained ever-wider currency and legitimacy.[22] Psychology and mysticism arose from liberal Protestantism in the nineteenth century, but eventually spilled beyond the banks of even that wide stream. Historians of religion in America, themselves often personally committed to institutional Protestantism, have too often simply failed to see the vitality and dynamism of this "shadow culture" or "invisible religion" occurring beyond the walls of church life.[23] The pluralist turn of American religious print culture by the 1940s further enhanced the importance of these alternative spiritualities. This story, then, is an ironic tale of initial resistance yet ultimate complicity in the transformation of American religious culture from Protestant dominance, in spite of sizable and significant minority traditions, to a much more open, democratic, even chaotic spiritual environment. The psychologically and mystically rooted cosmopolitanism that came to characterize much of American religion and spirituality after World War II first emerged as a popular reality from the liberal Protestantism and book-buying consumerism of the interwar years—but ultimately took on a life all its own.

Backstory: Book Culture and Liberal Religion before 1920

To promote a national program known as Religious Book Week, Rufus Jones wrote in the spring of 1921 a brief article, "The Habit of Reading," intended to initiate readers into the mysteries of earnest religious reading and book buying. Jones began by lamenting the poor reading habits of most Americans and noted, ominously, the impressive "experiment made by many of the new cults in America."[24] "They grow, expand, and flourish," he wrote, "largely through the use of books." Christians needed to be just as diligent, especially since, with the recent expansion in religious publishing and book promotion, "there exists today within the reach of everybody who can read a very remarkable assortment of transforming and enlightening books." Among the many worthwhile kinds of religious books available, Jones cited biography, biblical criticism, and especially texts exploring the implications of modern scientific and historical inquiry for persons of faith. As a historian and student of psychology himself, Jones implored, "No Christian man or woman today can afford to miss the fresh and vivifying light which will come to religious faith from . . . writers who unite great faith with exact and profound knowledge."

Jones aimed not only to make his readers aware of important new religious books, but also to advocate particular ways of reading those books and particular ways of relating to the entire marketplace of books. "It is not enough to read capriciously and sporadically, to borrow a book occasionally and then have done with it," he argued. "I am pleading for the ownership of books and for *the cultivation of the habit of reading*" (italics original). Proper religious reading, for Jones, meant reading in a very specific manner. "The true and effective way to read an illuminating book," he counseled, "is to read it, pencil in hand, to mark cardinal passages, to make notes, and to digest the message which the book contributes." He then added, just to make sure his point was clear, "That means that the book ought, if possible, to be owned rather than borrowed." Book buying might, incidentally, through the laws of supply and demand, stimulate the writing of more and better religious books, but for Jones the primary benefit of proper book reading and buying was personal. One must own religious books because "one needs to go back again and again to a good book, to reread marked passages, and to become literally possessed of it." A good book can possess us, according to Jones, only if we first possess it.

In this remarkable editorial Jones encapsulated quite neatly the tension between modern and earlier evangelical ideologies of the book, a tension at the heart of the religious book business in the decades after World War I. When he remarked that the proper way to read was with "pencil in hand . . . to go back again and again to a good book, to reread marked passages" he presented modern Americans with old advice about how to read. Nineteenth-century evangelicals spent considerable energy trying to persuade Americans to read in just this way. They worked tirelessly not only to write, produce, and distribute books, but also to educate American readers about how to read those books, and in the process established an ideology of reading religiously that continued to exert great influence well into the twentieth century. Yet Jones's enthusiastic endorsement of a for-profit promotional scheme signaled a new relationship to the marketplace of print. After at least a century of oscillation between fear of the market's corrupting powers and hope in its millennial possibilities, many advocates of religious reading after World War I abandoned their fears and fully embraced the market as the single greatest tool for the dissemination of their message. The religious leaders and bookmen who championed Religious Book Week sought to use the tools of modern business to advocate for an older culture of the book that, they hoped, might help counter the corrosive influences of the very consumer culture they now embraced.

Print mass media in the United States arose as an evangelical endeavor in the early years of the nineteenth century. The millennial dream of building God's kingdom in the new nation inspired the postrevolutionary generation of publishing pioneers to embark on the audacious enterprise of bringing the sacred word to every American; the rapid pace of change in this emerging society made such previously outlandish dreams plausible. In short order evangelical reformers founded the American Bible Society (1816), the American Sunday School Union (1824), and the American Tract Society (1825).[25] The overall output of books grew rapidly, and religious publishing added significantly to this vast expansion.[26] Though leery of blurring the sacred and the profane, religious publishers by midcentury became increasingly open to using secular culture for spiritual purposes. As a result, the book business became an ever more potent force in American religious life. The famed preacher Horace Bushnell, notes the historian Paul C. Gutjahr, even remarked in 1844 that his fellow American Christians "operated as if 'types of lead and sheets of paper may be the light of the World.'"[27]

Nineteenth-century print culture shared with the Protestantism that sparked it a democratizing impulse rooted in the ideology of the priesthood of all believers. In the vastly expanded world of print this impulse led to what one might call a priesthood of all readers, a situation ripe for religious turmoil rooted in interpretive chaos. As a result religious leaders devised ideologies of proper reading, strategies for vulnerable readers to navigate these uncharted and potentially treacherous waters. These modes of reading religiously exerted powerful cultural influence long into the twentieth century. The tract societies and colporteurs bringing reading material to the nation had great reason to fear, since, according to their implicit theory of print communication, "reading ... was a very dangerous activity."[28] So dangerous were books that evangelical writers in this age of the temperance crusades often "compared the power of reading to the intoxicating, addictive power of alcohol." Some even more succinctly "believed that books could kill" since they offered unregulated and unsupervised access to a whole universe of ideas, including the sinful and demonic.[29] Religious publishers throughout the nineteenth century sought to overcome the possible dangers of reading by teaching their readers how to read properly.[30] Noah Porter, the president of Yale College, used his widely reprinted 1870 reading guide, *Books and Reading: Or, What Books Shall I Read and How Shall I Read Them?*, to urge caution in the face of such power. "No force nor influence can undo the work begun by those few pages," Porter exhorted. "No love of father or mother, no temptation of money or honor, no fear of suffering or disgrace, is an overmatch for the enchantment conjured up and sustained by [an] exciting volume." Therefore, Porter continued, "we ought to select our books—above all our favorite books—with a more jealous care than we choose our friends and intimates" and read those books in the prayerful and attentive manner befitting their sacred power.[31]

George Philip Philes, the author of another reading guide, echoed Porter's exhortations and added, more practically, that each worthwhile book should be read four times in order "to master and use it; not only to swallow it, but to make it part of ourselves, and thereby strengthen all our powers."[32] When read in such a way, a text would lay bare for the reader its meaning, and the printed word would touch a human soul as a means of divine grace. This idea, so foreign to modern theorists of reading, rested, writes the historian David Paul Nord, on "the belief that the meaning of a text resides entirely in the text and that the text is hegemonic."[33] Prayerful reading would eliminate the anarchic possibilities inherent in both Protestant doctrine and the emerging mass media, allowing readers direct access to sacred, timeless truths.

Evangelicals such as Porter and Philes believed the modes of sacred reading they cherished were losing ground to what they called "shallow" or "passive" reading. This debate persisted throughout the twentieth century in various guises, secular and religious, as critics came to see the "shallow" reading that so vexed nineteenth-century jeremiahs as but one of the myriad vices of American consumer culture.[34] The philosopher Paul Griffiths, for example, contrasts religious reading—"as a lover reads, with a tensile attentiveness that wishes to linger, to prolong, to savor"—with consumer reading, which "wants to extract what is useful or exciting or entertaining from what is read, preferably with dispatch...all in the quick orgasm of consumption."[35] Just as nineteenth-century tract writers believed a good religious text to be "hegemonic," its meaning plain to any attentive reader, Griffiths asserts, "the basic metaphors [of reading religiously] are those of discovery, uncovering, retrieval, opening up: religious readers read what is there to be read, and what is there to be read always precedes, exceeds, and in the end supersedes its readers."[36] Griffith's stark divide between religious and consumerist modes of reading echoes the concerns of Porter from a century earlier. This continued concern throughout the nineteenth and twentieth centuries reveals an abiding conviction in the power of the printed word to mold character and faith, for good or ill.

The irony at the heart of this great reading debate, as the pioneers of religious mass media clearly recognized, is that religious reading in the nineteenth century depended on the market, and by the twentieth century not just the market but the culture of consumerism itself. For Griffiths, "the work read...can never be discarded because it cannot be exhausted," yet by the mid-twentieth century especially, books had became cheap and disposable commodities. Rufus Jones even contended in 1921 that to read religiously one *must* enter the marketplace, one *must* buy. Sharing books, reading aloud—none of these traditional modes of relating to sacred texts would suffice. Religion, of course, as one part of larger cultural systems, exists only as embedded in a web of cultural norms, beliefs, and practices; in America this means religion *happens* in a consumer market-place.[37] Though many have feared the dire consequences of American consumerism and mass production for proper religious practice, Americans of all traditions of faith in the nineteenth and twentieth centuries lived their religious lives in a culture profoundly shaped by the dictates of the market.[38] Gutjahr observes that in American practice by the early twentieth century, even Bibles, once "simply a religious guidebook for life...had become collectable commodities."[39] The anxieties and hopes embedded in these cultural developments—the promise of the market to bring good religious books to millions and the fear that one would never quite know just what they read or how—persisted well into the twentieth century, long after consumerism had thoroughly transformed every corner of American culture.

For all the fulmination of self-proclaimed reading arbiters, readers increasingly took the notion of a priesthood of all readers to its logical conclusions. While some read with the solitary fervor and intensity the evangelists hoped for, many blended such practices with communal and cursory styles of reading, all while sampling freely from available reading options. These flexible and pragmatic approaches to reading created new opportunities for engagement with a wide array of ideas about the self and the divine.[40] The most critical of these new religious developments for twentieth-century religious liberalism were a renewed and transformed emphasis on mystical practice and experience, the healing ministry known as mind cure, and the rise of modern psychology. These three interrelated spiritual innovations spread as significant components of popular religion in large part through the mass print media. Rather than religious movements dependent on revivalism or church life, these were first and foremost discourses, creatures of the printed word.[41] Initially explored only by an avant-garde of liberal intellectuals late in the nineteenth century, the new books and ideas emerging at the margins of liberal Protestantism eventually reached a nation-wide middle-class audience. The mass media unleashed by nineteenth-century evangelicalism enabled the alternative spiritualities of the twentieth century to flourish, especially with the rise of religious middlebrow culture in the decades after World War I.

Mysticism, mind cure, and psychology each arose, in their modern iterations, in the cultural milieu of nineteenth-century Anglo-American liberal Protestantism, and each reached a period of particular ferment in the years around 1900. In response to the economic, cultural, and social developments historians describe using the rubric *modernity*—positivistic science, corporate and government bureaucracies, the research university, Darwinism, historical-critical study of the Bible, consumerism, urbanization—liberals at the elite and popular levels fashioned the discourses of mysticism, mind cure, and psychology. These discourses in fact drew so deeply from the same liberal Protestant well that only slowly over the course of the twentieth century did they emerge from their common origins as distinct modes of language, thought, and practice.

In spite of critical differences, the appeal of each was the same: all three claimed access to universal truth, and all three built universal claims on the foundation of individual experience. Claims of universal truth often masked structures of domination rooted in race, gender, and nation, to be sure. But we need not accept the universal claims of these nineteenth-century liberal discourses to appreciate their appeal to later popularizers, or to so many twentieth-century Americans. As the historian Leigh Schmidt notes, "It was exactly the sui generis rhetoric that made 'mysticism' timely, not timeless."[42] Claims to universality, in other words, were very much of the moment, and mysticism, mind cure, and psychology, by offering universal truths rooted in individual experience, seemed to offer insight into the essence of the human condition.

Of the three, mysticism as a category of experience had the deepest roots in Western religious life and the longest relationship with liberalism.[43] Though the terms *mystic* and *mystical* are ancient in origin, the term *mysticism* in English dates only to the mid-eighteenth century, used then by Anglicans to critique the ecstatic "excesses" of sects such as Methodists and Quakers. Not until the 1840s and 1850s, in the hands of British and American romantics and transcendentalists, according to Schmidt, did the term begin to acquire modern meanings. Ralph Waldo Emerson, Margaret Fuller, Bronson Alcott, and others, Schmidt writes, refashioned mysticism from a term of sectarian critique into something "loosely spiritual, intuitive, emancipatory, and universal."[44] The notion of mysticism as the solitary soul's union with the divine, an experience at once ineffable and timeless, not bound by culture, language, history, or even self, was an invention of nineteenth-century liberalism, as was the notion that such mystical experiences served as "the fountainhead of all genuine spirituality."[45]

A host of American and British writers in the years around 1900 seized on the new discourse of mysticism to advance the cause of liberal Protantism. The historian T. J. Jackson Lears locates the vogue in mysticism at this time within a broad context of antimodernism, and certainly the fascination of many turn-of-the-century scholars of mysticism with the Orient or with medieval Catholic spirituality supports such an argument.[46] What the embodied ecstasies of Pentecostalism offered to the dispossessed at Asuza Street in Los Angeles in 1906, mysticism provided for elite liberals: pure experience of the divine. Critics note that the mysticism vogue in these years was mostly second order—it was a vogue in mysticism studies more than in mystical practice—yet this simply confirms that these were thoroughgoing moderns seeking refuge in a spiritual zone safe from the disenchantment of modernity. In addition to James's *Varieties*, the years around and after 1900 witnessed the Anglican William Ralph Inge's *Christian Mysticism* (1899); *The Mystical Element of Religion* (1908), a study of medieval Italian saints by Baron Friedrich von Hügel, a British Roman Catholic; Rufus Jones's *Studies in Mystical Religion* (1909); *Mysticism: A Study in the Nature and Development of Man's Spiritual Consciousness* (1911) and *Practical Mysticism: A Little Book for Normal People* (1914) by the Anglican Evelyn Underhill, a student of von Hügel; the Methodist John Wright Buckham's *Mysticism and Modern Life* (1915); and the German Lutheran Rudolf Otto's *The Idea of the Holy* (1917). From outside this wide array of Western Christian traditions, the German-American editor Paul Carus introduced many Americans to Buddhist mystical practice through his own writings and his collaborations with D. T. Suzuki. Carus's work was but one small part of a larger turn-of-the-century vogue in Eastern traditions that included the Vedanta of Swami Vivekenanda and Madame H. P. Blavatsky's Theosophy. Even this cursory review of mystical writings reveals the deep hunger for authentic experience of the divine among Protestant moderns at the dawn of the twentieth century.

Mysticism helped liberals at the turn of the twentieth century cope with science, especially with the positivistic conceptions of human nature most starkly represented by evolutionary biology and laboratory psychology. Many of the early scholars of mysticism in fact, including Rufus Jones, John Wright Buckham, James Bissett Pratt, and William James, were also ardent students of biological and psychological science. The critical bridge between mystical spirituality and the emerging science of the psyche was the popular religious ideology of mind cure.[47] Like mysticism and indeed like psychology itself, mind cure was an artifact of nineteenth-century liberal Protestantism. Mind cure shared with mysticism the use of altered states of consciousness (often hypnosis) and union of the self with the larger cosmos, what Emerson called the "Over-Soul" and later writers "More," "Supreme Mind," and "Universal Consciousness." The intense popular interest in metaphysical healing between 1885 and 1910 (and again the Pentecostal emphasis on faith healing) paralleled the scholarly focus on mysticism in these same years.[48] This ideology of mind cure proved a powerful allure for writers and readers throughout the twentieth century. Though mind cure frequently succumbed to the temptation of the easy answer—the historian William Leach accurately describes it as "wish-oriented, optimistic, sunny, the epitome of cheer and self-confidence, and completely lacking in anything resembling the tragic view of life"—it nevertheless attempted to meet the real needs of modern Americans.[49] Indeed mind-cure philosophies have remained into the twenty-first century as the inevitable companion of liberal religious efforts to forge spiritual practices that engage the problems of everyday life in modern terms.

Rather than an antimodern retreat, then, mind cure promised to harness modernity's advances for the enrichment of human life. The belief system of mind cure, often called New Thought by the late nineteenth century, postulated a correlation between the mind of the individual self and Mind as an expression of an omnipotent and omnipresent Divine. The techniques of mind cure—meditation, hypnosis, autosuggestion, prayer—all focused on removing blockages between mind and Mind and opening the self to Supply—of energy, of health, of wealth, of wisdom—that might then flow in infinite abundance. The title of the first New Thought bestseller, Ralph Waldo Trine's *In Tune with the Infinite* (1897), captured the means of mind cure perfectly; its subtitle, *Fullness of Peace, Power, and Plenty*, revealed its ends. Mind cure retained little of Calvinism's sense of divine mystery and otherness. God's power, it held, is here, to be used now. The trick was to figure out how, and thus mind cure developed intellectually along the lines of a science and in practice as a technology. Those who claimed to understand Mind possessed insight into the deepest secrets of existence, a gnosticism for modern times.

Mind cure as a religious ideology held particular appeal for women. The historian Donald Meyer describes mind cure as a post-Calvinist Protestant expression of "pure wish," but Beryl Satter more precisely characterizes New Thought as a "gendered discourse of desire."[50] Indeed the institutional history of New Thought reveals a preponderance of white, middle-class women among both the leadership and adherents, especially in the urban centers of the North and Midwest where the movement was strongest. The ways print culture facilitated the emergence of textual communities centered on the home was critical to mind cure's success among women, who often encountered these new teachings in print before reaching out to local communities. If the sudden transformation mind cure offered recalled the life-changing power of evangelical conversion, its focus on the feminine aspects of the divine marked a radical departure from mainstream Protestantism.

The new psychology of the 1880s and 1890s emerged in response to the same liberal Protestant crisis and with preoccupations about the nature of mind and consciousness that were similar to mind cure.[51] Like mind cure, academic psychology offered a metaphysical science of healing. In fact it makes little sense to distinguish psychology and mind cure prior to the 1880s, when the first academic psychology departments were founded in American universities. Indeed throughout the twentieth century the two discourses continued a regular intercourse in the arena of popular religion. Norman Vincent Peale, most famously, drew heavily on both psychoanalytic theory and the Unity School of Christianity, a New Thought denomination, in his hugely popular speeches and writings of the 1940s, 1950s, and later. The legitimacy of psychology in the twentieth century required it to renounce, sharply and deliberately, all ties with its popular religious cousins, but in the arena of lived religion such high/low distinctions mattered little.

Even a cursory glance at the biographies of the discipline's American founders—men such as William James, G. Stanley Hall, George Coe, James Leuba, Edwin Starbuck, and James Mark Baldwin—reveals the liberal Protestant origins of psychology as an academic discipline in the United States.[52] The young psychologists of religion that followed the pioneers James and Hall labored to use science itself as a means to keep religion viable in the modern age. Some, like Coe and Leuba, proved less willing than James to accept emerging theories of the subconscious as adequate to the task of accounting for mystical experience. Much of this later skepticism proved decisive as psychology began its long process of withdrawal from its religious roots. But in the realm of popular religious life, the more open and pragmatic categories of James prevailed. His famed definition of religion—"the feeling, acts, and experiences of individual men in their solitude, so far as they apprehend themselves to stand in relation to whatever they may consider divine"—indicates most clearly his determination to place experience at the center of religious life.[53]

The trait that made James's *The Varieties of Religious Experience* the most influential of all the early twentieth-century psychologies of religion is the deftness with which he bridged liberal Protestant intellectual culture and the wider religious currents of mysticism and mind cure, all while legitimating, rather than reductively dismissing, religious experience. James devoted considerable attention to the mind-cure philosophies he took as emblematic of what he called the "religion of healthy-mindedness." In *Varieties* he quoted extensively from Trine's *In Tune with the Infinite*, describing, without condescension or criticism, what he found there as "traces of Christian mysticism, of transcendental idealism, of vedantism, and of the modern psychology of the subliminal self."[54] *Varieties* proved so useful to later writers because it brought under the universal umbrella of science experiences ranging from evangelical conversion to mind-cure healing, psychical phenomena, and mystical rapport with the More, without reducing any of these to neurology or the psychology of the subconscious. In this enterprise many religious innovators and popular inspirational writers recognized a kindred spirit.

Coe, Leuba, Starbuck, and others in the years from 1902 through World War I continued to debate, in academic settings, the significance of what James achieved in *The Varieties of Religious Experience*. Rufus Jones's *Social Law in the Spiritual World*, as noted, was the first significant effort to translate *Varieties* for a popular audience. Jones had studied James's *Principles of Psychology* intensively when it appeared in 1890 and taught courses in Jamesian psychology at Haverford College in the 1890s. In 1900–1901 he went to Harvard for graduate study, though was disappointed to learn that James was in Europe preparing for the Gifford Lectures that would become *Varieties*. In spite of his appreciation of James's psychology, Jones—unlike James and his fellow psychologists—lived a life in regular communion with the world beyond. He was a birthright Quaker and therefore came by his mysticism as honestly as James did his post-Calvinist New England angst. After returning from Harvard to Haverford, he set out to produce the work that would make Jamesian psychology and his own Quaker mysticism available to a reading public also struggling with matters of faith, science, and authentic experience.

James taught that all knowledge and all experience are mediated through consciousness; yet as a mystic, Jones also held that God can be apprehended only through this very same medium: the conscious experience of an individual personality. The study of personality therefore became a critical tool of spiritual development. "If we could drop our plummet down though the deeps of one personality," Jones wrote in *Social Law*, "we could tell all the meanings of the visible world, all the problems of social life and all the secrets of the eternal Personal Self."[55] Critics have made the argument that liberal religion—Protestant liberalism in particular—suffered a spiritual malaise in the twentieth century largely due to an overeager embrace of scientific psychology.[56] Jones too embraced science and psychology, but he tempered it with mystical experience and thereby kept psychology from crowding out spiritual vitality.

In *Social Law* Jones took what he understood to be the fundamental lessons of the new psychology and applied them to the mystical heart of his Quaker tradition. He grouped mystics into two classes: negation mystics and affirmation mystics. The first class sought ecstatic rapture of union with the divine, which Jones regarded as spiritual escapism. The affirmation mystics, on the other hand, "do not make *vision* the end of life, but rather the beginning.... More important than the vision is obedience to the vision."[57] For the affirmation mystic, the solitary, personal, inward, mystical experience, which for Jones always lay at the heart of spiritual life, was to be valued only insofar as it empowered the participant to service in the world. "The truth test is to be sought, not in the feeling-state, but in the motor-effects,"[58] he wrote, reflecting James's philosophical pragmatism. For Jones, the test of mystical experience was its social utility. In *Social Law* he argued that modern psychology and timeless mystical practice, taken together, offered a path through the thickets of modern life, a path ultimately of personal and social salvation. Jones's vibrant adaptation of James foreshadowed a long line of similar twentieth-century efforts.

Rufus Jones wrote *Social Law* in 1904 to help distraught moderns find personally and socially useful religious experiences. Less than twenty years later, he joined a wide-reaching effort, Religious Book Week, designed to encourage Americans to read books like *Social Law in the Spiritual World* and the many others offering the latest wisdom. The 1920s witnessed a remarkable renaissance of religious publishing and a host of marketing innovations devised to get more books, and the right books, into the hands of readers, and to instruct those readers how to read those books. What emerged was a religious middlebrow culture that freshly asserted the centrality of books and reading in middle-class religious life and that reconfigured the relationships among individual autonomy, institutional authority, and cultural expertise. Liberal religious leaders like Jones turned to James—and the discourses of mysticism, mind cure, and psychology more broadly—in their efforts to create and promote a religious reading culture suited to modern life.

Religious middlebrow culture structured both the relationship of readers to texts and the expectations readers had for the transformative power of reading. As modern life challenged previously held assumptions about faith, character, personality, and the self, readers turned to inspirational literature for guidance, and the rules of middlebrow culture shaped the meanings readers made in those encounters. But religious middlebrow culture also shaped spirituality by introducing previously marginal ideas about the nature of religious experience into the mainstream of popular thought and by preparing readers for a spiritual engagement with religious "others." The corrosive "acids of modernity" forced liberal Protestants in particular to search for new tools, tools adequate to the task of guiding readers in a constantly shifting consumer culture. Middlebrow reading habits in the 1920s, 1930s, and 1940s became a central part of religious practice for countless Americans. The content of the books they read shaped middle-class spirituality for the remainder of the twentieth century.

1

Enlarging the Faith

*Books and the Marketing of Liberal Religion
in a Consumer Culture*

In the late winter of 1922 the Religious Book Week Committee received a brief note from President Warren G. Harding written "to endorse the program for the wider circulation of books of a religious character." The organizers of the fledgling enterprise, then in its second year, must have been elated. Harding's pronouncement had perfectly captured their sense of mission. Writing in the wake of World War I, with the carnage of Verdun and the Somme still clearly on his mind, he told the bookmen of New York that the wider reading of religious books was essential so "that the world may become morally fit. Unless this is done, trained bodies and trained minds may simply add to the destructive forces of the world."[1] Many Americans in the years before the war had placed great faith in technical expertise and reinvigorated masculinity—in "trained bodies and trained minds"—but now Harding understood such training to be inadequate to the challenges of a rapidly modernizing society. At a time when professionals, artists, and intellectuals were shedding ties to religion, Harding contended that America needed a moral center, a center to be found in religious books.[2]

The transformation of the religious book business in the 1920s—exemplified by Religious Book Week—grew out of the hopes and fears of liberal religious leaders as they grappled with their declining social influence, the increasing sway of consumer culture, and a pervasive postwar spiritual malaise. These bookmen and church leaders tried to use religious publishing to reassert cultural influence and generate spiritual renewal, and in the process created a thriving religious middlebrow culture. The dual aims of asserting influence and providing renewal required an expansion of the very idea of "the religious" itself, and the book weeks, book lists, and book clubs that characterized these new publishing and promotional enterprises brought this enlarged religious sensibility to the reading public. Religious middlebrow culture emerged in the 1920s as a primary framework through which middle-class moderns made sense of scientific advancements, theological controversies, and increasing social pluralism. As a carrier of broadened and liberalized notions of religion, middlebrow culture also transformed the ways American readers experienced spiritual community, tended to their psychological and spiritual needs, and encountered the transcendent. Middlebrow reading, in other words, became a fundamental middle-class religious practice. The promotion of a broadened sense of "the religious" through the marketplace for books encouraged and legitimated a culture of seeking that would become increasingly central to liberal religion in the twentieth century. But these profound shifts in religious and cultural life took decades to unfold and were difficult, if not impossible, to foresee. To many observers in the 1920s, the advent of this greater religious openness seemed more like cultural chaos.

Cultural Crisis and Religious Publishing in the 1920s

Harding's note to the Religious Book Week Committee—read from thousands of pulpits and reprinted in newspapers across the country—reflected widespread anxieties in the years after World War I, anxieties about the nature and direction of Western civilization itself. The sheer destructiveness of the Great War led critics to question liberal assumptions about progress that had prevailed for decades. Many religious leaders who had zealously championed American intervention in Europe, sharing Woodrow Wilson's evangelical faith in American democracy, now repented of their earlier militarism and turned instead to isolationism and pacifism. Walter Lippmann, writing at the end of the 1920s, simply declared, "The promises of liberalism have not been fulfilled."[3] In his brilliant *A Preface to Morals*, Lippmann announced that examples of liberalism's failed promises "lie all about us: in the brave and brilliant atheists who have defied the Methodist God, and have become very nervous; in the women who have emancipated themselves from the tyranny of fathers, husbands, and homes, and with the intermittent but expensive help of a psychoanalyst, are now enduring liberty as interior decorators; in the young men and women who are world weary at twenty-two; in the multitudes who drug themselves with pleasure."[4] Millions of Americans "at last free to think without fear of priest or policeman" struggled to cope with the disconnect between progressive expectations of spiritual emancipation and postwar realities and sought meaning, however hollow, in "the moving pictures and the popular newspapers."[5] Millions more in the United States found security in the certainties of an emergent fundamentalism.[6] But countless others, dissatisfied with orthodoxies old and new, found themselves unmoored. "These are the prisoners who have been released," Lippmann announced. "Yet the result is not so good as they thought it would be. The prison door is wide open. They stagger out into trackless space under a blinding sun. They find it nerve-wracking."[7]

President Harding had campaigned on a "return to normalcy" in his success-ful 1920 presidential bid, but there was no turning back, and observers like Lippmann noted just how much the world had changed in a few short years. Many of the most significant changes—increasing urbanism and pluralism, the rise of a mass culture, and pervasive middle-class consumerism, to name but a few—had roots stretching back before the war, yet these changes hit the American public with full force in the early 1920s. The historian Lynn Dumenil notes that many Americans in these years experienced "a growing consciousness of change, a perception that a yawning gulf separated them from the world of only a decade before." These social and cultural changes, she writes, "challenged tradition, religion, rational order, and progress."[8] American intellectuals embraced with renewed vigor Freudian psychology, literary modernism, surrealist art, the new physics, historical biblical criticism, and evolutionary biology. Other Americans turned their discontent into violent rage, as race riots swept the country in 1919 and the revived Ku Klux Klan gained a measure of political influence and legitimacy it had not enjoyed even during its previous heyday under Reconstruction.

This postwar turmoil added to already pronounced strains in American cultural and religious life, especially the twin crises of masculinity and churchly authority that had been developing since the 1890s and now reached a climax in the 1920s. When the Census Bureau effectively declared the frontier closed in 1890—with the concurrent rise of massive corporate bureaucracies that forced a generation of men to work behind a desk for the first time—many American men feared that "overcivilization" was sapping them of independence and virility. Theodore Roosevelt's 1899 oration on the "strenuous life" called for American imperialism, linking national and racial power to the strength of American manhood; in the struggle of nations, he proclaimed, "the one with the most superior manhood" would lead "human racial advancement toward a higher civilization."[9] Roosevelt's was far from a lonely voice. The national, racial, and spiritual dangers of diminished manliness in fact inspired numerous reform efforts, including a proposal from the psychologist G. Stanley Hall to allow boys to act on their "savage" and "primitive" instincts in play.[10] Hall's proposal met with a firestorm of criticism, yet other efforts to inculcate manly vigor were readily adopted across the nation, including football, which quickly emerged as a national passion in American educational institutions, and the Boy Scouts, brought to the United States from England in 1912 to allow boys yet another escape from the confines of civilization.[11] In religious circles, the crisis of mascu-linity spurred an enthusiasm for "muscular Christianity" among liberals and conservatives alike, including renewed efforts in art and literature to redefine Jesus in manly terms, in contrast to the perceived effeminacy of nineteenth-century evangelicalism's Savior.[12] The short-lived Men and Religion Forward Movement and the hyperactive revivals of the former baseball player Billy

Sunday were matched by a torrent of books, including Harry Emerson Fosdick's *Manhood of the Master* (1913) and Bruce Barton's *A Young Man's Jesus* (1914), all seeking to rescue American men, and American Christianity, from the emasculating and enervating onslaughts of feminized evangelical piety and stifling modern civilization.

The hope of those promoting this "muscular Christianity" was to make religion more appealing to men, who attended weekly services in far fewer numbers than their mothers, wives, and daughters.[13] The gender imbalance in the pews, a long-standing reality of American religious life, was mirrored, however, by the much greater gender imbalance in the pulpit, so for all the angst over feminized religion, the institutional church in the early twentieth century remained a bastion of male power. For most of American history, dominance of the pulpit carried significant cultural authority, but clerical power, as a force in the wider culture, began to erode in the late nineteenth century, and this erosion accelerated amid the cultural transitions of the 1920s. The church historian Robert Handy has called the 1920s the period of a "second disestablishment" and a "religious depression," noting, "The realities of postwar life were proving difficult to understand and address within the familiar styles of Protestant thought and piety." The loss of ministerial authority stemmed from numerous factors, including schisms over doctrine (the so-called modernist-fundamentalist controversy) and increasingly accepted scientific understandings of both the natural world and human nature. Yet even more broadly, notes Handy, "the direction of social change, demographic trends, and urban patterns was against the dominance of an acculturated Protestantism with its . . . rural nostalgia."[14] The sociologists Robert and Helen Lynd, in *Middletown*, their masterful study of Muncie, Indiana, conducted in the mid-1920s, reduced the matter of clerical authority to even simpler terms. They recorded "an impression of ministers as eagerly lingering about the fringes of things trying to get a chance to talk to the men of the city."[15] Liberal Protestants, unused to life on the fringes and struggling to maintain cultural influence, naturally felt the beginnings of this "second disestablishment" with great acuity, while critics such as H. L. Mencken howled with delight.[16]

The singular phenomenon of Bruce Barton, an advertising executive and the author of *The Man Nobody Knows* (1925), a bestselling biography of Jesus, perfectly encapsulated the confluence of commercial culture, religious publishing, theological liberalism, and gender anxiety in the 1920s. Barton's book received intense scorn from both conservative and liberal critics, mostly for its indisputable theological shallowness and naked celebration of American capitalism. In a typical commentary, Gilbert Seldes in *The New Republic* argued, "The author is a man so fanatic about American business that he must reduce his Savior to the terms of the executive and organizer and go-getter."[17] In his effort to craft a Jesus who would inspire urban, educated, professional men—a Jesus whom

Barton himself could respect, in other words—he may indeed have created a grotesque caricature of the man from Nazareth, but his ambition stemmed from the same cultural crises that bedeviled his fellow modern Americans. The stunning commercial success of *The Man Nobody Knows* and its sequel, *The Book Nobody Knows* (1926), testifies that Barton's ambition was at least to some degree realized, whatever the professional critics may have thought.

Like many of his generation and class, Barton struggled with religious faith, even though his father, the Rev. William Barton, was a well-connected and sophisticated liberal preacher and author. Nevertheless after an extended period of reflection and consultation with leading clergy, including the celebrity preacher and author Harry Emerson Fosdick, Barton eventually followed his father's example and embraced a religion that, according to his brother, was a "simple, rational, reasonable and pleasant part of life."[18] He wrote his book in the sincere desire that a relevant rendering of Jesus would serve "as a guide to the complexities of maintaining religious faith in an increasingly secular world."[19] In this way his project was much like that of William James in *The Varieties of Religious Experience*, Rufus Jones in *Social Law in the Spiritual World*, and a host of other early twentieth-century liberals. He would rescue the faith by modernizing it. As his biographer Richard Fried concludes, "He may have ended by sanctifying business, but he intended to show how religion could be made modern and relevant to contemporary life."[20] Seen in this light, Barton's agenda mirrored the aims of many liberals in religious publishing. He too despised the religious literature that was either abstruse and abstract or insipid and sentimental, what one newspaper wag of the time called "dusty tomes of doctrinal controversy or Sunday school books of the proverbial goody-goody, milk-and-water type."[21] In place of such reading, Barton offered a work "stripped of all dogma" that would speak to professional men about their everyday concerns and would offer them, in the words of the subtitle, "a discovery of the real Jesus."[22]

Critics and historians since the 1920s have often used Barton's writings as shorthand for phony 1920s consumerism—a consumerism built on the false promises of advertising, Barton's own craft. Yet his readers tell a different story. For many, Barton's manly, entrepreneurial Jesus was indeed the real thing. "Mr. Barton has succeeded as no other of whom I know," wrote a pastor from Oklahoma City to Barton's editor, "in making Jesus of Nazareth real."[23] "I think of him as a man like myself," wrote another reader, a hardware company executive from Cleveland. "So this book of Barton's brings him closer to me and makes him a more real personality than any that I have ever read."[24] A twenty-one-year-old student from Massachusetts wrote directly to Barton. "It is a wonderful book," he declared, "with just the kind of substance we young men desire. This wishy-washy, effeminate Christ must be shut out of Christendom."[25] The ability of Barton's book to speak to these and countless other readers—and to remain a top-ten bestseller for two years in the mid-1920s—reveals the remarkable convergence of the modern and the manly in the religious culture of the period. Even more, it demonstrates the willingness of many Americans to look outside the church, to an ad man rather than a preacher, to find a Christ worthy of their faith.

This array of cultural and spiritual anxieties—postwar disillusionment and anomie, the perceived crisis of masculinity, and the waning of liberal Protestant institutional power—lay behind the transformation of the religious book business in the 1920s. The historian William Hutchison describes the period as "an era in which, more than any other, the quest for cultural authority [by liberal Protestants] had become a matter of conscious intent and of programmed institutional expression."[26] Religious leaders, recognizing the threats to their cultural influence, turned to the mass medium of print to reassert their authority, and publishers seeking greater sales happily cooperated. At the center of liberal theology was the notion of redeeming the entire social order for Christ; integral to the expansion of religious book sales, therefore, was an effort to broaden and redefine what readers and authors understood a religious book to be. A more capacious understanding of religion and the aggressive marketing of these more expansive religious books allowed publishers and church leaders to accomplish their ends—increased sales, cultural redemption, and spiritual revitalization—while enhancing their own status as cultural arbiters. By marrying cutting-edge business practices with a liberal religious outlook, these leaders aimed to create new markets for books while fortifying the spiritual life of those middle-class Americans struggling to cope with the dislocations of modernity.

Religious Book Week was but one part of this sweeping transformation in the way religious books were marketed and sold. Publishing executives and liberal religious leaders, including leaders of the Federal Council of Churches, looked at the changing cultural, religious, and business environment—the perils and promises of modernity—and saw opportunity. In addition to creating the Religious Book Week, these leaders produced a variety of book lists, including a critical list from the American Library Association, and a variety of book clubs, beginning with the Religious Book Club, founded in 1927. In the process they created a thriving religious middlebrow culture, one that shared with the larger middlebrow sensibility both a democratic impulse to bring the latest ideas to the widest possible audience and, concurrently, an enhanced role for experts to guide readers through the confusing cultural marketplace.

For all the cultural and spiritual tumult of the decade, the 1920s was also a period of economic expansion and increasing material abundance, making hopes of salvation through literary consumerism seem not entirely outlandish. The historian Ann Douglas describes America in 1920 as "a Cinderella magically clothed in the most stunning dress at the ball," as if the nation had somehow escaped the drudgery of its past and entered a fairy-tale future. "Immense gains with no visible price tag," she writes, "seemed to be the American destiny."[27]

The nation was indeed prosperous, especially after the postwar depression of 1920–22 abated, and now finally at peace. The interwar years, according to the historian Richard Wightman Fox, were "the critical decades in the consolidation of modern American consumer society. It was in those interwar years that the characteristic institutions and habits of consumer culture—the motion picture, the radio, the automobile, the weekly photo-magazine, installment buying, the five-day work week, suburban living, to mention a few—assumed the central place that they still occupy in American life."[28] The now standard images of the 1920s as a decade of decadence—the "roaring twenties" of Gatsby and Harlem, flappers and jazz—capture the era as one of economic prosperity, cultural renaissance, and spiritual liberation.

The liberal religious agenda for books was therefore, from the beginning, characterized by fear and hope, by yearning for the past and faith in the future. The modern bookmen shared a sense of cultural and spiritual crisis, but also an optimistic faith in modern promotional strategies to bring their products to eager consumers. Among leaders of the book business and their allies in the churches, nostalgia for the moral and social life of the nineteenth-century village commingled with excitement over the advancing economic and intellectual possibilities of the twentieth-century city. The initiatives these publishers and clergymen created embodied these tensions and contradictions. By employing the marketing sophistication of the emerging mass culture, the promoters of the book weeks and book clubs made the consumer ethic a prevailing cultural norm. Yet even as it furthered the reach of consumerism, religious middlebrow culture also cut against the deadening emptiness of consumerism, offering countless readers an expanded spiritual horizon.

Religious Book Week (1921–1927)

The idea for a special week to promote the reading and buying of religious books was hatched in the fall of 1920. A group of twenty representatives of general religious publishers, including the Fleming H. Revell Co., Thomas Nelson & Sons, the Presbyterian Board of Publication, and the Association Press (the publishing arm of the YMCA), met in November at the New York headquarters of the National Association of Book Publishers, under the leadership of Frederic G. Melcher, executive secretary of the NABP. Inspired by the book campaigns of World War I, and even more by Melcher's successful Children's Book Week, inaugurated in 1919, these publishing leaders quickly set about the business of revolutionizing the way religious books were marketed and sold in the United States. A committee formed to devise improved marketing strategies for local booksellers, including strategies to enhance traditional advertising in newspapers and denominational journals, suggestions for cooperative ventures with churches and Sunday schools, and advice on better counter and window displays. The committee, with a budget of $1,940, produced a pamphlet containing these suggestions and distributed 3,500 copies to book dealers across the country. In addition the committee sent out ten thousand posters for display in churches, schools, libraries, women's clubs, and bookshops. This marketing blitz, conducted throughout the winter and spring of 1920–21, reached a climax with Religious Book Week itself, held March 13–20, 1921. When the first Religious Book Week arrived, so did modern marketing in the field of religious books.

Melcher, the chairman of the Religious Book Week Committee, was perhaps the most influential book promoter of the twentieth century and a driving force in bringing modern business practices to the selling of books.[29] After stints at bookstores in Boston and Indianapolis, beginning as a receiving clerk at age sixteen, Melcher came to New York in 1918 to assume the editorship of *Publishers' Weekly*, the flagship publishing trade journal, a position he held for the next forty years. In the early 1920s, in addition to his work with *Publishers' Weekly* and the National Association of Book Publishers, Melcher also served for a period as secretary of the American Booksellers Association. These positions, first in retail and later at the very center of the New York publishing establishment, afforded Melcher a unique opportunity to influence all aspects of the book business, and he made the most of it.

Melcher arrived in New York just as the book business entered a critical period of professionalization. Book publishers and sellers, steeped in the genteel tradition, had typically viewed their work as a vocation more than a profession, closer in spirit to teaching or the ministry than to standard business endeavors. For this reason publishers had long resisted professionalization, especially the trend toward scientific management that had transformed so many other business enterprises in the late nineteenth century and early twentieth.[30] A brief effort to establish a trade association, the American Publishers Association, foundered on antitrust grounds soon after it was organized in 1900. Incremental changes occurred—the American Booksellers Association was established in 1901, and publishers' advertising budgets increased significantly in the years around 1900—but in general industrywide change did not begin until after World War I.

These changes stemmed partly from shifting demographics and partly from a cultural and generational shift among book industry insiders. The 1920 census revealed that the United States had crossed a significant threshold: it had become an urban nation for the first time, with more than 50 percent of the population living in cities.[31] In addition, over the course of the decade the number of high school and college graduates each more than doubled. This urban population, wealthier and better educated than any in history and enjoying greater leisure time than ever with the spread of the eight-hour workday, made the 1920s a golden age for publishing. Book publishers seized the opportunity, and by the end of the decade were issuing over ten thousand titles annually, up from six thousand in 1920.[32]

While demographic change provided new opportunities, the modernization of the book business itself was the accomplishment of a new breed of executives. These young leaders were men "who came to publishing with interest and appreciation, rather than skepticism and contempt, for modern business practices, particularly advertising and marketing," and they quickly set about changing the old ways.[33] This new generation—future giants of publishing, including Alfred Knopf, Donald Brace, Alfred Harcourt, Richard Simon, Max Schuster, John Farrar, Stanley Reinhart, and Bennett Cerf—shared many of the traditional, noncommercial values so cherished by previous generations of publishers, yet nevertheless saw how advertising firms such as J. Walter Thompson, N. W. Ayer, and Lord and Thomas were transforming American business and hoped "advertising could help them increase distribution of books in the same way advertising had increased the distribution of other goods."[34] J. W. Clinger of the American Baptist Publication Society stated the case for advertising most succinctly. In an address titled "The Advertising of Religious Books" delivered in 1923, he pronounced advertising "a positive, creative force." "Modern advertising," he declared, "has made the luxuries of yesterday the necessities of today. It fills the human mind with new and fascinating yearnings."[35]

In addition to advertising, publishers turned to a variety of other marketing schemes. Some were flops, such as proposals to sell books by telegraph or aboard railways, but others proved to be lasting successes, such as the establishment of mass-appeal literary reviews like the *Saturday Review of Literature*, which first appeared in 1920 under the editorship of Henry Seidel Canby.[36] Many city newspapers also expanded their book review sections in the early 1920s, further increasing the public exposure of new books. Alfred Knopf instituted yet another innovation, bringing greater marketing sophistication to book design by "combining a commitment to high-quality paper and unique typefaces with jackets designed to look different from other company's books."[37] Perhaps most important in the professional development of the industry was the creation in 1920 of the National Association of Book Publishers, the first significant publishing trade association. The NABP functioned as the driving force behind many of the critical innovations of the decade, including Religious Book Week.

When Frederic Melcher arrived in New York in 1918, to work for *Publishers' Weekly* and soon the NABP, he quickly established himself as an important innovator in this new business climate. But Melcher did not begin his experiments in the field of religion; he first made his mark promoting children's books. In 1922 he instituted the Newbery Medal for the best children's book, followed in 1937 by the Caldecott Medal, awarded for the best children's picture book. Along with the Book-of-the-Month Club and, more recently, Oprah's Book Club, these awards have been among the most successful marketing devices in the history of

American publishing, continuing to drive sales of children's books into the twenty-first century. In addition to these lasting contributions, in 1919 he cofounded, with Franklin K. Mathiews, the librarian of the Boy Scouts, the Children's Book Week, the first effort to devote a week annually to the promotion of a particular kind of reading, and the direct inspiration for Religious Book Week. Melcher's innovations in the marketing of children's books were among the first efforts of the new generation of bookmen to experiment with modern marketing techniques, and the experiment proved a tremendous success.

Children's Book Week soon developed into a model for other book-promotion campaigns. As part of the shift toward scientific management, in late 1930 the NABP hired Orion H. Cheney, former vice president of the Irving Trust Company of New York, to lead a committee of researchers in a systematic review of the new business practices adopted across the industry in the 1920s. When the Cheney team published its report in 1931, among its many findings was the conclusion that Melcher's Children's Book Week had been a development of great significance in book promotion. Publishers had long known the difficulty they faced in developing a brand compared to marketers of other commodities; consumers simply did not consider the publisher when making a book-buying decision. In light of this challenge, Earnest Elmo Calkins, an advertising expert, had advised publishers in 1922 to focus their advertising dollars on general reading promotions rather than specific books. Though his advice was not widely accepted initially by industry leaders, Cheney concluded that precisely this aspect of the Children's Book Week made it a model promotional program. By simply advocating children's reading, the book week in effect made teachers and librarians into book-hawking accomplices, indirect collaborators in the encouragement of book buying.

Enlisting schools and libraries, and later churches, to promote books proved successful in large part because campaigns of this kind worked as advertising while remaining free of the stigma of conventional advertising. Children's books—and soon religious books—were the first books to receive systematic promotion precisely because they were the books least likely to be seen as mere commodities. Even as modern business practices transformed the industry in the 1920s, many publishers still saw their profession as cultural work rather than simply commercial, and they were loath to turn a book into just one among all other goods for sale to eager consumers. By promoting reading among children, or reading of religious books, publishers could experiment with innovative marketing practices without tarnishing either their self-image or their public reputation as stewards of cherished cultural values. As the Cheney survey noted, the effectiveness of the Children's Book Week "has been built up by the painstaking enlistment of the cooperation of the logical agencies concerned with education and child welfare—and by the careful conservation of the prestige and good-will of the industry."[38] Contrary to techniques that might work in other fields, "the principle of the work of the Children's Book Week has been as sound as that of any cooperative promotion campaign we have studied," the Cheney survey team wrote, "for the very reason that it avoided a big advertising campaign ... and press agent ballyhoo."[39]

When Melcher assumed the leadership of the Religious Book Week Committee in the fall of 1920, he naturally drew on his experience with Children's Book Week. Not surprisingly, Religious Book Week, like its predecessor, was quickly a smashing success. Accounts of the campaign appeared in *Literary Digest* and the book sections of the *New York Times* and *New York Herald*, in addition to other leading newspapers across the country. Stories in the *Idaho Statesman*, the *Fort Wayne News Sentinel*, the *Duluth News-Tribune*, and the *San Jose Mercury News* demonstrated the national reach of Melcher's public relations operation even in its first year. Denominational and other religious periodicals, including *The Intelligencer*, *The Christian Register*, *Lutheran Christian Herald*, *The Continent*, *The Watchword*, *Presbyterian of the South*, and *New Era Magazine*, devoted special issues to the book week, greatly enhancing national awareness. (The Rufus Jones essay on "The Habit of Reading" appeared in *The Watchword* that March.) Articles in *The Baptist* included "A Man and His Books" by the Baptist rising star Harry Emerson Fosdick; "The Place of Religious Books in the Home"; and "Books I Should Like My Pastor to Read," written by a layman, and "Books I Should Like My People to Read," written by a pastor.[40] The *Sunday School Times* carried a piece on "Reading to Steady One's Faith," while the *Central Christian Advocate* published "Is Reading a Lost Art?" by Clifton D. Gray, the president of Bates College.[41] Melcher himself trumpeted the undertaking in a long essay for the *New York Times*. Before the first book had even sold, Religious Book Week commanded the attention of the press, secular and religious, across the country.[42]

In addition to garnering free publicity, the organizers of Religious Book Week worked tirelessly to coordinate their efforts with local congregations, booksellers, libraries, women's clubs, and religious groups, applying strategies adapted from Children's Book Week. Churches across the country arranged books for display on the Sunday of book week, often tied to book-themed sermons. The influential pastor of the First Congregational Church in Detroit, Gaius Glenn Atkins, even noted in 1922 that there "is more preaching from books than possibly ever before," a boon to booksellers since "notice from the pulpit will set more people to reading a book than possibly any other advertisement."[43] Melcher meanwhile courted librarians at the 1921 meeting of the American Library Association, and in 1922 the ALA passed a resolution encouraging all public and theological libraries in the nation to "co-operate fully" with Religious Book Week.[44] *Publishers' Weekly* received reports of city newspapers displaying books on religious themes in their offices, and booksellers nationwide joined the effort. A headline in the *San Jose Mercury News* announced, "Interest by No Means Confined to Clerical Minds—Many Department Stores Fall in with Idea."[45]

Not surprisingly denominations and other national religious organizations proved the most enthusiastic allies of Religious Book Week. The YMCA sent a four-page leaflet to its six thousand branches with suggestions for ways to participate in the campaign, arguing that religious literature is "indispensable" because of "how close a relation it bears to questions of daily living."[46] Similar materials were sent to clergy from denominational headquarters, including seventeen thousand circulars from the Methodist home office, eight thousand from the Baptists, and six thousand from the Presbyterians. The Methodist denominational leadership encouraged every congregation in the nation to participate in Religious Book Week with a small circular entitled *Seven Good Reasons for Observing It in Every Methodist Church*. In addition to declaring that religious reading would "help to construct worthy ideals of living thru the inculcation of right ideas of life," the pamphlet encouraged buying and reading religious books because "it will enrich the atmosphere and increase the attractiveness of the home" and "it will encourage the assembly of the family about the evening lamp."[47]

The Methodists' encouragement to buy books to "increase the attractiveness of the home" and "encourage the assembly of the family" indicates how thoroughly values of consumerism and community intermingled in Religious Book Week. Indeed organizers frequently noted the importance of word-of-mouth advertising, a form of advertising through community, to religious book sales. "One reason why sales can run to such large figures," observed Melcher, "is because the man or woman who becomes interested in a book feels instinctively that it is his or her duty to urge its reading on another."[48] Another commenter explained, "A reader who has enjoyed a good novel may recommend it in a friendly way, but the reader of a book that has moved him in his innermost soul feels it his duty and privilege to get others to read."[49] The promotion of religious reading fostered the development of communities among those reading the same books at the same time, and publishers depended on those communities for further sales.

Consumer values coexisted with community and spiritual values at all levels of Religious Book Week. A bookseller "in the west" reported back to the Religious Book Week Committee that the campaign "really put his store on the map," while another strictly religious bookstore claimed "that the first days of Religious Book Week were like Christmas shopping days."[50] The Chicago Booksellers' League, recognizing the potential for such commercial gains, sent a Religious Book Week mailing to all the clergy in the city, made announcements at meetings of local ministers, and provided copy for stories about the campaign to local newspapers. Many book week boosters drew direct comparisons between the buying of books and the buying of other goods, for, as the YMCA noted in its book week leaflet, "the publishers and the distributors of books have felt that there was no good reason why people should not buy books for themselves and their friends as frequently as they now buy less desirable things."[51] An advertisement in the March 1921 issue of *Newsabout*—its special religious books issue—asked rather pointedly, "What shall it be on Easter morning? Handkerchiefs? Candy? Flowers? It is up to YOU to make it BOOKS."[52]

The references to Christmas and Easter shopping remind us that by the 1920s commercialism and religious piety already had a long shared history in the United States.[53] The Religious Book Week campaign certainly capitalized on this history of "selling God," yet endeavored at the same time to redeem it. Jesus may have driven the moneychangers from the temple in Jerusalem, but the organizers of Religious Book Week sought not to expel but to convert them. Numerous churches reported cooperative ventures with local bookstores, allowing booksellers to establish displays in the church during Religious Book Week. Such arrangements did not offend, apparently, because the commercialism served sacred ends. William H. Wooster of the Fleming H. Revell Co., the leading nondenominational religious publisher in the nation, expressed his version of redeemed consumerism when he wrote in support of the book week. "If all young married couples could realize how much their future happiness actually depends upon *creating the right religious atmosphere about their home* from the start," he remarked, "I am sure a number of religious books would be installed along with their very first furnishings."[54] Dr. W. J. Smith, manager of the American Baptist Publication Society's bookstore in Kansas City, also noted that commercial success in the selling of religious books might serve higher ends. "I am sending out letters to all the pastors in my territory soliciting their co-operation in the Religious Book Week," he declared, because "the right kind of advertising"— meaning advertising from preachers and Sunday school teachers—"is the gateway to a successful book business." Commercial success in selling religious books, according to Smith, served both God and Mammon. "It will not only mean the sale of books, but it will help to make the world safe for democracy," he proclaimed. "While doing this, we are advertising our store and will, no doubt, get in touch with many prospective customers."[55] Redeeming consumerism, for family, God, and nation, allowed booksellers like Smith to earn a living while serving the faith.

Religious Book Week may not have done much to fulfill Woodrow Wilson's vision of a world made safe for democracy, but William Jennings Bryan, formerly Wilson's secretary of state—and a leading evangelical—lent his celebratory endorsement to the crusade. The committee managed to secure an additional letter of support from Harry Emerson Fosdick, enabling the promoters to announce with pride that the first Religious Book Week was endorsed by the leading voices of conservative and liberal Protestantism.[56] Indeed given the intense ideological clashes in American Protestantism in the early 1920s, the Religious Book Week Committee achieved a remarkable feat by enlisting these two giants in a joint endeavor. Fosdick delivered his no-holds-barred "Shall the

Fundamentalists Win?" sermon from his pulpit in New York's historic First Presbyterian Church in May 1922, only a year later, and quickly thereafter he and Bryan began their fierce ideological struggle, one of the flashpoints of the fundamentalist-modernist controversy.[57] The two debated evolution in the pages of the *New York Times*, and Bryan, calling Fosdick "the most altitudinous higher critic," whose liberal theology simply deadened the "pain while the Christian religion is being removed," eventually succeeded in driving Fosdick from his Presbyterian pulpit in 1925.[58] Fosdick's departure ultimately led to his founding of the Riverside Church with the backing of John D. Rockefeller Jr., while Bryan's continued harangues against evolution and liberalism led to his humiliation in 1925 in the Scopes Trial. But on the eve of this great conflict, Bryan and Fosdick together supported Religious Book Week.

Religious Book Week: Beyond "Sectarian Propaganda"

The simultaneous endorsements of Bryan and Fosdick point to the very heart of the Religious Book Week agenda. While the organizers clearly designed Religious Book Week as a marketing campaign to boost sales, they also understood that better sales went hand-in-hand with a larger religious ambition: to circumscribe and unify a spiritual center in a divided and diversifying country. Promoters regularly denounced "sectarian propaganda" and in numerous speeches, editorials, and essays called upon publishers and booksellers to embrace the wider possibilities of faith. This was not a new refrain. For decades liberals had sought to strip Christianity to its essential core and thus liberate it from sectarian captivity. The same can be said of many religious movements, of course, such as the Disciples of Christ in the nineteenth century and the fundamentalists of the early twentieth, who each saw their movement as a return to the essence of Christianity. Religious liberals, however, located the essence of Christianity not in a return to the past but in an embrace of the present and future.

The characteristic principles of Protestant liberalism—optimism regarding human nature, emphasis on moral education and ethics, and an overarching faith in human progress—led modern liberals to pursue human unity beyond creed or sect and to believe in its possibility. Advocates of "muscular Christianity" had decried the "et cetera of creed," prompting the historian Stephen Prothero to characterize muscular Christians as thinking "doctrine was for sissies."[59] Fosdick himself vigorously championed the cause of a faith liberated from narrow doctrinal strife. In "Shall the Fundamentalists Win?" he lamented the "shame that the Christian Church should be quarreling over little matters when the world is dying of great needs." "What can you do with folks," he asked, "who, in the face of colossal issues, play with the tiddleywinks and peccadillos of religion?"[60] Religious Book Week married this expansive notion of religion with the tools of mass culture—the mass media of print and a consumerism stoked by sophisticated advertising campaigns—enabling its liberal Protestant organizers to use middlebrow literary culture to evangelize middle-class readers. The *Idaho Statesman*, in its announcement of the first Religious Book Week, reflected these concerns about the scope of religious reading: "Some of the greatest books of all time—most worthy of being read—would never be called 'religious' books. On the other hand, the great mass of religious reading on our bookshelves is pure tosh.... When one stipulates 'religious' books, one includes the works of minds hopelessly in a rut, the books inanely expository, totally denominational."[61] To counteract such impressions, a California bookshop reportedly carried a sign in its window proclaiming, "This Book Shop interprets religion as concerned with everything that helps humanity."[62] The agenda to move beyond creeds, itself a sectarian position of liberal Protestantism, shaped the spiritual focus of middlebrow reading for decades to come.

In Religious Book Week's second year the organizing committee, still under the leadership of Frederic Melcher, a committed Unitarian layman, added Arthur Kenedy of P. J. Kenedy and Sons, the nation's oldest Catholic publishing house, and Charles E. Bloch of the Jewish Book Concern, to the previous group of Protestant bookmen. The committee now boasted of "the breadth of the plan," a remarkable achievement, they believed, because "all types of religious houses— Evangelical, Catholic, Jewish, Liberal—were...included, using the same program and putting the same thought forward co-operatively."[63] The Religious Book Week Committee also gathered statements on the importance of religious reading from a wide range of church and synagogue leaders, to be used in promotional materials and to be made available to local newspapers across the country. To Fosdick's statement "A Man and His Reading," the committee added statements from William Barton, a leading Congregationalist minister and the father of Bruce Barton; Russell Conwell, a renowned evangelical orator, the first president of Temple University, and the author of the famed "An Acre of Diamonds" sermon and book; Rabbi Maurice Harris of Temple Israel, New York; and Charles W. Eliot, president emeritus of Harvard, the most celebrated reading promoter of the era.[64]

Each of these men, in his endorsement, echoed the central claim of Religious Book Week: good religious books must transcend the narrow, sectarian concerns that tarnish the public's impression of religion and speak plainly to higher, universal truths. In order to counter the "feeling that religious books were for a few devoted church-goers," as *Publishers' Weekly* later described the problem, advocates of Religious Book Week frequently stressed the widest possible scope for religious reading.[65] In his statement of support, Charles Eliot emphasized the importance of cooperation between religious and secular publishing houses, while another endorser added that public libraries might join the cause "so long as the religious teaching is in no sense sectarian."[66] To these voices of inclusiveness Rabbi Harris added his call for religious leaders to direct "the reading of the age into the right channels in a way to stimulate the noblest aspirations."[67]

Over and over in the early years of Religious Book Week, commentators remarked on the role of books in expanding religious possibilities. "Each year," book week organizers declared in 1924, "when the discussion of religious books comes to the front there is increasing evidence of the broadening definition of what is a religious book."[68] Some tied this enlarged spirituality to commercial success; since "those [books] which have the widest sale are usually of undenominational and general character," increased sales meant overcoming the "strong prejudice against the word 'religious'" by working "to broaden the understanding of the public as to what a religious book means."[69] But just as frequently the impulse transcended economic interest alone. Henry F. Cope of the Religious Education Association declared in 1921 that the Great War "projected at a common focus life's naked realities and its profoundest speculations." Out of this "hour of supreme crisis" arose "a literature of religion that has become popular . . . because it simply faced life." The new religious literature had captured the attention of so many readers, Cope declared, "by meeting our needs as beings who live seven days a week, rather than only one and, also, as beings who on all these seven days have infinitely deep hungers and infinitely high longings."[70]

Efforts to describe this broadened sense of religious possibilities came not just from publishers or religious leaders, but from a wide array of sources. Harold Hunting, a bookstore manager, echoed the notion that increased sales required rethinking the meaning of *religious*. A "much more broad and liberal definition of a religious book is called for," he declared, if booksellers hoped to turn Religious Book Week publicity into profit. Hunting proposed, in a paraphrase of William James, that "a man's religion is his idealization of what he cares most for" and that therefore "a religious book is one which helps us to get the really best out of any of the concrete interests of life." Books of technical theology, commentaries, and sermon outlines might interest clergy, but booksellers must understand that "religion is not confined to church people. It sometimes seems that there is as much religion outside the churches as in them." The "man in the street," Hunting declared, is not moved by "sectarian propaganda" but by broad-minded books that aid in the living of life.[71] An editorial writer in the Rock Island, Illinois, *Argus*, agreed, insisting that the focus of Religious Book Week must be on "modern religious books that discuss the practical problems of every day life." This writer argued, "A religious book is any book that turns the light of truth inward on the problems of human life and inspires men to follow the higher rather than the lower choices." Such books, modern religious books that speak to modern readers' needs, are books "the public can read . . . without being bored."[72]

The notion of avoiding boredom was not, perhaps, the loftiest of aspirations, but it brought together the twin aspects of Religious Book Week: providing relevant spiritual sustenance and doing so in an appealing consumer package. Indeed for all the elevated rhetoric about the intellectual, social, and spiritual contributions made by good religious books, the book week organizers recognized that their agenda of defining a spiritual center still required salesmanship. As Religious Book Week matured beyond its first year, Melcher and the rest of the committee carried this agenda for religious reading and national spiritual revitalization forward with an increasingly aggressive, sophisticated, and comprehensive marketing strategy. The committee more than doubled its publicity budget in 1922 to $4,000, and Melcher, ever the innovator, made an appearance from the Westinghouse radio station in Newark, New Jersey—a station whose signal carried well over one thousand miles at the time—to speak on the campaign's 1922 theme, "Great Books Are Life Teachers." Melcher's address, according to the publishing historian John Tebbel, represents the first known use of radio to promote reading.[73] The book week enterprise also made available in 1923 promotional slides for use in a "motion picture theater, or in [a] church, club or library motion picture projector or projectoscope," and moved more aggressively to woo general trade book stores, winning conspicuous support from the book departments at Macy's and Wannamaker's.[74]

The Religious Book Week organizers also reached out to the burgeoning film industry, indicating a clear effort to embrace rather than shun the medium many feared would bring about the demise of reading. The book week committee secured from the National Committee for Better Films a list of films based on popular religious texts that booksellers and churches might use to spur interest in religious literature. The National Committee, founded in 1916, was affiliated with the National Board of Review of Motion Pictures, an organization of concerned citizens dedicated to educating the public about controversial films.[75] The films recommended were all noncommercial, though the National Committee advised that churches without projection equipment "co-operate with some theater in their exhibition . . . urging the congregation to attend." The list included a fifty-two-reel collection of *The Holy Bible in Motion Pictures*, in addition to movies of special interest to Protestants, Catholics, and Jews. Among the recommended movies were *Methodized Cannibals*, a film on Methodist missions in the South Pacific; *God and the Man*, based on a fictional treatment of early Methodism; *Pilgrimage to Lourdes* and *Belgian Sisters of Luzon*; and *The Wandering Jew*, a life of Theodore Herzl. All the films listed were chosen to "fit in particularly with Religious Book Week showings" because "they will undoubtedly revive interest in religious books on kindred subjects."[76] Though radio, department store, and film promotions represented important innovations in the advertising of books, careful coordination with libraries, Sunday schools, and churches nevertheless remained the central focus of the campaign. Ultimately, according to the committee's own "Suggestions for Booksellers," "10,000 ministers talking about books are the most valuable allies that bookstores can win."[77]

The marketing strategies of Religious Book Week reveal the way religious liberalism resolved certain long-standing religious and cultural tensions while fostering new ones. Hawking religious books as commodities, religious leaders had feared for generations, might profane the sacred. To address these concerns, liberals employed the Social Gospel notion of embracing the world, in all its sordidness, as the proper arena of redemptive work, and stepped confidently into the marketplace. The market, however, engendered fear that the individualism of empowered consumers might erode clerical authority and even undermine the very idea of timeless, transcendent truth. And so liberals devised further adaptive innovations, marshalling the resources of modern mysticism and science and reframing their message in universal terms.

Yet these developments produced their own challenges and contradictions and never fully resolved the role of churchly or clerical authority, or indeed the role of religious bodies in the faith life of individuals. After all, leaders of Religious Book Week relied on churches to sell the message that religion is not bound by churches. Indeed for all the rhetorical effort employed to combat denominational or sectarian parochialism, mystical claims of spiritual universalism faced a fierce foe in the centrifugal force of consumerist eclecticism. Ten thousand ministers might sell a lot of books, but with all those books in the hands of all those freewheeling readers, what would become of ministers and their churches? And more important, what would become of the readers themselves, as their religious lives and their consumer habits became more and more entangled?

Religious Book Week: Advertising Posters and the Contradictions of Consumerism

No single artifact better exemplifies these cultural pressures than the posters used to advertise Religious Book Week. As pioneering as radio and film tie-ins were in the 1920s, the most important instrument for marketing religious books was the poster, produced annually and distributed by the tens of thousands to churches, public libraries, bookstores, YMCA branches, denominational offices, and other religious and civic organizations around the country. These posters became the public face of Religious Book Week. The best of them were not only visually compelling, but also communicated with clarity and simplicity the book promoters' vision of religious reading, informing pastors, Sunday school teachers, booksellers, and readers themselves why proper reading mattered and how books furthered well-ordered families and society. With their visual emphasis on male authority, the posters embodied, more clearly than any other artifact of the campaign, the tensions at the heart of Religious Book Week, and religious middlebrow culture more broadly, in the 1920s.

The posters themselves were products of modern advertising, often designed by leading practitioners of the graphic arts. Yet they visually evoked nostalgia for nineteenth-century genteel and evangelical ideologies of reading—forms of reading that adhered to preconsumerist values. The liberal religious mission at the heart of Religious Book Week—to promote a tolerant, practical, and modern spirituality transcending sect and tradition—stood side-by-side in these posters with references to an earlier America centered on home and family. While serving as guides for twentieth-century consumers, these posters harkened back to nineteenth-century producer values, especially the critical notion of character, before advertising and the ethic of consumption had so radically altered the cultural landscape. In keeping with their focus on character as a core value, the posters also reveal the organizers' concerns about male, clerical authority in an age increasingly defined by mass culture.

The mass-produced poster as a medium arose in the milieu of modern advertising in the late nineteenth century and achieved a greater degree of cultural currency as a nearly ubiquitous tool of government propaganda during the Great War. Technological advances in the 1880s and 1890s, especially in color lithography, enhanced the mechanical possibilities of poster making, while talented artists such as Edward Penfield and Will Bradley in the United States, and even more famously Jules Cheret and Henri Toulouse-Lautrec in France, brought aesthetic refinement, distinctive styling, and, most important, previously unimaginable cultural cachet to poster design.[78] In the early years of the twentieth century "the advertising poster was widely regarded as an exciting new art form," inspiring many businessmen to anticipate that "good posters would oil the machinery of economic progress" through "the harmonious conjunction of art and commerce."[79] American publishing houses became some of the earliest and most enthusiastic patrons of poster advertising, such that "elite-sector national publishing was largely responsible for the emergence of the commercial fine art poster" in the United States.[80] The high profile given to poster artists during the war, through the government's Division of Pictorial Publicity, and the increasingly important role of advertising in the American economy after the war made the 1920s a heyday of poster art. "During the 1920s," the art historian Michele Bogart observes, "advertising art directors moved, relatively successfully, to make the circles of art and advertising intersect" so that art for commercial purposes achieved unprecedented cultural legitimacy in this critical decade in the history of American consumer culture.[81]

Frederic Melcher, not surprisingly, played a leading role in bringing top-flight poster artists to the promotion of religious books.[82] Alongside the innovations he introduced with Children's Book Week, the Newbery and Caldecott awards, and radio book promotion, Melcher also showed a keen interest in the application of the graphic arts to the selling of books. He served as president of the American Institute of Graphic Arts in 1927–28, at a time when book jacket design, like so much else in publishing in the 1920s, transitioned from practices reflective of older book culture values to new methods that applied modern business sensibilities; in the case of dust jackets, this meant the gradual replacement of plain, utilitarian jackets with more ornate designs, signaling the book's status as a commercial good competing in a marketplace as well as a cultural object embodying noncommercial values.[83] In this new business climate, the Religious Book Week Committee, led by Melcher, understood from the beginning the importance of image making to a successful marketing campaign, and with the first book week commissioned a poster as a critical component of its public communication strategy. By the middle of the 1920s these posters came from some of the most celebrated poster artists in the country.

The Religious Book Week campaign produced four posters from 1921 to 1927, and though the designs changed considerably, each poster framed the reading of religious books as a counter to what Lippmann would call "the acids of modernity," as an activity to preserve timeless American values in a rapidly changing society. The 1921 image, for example, depicts two men, one a wanderer, overburdened, stooped, and perhaps lost, while another man, dressed as a Puritan, points forward, evidently guiding the wanderer on his way (Figure 1.1). In this poster, apparently intended to evoke John Bunyan's seventeenth-century Protestant allegory *Pilgrim's Progress,* the Puritan gestures toward an unseen horizon, but also, in the composition of the image, toward a shelf of books and a lit torch, symbol of truth. Under the heading "Religious Book Week" appears the caption "More Books for the Home," the slogan of the 1921 campaign. Though perhaps somewhat confused rhetorically—devoid of women, children, or an interior domestic space, the image fails to reinforce visually the theme of books in the home—this poster nevertheless clearly communicates that religious books might serve as guides to troubled moderns, wandering, as Lippmann wrote, "in trackless space under a blinding sun."

The 1922 poster also evoked the values of a bygone time, as a father reads to his family in the parlor of their home (Figure 1.2). His wife sits across from him, contentedly holding their daughter, while their son eagerly peers over the father's shoulder, reading along. A Bible rests on the side table—a mere prop? set aside just moments ago?—as the family happily reads together this other "good book." The scene might well be one of small-town family life, except the family's upper-class attire and fine furnishings and, most tellingly, the skyscrapers visible through the window behind, indicate that this is a modern, urban, sophisticated family. By engaging in the simple act of reading together, this urbane family avoids the disorientation of less well-grounded moderns. Furthermore, for all the evident wealth of the family this poster portrays, it, like all the Religious Book Week posters, avoids endorsing overt commercialism. While a 1919 poster for Children's Book Week showed two children captivated by a room overflowing with books—and the insistent demand "More Books in

Figure 1.1 Image from the 1921 Religious Book Week Poster, reproduced on the cover of *The Baptist*, March 5, 1921.

the Home!"—the Religious Book Week poster features only a modest collection, and the action clearly centers on the careful reading of the single open text, in accordance with traditional prescriptions for proper religious reading. The caption, the theme of the 1922 campaign, "Good Books Are Life Teachers," underscores the value of reading not for pleasure but for moral uplift.

Figure 1.2 Religious Book Week Poster, 1922. Miscellaneous Items in High Demand collection, Prints and Photographs Division, Library of Congress, LC-USZC2-181.

Combating the emptiness of modern consumer culture was indeed a central thrust of Religious Book Week, but in place of modern mass culture religious liberals proposed not a return to nineteenth-century evangelicalism, but a revitalized and modernized faith. To that end, the visual rhetoric of each of the Religious Book Week posters spoke of the twin emphases on vigorous masculinity and nonsectarian spirituality. Each poster symbolically represented male authority as central to the project of redeeming modern life. The posters perfectly captured the contrast between an outdated emphasis on doctrine, which "was for sissies" in Prothero's phrasing, and the broadened, liberalized, nonsectarian religion promoted by the Religious Book Week, which was, according to boosters, strikingly masculine.

The visual rhetoric of the posters reinforced the verbal rhetoric of book week promoters, who throughout the 1920s wrote about the nexus of modern spirituality and renewed masculinity. This rhetoric was an act of salesmanship to be sure, an effort to attract male readers and thereby provide greater legitimacy to the broadened faith of the imagined spiritual center. Henry Cope, the educator and book week supporter, vigorously championed masculine modernism in religion. He declared, "The man who reads in his library or on the train a religious book is a new type of man." Whether highly educated or not, this new man lives a "life full of immensely widened interests and intelligence. His mind is no longer parochial; it roves the whole world." The "new woman" may have attracted more attention in the 1920s, but Cope saw the "new man" as critical to the program for religious books. Alongside this new book reader, Cope proclaimed, "the man who writes the religious books is likewise a broader man. If he is a minister he has shared his educational experiences with his audience; they all went to the same or similar schools. The fact that he was destined for a religious profession did not prevent his making good on a ball team. And now he mingles with the crowd; he belongs to their clubs, plays their games and knows their life at first hand. His kind of book gets into their hands because their kind of books have come into his life."[84] It took a man's man, athletic, sociable, confident, and worldly, to write religious books in the modern world, books that might appeal to "the new type of man" striving ahead in America's bustling cities. As another book week editorial announced more succinctly, "The modern religious book is a very virile piece of literature."[85]

Evidence from the Cheney report indicates this talk of virile literature was no bluster. Though women outnumbered men by two to one in the pews, the Cheney team found that among readers who identified as religious in 1930, men devoted 48 percent of their reading to religious books, while women devoted only 31 percent. The discrepancy, the Cheney team concluded, was not due to "vocational interest in the men"—clergy doing their homework, in other words—but to the "forceful machinery for religious book distribution."[86] The efforts to promote religious books as virile, according to the Cheney survey anyway, evidently worked.

The Religious Book Week poster first introduced in 1923 powerfully depicts this relationship between modern religious literature and virility. This poster featured a close-up portrait of a robust Abraham Lincoln (Figure 1.3). As with previous posters, the 1923 design lacked any religious symbols that might reveal allegiance to a particular sect or doctrine; the books it promoted were as modern as its design. The poster simply announces, "Religious Book Week," and, along the bottom, the annual theme, "Good Books Build Character." The poster's designer, Charles Buckles "C. B." Falls, was one of the preeminent poster artists in America. Falls had designed the poster with the largest circulation in history, a 1918 propaganda poster encouraging donations of books "for men in camp and 'over there.'"[87] Born in Indiana, Falls found work in newspaper and book illustration in Chicago and New York before achieving international acclaim with

Figure 1.3 Charles Buckles "C. B." Falls's poster for Religious Book Week, 1923–26. Artist Posters collection, Prints and Photographs Division, Library of Congress, LC-USZC4-13135.

the success of his poster designs during the war. He completed his wartime "Books Wanted" poster in a single weekend under deadline, and its popularity solicited "more books for our armed forces than the training camps could house."[88] With the Abraham Lincoln poster for Religious Book Week, Falls employed his considerable skill and experience to render graphically the liberal religious agenda for reading.

The Religious Book Week Committee reissued the Falls poster for each of the campaigns from 1923 through 1926. The most striking feature of the design is the overt masculinity of the Lincoln image. This is the rail-splitter Lincoln, not the gaunt, haggard, war-weary president. Recruiting posters from the war had frequently appealed to men's sexual identity to encourage enlistment, and Falls himself had crafted sexually charged images in his own wartime propaganda work. With his portrait of Lincoln for Religious Book Week, Falls here too devised an image with a strongly gendered visual rhetoric. The central ambitions of

Figure 1.4 Adolph Treidler's poster for Religious Book Week, 1927. Artist Posters collection, Prints and Photographs Division, Library of Congress, LC-USZC4-13136.

Religious Book Week—increased book sales and reasserted cultural authority for Protestant elites—required a modernized faith stripped clean of doctrinal adornment, a faith that was practical and manly. In Abraham Lincoln, an icon revered as American everyman and martyred savior of the nation, unchurched frontiersman yet profoundly religious, author of American scripture in his great addresses at Gettysburg and the Second Inaugural, in this first among American men Falls found the perfect symbol for the aspirations of Religious Book Week promoters. The spirit of Lincoln was the spirit of virile modern religion.

In 1927 the final Religious Book Week poster appeared, Adolph Treidler's rendition of a Gothic cathedral interior (Figure 1.4). Treidler's image carried a slogan, "Religious Books Build Character," only slightly modified from the "Good Books Build Character" theme that book week promoters had used since the Lincoln poster was first introduced in 1923.[89] Treidler, like Falls, was a highly regarded illustrator when he received the book week commission, having studied at the California School of Design and with Robert Henri in New York. He worked for many of the leading mass-circulation magazines of the early twentieth century and achieved wide recognition for his poster designs for cruise ship lines.[90] *Publishers' Weekly* proclaimed his design for Religious Book Week "masterful," and his was indeed the most consistently praised of the promotional posters. Treidler's Gothic interior recalls the nostalgia for medieval order associated with Henry Adams and other turn-of-the-century American antimodernists, and like Falls's symbolically rich invocation of Lincoln, Treidler seemed to assert that the book week's emphasis on building character required a turning back to bygone times.[91]

Cultural historians have identified critical changes in the notion of character as it developed among the middle classes in the late nineteenth century and early twentieth. The most common formulation of these changes identifies a shift from a "character" ethic of the nineteenth century, rooted in material austerity and a production-driven economy, to a twentieth-century culture of "personality" tied to material abundance and a consumer-driven economy.[92] Central to the culture of character, according to this framework, were notions of duty, work, honor, reputation, self-sacrifice, morals, and manhood; the twentieth-century culture of personality, in contrast, described itself with adjectives, not nouns, including terms such as *magnetic, masterful, creative, dominant*, and *glowing*. The advertising campaign of Religious Book Week shows, however, that concerns over character persisted into the 1920s and were indeed expressed in and through advertising, the very cultural force thought most antithetical to the producer values of earlier times. The liberal Protestant leaders of Religious Book Week placed great rhetorical emphasis on character, rooted in disciplined, manly self-cultivation, even while simultaneously locating the tools for the cultivation of character—"good books"—in the consumer marketplace. Along these lines, the historian Richard Wightman Fox argues that liberal Protestantism in many ways fought to preserve an older culture of character until at least the mid-1920s through the characteristically liberal strategy of adaptation to the modern. The timeless values of Lincoln could last, in other words, only if Americans embraced new means for their acquisition. Character now would be found through properly directed consumption.

The slogans "Good Books Build Character" and "Religious Books Build Character," visually rendered with Falls's Lincoln and Treidler's Gothic cathedral, signified liberal Protestantism's simultaneous embrace of twentieth-century consumerism and its efforts to combat the spiritual corrosiveness of modernity. Lincoln and the medieval church each symbolized a unifying male authority structure, transcending schisms, factions, parties, and doctrines. The notion of character offered to confused moderns the same unifying center, a single integrated self, not the fractured and phony series of selves marketed as "personality." The editors of *The Baptist*, in their March 1921 Religious Book Week issue, stressed the role of books in shaping character. "Character is formed by the image one holds in his mind," they pronounced. "Whenever the story of any great man is told, there is certain to be mention of a few books which helped to shape his character. It makes a difference what is read."[93] The posters of Lincoln and the Gothic church reminded readers, in similar fashion, of the role of good books in sustaining the values of an earlier America in a rapidly modernizing society.

Religious Book Week, however, was itself a marketing campaign, a creature of twentieth-century consumer culture, and so found itself in the paradoxical position of marketing character. This paradox, according to Fox, permeated liberal Protestantism, which had "helped produce a twentieth-century consumer culture which knew no transcendent sources of value or judgment, yet . . . helped preserve an older producer culture that saw human responsibility as the cultivation of character in self-sacrificial service."[94] Perhaps most tellingly, neither the Falls nor the Treidler poster—each an advertisement designed, ultimately, to help sell books—featured a book, revealing the deep ambivalence of these publishers and churchmen to the very consumer culture they also embraced. Ideals of self-sacrificial service and character development never vanished from liberal Protestantism, of course, as the Social Gospel ethic of redeeming the social order fueled countless forms of social and political activism, large and small, throughout the twentieth century. The mass mobilization of World War II provided one great arena for service, as millions sacrificed overseas and at home as soldiers, workers, caretakers, and conscientious objectors; the civil rights crusades of the postwar decades provided another. Charges of self-absorption had haunted American forms of liberal religion from the moment Emerson embarked on his quest for self-reliance in the 1830s, and with the rise of consumer culture beginning in the 1870s this narcissistic potential received tremendous sustenance. To the extent liberal Protestants in subsequent decades sanctified the market as a site of self-realization they certainly abetted these historical developments. But the ambivalence of Religious Book Week promoters, even in the late 1920s, toward a thoroughgoing consumerism indicates that the liberal religious embrace of market logic was not complete. The antimodernism of Falls's Lincoln and Treidler's Gothic cathedral point toward aspects of liberal theology and practice, especially its abiding emphasis on the mystical, that remained deeply personal yet never fully domesticated, even at the height of liberal Protestant cultural ascendancy.

Frederic Melcher and the National Association of Publishers made the decision in 1928 to move on from a specific Religious Book Week to other promotional strategies, declaring the book week concept "having served its purpose."[95] The editor of *Church Management* magazine seemed to agree. "Sectionalism among religious books is passing," he declared in 1929. "I refer to the old sectionalism based on geographic and denominational lines. . . . For the first time a religious writer has a nation-wide constituency."[96] Division within American Protestantism was far from over, of course, but the late 1920s was indeed a time of great hope for writers and publishers of modern religious books. "At the heart of Religious Book Week," writes the historian Joan Shelly Rubin, "was a confident assertion of the expanding American readership for volumes on religion, together with a recognition of waning denominational allegiance among mainline Protestants." Religious Book Week and other "book-marketing strategies," she notes, "were an index of the cosmopolitanism by which liberal Protestants sought to define themselves in the early twentieth century."[97] Religious Book Week aimed to unite the promotion of religious books into a single, coordinated, national campaign, with the full resources of the New York publishing world devoted to broadcasting a simple message about modern books and a modernized faith. By the late 1920s, it seemed to those in charge, they had succeeded.

With the conclusion of Religious Book Week, in fact, religious books received, if anything, greater promotional attention, as the NABP declared the entire six weeks before Easter "Religious Book Season." The publishers' association marketed books more aggressively than ever to churches, sending 100,000 copies of its book circular to congregations and denominations across the country in 1928. In addition, noted *Publishers' Weekly*, "the famous Treidler poster is being given wider distribution, and with it can be supplied to any bookseller the famous Lincoln poster, so suitable for books of this character."[98] As Religious Book Week expanded into Religious Book Season, liberal Protestantism seemed to have rebounded from its postwar doldrums.

*   *   *

Fearful of declining cultural influence and spiritual malaise, publishers and church leaders responded in the 1920s by marketing a practical, virile, and modern faith. In the process they established the beginnings of religious middlebrow culture, a force that would transform reading choices, and middle-class spirituality, in the decades to come. Yet even as religious reading became increasingly commercialized, concerns about the spiritual consequences of consumerism remained. Leaders like Rufus Jones and Harry Emerson Fosdick championed religious experience and Social Gospel activism as the keys to sustained vitality, while the promoters of Religious Book Week invoked the notion of character as the antidote to modern consumer emptiness. But liberalism was broad and varied. Others championed liberalism's traditional individualism while disdaining its spiritual and ethical demands, and thereby wed theological modernism to a reactionary politics. These laissez-faire liberals embraced the prevailing consumer culture without the ambivalence that haunted the organizers of Religious Book Week and would remain a potent cultural presence from the 1930s onward.

Henry C. Link's 1936 bestseller *The Return to Religion* most clearly represented this fully consumerist liberalism in the years after Religious Book Week ended.[99]

Link had earned his Ph.D. in psychology from Yale in 1916, and in *The Return to Religion* told how he had abandoned for twenty years the strict Methodism of his youth, only to return once he saw it as the clearest path to success in modern society. His crisis of faith, he recounted, arose in typical fashion, when, as a student, he first realized, "in the light of modern science, how absurd much of the Bible was...that the concrete details of religion, the Church and the churches, the creeds and the doctrines, the rituals...all these were but the superstitious mistakes of uninformed minds trying to express the spiritual core of religion."[100] Nevertheless he returned to religion because "the findings of psychology in respect to personality and happiness were largely a rediscovery of old religious truths" and because "the greatest and most authentic textbook on personality is still the Bible."[101]

The key to a better personality, Link repeated throughout the book, was to be found in doing, not thinking, in practicing the habits of success rather than merely studying them. And religion was the social institution that most effectively compelled doing. "I go to church," Link wrote, "because I would rather read the Sunday papers," "because I shall meet and have to shake hands with people, many of whom do not interest me in the least," "because I might be asked to do something I don't want to do," "because I may disagree with what the minister has to say." "I go, in short," he summarized, "because I hate to go and because I know that it will do me good."[102] Link's conservative politics flowed from this understanding of the good. He railed against the New Deal, for example, as a danger to personality because it encouraged dependency and sloth, whereas "the effective personality must be primarily a producer, producing more than it consumes."[103]

Link's message of religion's utility was pitched to those, like himself, who had been educated out of old creeds and superstitions yet still needed guidance in a modern consumer society. It clearly resonated with a sizable segment of the reading public, as the book rocketed up the bestseller lists, selling out sixteen printings for Macmillan in its first ten months, thirty-four in three years; it was reissued as a Pocket Book, the first series of mass-market paperbacks, in 1941. Ironically, one of the clearest impediments Link noted to the achievement of a better personality, to practicing life rather than brooding over it, was reading. He recommended, for example, that one lonely, bookish client give up reading for a year and use the money saved to buy herself more stylish clothes. More particularly, he wrote in this bestseller, "I have warned probably more than a thousand people against the excessive reading of psychology. There is no more reason for the excessive study of psychology," he counseled, than for the healthy adult to study medicine or anatomy. "Both habits tend to produce hypochondriacs, and are symptoms of over-education, exaggerated habits of absorption."[104]

Link's opposition to reading arose from his fears of the narcissistic potential of consumerism, but his solution was to trade reading for stylish clothes, to abandon the inner life for a life of surface appearances. Like other laissez-faire liberals, he failed to recognize the contradiction at the heart of his own politics: that the unchecked market he lauded eroded the very values he aimed to protect. Most tellingly, in addition to his work as a clinical psychologist and author, Link had assumed in 1931 the position of director of social and market research for the Psychological Corporation in New York, where he directed "over 100 psychologists throughout the nation in making consumer surveys, product tests, employee morale and publication relations surveys."[105] As religious middlebrow culture took shape in the 1920s and 1930s, Link's laissez-faire liberalism represented one of its significant manifestations, the fully consumerist and therapeutic orientation later critics would decry as a soulless "culture of narcissism."[106]

Many religious liberals, such as those who organized Religious Book Week, understood these pitfalls. Even as they embraced modern marketing strategies, they remained wary of the spiritual power of consumerism, always endeavoring to redeem the market for their own purposes. Spiritually mysticism offered a way forward, a path that retained liberalism's focus on individual experience yet steered clear of the petty performances of personality. Culturally the mechanisms of middlebrow culture offered another path forward, a way to inhabit the marketplace while avoiding its anarchic and debasing potentialities. As consumerism gained an ever greater hold on all aspects of American life, psychology, mysticism, and the middlebrow increasingly defined the character of American religious liberalism.

2

The Religious Book Club

Middlebrow Culture and Liberal Protestant
Seeker Spirituality

Religious Book Week brought modern religious literature to the attention of the reading public. But a wide-scale effort such as this, for all its promise, also created significant problems. For the consumer, promotion on this scale posed the question of choice. "Who will decide for us which books are religious," asked a Western newspaper regarding Religious Book Week, "and which, being religious, are worth our while?"[1] In a vast marketplace, full of an ever-growing array of options, each compellingly presented and readily available, how was a reader to decide what to read? And who, if anyone, could help one choose? This overwhelming profusion of new books and new ideas, occurring in all fields of learning in the 1920s, both frightened and delighted Americans. "The growth of such new knowledge appeared to be a cause of great rejoicing," writes the historian Warren Susman, yet many simultaneously wondered "whether mass education and mass communication will allow any civilization to survive."[2] Was America on the verge of a golden age of understanding—of mastery of nature, self, and society in ways the world had never seen—or more ominously embarking on a path toward cultural chaos? Since the early nineteenth century American Protestants had entertained millennial hopes regarding the printed word. Was the millennium at hand, or simply a babble of confusion?

In response to these urgent questions, questions vexing both religious and secular culture, an industry of cultural expertise arose in the 1920s. This "spectacular eruption of highly popular efforts to popularize knowledge" included a vogue in outlines—summaries of an entire field of learning, often from acclaimed writers like H. G. Wells—that the historian Joan Shelley Rubin considers "the interwar period's most important nonfiction publishing trend."[3] Will and Ariel Durant's *The Story of Philosophy* (1927) and, more famously, *The Story of Civilization* series (first published in 1935) became the most celebrated such books in American history. Readers new to challenging texts like these might turn to how-to books, including Ezra Pound's *How to Read* (1931) or Mortimer Adler and Charles Van Doren's seminal *How to Read a Book* (1940), which proclaimed, "The more active the reading the better."[4] Adler and Van Doren offered guidance on "how to read practical books," "how to read history," "how to read science and mathematics," and "how to read philosophy." Other enduring institutions of this emerging culture included *Reader's Digest*, founded in 1922, and the Book-of-the-Month Club, established in 1926, each of which guided readers through the confusion of reading possibilities with expertly chosen texts.[5] These outlets offered readers engagement with the serious and vital ideas of the day, in forms that were reliable, affordable, and understandable. To meet these same needs for expert advice in the confusion of mass culture, the Religious Book Club opened in 1927. The Religious Book Club, like its model, the Book-of-the-Month Club, facilitated sampling—and buying—within the constraints of the club, among books chosen by experts, always with editorial guidance about what to read and how.

Religion and Middlebrow Culture

The term used in the 1920s, and still used today by scholars and critics, to describe this culture of outlines, readings programs, and book clubs was *middlebrow*. Borrowing from phrenological pseudo-science, critics by the 1880s began to use *highbrow* as a term of cultural distinction, and by 1900 or so *lowbrow* came into usage as the opposite, to denote lack of cultivation. By the 1920s middle-class Americans regularly fretted over their place in this pecking order; a publisher's advertisement in a 1922 issue of *The New Republic*, for example, playing on these fears, wondered worriedly, "Are We a Nation of Low Brows?"[6] By the 1920s a middle ground, the middlebrow, had also emerged, to be quickly engulfed in controversy.[7] Virginia Woolf in *The Death of the Moth* derided the middlebrow person as devoted to "no single object, neither art itself nor life itself, but both mixed indistinguishably, and rather nastily, with money, fame, power, and prestige."[8] Dwight Macdonald's famous screed decrying "masscult and midcult" in the *Partisan Review* in 1960, and other scathing accounts from Clement Greenberg and European academics sensitized by fascist propaganda, cemented the impression of many by midcentury that middlebrow culture was debased and even dangerous.[9]

Others, even at the time, however, used the term in a more neutral way. A writer for the *Saturday Review* in 1933 defined middlebrow readers as "the men and women, fairly civilized, fairly literate, who support the critics and lecturers and publishers by purchasing their wares." Neither "the tabloid addict class" nor "a tiny group of intellectuals," they are simply "the majority reader."[10] By the late 1940s American preoccupation with cultural hierarchy had only intensified. In February 1949 *Harper's* published the editor Russell Lynes's essay

"Highbrow, Lowbrow, Middlebrow: Which Are You?," which was picked up by *Life* magazine two months later, adding a humorous chart to help readers decide. These articles signaled perhaps the high-water mark of American taste-culture preoccupation.[11] The historian Lawrence Levine, in his masterful study of cultural hierarchy in America, elegantly captures the essence of middlebrow culture, calling fragmentation into separate taste cultures simply "the cultural consequences of modernization."[12] Indeed modern life presented unprecedented threats to individuals' sense of a unified self and also posed, through mass culture, a profound challenge to cultural authority. Middlebrow culture arose as a structural accommodation to these cultural crises.

Religion was not immune from these pressures, as advances in historical, scientific, and philosophical thinking disturbed previous certainties and forced modern American readers to seek guidance in the field of new religious knowledge, just as they were in all other areas of human inquiry. The war and its aftermath, and increasing urbanization and pluralism, further compounded the sense of bewilderment. In response a religious middlebrow culture, with its own experts and institutions, emerged in the 1920s as part of the larger middlebrow culture. For millions of American readers after World War I, religious middle-brow culture became what the cultural theorist Stuart Hall calls a "discursive formation," the social structure in which and through which new knowledge acquired meaning.[13] "The world," Hall observes, "has to be *made to mean*," and religious middlebrow culture shaped the meaning readers found in religious books, as they struggled to understand themselves and their relation to society and the sacred order.[14] Middlebrow culture provided a structure that helped make the confusing modern world *mean*. Beginning with the first Religious Book Week in 1921, religious leaders began to offer book lists and reading programs designed to help overwhelmed consumers sort through the mass of new books and new ideas. The most important of the new middlebrow frameworks was the book club, and the Religious Book Club, founded in 1927, one year after the Book-of-the-Month Club, quickly became a central institution for guiding reli-gious reading and book buying.

Religious middlebrow culture, like the broader middlebrow culture, partici-pated in modern consumerism through advertising and other mass media forms, but religious middlebrow also drew on the inheritance of nineteenth-century evangelical hopes and fears about print media. The clergymen, publishers, and other culture brokers who became the arbiters of the new religious middlebrow culture used the latest business and technological advances, as had their fore-bears, to market their religious messages. But in contrast to the evangelicals of the nineteenth century, these twentieth-century liberals were less concerned about maintaining purity, being *in* but not *of* the world, than with being fully present in the world, redeeming it from the inside out. Modern bookmen and bookwomen understood the anxiety and disorientation of their fellow educated urbanities and recognized with them as well the appeal of new approaches to the self and the divine that had engaged religious liberals since the nineteenth century. The transformative power of the 1920s innovations in bookselling came from the sensitivity of modern publishers and booksellers to the anxieties of the age. The book weeks and book clubs they organized united modern business practices, modern religious ideas, and a continuing faith in the wonder-working power of print, all in service of the liberal agenda of building God's kingdom on earth.

Though religious middlebrow culture differed from the larger middlebrow project in subtle ways, it nevertheless shared the same essential structure. Two dynamics provide a sense of the middlebrow rules. In navigating the contradictions and tensions of these prescribed practices, readers marked out what Rubin has aptly termed "the 'middleness' of middlebrow culture."[15] Middlebrow reading norms, first of all, dictated that one read earnestly, intensely, and with purpose, in the recognition that right reading would make one better, while refusing, at the same time, to accept the transcendent difference of high culture. Evangelicals like Noah Porter and George Philip Philes in the nineteenth century may have seen consumerist and religious reading as mutually incompatible, but middlebrow reading practices of the 1920s, 1930s, and 1940s called upon readers to engage in the consumer marketplace for books precisely in order to become more than just a consumer. In fact in his 1921 endorsement of Religious Book Week, Rufus Jones echoed the code of middlebrow reading just as surely as he did that of his religious reading predecessors when he told his audience to buy books and read them with pencil in hand. Yet even as middlebrow culture elevated and ennobled readers, it brought high thinking and eternal truths down to earth, to be sold alongside other commodities. Selling books as advertisers sold soap, according to Janice Radway, "threatened to rework the very notion of culture itself as a thing autonomous and transcendent, set apart and timeless, defined by its very difference and distance from the market," a notion of culture espoused most influentially by Matthew Arnold and other adherents of the nineteenth-century genteel tradition.[16] In the twentieth century middlebrow culture brought the lofty within reach, whether that was literary modernism, continental philosophy, or the latest output from American seminary professors. As the book club promoter Samuel W. Craig observed in 1924, "If books were merchandised in the aggressive manner of magazines, breakfast foods, toilet articles, or any other standard commodity, the increase in sales would be tremendous."[17]

The second dynamic of middlebrow culture was the simultaneous embrace of autonomy and expertise. This dialectic shaped reading practices, including the reading of popular religious books, by carefully shepherding readers through the chaos of reading choices, offering them the comfortable and limited freedom to act as guided consumers. Cultural changes, most centrally the standardization that accompanied economic growth, "made it more difficult for experts [by the 1920s] to insist that the route to autonomy lay in the self-abnegation the genteel tradition had demanded," yet, according to Rubin, "readers overwhelmed by the spiraling numbers of book titles required help in selecting the 'best.'"[18] The tension between autonomy and expertise had been, at a basic level, fundamental to the Protestant experience itself from the Reformation forward, as the doctrine of the priesthood of all believers, increasing literacy, and vernacular translations of the Bible undermined the clerical caste's monopoly on spiritual authority. In the twentieth-century United States, professional specialization, the Progressive emphasis on technical expertise, and simply the ever more complex nature of modern urban life pulled readers toward greater reliance on literary guidance, while the logic of consumerism, rooted in the all-powerful choice to buy or not to buy, further reinforced the notion of reader autonomy.

The overriding concern of middlebrow readers—the very reason, in fact, for bothering with all this difficult decision making—was the widely held assumption that proper reading would lead to self-improvement, what one critic calls, without condescension, the "take-your-vitamins earnestness [of] the middlebrow enterprise."[19] The exhortations of advertisers to improve one's appearance, hygiene, and personality and the competitive struggle of modern life fueled consumer anxieties and stoked demand for readily available solutions. The slogan for much of Religious Book Week, "Good Books Build Character," offered one such solution; read the right kinds of books, it said, and you can create a self immune from the push and pull of modern living, a character rooted in timeless values. The rise of religious middlebrow culture was both an indication of these individual and social anxieties and a central means by which middle-class Americans forged new identities in the changing environment. "Many Americans," Rubin writes, "adrift in uncharted waters . . . sought stability, insight, and pleasure in the books to which they were directed."[20] And enterprising publishers, booksellers, and religious leaders were eager to provide those directions.

Book Lists and Religious Middlebrow Culture

The most basic form of guided reading was the book list, a staple of middle-class culture since Dr. Eliot of Harvard introduced his famous "Five-Foot Shelf of Books" in 1909, and indeed already emerging in the Chautauqua reading programs of the late nineteenth century. Eliot was an early supporter of Religious Book Week, and from the beginning of the campaign in 1921 numerous other self-proclaimed experts stepped forward with reading lists to guide consumers newly awakened to religious reading. *The Continent*, for example, published in its 1921 Religious Book Week issue a list of one hundred recently published books on religious topics, compiled by a retired pastor. The reading program included books of modern scholarship on the Bible, history, and science, as well as books of spiritual interest, such as *Spiritual Voices in Modern Literature* and *Christ in the Poetry of Today*. Each book was chosen to be "helpful in clearing the mind and guiding thought in these interesting days."[21] Gaius Glenn Atkins, a prominent Detroit pastor and author, published two lists in the book review section of the *Detroit Free Press* during Religious Book Week in 1923. The first list consisted of books featuring "an intellectual approach," including works on faith and science, and new books from the theologically liberal philosophers Borden Parker Bowne and William Earnest Hocking; the second list featured devotional classics, including *Pilgrim's Progress* and *Imitation of Christ*.[22] Frederick D. Kershner, a professor of Christian doctrine at Drake University in Iowa, devised yet another list, a program of fifty-two books to be read over the course of a year. "Since the appearance of Dr. Eliot's famous five-foot bookshelf," he exclaimed, "the attention of the general public has been directed to almost numberless schemes for systematic reading," and Kershner, like Atkins, aimed to use his scheme to guide readers through the confusing proliferation of modern religious works.[23] Kershner's program started with outlines in biblical history and interpretation, moved to Hendrik Willem Van Loon's *The Story of Mankind*, and spent many weeks in modern thought and literature, including Sinclair Lewis's *Babbitt* and volumes from Bertrand Russell. Titles from the pacifist Sherwood Eddy and Williams College professor James Bissett Pratt's *The Religious Consciousness* and *Matter and Spirit* provided introductions to contemporary religious thought on social, psychological, and spiritual matters.

The most ambitious and influential list-making enterprise came from the American Library Association, the professional association for public and academic libraries.[24] Members of the ALA formed a Theological Libraries' Round Table in 1916—later called the Religious Books Round Table—to facilitate cooperation among theological librarians, but membership was open to any member of the ALA interested in religious literature.[25] Librarians from public libraries soon began to voice their unique concerns, and out of the persistent urgings of these public librarians, the Round Table eventually shifted its focus from the narrow interests of seminary libraries to the wider matter of religious literature in public libraries, and therefore to the enterprise of selecting the best religious books for the general public. The lists produced by the Religious Books Round Table from the mid-1920s to the mid-1950s constituted the official statement of the library profession on quality in religious reading and served as a key index of religious middlebrow sensibilities.

At the inaugural meeting of the Round Table, a meeting otherwise devoted to technical matters of indexing and cataloguing, Miss Colegrove, a librarian from the Newark Public Library in New Jersey, "asked the assistance of theological librarians in suggesting where she could secure lists of modern, popular religious books." She felt the need for such recommendations, the meeting minutes state, because ever "since 'Billy' Sunday had been holding meetings in New Jersey there had been an increased interest among the patrons of their library in books on religion written in a plain, popular style."[26] In 1920, after a number of Round Table annual meetings devoted once again to the concerns of seminary librarians, "librarians of public libraries in small communities" returned to the question of "the best method of securing really *valuable* religious works for the *public* library shelf." Many librarians found themselves inundated with free books "given wholly for sectarian interests" by members of aggressive "sects" and wanted assistance from the ALA in selecting "non-controversial, non-sectarian, religious works, sound in logic, strong in pedagogy, inspirational and constructive in real character building."[27] The leaders of the Round Table suggested, unhelpfully, that these public librarians turn to clergy in their towns for book lists, indicating a firmly held distinction in the minds of the Round Table leaders between marginal sects, which could not be trusted to select proper reading for the public, and mainstream churches, which could responsibly safeguard the public interest. In spite of this rebuff, the seed was planted for the professional library association to enter the business of choosing the best in religious literature.

In the early 1920s, as Religious Book Week drew national attention to modern religious books, librarians began to devote more serious attention to the problem of choosing religious literature for the public library. In response to the continuing concerns of public librarians, in fact, the Round Table chose as the theme for its 1921 and 1922 meetings "Religious Books in the Public Library." The kinds of books recommended as appropriate for public libraries closely matched the kinds of books promoted by Religious Book Week: modern, accessible, and "non-sectarian." Elima Foster, head of the Division of Philosophy and Religion at the Cleveland Public Library and secretary of the Round Table, told her fellow librarians at the 1921 meeting that "religion is coextensive with the whole realm of human experience" and offered the teachings of William James and his student James Bissett Pratt as models for understanding religious experience and guiding the selection of books.[28] Frank Grant Lewis, the librarian of Crozer Theological Seminary and founder of the Round Table, told public librarians they must "put aside their religious sectarianism" and "be ready to welcome to the library a religious book recognized as valuable to others even tho he himself would shrink from reading it." The only religious bias the public librarian should show, argued Lewis, was "generosity for the so-called modern or liberal points of view," because without exposing its readers to the latest developments in religious thinking, "the library will fail in meeting one of its large opportunities."[29] Librarians from across the country shared this goal of promoting modern religious thinking. Elizabeth Howard West, the state librarian of Texas, for example, advocated modern religious literature for public libraries, though she noted that "librarians have to be...wary, if their clientele is inclined to be conservative." The "righteous cause of breaking down narrowness and intolerance is best served by tact," West wrote, but ultimately "the hope of the future religiously" lies with those open to new books and ideas in religion, for "religious faith is not hurt, but only strengthened and rationalized by such reading."[30] The task of choosing the best modern religious books, according to West, Lewis, and other librarians, was one part of the larger pedagogical enterprise of middle-brow culture.

In 1925 the Round Table began to issue a list of the top forty or fifty (the number varied) books on religion published in the preceding year, culminating nearly a decade of discussion on the matter. In many ways the annual lists, though intended primarily as a buying guide for public libraries, carried forward the project of Religious Book Week. Frederic Melcher had addressed the Round Table in 1921 to brief them on the inaugural book week, and in 1922, after a presentation from Marion Humble, the assistant secretary of the National Association of Book Publishers, the Round Table passed a resolution encouraging all public and theological libraries to support Religious Book Week. The resolution commended "the efforts of the Religious Book Week Committee to spread the news of religious books among people."[31] In 1924 the Round Table officially changed its name to the Religious Books Round Table, reflecting its move away from the professional concerns of seminary librarians and toward the larger matter of the place of religious books in public and general-purpose libraries. When Frank Lewis at the 1925 meeting announced the first book list, which he had personally selected, he also noted the formation of a separate organization for theological librarians, a move indicating the Round Table's permanent shift in focus to general libraries and general readers. The organizers of Religious Book Week, in their effort to stimulate sales, advanced a vision for a national common ground of faith. And the professional librarians, in tackling the problem of choosing religious books for public libraries, now also arrived at the same crossroads.

The Religious Books Round Table's list quickly gained recognition beyond libraries and librarians, becoming a widely accepted public record of the most important new books on religious matters. From the list's inception in 1925 until the disbanding of the Religious Books Round Table in the late 1950s, newspapers across the country regularly published the Round Table's annual pronouncement as a public service. In May 1929, for example, the *New York Times* reproduced the list, declaring it, in a headline, "List of 'Most Important' Volumes of Kind of 1928." As he revealed the list at the ALA convention in Washington, D.C., Frank Lewis noted that the diversity of books on the list meant that Protestants and Catholics, whether conservative or liberal, were likely to find titles that both pleased and dismayed them. "Because of such varied characteristics and unwelcome points of view for nearly everybody," he wrote in the ALA announcement, "the list is in some sense representative and worthy of attention on the part of librarians and library readers."[32] Such inclusiveness, claimed Lewis and his fellow committee members, gave the ALA book list the legitimacy to serve as a national record of quality religious literature.

The Religious Books Round Table lists from 1925 through 1949 reveal a diversity of recommended books, but with its emphasis on new knowledge and its ethos of inclusiveness and wide-ranging inquiry, the lists ultimately reinforced the agenda expressed by Elizabeth Howard West of Texas: to use religious literature to make a tactful yet unmistakable brief for religious liberalism. The ALA's selection criteria, as expressed in the 1935 press release, "were the needs of the average public library and the interests of the general reader," but from these criteria the committee that year arrived at only one unanimous selection, *The Secret of Victorious Living* by Harry Emerson Fosdick, the leading liberal preacher and writer of the day.[33] Using the imagined categories "average public library" and "general reader" as selection criteria led the ALA inexorably in ecumenical and liberal directions. The 1939 committee, composed "of men who have a wide knowledge and a sound appreciation of modern religious literature," produced a list with a "non-denominational character" that would be of "great practical value in meeting the librarian's problem of selecting religious books."[34] The American Library Association gave its imprimatur each year to the "most outstanding books" in religion, and it consistently equated "most outstanding" with "modern" and "non-denominational."

Not surprisingly, for most of the Round Table's existence the annual selection committee consisted primarily of librarians from large public libraries and leading Protestant seminaries, including, on occasion, luminaries such as Halford Luccock and H. Richard Niebuhr of Yale Divinity School and Henry Sloane Coffin and Reinhold Niebuhr of Union Theological Seminary. With very few exceptions, the lists reflected the interests of such committee members. A fairly typical list offered in the spring of 1932 featured books from George Buttrick, Shirley Jackson Case, James G. Gilkey, E. Stanley Jones, Rufus Jones, Toyohiko Kagawa, Shailer Mathews, John R. Mott, Albert Schweitzer, Willard Sperry, and Ernest Fremont Tittle—a veritable who's who of interwar religious liberalism.[35] Evelyn Underhill, Georgia Harkness, William Earnest Hocking, and Jacques Maritain each made frequent appearances on the list throughout the 1930s. Beginning in the 1930s the committee added a Catholic and a Jewish member each year to the selection committee, noting that "in this way the total field of representative religious thought has been thoroughly explored."[36] The bewildering array of book choices led readers to rely increasingly on expert guidance, and the ALA book list, like lists from preachers and professors, offered reliable advice in confusing times.

Like book lists, book series provided expert guidance amid the proliferation of titles, while more explicitly offering publishers new sales opportunities.

Carefully edited series allowed publishers to market demanding texts, which generally saw limited sales, to new audiences eager for curated quality. The Modern Library, founded in 1917, achieved great success with this formula after its 1925 purchase by Bennett Cerf and Donald Klopfer, and has remained a staple for Random House ever since.[37] What the Modern Library did for modern fiction, the Hazen Books in Religion series, begun a decade later, aimed to do for modern religious literature. This series was a joint venture of the Hazen Foundation, established in 1925 by Edward W. Hazen, an executive with Curtis Publishing; the Association Press, the publishing arm of the YMCA; and the Federal Council of Churches. Hazen, who died in 1925, had been a devout Connecticut Congregationalist and eager YMCA supporter, and the Hazen Foundation funded the series "to present in compact and inexpensive form a number of the 'best available interpretations of the Christian philosophy as a guide to Christian living today.'"[38] The series, which appeared in twelve volumes from 1936 to 1940, published acclaimed scholars and preachers such as the Yale church historian Kenneth Scott Latourette (*Toward a World Christian Fellowship*), Haverford's Douglas Steere (*Prayer and Worship*), and the Social Gospel Methodist Ernest Fremont Tittle (*Christians in an Unchristian Society*), as well as John C. Bennett (*Christianity—And Our World*), Henry P. Van Dusen (*Reality and Religion*), and Georgia Harkness (*Religious Living*), all of Union Theological Seminary in New York. Most of these titles came in under eighty pages in length. By the appearance of the final two volumes in 1940, the first ten had already sold 100,000 copies, and the books continued to sell briskly, demanding numerous reprintings, throughout the 1940s.[39] The Hazen series presented to readers a robust Social Gospel ethics, social democratic politics, and a capacious understanding of the religious life, all in tidy, accessible, and affordable (50 cents) packages.[40] Cultural and religious experts in the interwar years, from clergy to librarians and publishers, understood the power of lists to shape taste and stimulate reading, and their innovations at the local and national level steered countless readers toward an expansive religious liberalism.

The Religious Book Club

For all the importance of various lists and series, no innovation of the 1920s proved as transformative as the book club. "Books are being made as accessible as milk on the stoop," observed a writer for *The Nation* in 1929 of the book club phenomenon, and "as compulsory as spinach."[41] For generations Americans had been buying books in a variety of ways, including directly from publishers and through agents of various kinds, but by 1850, according to the book historian Michael Winship, the independent retail bookstore had become the central mechanism of American book buying.[42] The problem, however, was that bookstores were heavily concentrated in urban centers and college towns. The Cheney report of 1931, in fact, found just over four thousands retail outlets that sold books in the United States, yet fully two-thirds of all U.S. counties, and nearly half of all cites with populations between 5,000 and 100,000, had not a single book retailer.[43] The mail-order book club filled this critical need. By 1945, when a large social scientific survey of American book buying and reading was conducted for the first time, book clubs accounted for 22 percent of all books sold (and 29 percent of all books sold to women), second only to bookstores, which sold 32 percent; fully 14 percent of all Americans were book club members, while another 13 percent were former members.[44] With the advent of the book club, for the first time the world of books was readily available to every American home, where the latest title from New York might arrive on the stoop alongside the bottle of milk.

By far the most significant club in the arena of religion was the Religious Book Club, though a host of smaller religious book clubs had tested the waters earlier in the 1920s. Many local churches created clubs for members, for example, such as a plan from a Presbyterian church in Detroit that the pastor described as aiming "not simply to induce men and women to read, but to direct them in their reading."[45] Twenty-four churches in Montclair, New Jersey, jointly created an interchurch reading program in 1925. An organizing committee devised a reading list and issued an invitation to members of area churches "to join in a Community Reading Plan along the lines of World-Friendship and Christian Internationalism." The committee arranged for the local public libraries to purchase the books and display them prominently on special shelves, while the Montclair *Times* published an "honor roll" of top readers. "It seems appropriate that this should be sponsored by the churches," the committee announced, "for it is our Christian ideals which are challenged by the manifold problems confronting us today. We, therefore, need a more unified, enlightened Christian opinion."[46]

As publishers and booksellers began to notice the increasing commercial viability of modern religious books, it became inevitable that the impulses behind the reading clubs of churches and endeavors such as Religious Book Week would lead to a book club for religious literature. Commercial opportunity, fueled by an attractive selection of new books and a deep yearning for expert guidance—this was the formula for book club success. And so in 1927, the final year of Religious Book Week and only a year after the founding of the Book-of-the-Month Club, the biggest names and most important institutions of the Protestant establishment opened the Religious Book Club for business.

"BOOKS, BOOKS EVERYWHERE! Are you overwhelmed each month by the flood of new books?" screamed the advertisement. "Have you the time and eyesight to spare to discover among these volumes the one or two which will minister to your spiritual needs? Can you find, among this vast outpouring, the one or two books which will add richness and depth to your religious outlook? Have you not often felt that for the sake of your own self-development you ought to read more of the great books on religious life and thought?" Whether one was a pastor or a lay reader, living in the country or the city, an answer was now at hand: the Religious Book Club. "Would it not be an ideal situation if you could find in your hands each month a book that is truly significant, truly inspiring, a book whose spiritual worth has been tested and endorsed by five great religious leaders?"[47]

The original idea for the Religious Book Club came from Stanley A. Hunter, pastor of St. John's Presbyterian Church in Berkeley, California. He wrote to Samuel McCrea Cavert, general secretary of the Federal Council of Churches—the central institution of Protestant ecumenism, founded in 1908—asking if the FCC might offer a service to ministers across the country overwhelmed by the problem of selecting the best new religious books.[48] Cavert spoke with Maxwell Geffen, president of Select Printing Co., and the two devised the outlines for a book club. Geffen would serve as business manager, and Cavert as editorial secretary. An editorial committee of eminent church leaders would choose the main book of the month, as well as a number of alternate recommendations, and write the reviews for the monthly bulletin. The Religious Book Club, formed according to this plan, launched in November 1927.[49] Critics, echoing genteel and evangelical fears about the marketplace, denounced Cavert's involvement in a "commercial organization," but the Religious Book Club's founders sought to transform the culture through engagement, not withdrawal, and the Religious Book Club was born.[50]

The editorial committee, like the committees responsible for Religious Book Week and the religious book list of the American Library Association, came from the ranks of the Protestant establishment; in this case, in fact, from the very highest ranks. S. Parkes Cadman, the English-born pastor of Brooklyn's Central Congregational Church, served as chairman. He was the leading Congregational preacher in the country, and perhaps the leading preacher of any stripe, famous as the country's first radio preaching star; he also wrote a nationally syndicated newspaper column, authored numerous books, and since 1924 had served as president of the Federal Council of Churches. Serving with Cadman on the selection committee were the Rev. Harry Emerson Fosdick, of Union Theological Seminary and Park Avenue Baptist Church, also a celebrated author and preacher; the Rt. Rev. Charles H. Brent, Episcopal bishop of Western New York and former chief of chaplains of the American Expeditionary Forces during World War I; the Methodist bishop Francis J. McConnell of Pittsburgh, president of the Religious Education Association; and Mary E. Woolley, president of Mt. Holyoke College, president of the American Association of University Women, and a member of the board of the YWCA. From its inception and for many decades to come, the Religious Book Club endeavored to set the nation's religious reading agenda, drawing on the expertise and celebrity of the most well-known and well-regarded religious leaders in the country.

In announcing the formation of the club, Cadman captured the spirit of the times, both Lippmann's sense of crisis and the business boosters' optimism. "Some gravely question whether civilization will go down in a crash" while "others give way to an acrid cynicism," he proclaimed. "The sweeping developments in science and world affairs," developments not to be feared in their own right, nevertheless demand "all thoughtful people to be rethinking constantly the meaning of religion for human life. Unless one does this," Cadman warned, "he is in danger of finding himself swept loose from his moorings and not knowing how to anchor himself to any spiritual realities." Fortunately, in spite of the unsettling pace of modern life and the rapid and confusing proliferation of new ideas, new religious thinking offered even disillusioned moderns "faith in the reality of the unseen world" and in the "goodness and righteousness at the heart of the universe." Americans in the 1920s were awakening to the hope offered by the latest religious thinking, insisted Cadman, and the "Religious Book Club is one more indication of the extraordinary interest in religion today."[51]

Cadman's vision for the Religious Book Club placed it squarely alongside *Reader's Digest* and the Book-of-the-Month Club as a tool for earnest, intelligent, and curious readers seeking guidance in confusing times. "The undertaking was born in the conviction that hosts of men and women all over the United States are hungrily seeking for light on the great problems of religious life and thought," Cadman announced. "The Religious Book Club hopes to make a modest contribution, by drawing larger attention to the most worthwhile publications, now too much neglected because of the notoriety achieved by sensational volumes of no enduring significance." The mass market simply overwhelmed readers with hyped bestsellers and sheer consumer excess, leaving those seeking to better themselves helplessly adrift. "The man in the street, who often seems concerned only with the stock market and the World Series, is really immensely interested in religion," Cadman proclaimed. "Such people are eager to avail themselves of the best opportunity to keep abreast of the best insight and scholarship in the realm of religion."[52]

Here, quite simply, was what the Religious Book Club offered: the best. It delivered the best books written by the best minds selected by the best religious leaders offering the best solutions for the vexing problems of modern living, at a discount, to your home, once a month. "I appreciate, more than I can express, the service which the Religious Book Club is rendering," wrote a Seattle minister to the book club offices. "A man who is free to read what he will does not always read what he should!" Another letter writer announced his delight at "having [his] books selected by master minds," while a third, a minister from Mount Pleasant, Michigan, described the book club experience as "like being taken into the study of each of the members of your committee and given a share of an intimacy of which ministers in small towns are sorely in need."[53] Ministers and lay readers alike hungered for uplifting religious conversation and community, and the Religious Book Club allowed its members, scattered across the country and the world, to share the same texts, ideas, and experiences.

Under the direction of Cavert, Geffen, and Henry Smith Leiper, Cavert's successor as editorial secretary, the Religious Book Club grew rapidly in membership and influence in its early years. In May 1927, just months before the club's November debut, the Rev. Joseph Fort Newton, an editor at the *Christian Century*, had remarked, "We ought to have some competent guidance in the midst of the maze of books....It is amazing to me that the Literary Guild and the Book of the Month Club have apparently excluded religious books from their lists."[54] Many others evidently saw the need as well, as membership rose quickly after the club's launch. In only its second month it could boast of members in every state and in China, Mexico, Canada, Switzerland, England, Scotland, Hawaii, and Puerto Rico (most members outside the United States appear to have been American missionaries). Total membership increased more than sixfold in the first seven months, from 980 to nearly 6,500. By 1929, according to one account, fully 40 percent of members were neither preachers nor professors, but rather ordinary lay readers.[55] The club regularly touted its selections for topping the bestseller list of *Church Management*, a leading ecumenical periodical.

Reports also came back of libraries, bookstores, and community reading groups using the book club's selections as guides for choosing their own stock or reading lists. The problem of proper selection was especially critical for libraries, noted one librarian, since the public librarian "represents a non-sectarian institution and therefore shuns the sectarian and highly controversial book." Marcia M. Furnas, chief of circulation of the Indianapolis Public Library, addressed this problem with the assistance of the Religious Book Club. "We have usually prepared for distribution during Lent or for Religious Book Week a list of the most interesting titles," she reported. "In our present list, we have used the appeal which we thought the Religious Book Club selection would have, to advertise the books." With this method of selection, she added, "a title on the list can rarely be found on the shelves even long after the list has gone out."[56] A bookstore in Concord, New Hampshire, sent its clients a card each month, on which were printed the titles selected by the book club. The bookstore "finds that if the titles are good enough to be selected by the committee of the Religious Book Club," the titles were likely to sell well among its regular customers.[57] The *Religious Book Club Bulletin* called attention to yet another "recent and outstanding trend" in the use of its selections: local reading clubs based on the religious book of the month. "Leading citizens in many communities," the editors noted, "are bending every effort to further the interest already aroused in this excellent method of religious education and group thinking. If you think this idea is a worthy one we shall be glad to send you further information."[58]

The membership of the Religious Book Club never grew terribly large, at least by the standards set by *Reader's Digest* or the Book-of-the-Month Club, but given its celebrity editorial committee, its close ties to the Federal Council of Churches, and its status as the first book club in the nation devoted to religious reading, it nevertheless served for decades as the model institution of religious middle-brow culture. Henry Ormal Severance of the library at the University of Missouri summarized the importance of a Religious Book Club selection when he told a gathering of professional librarians in 1932 that the club was simply "the best source of information for the most readable books" in religion.[59]

Not only bookstores and libraries followed its lead. In 1928 the Rev. Francis X. Talbot, literary editor of *America*, the leading Jesuit magazine, and Thomas D. Kernan of *Vanity Fair* formed the Catholic Literary Guild of America, the administrative structure for the new Catholic Book Club.[60] To help Catholics choose "the books they should read and the books they should leave unread," the Catholic Literary Guild announced it would endorse "the work of any author, regardless of his or her religion ... if it measures up to our literary standards and at the same time does not violate our teachings."[61] This Catholic effort to produce a parallel cultural institution, similar in structure and purpose to its Protestant counterpart but more hospitable to Catholic religious and cultural sensibilities, emerged from the same impulses that led to the parochial school movement and, more specifically, the Columbian Reading Union in the late nineteenth century, a Catholic competitor to the Protestant Chautauqua reading curriculum.[62] Mary Elizabeth Downey of the Chautauqua School for Librarians in fact remarked in an address to the ALA's Religious Books Round Table on the role of both the Religious Book Club and the Catholic Book Club in publicizing new religious works and driving patron library requests, an indication of the success of these Catholic efforts.[63] The Catholic Book Club claimed responsibility for introducing the French convert Jacques Maritain to American readers in the 1930s, and over the next two decades featured books from Fulton Sheen, Thomas Merton, G. K. Chesterton, C. S. Lewis, and Clare Boothe Luce. The Freethought Book-of-the-Month Club appeared in late 1928, founded by Joseph Lewis, the leading atheist crusader of the 1920s and the author of *The Tyranny of God* (1921) and *The Bible Unmasked* (1926); it boasted between thirty thousand and forty thousand members by the early 1930s.[64] The Spiritual Book Associates, another Catholic club founded by Francis Talbot, followed in 1934, and by the 1950s more than fifty similar religious book clubs were in operation, including a range of Catholic, Protestant, and Jewish enterprises.[65]

More important than the host of imitators the Religious Book Club inspired, however, is the lofty position it occupied within American Protestantism. The club functioned for decades as perhaps the most influential arbiter of religious reading among mainline Protestants. Endorsement by the Religious Book Club placed a new book, thinker, or idea before the most powerful people in American religious life, especially after October 1930, when the Religious Book Club absorbed the *Christian Century* Book Service, prompting Charles Clayton Morrison, editor of the *Christian Century*, to join an expanded editorial committee.[66] For the cultural historian, therefore, the Religious Book Club serves as a reflection of the Protestant establishment's sense of itself, of its values and the role it imagined for itself in society. The 1920s and 1930s witnessed great campaigns for interreligious cooperation, such as the Interchurch World Movement, the continued expansion of the Federal Council of Churches, and historic global ecumenical gatherings at Stockholm in 1925 and Lausanne, Switzerland, in 1927, all heavily supported by American Protestants. The Religious Book Club, though an independent corporation, functioned as the de facto voice of the Federal Council in the world of books, with Samuel McCrea Cavert, general secretary of the Council, serving as the founding editorial secretary, and editorial committee members S. Parkes Cadman (1924–28) and Francis McConnell (1928–32) each serving terms as president of the Federal Council. The Religious Book Club embodied the same spirit of earnest inquiry, high civic mindedness, social tolerance, and self-important noblesse oblige that animated ecumenical Protestantism. In a culture it saw as drifting farther and farther from its steadying influence, the Protestant establishment used the Religious Book Club and the power of print to promote its vision of the American spiritual center. Along the way the Religious Book Club also gave the Protestant establishment's stamp of approval to the kind of spiritual seeking that would increasingly characterize liberal religion in the twentieth century.

The Religious Book Club: Religious Education for the Imagined Center

So what did this imagined center look like? And what shape did this seeking take? In other words, what kinds of books did the Religious Book Club promote, and what kinds of books did its members actually read? Essential to liberal Protestant self-identity was an ethic of intellectual openness rooted in a belief in progress, and the book selections of the club clearly reflected this. Books on matters of science and faith, new biblical scholarship, and new works in the history of Christianity were the most common selections. Books on contemporary social problems, especially volumes addressing matters of the church in society and in the world, also appeared with regularity, a trend reflecting the Social Gospel tradition in American Protestantism. Finally, the Religious Book Club presented inspirational titles nearly every month as either the main or alternate selections. These books, aimed at enhancing personal devotion and spiritual well-being, often presented psychological and mystical approaches to spiritual life, two highly complementary discourses stemming from the efforts of late

nineteenth-century Anglo-American liberals to reconcile modernity and religion. Psychologically informed spirituality made science an aid to religious life,
while mystical approaches, by emphasizing ineffable encounters with the divine,
safely removed religious experience from the encroachments of materialistic
positivism. Psychology and mysticism, as most powerfully articulated by William
James in *The Varieties of Religious Experience* and Rufus Jones in *Social Law in the
Spiritual World*, each claimed to speak of the universal in religious experience, a
claim with great appeal for anxious modern readers seeking a unified self and for
modern religious leaders seeking a unified culture. Along with psychology and
mysticism, perhaps inevitably, came more esoteric forms of spirituality, from
Eastern spiritual practices to various forms of positive thinking.

A nominee for the first editorial committee, the Princeton Presbyterian
Robert E. Speer, turned down the club's offer for fear his participation would
"brand him as liberal," a fear borne out by the club's selections over the years,
which demonstrated a liberal search for truth beyond doctrinal particularities.[67]
The guiding principle of the book club's selection process, it seems, whether
choosing books of pure scholarship or of social or personal application, was the
idea that modern faith transcended sectarianism—the same idea that animated
Religious Book Week and the rest of religious middlebrow culture. This did not
mean the editors made no room for disagreement; on the contrary, reviews in
the *Religious Book Club Bulletin*, the club's monthly newsletter, routinely reflected
the controversies within American Protestantism that were so heated in the
1920s. Nor did the editors shy away from the difficult issues raised by
Christianity's contact with other religious traditions, whether in the United
States or, through missions, around the world. Rather than adhere to a single
party line, then, the Religious Book Club simply operated on the presupposition
that hearty disagreement and the give-and-take of honest intellectual inquiry
constituted the best way to sort truth from error. As informed experts, committee
members would steer readers toward the best books, and as autonomous consumers, readers would select those texts that best suited their intellectual and
personal needs. Through this process of guided inquiry a faith robust enough for
modern living would emerge.

This was the logic of the marketplace, and the logic of middlebrow culture
itself. As part of its ambition to present the best for an intelligent and inquisi-
tive reading public, the editorial committee strove to address the central topics
of the day from multiple points of view. In April 1930, for example, the editorial
committee selected *The Atonement and the Social Process* by Shailer Mathews, the
liberal dean of the Divinity School at the University of Chicago, and, as an
alternate selection, *The Virgin Birth of Christ* by Princeton Seminary's J. Gresham
Machen, the foremost fundamentalist thinker in the nation.[68] In May 1933 the
club chose Henry Pitt Van Dusen's *The Plain Man Seeks for God*, a plea by the dean
of students at Union Theological Seminary for less intellectualism and more

personal piety among liberals, which was followed a few months later by John Dewey's *A Common Faith*, a book calling for a rationalized faith stripped of super-naturalism. Since modern faith eschewed what Fosdick, an editorial committee member, had called in 1922 the "tiddledywinks and peccadillos of religion," the Religious Book Club fretted not about theological purity. Its commitment was to the best, a commitment that transcended doctrine or tradition.

Not content simply to juxtapose competing points of view, the club often went so far as to present books with which the committee members personally disagreed, so long as the book presented its case intelligently and lucidly. When in February 1941 the club chose, as an alternate selection, *How to Find Health through Prayer* by the bestselling author and Macalaster College professor Glenn Clark, for example, the committee recommended the book in spite of "highly extreme and dubious positions" because of its other merits in addressing this critical topic.[69] With great regularity this willingness to select books represent-ing unconventional thinking on religious matters meant endorsing texts written by non-Protestants. Rabbi Ernest Trattner of Los Angeles had the first such book chosen, in April 1929, a work of biblical scholarship called *Unraveling the Book of Books* that addressed both the Hebrew and Christian scriptures. The first Catholic book came in June 1932, Abbe Ernest Dimnet's *What We Live By*, a book on "how to be happy" that soon became a national bestseller. Many more vol-umes from Jewish and Catholic writers appeared in the ensuing years and decades, and the breadth of the club's selections eventually reached even beyond the Judeo-Christian tradition to include Buddhist and Hindu texts, such as Swami Akhilananda's *Hindu View of Christ* and *Mental Health and Hindu Psychology*.[70] Overall the diversity of recommended authors was quite remark-able in the decades after the club's founding. Fulton Sheen and Paul Blanshard, Billy Graham and Aldous Huxley, Martin Buber and Karl Barth, Reinhold Niebuhr and Alan Watts, C. S. Lewis and D. T. Suzuki, Kahlil Gibran and Howard Thurman, Ralph Waldo Trine and W. E. B. Du Bois, Theodore Dreiser, Paul Tillich, Kirby Page, Gerald Heard, Jacques Maritain, Walter Lippmann, Roland Bainton, Norman Vincent Peale, Toyohiko Kagawa, Rollo May, T. S. Eliot, John Foster Dulles, William F. Buckley Jr., Carl Jung, Henry Steele Commager, Merle Curti, Henri Bergson, Mary Pickford, and Albert Schweitzer all had books chosen as primary or alternate selections between the late 1920s and early 1950s.

In spite of this openness—or, to be more exact, precisely because of this openness—the Religious Book Club remained solidly and consistently a creature of the liberal Protestant establishment. The openness to new ideas characterized by the remarkable roll call of recommended authors stemmed from the "take-your-vitamins" quality of the middlebrow project, an effort on the part of the better educated and more sophisticated editorial committee to inform the club's members of the world beyond the safe confines of Euro-American Protestantism. The committee sometimes signaled quite clearly when it was offering vitamins to its members. The October 1928 main selection, for example, James Bissett Pratt's *The Pilgrimage of Buddhism*, aimed to teach readers "how it feels to be a Buddhist," but the editorial committee, recognizing that Buddhism was an "alien faith" for its members, drew attention to an alternate selection from the liberal theologian John Wright Buckham for those unwilling to try Pratt's volume. Many members accepted this alternate offer, making Pratt's book the most substituted of all main selections in 1928. Pratt's work on Buddhism "was apparently too far removed from the ordinary experience of most Americans," Cavert commented, though he found consolation that nevertheless a majority of the members were "ready to explore a realm that a few years ago was almost *terra incognita*."[71] Reading a work on Buddhism or any other "alien faith," or a book with challenging new ideas on science, history, politics, or biblical interpretation, was intrinsic to the middlebrow agenda of reading for self-improvement. Through the reading practices of the club—through this exercise in intellectual inquiry unfettered by doctrine—the club and its members performed, in their selecting, reviewing, and reading, the liberalism of liberal Protestantism. The Religious Book Club used the reading practices of middlebrow culture to evangelize a broadened and liberalized faith among mainline Protestants.

The most common books recommended by the club were titles on science and faith and modern approaches to church history and biblical scholarship. These books most directly allowed club members opportunities for self-improvement through educational reading. The main and alternate selections from the 1920s and 1930s that addressed topics of science and religion—titles like *Science and Human Progress*, *Science Rediscovers God*, *Does Science Leave Room for God?*, *Science and God*, *Science and Religion*, *Through Science to God*, *From Science to God*, *Science in Search of God*, and *Christian Faith and the Science of Today*—reveal the club's core belief in intellectual engagement with the most controversial topics of the day. In recommending *From Science to God*, a highly philosophical tome aimed at skeptics, the committee remarked that the findings of this book "may not seem adequate to those who have been reared in an atmosphere of Christian faith," yet they found the book compelling because it demonstrated "a sound scientific and philosophical basis for religion."[72] Intellectual rigor, not piety, commanded the selection committee's attention—but only intellectual rigor that was simultaneously accessible. When recommending *The Literature of the New Testament*, one of many biblical studies offered over the years, the committee praised it as "the best single book interpreting modern knowledge of the New Testament—non-academic and superbly readable." Likewise the book *Faith: An Historical Survey* was offered because of its valuable service in "tracing varying concepts of faith through history." Like the outlines of Will and Ariel Durant or H. G. Wells, *Faith* "summarizes modern developments" for the busy modern reader.[73] Other titles on biblical and historical matters, including *Revaluing Scripture*, *The Background of the Bible*, *The Social Triumph of the Ancient Church*, *The Church through the Centuries, John Wesley and Modern Religion,* and *The Makers of Christianity from Cotton Mather to Lyman Abbott,* also appeared in the first decade of the club's existence, among many other titles in these fields. R. L. Duffus, who produced a Carnegie Corporation study of the book business in the 1920s, noted that book clubs exhibited "some of the attributes of a correspondence course," and indeed a reader who faithfully followed the reading plan of the Religious Book Club would have received an education on par with that offered by the leading academic seminaries in the country.[74]

The Religious Book Club and Seeker Spirituality

These books of modern learning clearly reveal the Religious Book Club's middle-brow agenda. But the greatest legacy of religious middlebrow culture was not as an institution of popular education in matters of the mind, but as a guide for personal betterment in matters of psyche and spirit. The "new knowledge," to use Warren Susman's term, that poured forth in increasing abundance from the pens of America's intellectual elite clearly mattered deeply to the religious leaders who ran the Religious Book Club, and they saw guiding their readership through the thickets of this new knowledge as critical to their mission. But ultimately new knowledge only mattered to the liberal Protestant leaders of the club to the degree that it served the higher purpose of sustaining religious vitality in modern times. And so for all the books on science or history or even the Bible, the Religious Book Club lavished special attention on books of personal spiritual application, books written to aid happiness, health, well-being, and intimacy with God. Here, just as with books on scholarly matters, an ethic of free inquiry reigned, and so, by promoting spiritual exploration through reading, the Religious Book Club and the religious middlebrow culture it epitomized advanced and legitimated a culture of spiritual seeking.

Books of personal spirituality were the most popular of the Religious Book Club's selections from the start. "The fact is," wrote Samuel McCrea Cavert, "that the 1929 volume which proved most popular among members of the Religious Book Club was one dealing not with any of the philosophical or social problems of religion, but rather with the personal inner life and the ways of making religion produce actual observable results in the experience of the individual."[75] The book, *Methods of Private Religious Living* by the University of Chicago philosopher Henry Nelson Wieman, addressed mysticism, joy, and prayer life from a psychological perspective, and achieved its success with club members despite the editorial committee's calling it an "unusual treatise on the practical development of the religious life."[76] Following this precedent, the book club offered numerous books on psychology, mysticism, and spirituality in the ensuing years, introducing readers to new practices and ideas regarding spiritual life. In essence the Religious Book Club offered a middlebrow education in being spiritually modern to complement and enhance the education it offered in being intellectually modern.

Books on psychology offered the most readily available bridge between modern science and the life of the spirit. As the historian Christopher White has described, since the late nineteenth century psychology had served as a critical field of study for liberal Protestant intellectuals searching for modern understandings of the self and of the self's apprehension of the divine—a search, as noted earlier, most influentially practiced and promoted by William James.[77] American Protestants embraced psychology as part of the intellectual and spiritual revolution that accompanied modernity, though the turn to psychology was not without controversy. Charles Clayton Morrison, the editor of the *Christian Century* and after 1930 a member of the editorial committee of the Religious Book Club, was a chief advocate of psychology within the ranks of the Protestant establishment. Morrison and others like him, the psychiatrist and theologian Kevin Meador claims, "embraced psychology ... as a way to make Christianity 'scientific,'" because "science heralded the dawn of a new era of Christian unity."[78] Critics, including most famously H. Richard Niebuhr in an influential 1927 *Christian Century* article, lamented psychology's ties to theology as "a sterile union," blaming "the revolution ... introduced by William James and his followers" for degrading historic Christian teachings.[79] The psychological turn, stemming from Berkeley, Hume, Kant, and Schleiermacher in Europe as well as James in the United States, wrote Niebuhr, "has substituted religious experience for revelation, auto-suggestion for communion with God in prayer and mysticism, sublimation of the instincts for devotion, reflexes for the soul, and group consciousness or the ideal wish-fulfillment for God."[80] While Niebuhr acknowledged that James himself had steered safely clear of such reductionism, his followers aimed to "show that religion is an epi-phenomenon—a fiction, indeed, explicable but quite unnecessary."[81] Niebuhr's criticisms represented one influential thrust of the neo-orthodox reaction against religious liberalism, but the reaction itself indicates the importance of the changes occurring in American Protestantism—the term *revolution* is not out of place—as increasing numbers of clergy and laity after the war turned to psychological science for spiritual guidance.

Popular culture in the 1920s and 1930s also reflected this ongoing fascination with mind and personality. On the bestseller lists in these years appeared James Harvey Robinson's *The Mind in the Making* (1922); *Self-Mastery through Auto-Suggestion,* by Emile Coué (1923);[82] *Why We Behave Like Human Beings,* by George Dorsey (1926); *The Art of Thinking* (1930), by the French cleric and philosopher Abbe Ernest Dimnet, and his follow-up, *What We Live By* (1932), a Religious Book Club selection; *Power through Constructive Thinking* (1932) and *Sermon on the Mount* (1934), positive-thinking classics from the New York Divine

Science preacher Emmet Fox; and the consumer psychologist Henry C. Link's 1936 bestseller *The Return to Religion*.[83] The American fascination with psychology, spurred by late nineteenth-century Protestant angst, by the 1920s had become a central cultural paradigm for understanding the self, society, and the experience of the divine.[84]

Offerings from the Religious Book Club in its first twenty years, either primary or alternate selections, included at least forty-five titles containing the words *psychology, psychiatry,* or *psychoanalysis,* from such leading scholars as Leslie Weatherhead, Henry Nelson Wieman, and Carl Jung. The first book club offering on psychology, Harrison Sacket Elliott's *The Bearing of Psychology upon Religion*, appeared in April 1928, and in 1930 alone *Psychology and Religious Experience, Psychology in Service of the Soul*, and *Sin and the New Psychology* were all book club selections. Many of these titles over the years were books of professional interest in the burgeoning field of pastoral counseling—July 1932, for example, featured both *Psychology for Religious Workers* and *Pastoral Psychiatry and Mental Health*—but most of the titles offered on psychology were of interest to lay readers as well. In reviewing *Mental Hygiene for Effective Living* by Edwin A. Kirkpatrick, a former professor of psychology and education at Columbia and Boston Universities, the committee stated the central concern of these books succinctly. "How may we maintain or rebuild a healthy personality," they asked, "in the face of the disintegrating forces of modern times?"[85]

The Religious Book Club presented its members with myriad answers to this basic question. James Gordon Gilkey offered his thoughts on the matter in a 1933 selection, *Managing One's Self*, a book covering ten common problems from the point of view of applied psychology. Other books of inspirational psychology from the 1930s included *Christianity and the Individual in a World of Crowds* by the Yale professor Halford Luccock, which, the committee wrote, "gives [a] keen diagnosis of social forces that are crushing personality today," and *Health for Mind and Spirit* by the English pastor W. L. Northridge, which argued for "intelligent cooperation between religious leaders and the medical profession" in "language that is readily understood by the non-technical reader."[86] A more influential voice was featured in July 1939, when Charles T. Holman's *The Religion of a Healthy Mind* was the main selection. Holman, the director of vocational training at the University of Chicago Divinity School, wrote this book not for his students or other religious professionals, but for "the thoughtful layman." Using James, Freud, and Jung as guides, Holman's path to a healthy mind involved "the discovery of a cosmic Purpose in relation to which one becomes a larger self." "Christian faith," the editorial committee summarized, "is pictured not as an escape from the real but as a discovery of reality.... To become 'God conscious' is, in the last analysis, the basic factor in mental health."[87] Carl Jung's *Psychology and Religion*, a March 1938 alternate selection, and Rollo May's *The Springs of Creative Living: A Study of Human Nature and God*, the November 1940 book of the month, offered yet more choices for those seeking psychological enlightenment.

Of all the authors championed by the Religious Book Club, perhaps the most important in the Protestant embrace of psychology were Elwood Worcester and Samuel McComb, disciples of William James and founders of the Emmanuel Movement. Begun in 1905, the Emmanuel Movement was the first sustained effort to bring academic psychology into the life of the church. Worcester, rector of Emmanuel Episcopal Church in Boston, and McComb developed a style of group therapy aimed at healing mind and body, with loose similarities to Christian Science and New Thought. The movement quickly spread through the urban centers of the Northeast, especially among middle- and upper-middle-class women, and retained a sizable following into the 1920s.[88] The Emmanuel Movement "helped introduce the new psychology into the church at a time when it was barely understood within the hospital" and anticipated the cultural fascination with psychology after the war.[89] Harry Emerson Fosdick was among an avant-garde of liberal Protestant leaders, influenced by James, Worcester, and McComb, who in the 1920s turned to the new psychology to aid in pastoral counseling. In choosing Worcester and McComb's *Body, Mind and Spirit* as a Religious Book Club main selection in March 1931, Fosdick and the rest of the editorial committee conferred the legitimacy of the Protestant establishment upon a field still viewed with suspicion in some quarters.[90]

The editors knew the book would push the club's members beyond the bounds of familiar religious thinking, yet in the spirit of free intellectual inquiry and expert leadership they nevertheless offered it as a book of "creative significance," useful as a "guide to the exploration of this new and little known field." The book offered "a simple and comprehensible interpretation of psychoanalysis" with regard to religion, including a high regard for the contributions of Freud, in spite of his "undue preoccupation with sex." Freudian psychology, the committee told its presumably skeptical audience, in fact made room for the notion of the soul and allowed for psychological interpretations of such phenomena as prayer and the healing miracles of Jesus. By releasing the soul from anxiety, fear, and guilt, psychological treatment offered a path to "a more serene inner spirit." Likewise, the review stated, Worcester and McComb demonstrated that faith and prayer facilitated psychological well-being and therefore aided bodily and mental health. While many popular books made outlandish claims about mental healing, here "is a treatise," wrote the editorial committee, "that is marked both by sanity and by a spirit of cooperation" between psychological science and spiritual insight.[91] The Religious Book Club featured other books from Worcester and McComb throughout the 1930s, including the April 1933 selection, *Making Life Better*.

Psychology brought modern scientific knowledge to bear on matters of psyche and spirit, but, like other modes of scientific thinking, it also threatened spiritual life with a purely naturalistic understanding of the human self. For decades liberal Protestants had lavished theological attention on the concept of personality, given their characteristic concerns for conscience, experience, and the sacredness of the individual. The historian of theology Gary Dorrien contends that "every liberal Protestant of the Progressive era preached...the religion of personality," and indeed a critically important strand of liberal theology, known as personalism, argued that sacred meaning inhered in, and only in, personhood.[92] The Religious Book Club frequently featured works from the personalist school—not surprising since one of the club's original and longtime editors, the Methodist bishop Francis J. McConnell, was a leading personalist and a student of the founder of the movement, the philosopher Borden Parker Bowne of Boston University. Personalism bore considerable fruit in the twentieth century, directly contributing to the theological foundations of the civil rights movement and the midcentury declarations of universal human rights, each an astounding liberal accomplishment.[93] Empirical psychology of the Jamesian variety aided in this endeavor through its own recognition of experience as the key linkage between the self and the other, including the divine Other. When Rufus Jones in *Social Law in the Spiritual World* argued, "If we could drop our plummet down though the deeps of one personality we could tell all the meanings of the visible world...and all the secrets of the eternal Personal Self," he perfectly captured the Jamesian, and personalist, insight.[94] From this vantage point, H. Richard Niebuhr's concerns about the "sterile union" of psychology and theology seem unfounded, since psychological exploration abetted in many ways both ethical progress and spiritual vitality. Nevertheless a purely positivistic psychology indeed threatened to become an updated version of the "medical materialism" James railed against in the opening pages of *Varieties*. And so, like James and Jones, the editors of the Religious Book Club turned to unmediated religious experience—to the mystical—to temper this reductionistic and dehumanizing tendency. In this way the mystical, rooted in and understood through human experience, brought together psychological knowledge and spiritual insight.

As with psychology, the book club's interest in mysticism was evident from the beginning. In November 1927, the club's first month, the committee chose *New Studies in Mystical Religion* by Rufus Jones as an alternate selection, and over the ensuing months and years it featured a steady stream of books on mystical spirituality, including both academic studies and devotional guides. Albert Schweitzer's *The Mysticism of St. Paul the Apostle*; *Christian Mysticism* and *Mysticism in Religion* by William Ralph Inge, dean of St. Paul's Cathedral in London and a professor at Cambridge; and Evelyn Underhill's *Worship* all were book club recommendations, and each placed mystical experience at the center of Christian faith and tradition. These theological and historical studies, like other book club recommendations, introduced club members to the latest scholarship on critical matters. But in addition to serving a pedagogical function, these books also aimed to inspire, to provide resources for spiritual living in a modern scientific age.

Regardless of specific form or content, in fact, the book club invariably recommended mystical spirituality as the means of keeping religion vital amid the encroachments of modernity. The challenge of science, argued numerous recommended books, posed no threat to a faith predicated on mystical awareness of the divine, and so mysticism became a bulwark against materialistic reductionism. The committee recommended for August 1928, for example, *Science in Search of God* by Kirtley F. Mather, head of the Geology Department at Harvard, because Mather argued that religion must not attempt to counter scientific thinking, but rather chart a course for living a spiritually abundant life, including prayer and meditation, within a scientifically modern society. Likewise *Beyond Agnosticism,* the May 1929 selection from Columbia University's chaplain, Bernard Iddings Bell, was recommended because it too offered mystical spirituality as a path that allowed one to live in concert with, rather than against, scientific thinking. Bell's book, wrote the committee, gave readers an "arresting presentation of the inadequacy of any materialistic interpretation of life."[95] Georgia Harkness's *The Resources of Religion*, the March 1936 main selection, argued that the main purpose of religion was to give "'a sense of direction' so that one no longer feels 'lost.'" The committee recommended the book because "of its exceptionally lucid portrayal of religion and its high significance for modern life," a case made with "intellectual vigor and an inspirational quality." "It is not merely an argument about religion," the editors exclaimed, "it is vital religion revealing its secret to others."[96]

Of all the books on mysticism recommended by the Religious Book Club, the committee members praised most exuberantly the works of Rufus Jones, a professor at Haverford College, a leader of the American Friends Service Committee, and "the best known of living American mystics."[97] After choosing *New Studies in Mystical Religion* in the first month, the club recommended fifteen Jones books in the next twenty years, including four as main selections. The writings of Jones combined modern scientific knowledge with mystical vitality and social engagement, all written in a lively prose style replete with personal anecdotes and folksy yarns, a perfect blend of ingredients for the book club's purposes. The committee, in reviewing Jones's *Pathways to the Reality of God* as the main selection for September 1931, noted the "revival of interest in mystical experience" and commended Jones for his discussion of mystics as "practical men," not dreamy spiritual escapists. The April 1936 featured title, Jones's *The Testimony of the Soul*, offered "a winsome summary of his life-long reflections and scholarship."[98] Jones's works, as the reviewers noted, were the essential texts in the revival of mysticism between the wars, and the Religious Book Club played a pivotal role in bringing his work to wide public attention.

Rufus Jones, Dean Inge, Georgia Harkness, and Evelyn Underhill all presented mysticism from within established churches and the broad parameters of historic Christian teaching. But in its ambition to offer the best modern religious literature regardless of doctrine or tradition, the Religious Book Club also featured works of mystical spirituality that reached even farther afield. As an alternate selection in 1935, for example, the club presented *My Adventure into Spiritualism*, an autobiographical account from a Congregational minister. "It constitutes a sober and factual recital of experiences which will be read with profit by an open-minded person," the committee wrote. "The author did not find spiritualism any substitute for his Christian faith. But he found psychics possessed of something which enriched and deepened that faith." The book "might well be studied by those who have preached immortality and who may be all unconsciously avoiding one of the avenues by which that faith stands abundantly justified."[99]

In addition to spiritualism, the Religious Book Club also presented texts from the mind cure strand of liberal religion. Mind cure had developed in concert with psychological science and mystical spirituality in the late nineteenth century and remained an important form of popular religious thought and practice throughout the twentieth century. Mind cure, or positive thinking, formed the key ideological component of laissez-faire liberalism, combining deep-seated individualism with a version of psychological theory to deny any limitations imposed by social, political, economic, or cultural structures or institutions. The book club reviewers often remained skeptical of mind cure claims, yet nevertheless offered books from positive-thinking celebrities like Glenn Clark and Norman Vincent Peale throughout the 1930s and 1940s. Clark's claims about healing were suspect in the eyes of the editors, according to their 1941 review of *How to Find Health through Prayer*, and Peale's 1948 *A Guide to Confident Living* might "unintentionally create the impression that 'success,' in the worldly sense of the term, is the main contribution of religious faith," a nice summary of the moral and intellectual outlook common to laissez-faire liberalism. Nevertheless the editorial committee featured these titles as alternate selections so readers, as free consumers and fellow spiritual explorers, might decide for themselves.[100]

By the mid-1940s the Religious Book Club began to receive criticism for its wide-ranging book choices. *Time* magazine in November 1946 wryly commented, "The Religious Book Club has no Index Librorum Prohibitorum—it is proud of its lack of religious rigidity in the books it recommends to subscribers. But this month many a Christian thought the club's board of editors might well be ashamed of its religious laxity" for its choice of the Robert Graves novel *King Jesus*.[101] The editors of *Time*, in fact, might well have directed their scorn at any one of a number of choices, for in the preceding years the club had chosen as alternates Aldous Huxley's *Ends and Means* (December 1937) and *The Perennial Philosophy* (January 1946), the classic statement of the essential unity of the world's mystical traditions. The club also chose as an alternate selection in April 1944 Huxley's friend and colleague Gerald Heard's *A Preface to Prayer*. Huxley and Heard had emigrated from England in 1937, and together with the writer Christopher Isherwood immersed themselves in Vedantism in southern California.[102] Heard's book discussed three levels of prayer, the highest being the mystical "pure concentration upon God." "Mr. Heard," the Religious Book Club's review noted, "draws in part on the Christian mystics but almost as much upon Hindu and Buddhist philosophy." In describing Heard's treatment of prayer, meditation, and "universal Consciousness," the reviewers noted, "Some of these suggestions will seem rather strange to those not familiar with mystical disciplines."[103]

*   *   *

The examples of spiritualist and mind cure texts and the writings of Huxley and Heard demonstrate the way middlebrow culture and the ethos of consumerism fostered spiritual seeking in the 1920s, 1930s, and 1940s. Though the reviewers on occasion expressed skepticism toward these more unconventional forms of spirituality, the commitment to intellectual openness and free spiritual inquiry that led them enthusiastically to embrace psychology and Christian mysticism led as well to these farther-afield teachings. The very mission of the Religious Book Club, in fact, as the leading institution of religious middlebrow culture, was to introduce readers to new ideas, to challenge staid teachings and practices, to give readers their intellectual and spiritual vitamins. Psychology and mysticism attracted liberal Protestants in the first half of the twentieth century because they offered modern universal vocabularies to compass the life of the spirit. In this quest for a universal spiritual idiom, the Religious Book Club and religious middlebrow culture became agents of wider and wider spiritual exploration.

Remarkably, even as the Religious Book Club offered members texts from the edges of liberal spirituality, it remained firmly rooted in the very center of American Protestant institutional power. The founding editorial committee member Harry Emerson Fosdick, the most famous preacher in America after his move to the Riverside Church in the late 1920s, remained on the committee into the 1950s, as did Samuel McCrea Cavert and Charles Clayton Morrison. In the late 1930s Rufus Jones briefly served as an editor, and after an expansion of the committee in 1946 the novelist Lloyd C. Douglas, the diplomat John Foster Dulles, and the Episcopal bishop Angus Dun joined, along with Charles Seymour, president of Yale; the Methodist bishop G. Bromley Oxman, president of the Federal Council of Churches; the sociologist and author Pitirim A. Sorokin of Harvard; Mildred McAfee Horton, president of Wellesley College; and Rear Admiral William N. Thomas, chief of navy chaplains.[104] In the late 1950s, in yet another reorganization, H. Richard Niebuhr, D. Elton Trueblood, and a young Martin Luther King Jr. joined the editorial committee.[105]

This group of men and women, drawn from the very pinnacle of the religious establishment in the United States, used their influence in the Religious Book Club not only to introduce American readers to the latest scholarship in science, history, biblical studies, and social problems, but also to push Americans toward ever farther spiritual horizons. In this way the religious middlebrow culture of the twentieth century recapitulated the story of Protestantism itself, in which print, from the beginning, has functioned both as an instrument of central authority and as the single most important force in undermining that authority. In the years after World War I the priesthood of all believers merged with the kingship of the consumer. Though firmly rooted in institutional liberal Protestantism, religious middlebrow culture catalyzed the culture of seeking that revolutionized middle-class religious life in the mid-twentieth century.

3

Publishing for Seekers

*Eugene Exman and the Religious Bestsellers
of Harper & Brothers*

Mary Rose Himler, an executive with the Bobbs-Merrill publishing house, did not mince words in her assessment of the religious book business in the mid-1920s. "Most religious books never reach the great bulk of the reading public," she declared, "because most religious books are bigoted and prejudiced, because a great many of them can be classified as textbooks for divinity students. Meanwhile, the American public knows exactly what it wants, whether it be automobiles, chewing gum or books and it buys that which gives it the most enjoyment, the better inspiration, the more interesting experience."[1] What many Americans wanted, it turned out, was precisely the modern inspirational literature promoted by the Religious Book Weeks and offered for sale through the Religious Book Club. Sales of new religious titles increased steadily enough by the mid-1920s that book industry insiders announced the advent of "a decided religious renaissance." "Religion and religious books," according to *Publishers' Weekly* in 1927, had quickly become "a very live topic."[2] Publishers and booksellers looked at the modernization and professionalization of the publishing industry, in particular at the sophisticated marketing of new, "virile" religious literature, and recognized an important shift in the fundamentals of their business. The numbers supported the claim of a renaissance. In 1900 religious books had been the sixth most widely purchased category of new books; by 1928 they were second only to fiction, ahead of biography, history, poetry, and even juvenile literature.[3] The portion of total book sales accounted for by religious books increased 34 percent, according to one measure, from 1925 to 1929 alone.[4]

Then came the Crash. In October 1929, when the bottom fell out of the stock market, and then in the coming months and years as the Crash metastasized into the Great Depression, the sense of jubilant optimism surrounding religion and religious books crashed as well. Commentators soon began to speak and write of a "religious depression" that corresponded with the economic depression, and the business of buying and selling books, including religious books, suffered greatly.[5] Total book sales dropped from 219,276,000 in 1927 to 197,259,000 in 1937, but within this drop religious books suffered particularly severe losses; as a percentage of total books sold, religious books declined by 45 percent in the years from 1931 to 1935.[6] This sharp decline in the sales of religious books occurred not simply as a function of the generally dismal economic climate, since religious books suffered a significantly greater drop in sales than others kinds of books. Rather the sales of mass-market religious books plummeted as part of the broader fate of liberal religion in these years.

The core liberal affirmation of progress and the American Protestant establishment's sense of its custodial relationship to the culture meant that the crisis shaking the nation shook liberal Protestantism especially hard. Jewish and Catholic congregations, by contrast, grew steadily in membership throughout the early 1930s. Right-wing religious and political movements, such as Frank Buchman's Moral Re-Armament and William Dudley Pelley's Silver Shirts, and vocal firebrands like Father Charles Coughlin and the Rev. Gerald L. K. Smith, all attracted considerable followings. New sects and religious movements, such as Father Divine's Peace Mission, briefly flourished as well. But Protestant mainline churches flagged in membership, financial contributions, support for domestic and global missions, and just plain zeal.[7] When Robert and Helen Lynd returned to Muncie, Indiana, in the mid-1930s to follow up on their pioneering *Middletown* study of the previous decade, they found that the congregations of the mainline churches seemed "older than formerly," perhaps because "sermon topics in 1935 are interchangeable with those of a decade ago."[8] In spite of a resurgent Social Gospel, institutional liberal Protestantism had failed to mount an adequate response to the national emergency. As one informant in the Lynds' study remarked, "The depression has brought a resurgence of earnest religious fundamentalism among the weaker working-class sects...but the uptown churches have seen little similar revival of interest."[9] The long-term, historic decline in the Protestant mainline, generally described as a phenomenon of the 1960s and later, can in many ways more sensibly be understood as a trend beginning in the 1930s. The revival of the 1950s, a result of World War II, the baby boom, and suburbanization, appears now as a significant but nevertheless fleeting interruption of this larger historical process.

The crisis in the churches accounts to a large degree for the drop in the overall sales of religious books, since the largest sectors of religious publishing consisted of texts for clergy and devotional literature for the laity. Yet the Depression cut deeper than economics, deeper even than institutional religion—and here, paradoxically, was hope for religious publishing. In its most intimate manifestations, in the hearts and minds of men and women, the crisis of the 1930s furthered rather than set back certain spiritual trends emerging from the fringes of

liberal Protestantism in previous decades. The Depression, remarked the journalist and social historian Frederick Lewis Allen, "marked millions of people—
inwardly—for the rest of their lives." Behind the raw numbers measuring
joblessness and foreclosures "were failure and defeat and want visiting the ener-
getic along with the feckless, the able along with the unable, the virtuous along
with the irresponsible."[10] While many contemporary observers, such as the
informants of Helen and Robert Lynd, saw the churches as offering little to those
in spiritual as well as economic crisis, those hurting in the Depression years were
not without recourse. The modern literature of soul care that was marketed so
aggressively in the 1920s found a steady audience among the American middle
class of the 1930s. Indeed the religious establishment represented by the editorial committee of the Religious Book Club began its period of long decline in
these years, but the spirituality they promoted only continued to rise. Formal
liberal religious theology in prominent pulpits and seminary professorships gave
way in many places to the emerging neo-orthodoxy, yet popular religious explorations at the margins of liberal Protestantism continued to flourish.

The most important firm in liberal religious publishing in the 1930s, and perhaps the most important of the twentieth century, was the venerable New York
house of Harper & Brothers. In the 1930s Harper's printed a series of bestsellers
from Harry Emerson Fosdick, Emmet Fox, and Glenn Clark, among others,
under the guidance of its religion editor, Eugene Exman. Exman, a towering
figure in twentieth-century religious publishing, embodied as no one else the
interplay of modern bookselling, the liberal religious establishment, and the
expanding culture of cosmopolitan spirituality. With a mission to "aid the cause
of religion" without advocating for "any particular sect," Exman built the most
significant list of religious authors in the publishing business, even as he himself
embarked on a prototypical quest for spiritual enlightenment.[11]

The Modern Book Business: Consolidation and Transformation in Religious Publishing

The religious middlebrow culture that emerged in the 1920s and 1930s, though
rooted in liberal Protestantism, encouraged and institutionalized a wide-ranging
ethos of spiritual seeking. Leaders in book publishing saw these developments
and adapted their businesses accordingly. Beginning in the mid- and late 1920s,
as the publishing industry professionalized and modern religious literature rose
in prominence, a number of distinguished New York general-trade presses
restructured their religious publishing practices, frequently by establishing specialized religion departments, and emerged as key players in this new field. These
houses, especially Harper & Brothers, Scribner's, and Macmillan, embraced the
marketplace with renewed vigor in the late 1920s and 1930s, and despite their

deep connections to institutional Protestantism recast their businesses in more explicitly commercial terms.[12] The drive to expand sales meant promoting books pitched at the imagined spiritual center and therefore continuing, in many ways, the agenda of religious middlebrow culture established by Religious Book Week and the Religious Book Club. As the Depression undercut faith in the mainline churches, these modern religious publishing houses continued to provide a steady stream of books, many reflecting traditional Protestantism, but many others emphasizing newer spiritual vocabularies. All told, the business of religious books from the Depression years forward greatly accelerated the already significant popular trend toward liberal religious sensibilities.

By the late 1920s industry leaders knew that modern religious books would sell. "Man to man," declared Charles Ferguson, former head of the Religious Books Department at Doubleday, Doran, to his fellow bookmen, "there is reward on earth for some bookseller or group of booksellers who will take religious books seriously and make a normal, intelligent effort to handle them on a sound, commercial basis." "I believe," he added, "with all the fervor of a salesman that there is money in religious books, just as there is in stories of crime and stories of sex."[13] Like their evangelical predecessors in the nineteenth century, many leaders in the religious book business in the 1920s remained wary of treating their product as just another commodity, and Ferguson hoped to goad the trade into more aggressive salesmanship. Religion—the right kind of religion—could be as tantalizing as crime and sex. Why not sell it as such? At the same time, as Ferguson was well aware, many in general-trade publishing and bookselling remained wary of religious books, thinking of them as either dull "textbooks for divinity students" or beneath the intellectual and aesthetic standards of serious book culture. But Ferguson would have none of this either. "I often hear urged the irrelevant objection that religious books are full of piffle," he proclaimed. "What of it, when books on philosophy, self-improvement, the care and feeding of dogs, and contract bridge are open to the same criticism? If the bookseller is to clear his shelves of piffle, he will be in a sad way, and publishers of religious books will suffer less than the rest from the returns for credit. I don't know why it is that a bookseller will think he has to be an apostle to sell religious books."[14]

Ferguson proposed a quintessentially capitalist solution to these dilemmas, a solution designed to appease both religious concerns and secular book dealers: sell "piffle" along with quality and let the market sort it out. Religious middlebrow culture, especially the various book lists and book clubs established in the decade after World War I, had emerged as an accommodation to such marketplace thinking by offering a mediating structure between the consumer and the free market. Middlebrow culture addressed the profusion of piffle by offering expert guidance, allowing readers to act as independent consumers, yet with the assurance that they were reading only the best. The mediation of middlebrow culture in this way allowed those with religious interests to embrace the marketplace without trepidation, and those with commercial interests to embrace religious books without theological expertise or evangelistic ambitions. Middlebrow culture, in other words, allowed trade presses to compete in a more thoroughly commercialized religious book business with both entrepreneurial intent and clean consciences.

The changes in religious publishing in the 1920s were indeed profound. In the nineteenth century the vast majority of religious literature had been published by denominational houses or by nondenominational evangelical enterprises such as the American Tract Society and the American Bible Society; by the end of the nineteenth century nondenominational evangelical houses, including the Association Press and the Fleming H. Revell Co., emerged as significant publishers as well.[15] Also important were family-run trade presses with strong connections to institutional religion, such as the Presbyterian house of Charles Scribner and the Methodist Harper's.[16] By the late 1920s, however, new business practices were rapidly transforming the field. In response to the booming business climate of the decade as well as the emergence of the new religious literature and the rise of religious middlebrow culture, many of the most prominent general-interest houses created new religion departments to handle the increasingly sophisticated trade. Macmillan, Harper's, Henry Holt, and John C. Winston all established religion departments in the late 1920s, and soon the most commercially successful religious and inspirational titles were coming from presses such as these. Macmillan, for example, published Henry C. Link's *The Return to Religion* in 1936, and Harper's produced a series of bestsellers throughout the 1930s. The irony here is abundant: as liberal religious thinkers increasingly blurred the boundaries of the religious and the secular—by integrating the latest science into their theologies, for example—general-trade publishers felt compelled to establish separate religion departments. The turn toward professionalization and scientific management techniques and the growing awareness of the unique challenges of marketing and selling religious books led publishers to segregate religion into separate departments, just as writers, booksellers, and religious leaders were championing the new integration of religion into every facet of life.

The increasing prevalence of commercialism in the religious book trade and the critical importance of middlebrow mediation to facilitate modern salesmanship were evident to booksellers as well as publishers. "Not long ago, if the bookstore carried religious books at all, they were relegated for the most part to the shelves in the extreme rear of the store," announced J. W. Clinger, advertising manager of the American Baptist Publication Society. In this not so distant past, "the austere label of 'Theology' hung over the shelves," yet now, in the late 1920s, "conditions are changing," he declared. "Religious books are coming into their own. They are being brought to the front in more and more bookstores, and the ways of marketing them are being studied."[17] Ideas for marketing religious books abounded. The Rev. Joseph Fort Newton, for example, an editor at the *Christian Century* and a leading liberal Protestant, told a gathering of booksellers that it was "a mistake...that religious books are advertised in a department by themselves," and others called for the abolition of separate religious bookstores, arguing that such arrangements kept religious books out of the hands of many who might otherwise be reached.[18] Gilbert Loveland of Henry Holt stated the case most clearly. "I, for one," he announced in 1929, "should be glad to see the break-down of the false disjunction between sacred and secular, and, correspondingly, between 'religious' and 'trade' books."[19]

On the eve of the Depression the business of publishing and selling religious books was in the midst of this significant transformation. Modern advertising and merchandising; book clubs and book weeks; new, popular, practical, and accessible books; and an aggressive move into the general trade arena made religious books more attractive than ever to booksellers and book consumers. "It is becoming quite evident to the book-trade that something is happening with regard to religious books," wrote Wilbur Hugh Davies, a trade publisher at Pilgrim Press, in February 1929. "Now we find not only the denominational houses, Doran and Revell continuing, but also Macmillan, Scribner's, Harper's...either with sizeable religious book departments or building such departments." The reason for this, Davies contended, was the quality of new religious literature and the potential for selling these new books not just in specialized religious bookstores, but also, and especially, through the general trade. Davies firmly believed that sustained growth in the religious sector required these new opportunities to reach the public. "It is the opinion of some of us," he proclaimed to his fellow publishers and booksellers, "that the general retail bookstores are best able to furnish this new outlet." He admonished his colleagues therefore to "read one of the newer, more popular religious books, [and] discover how different it is from what you have probably thought it was going to be."[20] The new business model, after all, depended on these new books, and booksellers needed to shed their misgivings about religious books if they hoped to capitalize on the emerging opportunities.

After the onset of the Depression, leaders in religious publishing pushed even harder than they had in the late 1920s to distinguish the newer religious books from the dreaded churchly tomes whose sales were plunging. In February 1931 William Savage of Scribner's wrote to his fellow publishers, "We must force home in this religious book business of ours that a religious book is not necessarily a theological book.... This is an important maxim that must be recognized in selling religious books today." The new, nontheological books, now more important than ever in the midst of the Depression, according the Savage, were books designed "that man might have a more abundant life" and as "a help in the human adventure." Religion was just plain good business, since "there are

religious books for all, from the orthodox fundamentalist to the extreme
wing of the humanist group." In the dark hours of the present crisis, Savage
concluded, "religious books are making their contribution. Interest in them
increases."[21]

The new books that so galvanized these trade publishers and general bookstores in the late 1920s and early 1930s were precisely the kinds of inspirational
works of psychological and mystical spirituality advanced by the Religious Book
Weeks and recommended by the Religious Book Club, along with an increasing
number of more explicitly mind-cure offerings. "Now, religious books have
changed incredibly during the past decade," declared Charles Ferguson in 1930,
referring to these trends in modern religious literature. "The black line of demar-
cation between saint and sinner has faded, and with it has gone the disparity
which once prevailed between books of the Church and books of the world." The
older "books of the Church" no longer spoke to vast numbers of Americans, and
so their sales figures had plummeted. But modern religious books "are for the
most part intelligent discussions of factors which concern us all," and their sales
remained strong. The reason, according to Ferguson, was simple: "The clerics
have learned to write."[22]

Of course more was at work in the success of inspirational literature than
simply better writing, yet the new approaches to popular religious writing were
indeed significant. The bestselling authors of the 1920s and 1930s, figures like
Bruce Barton, Henry Link, Glenn Clark, Harry Emerson Fosdick, and Emmet
Fox, whom Charles Ferguson declared "deft at popularizing" and "speak the language of the people," crafted new books designed to transcend denomination
and creed.[23] The churches suffered because many Americans were critical of their
failures in the face of the Depression. For this reason, noted Gilbert Loveland of
Henry Holt, these readers "resent being tagged 'religious,' for its history has
made hateful the very word, religion, and all its theological word-children."[24]
Charles Francis Potter, an official with the National Association of Book
Publishers in the late 1920s—and a former Unitarian minister who once publicly debated evolution in New York with the fundamentalist John Roach
Straton—described this new market as "the Non-church-going Religious Group."
"A great many people in the United States," he declared, "have no connection
with any organized religion. They attend no church or temple. Statisticians say
there are at least sixty million such in our country."[25] Charles Ferguson, naturally, was ready as ever to see the business potential here. "There is between religion and irreligion today an interplay which has given a decidedly new lustre to
religious books," he wrote. "Whatever the theological implications of this fact
may be, the message to the book dealer is clear: He will find in the religious
books of this hour a legible imaginative piece of work which he can sell."[26] The
experts and arbiters of culture would sort out the theological implications; the
job of business was to sell.

As many booksellers and publishers were quick to realize, the kinds of religious books that in fact sold in the 1930s were works, by and large, with mystical, psychological, and positive-thinking orientations. Charles Francis Potter, the Unitarian minister turned publishing executive, saw these trends very clearly. "Booksellers who have the habit of studying types of customers," he wrote, "know that there are many who will not buy an obviously religious book of the standard sort, but who welcome inspirational books which are called practical psychology, science of the inner life, philosophy of the soul, the art of living. . . . What many of them want in a book is religion without the conventional label, and the astute book-dealer will be ready for them."[27] Wilbur Davies, who had so ardently counseled booksellers not to fear religious books, likewise recognized "that the inspirational type of book and 'Name Authors' are more likely to sell in the newly developing religious book departments of the general bookstores."[28] As William Savage of Scribner's described the matter, "Many years ago it was science *vs.* religion, now science *and* religion is nearer the truth. Doesn't this very spirit create a more fertile field upon which the religious book can fall?"[29]

The general-trade publishers entered the religious field in the heady days of the late 1920s, in the midst of the sweeping professionalization programs transforming the industry, and the dramatic upswing in religious books sales in particular. But before long the grim reality of the Depression determined the fate of their new enterprises. "The vast majority of the . . . titles issued annually in the religious field are technical books—books designed chiefly for ministers and religious workers," Ferguson wrote in 1932, in the depths of the crisis. Given the low pay of most clergy and the falling donations to most churches, a drop in sales of such titles was inevitable, and these losses impacted the whole field. "The preacher is generally a man of the family, and he knows that he has a choice between a new book by Dr. [George W.] Truett and a new pair of shoes for Freddie," he sensibly noted. "It is useless, then, to deny that the depression has sadly influenced the bulk of the religious book business." Yet at the same time Ferguson was astute enough to see the signs of hope, for "what few inspirational books the publishers have to offer are enjoying steadily increasing sales in these times." Book buyers in a time of distress, even in the face of dire economic hardship, Ferguson believed, will still "turn to any book which gives them courage, faith, and a sense of strength in the presence of reality."[30] In the variety of spiritual forms that had emerged from American religious liberalism in the nineteenth century—and that had been marketed to American readers with such vigor in the 1920s—the most successful publishers of the 1930s found the voices to give just such courage and faith and presence of reality. As religious publishing professionalized and commercialized in the late 1920s and 1930s, the books produced by religion departments at the major general-trade presses became increasingly central to American reading habits and the practices of middle-class spirituality.

Figure 3.1 Eugene Exman, dust jacket photo from *House of Harper: One Hundred and Fifty Years of Publishing* (New York: Harper and Row, 1965). Used by permission of HarperCollins Publishers.

Eugene Exman and Religion at Harper & Brothers

The most significant of the new religion departments established in the late 1920s was at Harper & Brothers. Under the tremendously successful and influential leadership of Eugene Exman (Figure 3.1), who ran the department from 1928, just over a year after its founding, until his retirement in 1965, Harper's ushered into print a remarkable range of important books, from huge bestsellers to erudite professional theology to works from leading activists and clergy. Because of his long tenure, skillful leadership, and keen insight, Exman not only became synonymous with the religion department at Harper's but also eventually became the leading figure in American religious publishing in the middle decades of the twentieth century, frequently asked to write and comment on the state of the field. Not insignificantly, his personal story closely tracked that of liberal Protestantism, and much of American spirituality, in this same period. Exman's journey took him from the center of the liberal Protestant establishment to the far reaches of seeker spirituality, all while retaining his stature as a leading figure in religious publishing.

When Harper & Brothers established its religion department in late 1926, it turned first to Walter S. Lewis to guide its operations. Lewis had managed the Book Department of the Presbyterian Board of Publication for ten years and had been active in the American Booksellers Association and in the planning of Religious Book Week. The firm of Harper & Brothers was one of the esteemed New York houses, dating back to 1817, and for much of the nineteenth century was perhaps the nation's leading publisher of books and magazines. For many decades each succeeding Harper generation that ran the family firm consisted of remarkably devout Methodists and shrewd businessmen, and the firm flourished. This record of prosperity persisted into the 1890s, when a national economic downturn and uncharacteristic mismanagement required a bailout from J. P. Morgan and ultimately the imposition of outside control. Harper's subsequently struggled through the early years of the twentieth century, but by the mid-1920s a regime of strict financial discipline and the hiring of a new generation of young, professional-minded executives set the firm back on a promising course, finally clear of debt. The new direction featured a program of professionalization and specialization that resulted in a textbook department and a business book department, and with the renaissance in religious books in the 1920s the firm decided to enter that expanding field as well. Harper's turned to Walter Lewis, who had a solid track record in the field, and eagerly launched its foray into religious books.

In a published statement entitled "Why Harpers Have Entered the Field of Religious Books," the firm noted that "the last ten years have witnessed a widely-recognized increase in the demand for this type of literature" and promised to "devote all possible energy, discrimination and enterprise in promoting the publication and distribution of these books with the intention of making the new department an important part of their general business."[31] The announcement noted the passionate interest in religious matters due to the simmering modernist-fundamentalist controversies and the significant emergence of radio preaching as factors that seemed to drive readers to the bookstores in increasing numbers. Harper's lured Lewis with the intention to produce "outstanding books of a religious, ethical, and theological character," but Lewis was unable to see that agenda develop in any significant way. He died in February 1928, just over a year after his appointment as the founding head of the department, and in April Harper's hired the young Eugene Exman as his replacement.

Exman came to Harper's from the editorial staff of the University of Chicago Press, where he had managed both the trade and religion departments for the three years since his graduation from the University of Chicago Divinity School in 1925. His early years at Harper's saw a rapid and aggressive expansion, often at the expense of his competitors once the economic downturn struck. In 1929 Doubleday sold its list of religious titles—a backlist acquired in a merger with George H. Doran, one of the premier publishers of religious materials—to Richard

R. Smith, who aimed to establish an independent religious publishing house. Smith hired Charles Ferguson from Doubleday, Doran when he bought the religion list, but Smith's fledgling venture succumbed to the Depression, and Exman and Harper's bought the list in 1932 for a few thousands dollars, which they were able to recoup within two years. Also at that time, in the early 1930s, George Brett of Macmillan fired its long-time religion editor—another casualty of the Depression—and Exman lured many of the best writers away from Macmillan as a result.[32] Exman, in his early thirties, was now positioned as the key broker in the business. As he rose through the ranks at Harper's, becoming a director in 1944 and a vice president in 1955, he retained throughout his responsibilities as primary editor of religious books and manager of the religious book department, a role he did not relinquish until his retirement in 1965.

The key challenge Exman faced early in his tenure, of course, was the crisis of the Depression. Like his colleagues elsewhere in religious publishing, Exman saw the need to tap into the existing market provided by the churches whenever possible, but ultimately to disentangle religious books from theological books, so they might continue to sell even as the churches, and books aimed at church workers, faltered. Echoing others in the field, Exman proposed that the trade identify books for clergy and the churches as "theological," reserving the term *religious book* for books of inspiration and devotion, "the kind of book that for these many years has called the sinners to repent and the saints to rejoice." Though an active church member himself, Exman recognized nevertheless that "vast numbers of persons find little satisfaction in the activities and rituals of ecclesiastical bodies, yet are intelligently interested in religion." To sell modern religious books, Exman argued, the trade needed to cultivate these customers alongside reliable churchgoers. And wasn't this the mission of liberal Protestantism itself—to redeem not the elect, not those called out from the world, but the entirety of society? To fulfill this expansive commercial and cultural mission, Exman saw that the future of modern religious publishing lay not in particular creeds and denominations, but rather with "those who want above all else to be intellectually honest, who, weary of their own conceit, search for reality wherever it may be found."[33] This open-ended search for spiritual bedrock became the principle animating his work throughout his long career as the most influential religious publisher in the country. Exman's continuing sympathy, even yearning, for wider spiritual horizons shaped his work as an editor, and therefore the output of the most important house in American religious publishing.

When Exman began his career as editor of religious books at Harper's, he was a fresh graduate of the University of Chicago Divinity School. By the end of his career he was a regular speaker at Vedanta Centers, a leader of Wainwright House, a community in suburban New York devoted to spiritual exploration, a writer and speaker on mystical and psychological spirituality, and a participant in pioneering investigations of the spiritual significance of LSD. His journey from the center of the liberal Protestant establishment to the forefront of spiritual exploration exemplifies in many ways the similar journeys of fellow seekers of the nineteenth and twentieth centuries. In this regard he carried the torch passed down from Ralph Waldo Emerson, William James, and other elite spiritual adventurers of previous generations. As editor and manager of a leading religious book department, he brought this sense of free intellectual and spiritual inquiry to the mass market. Under Exman the religion department at Harper's became, like the Religious Book Club, an institution at once firmly rooted in liberal Protestantism yet simultaneously fostering a rapidly broadening spirituality.

Exman experienced a profound religious transformation in midlife, but his spiritual interests and penchant for personal awakenings had deep roots. Born in Blanchester, a small town in southwestern Ohio, on July 1, 1900, to the farmers Emmet and Mary Etta Exman, young Gene, as he was called, had at age seventeen what he later termed a "mystical experience."[34] Reflecting back on this and other spiritual awakenings in his life, Exman described "a heightening of reality; a higher sense of unity and a more profound sense of being, a sense of order and of beauty." Such "ecstatic experiences" induced "a sense of belonging to that which is . . . a feeling of participation, of being a part of the creativity that is the base of the universe."[35] This early moment of transcendent clarity obviously impressed Exman greatly, as it became the touchstone against which he measured similar experiences nearly forty years later. Though he would struggle as a young man with religious doubt, he took this adolescent experience with him to divinity school at Chicago and later into his professional life.

After primary and secondary education in the public schools of his hometown, Exman attended Denison University, graduating Phi Beta Kappa in 1922. From Ohio he ventured to the Divinity School at Chicago, where he earned a master's degree in the Department of Practical Theology in 1925, with a focus on religious education. His thesis examined the efforts of the United Christian Young People's Organization, a campaign of young adults from various churches across Oak Park, Illinois, to defeat a proposal to allow the showing of movies on Sundays. Exman's study never revealed his own feelings on the matter of Sunday movies, but rather engaged in a technical investigation of various organizing techniques and how they related to current concepts in social process and organization theory—just the kind of detached, social scientific inquiry expected from a Chicago graduate student in those years. "I remember saying," he wrote later in life, "after that adolescent experience [at age seventeen], that I would never need to doubt God again," but "the unity of knowledge I had then was not intellectually retentive." The rigorous environment of the Divinity School at Chicago, the leading center of rationalized liberal theology in the country, brought Exman to a period of doubt.[36] "Living in a secular, cynical society, as

I did as a graduate student in Chicago," he recalled, "I swung completely away from this belief" in God and the unity of all things, beliefs that had seemed so certain only a few years earlier.[37] Yet as strained as his own beliefs were, Exman still recognized the power of religious experience itself. When summarizing the value of the Oak Park campaign against Sunday movies, he declared, "It must be counted of particular worth because of the emotional attitudes which it developed."[38] Chicago introduced Exman to the world of high-powered liberal theology that would constitute much of his publishing record at Harper's, and though his seminary education precipitated a crisis of faith, it failed to extinguish entirely his early recognition of the transforming potential of personal religious experience.

Exman arrived at Harper's deeply formed by these early experiences, experiences of personal mystical revelation, of intensely rationalized but intellectually exciting liberal theology, of the social utility and ethical force of organized religion, and of the existential travail suffered when one faced the simple yet profound reality of doubt. This personal story meshed with the larger story of liberal religion and print culture in the interwar period, allowing him to use his own experiences to craft a successful vision for the religion department at Harper's. He guided the work of the department throughout his career according to a simple mission statement, printed on the back of each catalogue the department produced: "to publish books that represent important religious groupings, express well-articulated thought, combine intellectual competence and felicitous style, add to the wealth of religious literature irrespective of creedal origin, and aid the cause of religion without proselyting [sic] for any particular sect."[39] The motto certainly made good business sense, allowing Exman and Harper's to find and develop books that would sell "irrespective of creedal origin," but the mission of his department also reflected his personal commitment to "search for reality wherever it may be found." This combination of good business sense and an earnest "search for reality" drove his openness to the bestselling authors that made Harper's such a success in the 1930s and beyond.

Harry Emerson Fosdick's *As I See Religion* (1932)

The most prominent author Exman shepherded into print was his own pastor, Harry Emerson Fosdick of the Riverside Church in New York. A professor at Union Theological Seminary and the author of many popular books since the 1910s, Fosdick had gained the national spotlight with his 1922 sermon "Shall the Fundamentalists Win?," which directly challenged what he perceived as the growing threat of fundamentalism to progressive religion. Fosdick's passionate and articulate defense of a modern, liberal faith won him the support of John D.

Rockefeller Jr., liberal Protestantism's greatest (or at least wealthiest) champion in the 1920s.[40] Rockefeller actively supported Fosdick for many decades, most notably by building for him the grand Protestant cathedral on Manhattan's Morningside Heights, the Riverside Church. By the late 1920s Fosdick had become one of the nation's most famous preachers due to his prominent pulpit at Riverside and his hugely successful *National Vespers* show on WJZ, a New York radio station that was carried nationally on the NBC network.[41]

Fosdick published his early books—including *Manhood of the Master* (1913), *The Meaning of Prayer* (1916), *The Meaning of Faith* (1918), and *The Meaning of Service* (1920)—with the Association Press, and his bestseller of the 1920s, *Twelve Tests of Character* (1923), with George H. Doran. But after Exman arrived in New York in 1928, Harper & Brothers published all of Fosdick's prodigious output for the remainder of his career, including many volumes of sermons and the national bestsellers *As I See Religion* (1932) and *On Being a Real Person* (1943). Over the years the association of Exman and Fosdick developed into a warm friendship. Exman was an active member of Fosdick's Riverside Church from 1929 on, serving on numerous boards and committees, and the two worked together on a number of civic projects in addition to their relationship as author and editor. "You are not only my publisher," Fosdick told Exman after years of productive collaboration, "but my friend, and you have displayed that fact in many ways."[42] Fosdick considered Exman his "guide, philosopher, and friend in the realm of publishing," and he extolled Harper & Brothers for its "notable contribution to the religious literature of the English-speaking world," for which, he was happy to say, a "large share of the credit ... goes to Mr. Exman."[43] Fosdick and Exman worked well together in large part because of their shared formation in liberal Protestantism and their shared commitment to free spiritual exploration.

As I See Religion, Fosdick's 1932 bestseller with Harper's, arose from his ministry at Riverside and his ardent defense of religious liberalism, and in many ways paralleled his work with the Religious Book Club. In fact the book reads more than anything else like a manifesto for the Religious Book Club and the Harper's religion department. In this book, which received wide attention in both the mainstream and the religious press when it appeared, Fosdick articulated an interpretation of religion deeply indebted to William James, a view that positioned religious experience, rather than church, creeds, or systematic theology, at the center of religious life. In this way the book perfectly captured the mood of many Americans in the dark years of the early 1930s, disenchanted with the churches yet still yearning for religious meaning. As a popularization of Jamesian categories of religious understanding, *As I See Religion* followed in the footsteps of a number of previous texts, including Rufus Jones's *Social Law in the Spiritual World* (1904), Harold Begbie's *Twice-Born Men* (1909), and Dr. Richard Cabot's *What Men Live By* (1914). Fosdick's debt to James matched that of

Exman, and their shared religious sensibility formed the basis for their enduring relationship as pastor-parishioner, editor-author, and friends.

Fosdick's account of authentic faith, for all its theological openness, presented serious challenges to American Christians, and in the first chapter he addressed the foremost of these challenges: simply put, in the words of the chapter title, "What is religion?" The continual expansion of boundaries threatened the entire enterprise of institutional religion, and the matter of definition that had plagued scholars of comparative religion and promoters of religious reading now confronted Fosdick. "With widening horizons," he wrote in the book's opening lines, "religion has become ambiguous. It includes Christ and Buddha, Lao-tse and Mary Baker G. Eddy. It takes in polytheist, monotheist, and humanist. Bishop Manning, Billy Sunday, Gandhi, Professor Whitehead . . . are all religious."[44] Fosdick, of course, advocated such widened horizons himself as an editor of the Religious Book Club, and now in this popular account of the nature of religion he sought to help modern Americans find their way amid the confusion.

In the mystical communion of the individual and the Eternal, a union that occurred in consciousness and therefore psychologically, Fosdick located the essence of religion. His work in this way revealed the influence of James and Jones, yet he moved beyond their pronouncements by offering the first truly popular work of religious inspiration to place the union of psychology and mysticism at the center of religious life. According to the sociologists Louis Schneider and Sanford M. Dornbusch, As I See Religion was the first book in America to make the case for "psychology as an aid to man's attaining something like salvation in this life."[45] Even more, Fosdick argued, echoing the mystics as much as the scientists, religion "cannot be essentially described in terms of its temporary clothes, its churches, and its creeds. Religion at its fountain-head is an individual, psychological experience."[46] Mystical and psychological approaches to religious experience often blended together in early twentieth-century liberalism, as Fosdick's formulation clearly reveals, yet he offered the deft touch of a skilled rhetorician, a man thoroughly acquainted with the pulpit and the marketplace, to bring this message to the public in compelling form.

Fosdick's answers to the problems modern life presented to religion came in a series of typically learned essays. His book even included endnotes, a true rarity among popular religious writings. Nevertheless as a writer committed to reaching a mass audience he was quick to distance his endeavor from the work of formal theologians and social scientists, noting that when "the intelligentsia try to clarify this situation by their definitions they only confound it the more. If anyone, confused about religion's meaning, wishes to make his bewilderment more complete, let him become a connoisseur in definitions of religion."[47] The effort to bolster religion either through social scientific exactitude or dogmatic syntheses Fosdick considered "senile," since these efforts were attempts to resuscitate a dying tradition rather than search for continued relevance. "Our real task," he posed by contrast, "is to achieve a religion which saves people," and such religion must begin with the "inward communion from which come peace and power.... No one who has followed the work of religious psychology from William James to Starbuck and Coe will doubt the reality of such experiences."[48] Unfortunately, thought Fosdick, the leader of one of the most prominent congregations in the nation, "the present churches and the present theologies have too little to do with this saving experience.... A great deal of this vital religious experience has already fled from the churches and shaken off the dust of orthodoxy in order to get air to breathe and room to move about in."[49] Fosdick's work with the Religious Book Club and Exman's in the religion department at Harper's offered readers just such "air to breathe" free from the "dust of orthodoxy," and *As I See Religion* served as a theological rationale for precisely these kinds of endeavors.

Fosdick's approach, however, despite its focus on personal religious experience, was not simply to reduce religion to individual religious experience and leave it at that. For all his polemics against stale orthodoxy, Fosdick was a vigorous defender of religion in general and Christianity—at least as he framed it—in particular. In fact one of the remarkable contributions of *As I See Religion* was his respectful, smart, and sensitive rejoinder to those loud voices in interwar America denouncing all forms of faith. In good middlebrow fashion he used his popular book to introduce his readers to the ideas of critics such as Walter Lippmann, Bertrand Russell, Joseph Wood Krutch, and Sigmund Freud, devoting more than a third of the text to an explication of their ideas about faith, God, humanism, and atheism. A skilled debater, he began by conceding the many valuable contributions of his interlocutors: "Anyone acquainted with even the environs of modern psychiatry knows that not only religious imagination but every other function of the human mind is commonly used as a means of substituting desire for reality."[50] Bertrand Russell, Fosdick forthrightly acknowledged of the world's most renowned atheist, certainly "cannot be accused of fooling himself with desirable optimisms," while humanists such as Lippmann and Krutch had shown convincingly that "ethics can exist without religion."[51] Indeed, Fosdick concluded, "religion in America does desperately need to be humanized," and if he himself were to lose faith in God, he wrote, "undoubtedly I should try to be a humanist."[52] Humanism might help liberate the churches from their petty obsessions and obsolete supernaturalism and restore in religion "a real and inward worship of the Divine made concrete in an experience of goodness, truth, or beauty."[53] Yet for all his honest and effective concessions to the contributions of the humanists, Fosdick nevertheless mounted a resolute defense of faith in God, and of Christian faith in particular.

Fosdick chose to stand his ground on the matters of beauty and personality, matters he considered central to the meaning of human existence, and matters about which, he believed, humanism could offer no adequate account.[54] Modern science had rendered a service to religion "beyond all computation," for it had "calcined old fables and cleaned up a mess of rubbish in religious tradition," yet when science became the ultimate yardstick of truth it greatly diminished the scope of human understanding, for "the loveliest things in human experience are not adequately covered by the word 'scientific.'"[55] This assessment of science was not a retreat from the search for truth but an affirmation that in beauty resides higher truth, since "as always, beauty will prove to be timeless and when Einstein is as outmoded as Ptolemy this native speech of religion will still be the language of the soul."[56] Fosdick's personal tastes were decidedly Victorian—he lambasted the sex-saturated modernism of post–World War I literature and the stage, and he found jazz and most movies insufferable—yet he heralded the aesthetic dimensions of a modernized, postdogmatic liberalism all the same.[57] "Beauty subdues, integrates, and unifies the soul, washes the spirit clean," he poetically concluded, "and sends one out with a vision of the Divine, not simply believed in but made vivid."[58] Just as music and art cannot be reduced to the wavelengths of sound and light, so also, Fosdick maintained, religious faith must not be equated with the findings of sociological or psychological science or the pronouncements of systematic theology.

Fosdick's mystical vision of the life of the soul, transcending the material, the scientific, and the dogmatic, and finding God in the beautiful, proved a powerful conception at the depth of the Depression, when large impersonal forces were shaping so much of life, and faith in technocratically engineered progress had crumbled. He clearly understood the implications of his thought and the outrage it would spark from critics. He freely admitted the "vagueness of all this, its disembodied churchlessness and its intellectual vacuity," yet he found greater danger in the alternatives. "Rigid definitions of reality are insufficient," he asserted by way of rebuttal, and any "adequate thinking must have fringes.... Theological dogmatism has nearly been the death of religion, and only by outgrowing its strangling constrictions has religion managed to survive."[59] When faced with the choice between the vaguely mystical and the narrowly rational, Fosdick chose the mystical, the path blazed by his namesake, Ralph Waldo Emerson, a century earlier.[60] Like Emerson, Fosdick proclaimed that authentic experience rather than inherited certainty remained the higher spiritual calling.

The spiritual power of beauty mattered because it enabled the larger end of human intimacy with the divine. The greatest beauty and the highest truth in all of creation therefore was the mystery of individual consciousness, that uniquely human faculty that allows us to apprehend divine beauty and truth. Like other theological personalists, Fosdick used the term *personality* to describe each human person's sacred uniqueness; to Fosdick, in other words, personality was the soul for the modern age, precisely the opposite of the manipulative exterior described by success-oriented liberals like Henry Link. The special contribution of Christianity, Fosdick maintained, was not in its dogma or creeds, which any sophisticated study of comparative religions would reveal had clear cognates in other traditions of faith. "The genius of Christianity," he claimed, echoing a key refrain of personalism, "lies in reverence for personality."[61] He approvingly cited Emerson's claim about Jesus—"alone in all of history he estimated the greatness of man"—and asserted that from Christianity's affirmation of the "divine origin, spiritual nature, infinite worth, and endless possibilities" of human personality flowed both mystical rapport with the divine and the ethical imperatives of human society.[62] Jesus, according to Fosdick, "came at the matter" of personality "not theoretically, but practically. . . . His major parables concern the treatment of humans."[63] Regardless of the accuracy of Fosdick's claims of Christian distinctiveness, his core mystical and psychological affirmations—affirmations about the centrality of beauty and human personhood to both personal religion and ethics—functioned as highly perceptive critiques of the spiritual crisis engendered by life in a mass consumer society, especially a society in such evident disarray.

Though he was indebted to Emerson, James, and the Boston personalists, Fosdick's most direct mentor in mysticism was Rufus Jones, whose *Social Law in the Spiritual World* had greatly impressed the young Fosdick.[64] From Jones, Fosdick learned especially of the social and ethical aspects of mystical experience, and Fosdick's political activism during the Depression years demonstrated the prophetic dimensions of his religious vision. Only months after *As I See Religion* appeared, Fosdick's Union colleague Reinhold Niebuhr published *Moral Man and Immoral Society*, a devastating critique of liberalism's political failures, yet Niebuhr found the liberal Fosdick sympathetic on nearly all ethical and political matters.[65] The socialist Niebuhr surely approved when Fosdick preached, soon after the Crash, of the need to "begin drawing the basic industries of our nation together in co-operative planning under wise social control."[66] Like Roosevelt's New Deal, which Fosdick supported—and indeed like liberal theology itself—the overarching motivation behind Fosdick's economic philosophy was the imperative to restructure in order to survive. "Can capitalism so adjust itself to this new world, so move from its old individualism dominated by the profit motive," Fosdick wondered aloud to his radio audience at the depth of the Depression, "that it can become a servant of the people? If it can, it can survive."[67] At the same time as he was telling Depression audiences of the path to God found in beauty, he was preaching powerfully for social reform.

Fosdick fought most of his battles with words in pulpit and print, but during the Depression years, as throughout his career, he also entered the arena of direct action. He supported Angelo Herndon, an African American communist organizer arrested for "insurrection" in Georgia in 1932, and allowed the socialist leader Norman Thomas to hold meetings in the Riverside Church, despite complaints from Rockefeller. Indeed throughout his career Fosdick stood as a champion of civil liberties and free speech, vigorously denouncing the crackdown on radical dissent in the wake of World War I and serving in various leadership capacities with the ACLU. He also helped organize clergymen in support of striking New York garment workers in the early 1930s, and in 1932 lobbied the U.S. Senate on behalf of striking miners in Kentucky. These sincere but measured efforts for economic justice, however, were soon overshadowed by the cause that more than any other defined the political dimensions of his ministry. On Armistice Day 1933 he preached a rousing sermon, "My Account with the Unknown Soldier," in which he painfully repented for his militaristic zeal on behalf of the American war effort in 1917. "I renounce war," he told his mesmerized congregation, "and never again, directly or indirectly, will I sanction or support another." He barnstormed college campuses with this message, delivering it to thunderous applause, and preached it again before hundreds of rapt peace activists at the Broadway Tabernacle in 1934, an event the *Christian Century* dubbed "the greatest address of his life."[68] Fosdick maintained this pacifist stance for the remainder of his life, unwavering even in the lonely years of World War II.[69]

Fosdick's liberal political commitments—his concern for economic justice, for civil liberties, for racial equality, and, above all, for nonviolence—all flowed from his theological commitments to mystical experience and the sacredness of all human beings. Here too Fosdick followed in the footsteps of Jones. Jones asserted, and Fosdick agreed, that mystical experience was not for the privileged few, not only for "for saints or apostles," but also for "common every-day people like ourselves."[70] Jones's Jamesian theology—he at one point defined mystical experience as "consciousness of direct and immediate relationship with some transcendent reality which, in the moment of experience, is believed to be God"[71]—made mystical experience accessible to those of almost any theological orientation. Fosdick followed Jones as a mystical egalitarian, and in *As I See Religion* he presented a clear and accessible vision of the religious life rooted in mystical awareness of the beauty and truth of the divine, a reverence for human personality, and a commitment to the social and ethical implications of authentic religious experience. Fosdick's vision of the religious life—a life of the spirit larger than churches, theologies, or creeds and available to all, not only the spiritual virtuosi—represented a theology perfectly suited for the culture of seeking and the practices of religious middlebrow reading.

A new book from Harry Emerson Fosdick was a notable event in American culture in the interwar years, and *As I See Religion* garnered significant attention from both the secular and the religious press. The *New York Herald Tribune* wrote approvingly of his liberalism. Fosdick's audience of "thinking people, well read people, educated people," the review declared, "do not want to scrap religion for the fun of getting rid of it. They would prefer to keep it if it could be fitted into their concepts of the world we live in."[72] The *New York Times* wrote that Fosdick's book "may be read by the freethinker without danger of contamination" because it is "a book to make people think, not a book to tell them what to think."[73] Even the tiny *News Journal* from Murfreesboro, Tennessee, took note. Its reviewer declared, "I think I've read no book on religious philosophy in my life that seems so sane, so intelligent, as this book by Fosdick."[74]

Fosdick's fellow religious liberals, not surprisingly, were overwhelmingly pleased with *As I See Religion*. The Religious Book Club, which had a policy against recommending the books of editorial committee members as main selections, chose Fosdick's work as an alternate, declaring its conclusions to be "positive, constructive, invigorating."[75] Exman personally sent the review in the *Christian Century*, the leading journal of ecumenical liberalism, to Fosdick. The *Century* noted with admiration that the book's argument "was not stated in the jargon approved by academic conventions" and yet managed to address "squarely the religious issues which multitudes of intelligent people are now facing."[76] Other critics picked up on the book's ability to appeal to a mass audience while remaining intellectually substantive, such as the reviewer in *World Tomorrow*, who recommended the book for its "intellectual robustness, spiritual insight and knowledge of personality," presented in "an English style that is a rare instrument of strength and beauty."[77] Even the critic in the Calvinist *Reformed Church Messenger*, hardly a liberal publication, was largely enthusiastic. The book rendered a valuable service, this reviewer noted, to "those who, in the confused welter of modern thought...have lost all faith both in God and themselves." Though the reviewer hoped readers "might eventually discover that there is more in Christianity than Dr. Fosdick gives us," he ultimately declared it "a brilliant book."[78]

Reviews in the secular and religious press provide one measure of the response *As I See Religion* received at the depth of the Depression. But Fosdick did not write for his colleagues or his critics. Above all else he was a pastor, and he wrote his books as extensions of his ministry, to reach ordinary Americans. Over his long career Fosdick received a tremendous number of letters from those who read his books and columns and listened to his radio preaching, and certainly thousands of these letters came in response to *As I See Religion*. Sadly, all of this correspondence from readers and listeners in the 1920s and 1930s was destroyed, though his staff did transcribe selected brief summaries. A woman from Greenville, Mississippi, for example, apparently wrote to Fosdick to inform him of the joy the book had provided her and to tell him it had changed her thinking about both God and her fellow men and women. Specifically she noted that, with the insights Fosdick provided, she had overcome the racial prejudice she had previously felt and was now teaching others to do the same.[79] Fosdick was a polarizing figure in American religious life, and alongside readers such as this his book certainly generated vociferous critics. Indeed for all his talk of transcending orthodoxy, Fosdick's brand of liberalism constituted its own form of orthodoxy, though one with the characteristically liberal capacity for searching self-critique. Rather than the resolution of controversy, *As I See Religion* stands as a witness to it, perhaps the clearest testament of the culture of seeking that emerged from liberal Protestantism and mass-market book culture.

Emmet Fox and Glenn Clark: New Thought for a Depression Audience

In Fosdick's *As I See Religion* Exman published the work of his own pastor, who represented two of the most influential institutions in American Christianity: the Riverside Church and Union Theological Seminary. Yet Exman also used his position at Harper's to nurture and promote other widely popular books in the 1930s, books that arose from other strands of the American religious tapestry. Most notable among Exman's other bestsellers during the Depression were the positive-thinking works of Emmet Fox and Glenn Clark. These books, though in the broad family of liberal religious thought, deviated significantly from Fosdick's brand of liberal Protestantism. While Fosdick wrote of beauty, personhood, and ethical concerns, these laissez-faire liberals saw religion as a means to health, wealth, success, and power. The historian Donald Meyer concludes of Fosdick that while he gave "a somewhat more positive assurance than did James that objective spiritual power did exist," nevertheless "he like James was repelled by any wish that this objective power take care of everything."[80] Not so Emmet Fox and Glenn Clark. Fosdick stood in the tradition of William James and Rufus Jones, but Fox and Clark followed more closely the trail blazed by Phineas Quimby, Mary Baker Eddy, and Ralph Waldo Trine. James had been fascinated by such figures, the progenitors of the "religion of healthy-mindedness," and even envied them in many ways, but was never able to count himself among them. Fosdick and Exman, each of whom had suffered youthful religious ecstasy and despair, likewise rejected mind cure as untenable. And yet the Religious Book Club recommended the works of Clark, the less extreme of the two, and Exman happily published them both. Emmet Fox in fact became Exman's best-selling author of the 1930s, producing the most successful works of positive thinking in American culture in the half-century between Trine's *In Tune with the Infinite* (1897) and Norman Vincent Peale's *The Power of Positive Thinking* (1952). In Fosdick's work Exman had found his manifesto, and in publishing and promoting the works of Fox and Clark he put that manifesto into practice.

Emmet Fox was a New Thought superstar. In the depths of the Depression he held spellbound the throngs at his Church of the Healing Christ in New York City, which outgrew venue after venue: first the ballroom at the Astor Hotel, then the Hippodrome just off Times Square, and the Manhattan Opera House, which seated four thousand, and finally Carnegie Hall, where he addressed crowds of six thousand. An electrical engineer by training, "sensitive and delicate in appearance," according to a biographer, Fox commanded the rapt attention of the largest positive-thinking congregation in the world with a preaching style that was "quiet and thoughtful, simple and direct."[81] Born in Ireland in 1886 to a prominent family, he became convinced as a child that he had special healing powers, even wondering at times if he might perhaps be a saint. After reading mind-cure literature as a teenager, he determined instead that he simply possessed an intuitive understanding of natural spiritual law. Though he eventually studied engineering and worked professionally in that field in England, Fox never lost his interest in New Thought (called Higher Thought in England), reading widely and attending lectures and conferences throughout his twenties and thirties. He gave his first public lecture in metaphysics in London in 1928 and soon began touring widely across England and Scotland. In 1930 he moved to New York—to the Astor Hotel, his home for twenty years—and began giving talks in auditoriums, lecture halls, and hotel ballrooms around the city. He quickly received ordination through the College of Divine Science in Denver, and before long emerged as one of the most successful preachers in the country.

Nearly as soon as Fox became a preaching sensation, he produced a bestseller for Harper's. In 1932, only two years after arriving in New York and a year after his appointment as the pastor of the Church of the Healing Christ—an established congregation affiliated with the Divine Science branch of the American New Thought movement—Fox compiled a collection of his sermons and essays into a book called *Power through Constructive Thinking*. He eventually published five bestsellers with Exman at Harper's, including a tremendously influential New Thought analysis of the teachings of Jesus called *The Sermon on the Mount* (1934), but in *Power through Constructive Thinking* he outlined his philosophy most directly. This book went through eight printings by 1940, reaching hundreds of thousands of readers with a wildly eclectic mix of New Thought, transcendentalism, Christianity, Hinduism, and a variety of other metaphysical teachings. Like Fosdick, indeed like all those who served as successful experts in religious middlebrow culture, Fox understood the anxieties engendered by mass culture. "So many schools of thought seem to be competing for the attention of the student," he wrote in *Power through Constructive Thinking*, "so busy is the printing press; so many new books and pamphlets are written; so many magazines come and go; that people have told me that they have felt quite in despair of ever discovering what it really is that they must do to be saved."[82] In a book that covered the Lord's Prayer and the Yoga of Love, the Bible and the Law of Karma, the Seven Day Mental Diet, the Garden of Allah, the Golden Key, and reincarnation, Fox proposed to guide his readers through this welter of confusion and reveal the true secrets of spiritual knowledge.

The book proved a great success, and the secret of its success lay in the force-ful clarity with which Fox articulated his ideas. His central contention, as with all New Thought proponents, was that the spiritual world, just like the natural, operated according to identifiable laws, and that those laws, through a kind of gnostic insight, were knowable to those able and willing to see. "The universe operates strictly in accordance with Law," Fox wrote, "for God, among other things, is Principle, or Law."[83] A harmonious, happy, and healthy life resulted from knowledge of these laws, and Fox proclaimed that "mystic power" can "impart new and wonderful kinds of knowledge as soon as you really want such knowledge—glorious knowledge—strange things not taught in schools or writ-ten in books."[84] The key to unlocking such hidden knowledge was the "Golden Key" of "scientific prayer." Modern psychology, Fox believed, offered valuable tools in the science of the spirit and might aid in the pursuit of knowledge, but ultimately psychology simply reaffirmed the eternal truths of the wisdom tradi-tions. "The great Illumined Ones who wrote the Bible under Divine inspiration well knew all the teaching of modern psychology," Fox asserted. "The ideas concerning the subconscious mind and the part it plays in our scheme of things, which have lately been put forward by investigators like Freud and Jung and others, novel though they appear to the modern world, were all quite familiar to the great Initiates of the Bible."[85] In these pronouncements Fox stood squarely in the New Thought tradition that had had a long history in American religious life by the 1930s.

Yet Fox demonstrated a more voracious spiritual eclecticism than was typical even among his rather freethinking forbears in New Thought. He not only pro-duced widely read commentaries on the Sermon on the Mount and the Ten Commandments, but also aggressively appropriated ideas from an array of spiritual and metaphysical traditions beyond Christianity.[86] Sometimes his bor-rowings were more linguistic than substantive, such as when he used the phrase "The Yoga of Love" to describe his notions of "the true Christian idea of Love." In other areas, however, especially in matters of death and the afterlife, he ven-tured deeply into what was for most Americans uncharted territory. He taught reincarnation, for example, with the idea that the purpose of human existence was to gain complete spiritual understanding, a process that might take more than one lifetime. He also taught the Law of Karma, a borrowing from Hindu and Buddhist traditions that had entered Anglo-American New Thought through transcendentalism and Theosophy. Fox claimed evidence for his teachings on karma and reincarnation from the Bible, but readily acknowledged in *Power through Constructive Thinking* that such ideas had long and fruitful histories of exposition in the religious traditions of the East.

Regardless of the extent of his spiritual borrowings, all his teaching, like his teaching on reincarnation, returned to the core affirmation of right thinking as the key to spiritual success, health, and happiness. Such notions drew from the deep well of Anglo-American New Thought, and from this mind-cure tradition Fox also knew that harnessing the power of right thinking required careful attention to technique, which he called "treatments." For Fox, the most critical kind of treatment was right reading, and here he sounded much like the evangelical exponents of reading in the nineteenth century, and indeed like centuries of Christian advisors on proper spiritual reading. "The mistake made by many people, when things go wrong," he taught, "is to skim through book after book, without getting anywhere."[87] Rather, he counseled, one ought to read slowly and meditatively. When reading a Psalm, for example, "it is of very little use merely to read one of them through hurriedly and then put it aside. A Treatment such as [a] Psalm should be read over slowly many times. As you read, you should pause frequently to become receptive for a moment in order to give a chance for inspiration to come through."[88] While the Bible, as a unique book in human history—what he called "a spiritual vortex through which spiritual power pours from heaven to earth"—offered the best material for such reading, Fox also advocated "the reading of a page of any spiritual book that appeals to you."[89]

This eclectic and adventurous program of spiritual reading mirrored the agenda that Exman had outlined for the religion department at Harper's and that the Religious Book Club advanced through its wide-ranging recommendations. None of Fox's books was carried by the Religious Book Club or chosen by the selection committee of the ALA's Religious Books Round Table, indicating that his teaching had crossed the boundaries of taste, erudition, and spiritual acceptability policed by these guardians of Protestant culture. Nevertheless Exman aggressively promoted Fox's books, lavishing his various bestsellers with extensive advertising. Furthermore Exman ensured that *Power through Constructive Thinking* was carried at leading bookstores across the country. Harper & Brothers records indicate that the title was featured in general trade and department store bookstores, such as Brentano's in Washington, D.C.; Carson, Pirie, Scott in Chicago; Dayton's in Minneapolis; and Wanamaker's in Philadelphia, among many others. But more significantly, Harper's sold Fox's bestseller through Methodist Book Concern outlets in Chicago, Cincinnati, Pittsburgh, Baltimore, Boston, and Philadelphia as well as in the Presbyterian Bookstore in Chicago, the American Baptist Publication Society in Kansas City, and the Episcopal Book Shop in Detroit.[90] Fox did not pass muster with the brokers of religious reading at the Religious Book Club or the American Library Association, but in the more worldly world of book publishing and bookselling his writings were eagerly embraced.

For all the commercial success of Fox's bestsellers at Harper's, these books may not have been his most significant contribution to American religious life. His most lasting influence, almost certainly, was through Alcoholics Anonymous, which was just getting organized in New York City in the mid-1930s. The founders of AA drew substantially on his writings in their early work and eventually produced a seminal text in the history of American spirituality, *Alcoholics Anonymous*, more commonly known as the "Big Book."[91] One of the first alcoholics that Bill Wilson, the cofounder of AA, worked with in the early years of his recovery ministry, in fact—even before the formal establishment of Alcoholics Anonymous—was a man named Al Steckman, whose mother was Fox's secretary.[92] In addition to this personal connection, five of the accounts depicted in the Big Book, according to one historian of the movement, were of drunks who had overcome their addiction through the help of Fox's writings. Harry Emerson Fosdick and John D. Rockefeller Jr. became early supporters of Bill Wilson's efforts, and through Fosdick and Rockefeller, and because of the connections with Fox as well, Exman was also drawn early on into the circle of Wilson and Alcoholics Anonymous.[93]

In May 1938 Wilson, sober only three and a half years, began writing what would appear the next spring as *Alcoholics Anonymous*, the book that first introduced the twelve steps to the world. In 1932 Exman had published *For Sinners Only*, the highly successful collection of conversion narratives from the Oxford Group, an evangelical organization that had greatly influenced Wilson.[94] Because of this earlier connection, and because of the mutual personal ties to Fosdick and Rockefeller, Wilson came to Exman for editorial guidance soon after he began drafting his book. Exman offered Wilson a $1,500 advance based only on incomplete rough drafts, recognizing immediately the valuable contribution and commercial possibilities of the work. Eventually Wilson decided to form Alcoholics Anonymous, Inc., and self-publish the Big Book in order to control the promotion, and the profits, from the book more directly. Exman supported, even encouraged this move and remained a backer and friend to AA over the years. He eventually edited *Twelve Steps and Twelve Traditions* (1953), a significant follow-up to *Alcoholics Anonymous*, exploring in greater depth each of the twelve steps. Even years later Exman still considered AA "the most exciting modern movement in religion" and *Alcoholics Anonymous* "the best modern testimony I know of the power of religion to save sinners." "Religion, medicine, and psychology," Exman declared, "have together diagnosed the disease and provided a cure. These men and women of AA have been deeply moved by a religious experience."[95] That religious experience came in part through the writings of Emmet Fox, writings that Harper's, because of Exman's commitment to free spiritual exploration, had brought to the world.

Glenn Clark, in his books with Harper's, followed this same line from Fox and AA, focusing primarily on prayer and bodily health. Though both less successful and less radical than Fox, Clark nevertheless represented a significant voice of positive-thinking spirituality in the 1920s, 1930s, and 1940s. A football and track coach at Macalester College in Minneapolis, as well as a professor of "creative religious living," Clark wrote two books that became Harper's bestsellers, *I Will Lift Up Mine Eyes* (1937) and *How to Find Health through Prayer* (1940).[96]

Clark's writings, especially on prayer, relied extensively on mind-cure principles. More acceptable than Fox to liberal Protestant leaders such as Fosdick and Jones, Clark nevertheless elicited deep intellectual and moral concern, along with a tepid embrace, from the cultural gatekeepers. In this way his career demonstrates the abiding division in American religious liberalism between those attuned to its ethical and mystical dimensions and those laissez-faire liberals, like Link, Clark, and later Norman Vincent Peale, who promoted positive-thinking theologies of success. The Religious Book Club, as noted, articulated this ambivalence toward Clark in its recommendation of *How to Find Health through Prayer*, an alternative selection it presented despite significant reservations. Similarly another Clark book, published as *The Way, the Truth, and the Life* in 1946, received both endorsement and criticism. Exman recruited Jones as a reader for this manuscript in 1945, and though recommending it for publication because "the reader who wants an uplifting spiritual message will get it," Jones confidentially warned Exman that he found the book "decidedly lacking in scholarly insight" and often "far-fetched and forced."[97] Clark's mind-cure philosophy gained reluctant acceptance from the gatekeepers not on intellectual or theological grounds, but because of their faith, ultimately, in the transformative power of religious experience and in the ability of readers to find meaningful experiences in the most unlikely of places. For these reasons—and because he never ventured into realms such as karma and reincarnation that so clearly marked Fox as a religious eccentric—Clark, a lifelong Presbyterian, became an important advocate for positive thinking from within the broad compass of liberal Protestantism, rather than, like Fox, a voice from without. Clark's writings, and the summer camps he founded, which he called Camps Farthest Out, helped legitimate mind cure within the ever-widening liberal Protestant circle.

Like all New Thought exponents, Clark stressed the critical power of right thinking, especially the need to affirm the positive and squelch the negative. He had come to his own realizations about the power of mind in 1918 and 1919, in the wake of the Great War and in the midst of the global influenza pandemic, a period in his own life that also witnessed the birth of his son and the death of his father. "The secrets of the mighty works of Jesus," Clark realized while on the train to see his dying father, "lay in the fact that he gave himself in totality and entirety to the Father—his front mind, his subconscious mind, his unconscious mind, his entire mind."[98] This insight set Clark on a course of intense reading in American and English metaphysical writings. He first expounded on his newfound spiritual understanding in the 1925 bestseller *The Soul's Sincere Desire*, a book that, among other things, discussed the parables of Jesus as models for prayer and then spun its own parables through extended analogies involving golf.[99] Clark's most far-reaching and influential statement, however, came in *How to Find Health through Prayer*, which became a locus classicus, along with the writings of Mary Baker Eddy, for positive-thinking teachings regarding the body.

"Today we are on the very brink of discovering," he claimed, "the secret of that Elixir of Life that Ponce de Leon and all those earlier seekers...failed so miserably to discover."[100] That secret, of course, was right thinking and proper prayer.

To effect this seemingly miraculous power of healing, Clark offered a series of clear techniques and affirmations, but with a measure of nuance that allowed his work greater acceptability among his fellow liberal Protestants than was afforded the writings of Fox. Clark never equated illness with sin, for example, but only more narrowly with poor habits of mind. Sickness, he declared, building on an analogy to telephone transmission, "is merely a vibration set up in the sensitive responses of our marvelously responsive body, which will cease as soon as we reverently put the receiver to our ear and promise to obey the command that is being sent."[101] The "spiritually minded," those "most responsive to...vibration," were "the quickest to catch the reaction called illness."[102] Clark catalogued a very specific list of ailments and the ways sufferers evidently failed to respond to the spiritual commands being sent. Heart ailments, for example, might be relieved through the practice of forgiveness, whereas arthritis stemmed from rigidity of character, "our attempt to achieve too definite and perfect results in too short time."[103] In this same psychosomatic vein he declared, "Holding back ideas, or failure to express them, due to shyness, diffidence, or undue secretiveness tends to cause constipation."[104] Most astonishingly, and least subtly, Clark declared, "When respiratory infections become very dangerous, as the Spanish influenza did during the World War...it is due, I contend, to a great inflooding of wrong thinking and wrong feeling of entire nations."[105] Whether to address extreme instances such as this or more mundane ailments, Clark advocated a series of simple affirmative strategies to right what was wrong; he called these "deny it away," "laugh it away," "relinquish it away," and "know it away," and each involved positive thoughts, prayer, and directed scripture reading.[106] The short book concluded with an appendix of Bible verses and meditations appropriate for the treatment of a variety of specific illnesses.

The bestsellers of Fox and Clark, along with the writings of Fosdick, helped the religion department at Harper's survive the Depression, and even flourish, while other houses floundered. Exman's agenda to "aid the cause of religion without proselyting for any particular sect" resulted in an openness to spiritual innovation that served the department well in the mass marketplace. With an emerging culture of religious expertise available to guide readers in their reading choices and practices, firms like Harper's were free to pursue commercial success without fear of spiritual malpractice. In this way the middlebrow and the marketplace together forged a culture of spiritual exploration through reading. As it turns out, Eugene Exman was soon to become a living embodiment of that culture. After a period of doubt brought on by his graduate training at Chicago, Exman at midlife rediscovered—and then remarkably redirected—the spiritual energies of his youth.

Eugene Exman: Bookman as Seeker

Exman guided the religion department at Harper's through the difficult years of the Depression, expanding its catalogue and producing a series of highly successful works. As the Depression abated and the nation mobilized for war in the early 1940s, Exman himself underwent his own significant transformation. From this point forward the divinity school graduate and Riverside Church member who led one of the most prestigious and productive religious publishing departments of the period embarked on a brave, ambitious, and far-reaching spiritual quest, even while editing the works of some of the most significant Christian thinkers and activists of the twentieth century. Exman's personal journey—which requires a brief look ahead, into the 1940s and 1950s—provides an instructive instance of the intertwining of liberal Protestantism, book culture, and the rise of free-ranging spiritual seeking in the mid-twentieth century. His story vividly demonstrates, at the elite level, the emergence of modern spiritual cosmopolitanism from the free marketplace of religious reading, a marketplace he did so much to build during his career at Harper's.

Exman's personal story also points to the limits of spiritual openness, to the parameters of the possible that defined those avenues available for exploration and those that were out of bounds, either too dangerous socially or literally unimaginable. All spiritual journeys, even the most radical, draw on preexisting resources, including material resources such as social networks, education, travel, and access to books. But spiritual exploration is also constrained by cultural factors that operate to define legitimate and illegitimate sources to draw on, even as those very notions of legitimacy are tested, questioned, and reworked. Exman was privileged economically and culturally and therefore able to explore more widely than most, yet his search never ventured into African-derived religions, for example, or Native American religions, or Islam. Instead he followed the trail blazed by nineteenth-century liberal and transcendentalist elites, looking to Christian mysticism, the contemplative and meditative practices of India, and psychological science for the secrets of spiritual reality, both inner and outer. Nevertheless, though it was a trail already blazed, Exman's journey was still remarkably adventurous and consequential. In addition to setting a new course for his own life, he worked to bring the spirituality of the avant-garde to the reading public.

Exman resembled other nineteenth- and twentieth-century seekers not only in the paths he followed, but also in the way he was inspired by books; in his case, they were books, and authors, he knew intimately. Harry Emerson Fosdick, of course, was an Exman author and his longtime pastor at the Riverside Church, but by the early 1940s another of his authors at Harper's, the British expatriate Gerald Heard, had become his guru. Heard arrived in the United States in 1937 with his friend and fellow writer Aldous Huxley, and before long was settled in southern California expounding an eclectic mix of liberal Christianity, Vedantism, psychology, evolutionary science, and libertarian politics.[107] His first book published in the United States, *Pain, Sex, and Time: A New Outlook on the Evolution of Man*, was published by Harper's in 1939, and over the next decade and a half he published nearly a book a year with Exman, including *The Creed of Christ* (1940), *The Code of Christ* (1941), *Man the Master* (1941), *A Preface to Prayer* (1944), *Is Another World Watching? The Riddle of the Flying Saucers* (1951), and *The Human Venture* (1955). Heard sparked in Exman a transformative midlife awakening. "I've been [led] recently to enlarge my own spirituality," the forty-year-old Exman confided to the Quaker writer Thomas Kelly in early January 1941. Despite deep roots in liberal Protestantism, Exman now described himself as a "seeker," and in Heard he found both a kindred spirit and a guide. "A few of us...have lighted a torch from Gerald Heard," Exman confided to Kelly, and "meet in N.Y. regularly—a kind of 'Beloved Community.'"[108] From the early 1940s onward he ventured far and wide in search of his enlarged spirituality, guided by Heard's infectious spiritual curiosity and prodigious literary output.

Exman had been a key organizer of the Heard-inspired New Yorkers, and these spiritual gatherings soon led to much more consequential collaborations with Heard himself. The first step came in July 1941, when Exman traveled to southern California to participate in a month-long seminar with Heard co-organized by the American Friends Service Committee. These meetings, held at a Baptist college in La Verne, included thrice-daily sessions for meditation intermixed with periods for spiritual and intellectual discussion among the twenty-five attendees, with Heard acting as host and inspirational leader. Participants at the La Verne seminar immediately began planning for an even more significant enterprise. Using money from Heard's inheritance, the La Verne group negotiated the purchase of three hundred acres in Trabuco Canyon, southeast of Los Angeles, for the establishment of a college dedicated to spiritual training. Exman and other La Verne attendees became the first board of trustees of Trabuco College, which was under construction by the summer of 1942. The college quickly grew into a red brick and stucco retreat center and monastery, where acolytes meditated in the central domed hall, attended lectures in the auditorium, and generally imbibed Heard's philosophy of "mystical anarchism."[109] Exman soon published Heard's manifesto for Trabuco in two pamphlets, gathered under the title *Training for the Life of the Spirit* (1941, 1942), and later published *Prayers and Meditations* (1949), a collection of the devotional materials used at Trabuco.[110]

Not surprisingly, the Trabuco experiment was short lived. Heard closed the college in 1947, exhausted and disillusioned, and turned the grounds over to the Vedanta Society of Southern California in September 1949. Nevertheless in its few years of operation Trabuco served as an important meeting ground for religious seekers and activists and helped lay the groundwork for the human potential movement to come; the Esalen Institute in Big Sur, which opened in 1962, was inspired by Heard's experiment at Trabuco.[111] Significant pilgrims to Trabuco included Bill Wilson, the founder of Alcoholics Anonymous; Heard's friend Aldous Huxley, then preparing his opus *The Perennial Philosophy*, much of which was written at Trabuco; the writer Christopher Isherwood, who had been an attendee at the original La Verne seminar; and a number of influential war-time conscientious objectors. Exman himself eagerly explored the spiritual smorgasbord of Trabuco and discussed the writings of Heard and the ongoing spiritual revival at Trabuco with associates and authors, including the novelist Jean Toomer, another mystical seeker and Trabuco acolyte.[112] A decade later Exman was still enchanted by what had happened at Trabuco. Heard was a "genius," Exman exclaimed in the early 1950s, for his "spiritual synthesis of modern knowledge. He correlates the findings of the scientists, the psychologists, and the mystics."[113] The effort to reconcile psychological science and mystical insight had been the quest of liberal Protestants since William James and Rufus Jones wrote their seminal works at the dawn of the century, and was key to Fosdick's vision in *As I See Religion*. In Heard, Exman thought he had found the genius who finally fulfilled this dream.

Heard envisioned Trabuco College as a training ground of and for a spiritual elite, and he did manage to attract significant thinkers, writers, and celebrities to his cause. But perhaps the most significant of his elite devotees was his editor, since it was largely through Exman and Harper's that the influence of Trabuco's short-lived experiment spread into the wider culture. Exman published Heard's writings, but through Trabuco he also made connections with other writers drawn to Heard and Huxley, including, most important, Huston Smith and Jiddhu Krishnamurti, who would lead him and Harper's deeper and deeper into the emerging seeker culture. After Exman's midlife awakening, Harper's remained a key publisher of liberal Protestant theology and social thought, but it would develop as well into a leading purveyor of more expansive and cosmopolitan spiritual alternatives.

The comparative religion scholar Huston Smith best exemplifies the relationship between the old Harper's—liberal, ecumenical, adventurous, but solidly Protestant—and the changing Harper's of the postwar years. Like Exman and Heard, Smith emerged from liberal Protestantism in the 1940s into a world of greatly expanded spiritual possibilities. Raised in China by Methodist missionary parents, Smith studied theology at Chicago under Henry Nelson Wieman, a nonmetaphysical theologian working to adapt Protestant theology to modern science. Like Exman, Smith found the environment at Chicago enriching but spiritually enervating (though he did marry Wieman's daughter) and found in Heard a guide who reconciled science with a living awareness of the mystical. Heard's *Pain, Sex, and Time*, Smith later proclaimed, was "one of the...most important reading experiences" of his life, and as soon as he could Smith hitchhiked from Denver, where he was teaching, to Trabuco to sit at the feet of the master.[114] Heard and Huxley sent Smith on the seeker's path by recommending to him a swami in St. Louis, and soon Smith was embarked on his experiential quest to explore the world's wisdom traditions. Smith's hugely successful *The Religions of Man*, first published with Harper's in 1958 and revised and republished ever since (later under the title *The World's Religions*), captured for generations of students this firsthand wonder at the spiritual life in all its diverse beauty and mystery. Through this work and his numerous other scholarly and personal writings, lectures, and television appearances, Smith became one of the most important public figures arguing for the common essence of all world religions in mystical experience.

Smith's journey embodies, in extreme form, the creed of Exman, Fosdick, and, increasingly, their readers at Harper's. He used the mystical and psychological categories of liberal Protestantism to explore new spiritual insights and experiences, especially the meditative traditions of Hinduism, Islam, and Buddhism. Jiddhu Krishnamurti, by contrast, represented the other side of this global cultural transaction, a man of the East empowered by American mass-market publishing to reach Western seekers. Born in India, he was the adopted son of Annie Besant, the leader of the Theosophy movement, who proclaimed him to be a prophesied World Teacher. Krishnamurti renounced this messianic status in 1929 and thereafter pronounced a message of no self, social change, and limitless psychological freedom from his home in southern California and on the lecture circuit. Krishnamurti's following among Theosophists had dissipated in the 1930s and during the war, but he burst into prominence again after the war with the aid of Heard, Huxley, and Harper's. Through Heard, whom he first met in 1938, he forged a long friendship with Huxley, who urged him to write for a wider public. Soon he produced a string of important works for Harper's, the most significant of which, *The First and Last Freedom*, appeared with a foreword by Huxley in 1954.[115] In addition to Huxley, countercultural religious and spiritual figures such as Alan Watts and later Deepak Chopra claimed Krishnamurti as an influence and inspiration. The psychological and mystical esotericism Krishnamurti offered blended easily with Exman's ambition for Harper's, articulated two decades earlier, to "search for reality wherever it may be found."

The wide-ranging spiritual writings of Heard, Smith, and Krishnamurti heralded the future for both Harper's and Exman. Later Harper's executives, seeing the tremendous spiritual vitality in California and fretting the apparent decline of mainline Protestantism, relocated the religion department from New York to San Francisco in 1977.[116] Called HarperSanFrancisco (now HarperOne), it became a major publisher of alternative, Eastern, New Age, and recovery-focused spirituality, while continuing to produce important books in Christian theology and spirituality. Exman's personal explorations of mystical and psychological horizons, meanwhile, continued throughout the 1940s and 1950s. Soon after his spiritual awakening in the early 1940s, he joined the Laymen's Movement, a group of lay Protestant leaders, including John D. Rockefeller Jr. and J. C. Penney, endeavoring to bring Christian values into the affairs of business and politics. Exman wrote of the group, "Our venture, our research, should be directed to a new understanding of God, of our fellows, and of ourselves."[117] He proposed a science-like program of rigorous investigation, for "each of us has his laboratory of daily living in which he can work...with the same skill and persistence as at Oak Ridge."[118] Only through such research into the spirit, proclaimed Exman, would love, ethical concern for others, and Christian civic engagement be possible. "A man's job is to grow a soul," Exman explained, "a continuum of experience that begins here and extends beyond."[119] To further these ends, he and other members of the Layman's Movement established the Wainwright House in Rye, New York, in 1951, as a study and retreat center "devoted to a greater understanding of God."[120] Part of Wainwright House's special mission was to serve as a religious retreat center for the United Nations, and as such it advocated a mystical rather than a creedal approach to religious enlightenment as a cornerstone of emerging internationalism. Exman eventually served as chairman of the board of trustees of Wainwright House.

In the late 1950s Exman embarked on his most colorful spiritual adventure: participation in a study of the spiritual significance of LSD.[121] Huxley, Heard, and others in southern California had been experimenting with acid since 1955 and introduced AA's founder Bill Wilson to the drug in 1956. In the spring of 1958 Wilson and Exman—friends and collaborators for twenty years by this time—partook in an LSD investigation with a group in New York that included the actress Lucille Kahn and the Jesuit priest Ed Dowling.[122] Exman later told an international conference on parapsychology and pharmacology that the experience induced the strong sense that his "personality had to be crucified," a loss of ego he found painful and frightening, yet which led, "at the height of the experience," to the insight that he "could not have salvation alone."[123] He concluded, however, that while it did provide "an empirical basis on which to go to people who are skeptical...we should not by any means think that this is something we can discuss openly," for "whether you have the mystical experience, noninduced by the drug, or the experience of spiritual reality induced by the drug, you are open to suspicion."[124] Rather than LSD, then, Exman hoped for the transformation of American churches and religious life through mystical experience more broadly understood. "We have many orthodox people in theology," he wrote. "This is my field. I know something about the organized church, and some of my best friends are theologians. I know how awfully hard it is for them to break the shell of orthodoxy. They verbalize, they intellectualize, and this is the spiritual experience, paradoxically, that they are talking about."[125] Exman found the drug spiritually instructive but ultimately limiting, and did not continue to pursue the divine through psychedelics; Smith reached a similar conclusion, and Huxley too urged caution, while the acid evangelists Timothy Leary and Richard Alpert merrily pressed on. But Exman never lost his faith in the centrality of mystical experience to the life of the spirit. In 1960 he wrote an essay for Wainwright House, "The Search for Meaning," in which he continued the same focus on depth psychology, mystical ways of knowing and experiencing the divine, and the search for God beyond any destination as the very essence of what it means to be human.[126]

Alongside these ever-expanding spiritual explorations, remarkably, Exman carried on his highly successful work in the religion department at Harper's, eventually acquiring an informal status as a leading spokesman for the field.[127] He certainly brought a stellar group of writers into the Harper's fold. In addition to Fosdick, Fox, Clark, Heard, Smith, and Krishnamurti, the theologians H. Richard Niebuhr, Paul Tillich, Dietrich Bonhoeffer, Karl Barth, and Rudolf Bultmann were all Exman authors in the 1930s, 1940s, and 1950s, as were Pierre Teilhard de Chardin, the French paleontologist, philosopher, and Jesuit priest, whose *The Phenomenon of Man* (1959) Exman edited; D. Elton Trueblood, the Quaker philosopher, author of three mid-1940s bestsellers, *The Predicament of Modern Man* (1944), *Foundations for Reconstruction* (1946), and *Alternative to Futility* (1948); the founder of the Catholic Worker movement, Dorothy Day, who published her acclaimed autobiography, *The Long Loneliness* (1952), with Exman at Harper's; and the African American mystic Howard Thurman. Many of these writers published under the Torchlight imprint Harper's established in the 1950s. After the Montgomery bus boycott of 1955–56, Exman personally traveled to Montgomery to convince Martin Luther King Jr. to write about the boycott and the civil rights movement, resulting in *Stride toward Freedom: The Montgomery Story* (1958).[128] Exman himself became actively involved in the campaign against nuclear arms and the American war in Vietnam in the late 1950s and 1960s, an example of the frequent connections between mystical spiritual exploration and active social and political engagement. He also wrote the text and captions for an important photodocumentary book on the life and work of Albert Schweitzer, the great German physician, missionary, and mystic, about whom he spoke widely, including at the Riverside Church and the Ramakrishna-Vivekanada Center in New York City.[129]

These transformations in Exman's life took place over two decades and matured in a culture and a country quite different from the world of the Riverside Church and the mainstream of religious publishing in the late 1920 and 1930s, when he first began his work at Harper's. The corner of American religious life that he inhabited, that of liberal and bookish New York society, was by the late 1950s more open to this kind of wide-ranging spirituality than it had been thirty years earlier. Much of this change, in elite New York circles as much as in American middle-class culture, was due to the religious and psychological trans- formations and new orientation toward religious reading that emerged during World War II. Yet Exman's journey into Vedantism and mystical and psychological and even pharmacological spirituality was a natural if not an inevitable out- growth of the culture of religious reading that he helped build through the reli- gion department at Harper's. The ethos of religious openness so ably expressed in Fosdick's *As I See Religion* in this way came to fruition in the life of its editor and publisher.

* * *

Under Eugene Exman the religion department at Harper & Brothers became in the 1930s a leading publisher of religious books. Along with the other general- trade presses that aggressively entered the religion field in the late 1920s, Harper's brought with full force the logic of consumerism to the publishing and marketing of religious books. With the structures of middlebrow reading avail- able to guide readers through the open waters of the commercial marketplace, Harper's, Macmillan, and the new religious publishers of the era were able to free themselves from the burden of genteel cultural responsibility. Though the fear of commercializing and thereby cheapening both reading and faith never entirely subsided, the turn toward professionalized and specialized religion departments in the late 1920s nevertheless marked a critical turning point in the history of American religious publishing. A central tenet of religious liber- alism, after all, was to redeem the culture through participation in it, and partic- ipation in the commercial marketplace emerged as a natural development of this fundamental liberal impulse. The new spirit of religious exploration through consumer-oriented reading and publishing achieved great success at Harper's under Exman, who in his work and in his life embodied this culture as fully as any other twentieth-century American. The manifesto of his religion department was Fosdick's *As I See Religion*, and its bestsellers in the 1930s the positive- thinking guides of Emmet Fox and Glenn Clark, but the ethos of spiritual open- ness and eclecticism that Exman brought to Harper's increasingly permeated religious middlebrow culture.

Religious publishing continued to struggle through the Depression years, though by the late 1930s observers began to note an increase in sales and interest. Observers also noted continuing trends in the content of those books. "The quarrel between faith and science is now, broadly speaking, at an end," wrote P. W. Wilson, a bit optimistically, in an important survey of the field in 1938.[130] He also noted the decline of rigid sectarianism, declaring that in recent years "the religious bookshelf has suggested that frontiers between churches are breaking down." Yet in addition to these commonplace observations regarding American spirituality, Wilson fretfully perceived something new on the world stage. "The new chasm within civilization," he wrote, "lies between religion and contempt for religion," and here he saw ominous signs. The new "contempt for religion" came not from the crusading and condescending humanism of Mencken and Lippmann and Krutch, with which Fosdick and other liberals had achieved an amiable truce. The dangerous new development in religious life was "not that people go to movies when they ought to be listening to sermons," as he put it, "but an apocalyptic conflict between authorities over the human spirit." Wilson was speaking, of course, of the rise of fascism in Europe, and especially Nazism in Germany. In the contest between religion and contempt for religion, Wilson proclaimed, "Germany, at the moment, offers the most spectacular battlefield."[131] Heard had founded Trabuco in part because of his own apocalyptic worries about world affairs. His radical college never trained the spiritual world-changers he imagined, but he was right about this: the war with fascism had profound religious dimensions, and the United States would engage that battle along front lines in American schools, churches, libraries, bookstores, and individual religious lives.

4

Religious Reading Mobilized

The Book Programs of World War II

World War II pushed the American middle class in new directions religiously. For decades liberal Protestants had been working to craft a modern, nonsectarian spirituality, a faith suitable for an increasingly urbanized, scientific, and consumer-oriented society. They did this work largely for their own purposes, energized in equal measure by hope and fear regarding the changes they witnessed around them. But during World War II these liberal Protestant ambitions became national priorities. As the nation mobilized, religious and political leaders fretted over many things, including the effect of war on religious faith and the role churches might play in the war effort, but all agreed that sectarian divides must be overcome to face the existential threat posed by fascism abroad. In such a climate religious reading in the 1940s became a national concern. Industry executives, flush with patriotism, sought to enlist books as "weapons in the war of ideas," all the while working, as businessmen, to profit from an evolving and expanding marketplace. The reading and publishing initiatives of the Council on Books in Wartime (the subject of this chapter) and the Religious Book Week campaign of the National Conference of Christians and Jews (the subject of the next) sought to mobilize books, and readers, for this "war of ideas." Sales of religious books as a percentage of all books sold rose steadily from 1939 to 1945, perhaps one indication that the American reading public, along with industry and national leaders, recognized the importance of religious reading in a time of war.[1] In previous decades liberal Protestants had deployed their considerable cultural capital to promote their visions of right religion and right reading. Now, in the midst of war, previously unimaginable national resources were mobilized to aid the cause.

One consequence of this cultural mobilization was the training of a new generation of readers. Cultural arbiters and entrepreneurs had worked to shape American reading habits for decades through the institutions of middlebrow culture, and liberal Protestants had been eager participants in these enterprises.

Yet none of these transformed American reading practices like World War II. Through the greater availability of cheap books and increased access to higher education, the war laid the foundation for the mass reading environment of the postwar decades. Even more fundamentally, the war created new social arrangements that increased socialization into the practices of book culture, including the habit of reading itself, but also habits of book buying, book borrowing, and book talk with friends, family, and fellow book club members. In these ways the war took middlebrow reading values—reading for pleasure, for status, for sociability, for solace, and for self-improvement—and democratized them even further, habituating new readers to these middle-class cultural mores. New professional organizations that took shape after the war, such as the American Book Publishers Council (established 1945) and its Committee on Reading Development (established 1950), helped solidify these changes, but the war itself was the real catalyst of change.[2] And few arenas of American culture were more affected than religion. For the remainder of the century religious publishing would consistently outpace the overall book industry in sales, and the practices of book culture became ever more important as fundamental American *religious* practices.[3]

As this and subsequent chapters detail, however, the war did more than promote religious reading. It also pointed middle-class Americans down new spiritual paths, paths that mass-market reading allowed more and more to follow. Social and cultural historians have extensively catalogued the changes war and war mobilization brought not only to the military, government, and the economy, but also to areas of American life as diverse as race relations, the status of gays and lesbians, popular culture, education, the built environment, the fine arts, and organized religion. Few have turned their attention, however, to the more intimate arena of private spirituality and the war, though the war's impact here was no less profound than in other areas of culture. Those scholars who attend to the spiritual in the late twentieth century often take the 1950s, the postwar world, as the baseline from which to measure more contemporary developments, thereby obscuring the effects of the war.[4] Such approaches miss the profound role the war played in popularizing forms of spirituality rooted in religious liberalism.

The religious reading programs of World War II built on the work of previous decades, which had successfully drawn national attention to modern religious books and to new spiritual vocabularies. In particular the reading programs of the 1940s built on and accelerated the liberal Protestant search for the universal in religion, represented most significantly during the war, as before, by psychology and mysticism. But now, amid the exigencies of war, political and publishing leaders used psychological and mystical liberalism as a springboard for more ambitious interfaith endeavors among Protestants, Catholics, and Jews. Wartime pressures augmented the ongoing search for common spiritual ground with a new emphasis on forms of faith committed to pluralism, democracy, and national unity. While Eugene Exman and the spiritual avant-garde at Trabuco were exploring Hindu meditation and the early human potential movement, the war brought less exotic but ultimately more revolutionary interfaith practices and sensibilities to the mainstream. Primarily intended to foster goodwill and effective citizenship, the interfaith project also promoted reading across the boundaries of tradition, a novel religious practice for most middle-class Americans. The reinvigorated religious middlebrow culture that first emerged in the 1940s therefore further broadened the notion of a common ground of faith and played a critical role in promoting the new spiritual sensibilities, marked by cosmopolitan openness to difference, that characterized middle-class seeker culture in postwar America.

The Mobilization of Readers

World War II was indeed a good war for publishers and booksellers. The war brought the book business, like the rest of the American economy, out of the doldrums and into a period of tremendous growth. The total dollar value of books sold doubled from 1939 to 1945, an unprecedented increase.[5] As the war in Europe ground to its conclusion in the late spring of 1945, the Book Manufacturers' Institute commissioned a large-scale survey of American book reading and buying habits to better understand this remarkable upsurge. Using the statistical sampling methods developed by pollsters in the previous decade, hundreds of investigators fanned across the country, interviewing four thousand randomly sampled Americans. "The large increase in earnings, especially in the middle- and lower-income groups enabled many more people to buy books," the researchers concluded, while "neither shortages of labor and materials, nor distribution difficulties, nor drastic curtailment of advertising allowance seemed to slow down the pace."[6]

The study was led by the consumer psychologist Henry C. Link of the Psychological Corporation, the bestselling author of *The Return to Religion* (1936). Link's study asked subjects about the frequency of their reading, how they acquired books, the types of books read, and how reading related to other leisure habits such as radio listening, and correlated these findings, in good social scientific fashion, with age, sex, region, income, education, and religion. The solidly statistical results—94 percent of all books were read by "active" readers (those who read at least one book per month); 58 percent of books read in the previous month were fiction; 34 percent of Americans claimed to have more than one hundred books in the home; 57 percent of all books read in the previous month were borrowed, either from friends or family or from libraries (a finding that did not vary by income level); reading books occupied 8 percent of leisure time, well behind radio listening (49 percent) but comparable to movie going (11 percent) and magazine reading (11 percent)—were tabulated in colorful charts and tables, ready for an industry eager to keep the boom going in the postwar years. Mass-market paperbacks, priced at 25 cents, had been introduced by Pocket Books in 1939 but accounted for only 13 percent of books sold in 1945 (and therefore a much smaller fraction of total dollar share), indicating the upsurge was not due simply to the new availability of these inexpensive books, but rather to the economic and cultural shifts of the war years.[7] The most clearly and forcefully articulated finding—that book reading correlated more strongly with education level than with any other demographic statistic—boded well for the future, especially with the passage the year before of the Servicemen's Readjustment Act (the "GI Bill") and its education benefits for returning veterans. The president of Harper & Brothers, Frank MacGregor, looked back over the book boom of the war years and saw only bright days ahead. "It would seem," he told the survey researchers, "that the product of our industry has a future that knows no bounds."[8]

Religious books did more than ride this rising tide. Their figures swelled beyond the astounding growth in overall book sales, an increase far surpassing even the renaissance years of the 1920s. In response to a March 1943 questionnaire sent by New York publishers to religious booksellers across the nation, the Sunday School Board of the Southern Baptist Convention reported that their 1942 sales had run 29 percent ahead of 1941, and 1943 was already 31 percent ahead of 1942. A bookstore manager in Alabama reported his best sales in religion in sixteen years, and one in Florida his best in the previous eight; all agreed the new sales were coming from "laymen" or "the man in the street." As one respondent observed, "It is apparent ... [that] people who never read a religious book, or a book with religious implications, are taking time to temper their thinking with inspirational and devotional literature."[9] By April 1943 *Publishers' Weekly* could boldly and simply declare, "Reports are consistent that more religious books are being sold this year than ever before."[10] And the following year, 1944, a follow-up survey found even stronger growth. The Old Corner Bookstore in Boston reported religion sales in early 1944 running 50 percent ahead of the record year of 1943, while at the Methodist Cokesbury store in Dallas totals had soared by 300 percent. When asked to identify types of readers and books, respondents again reported the greatest sales in devotional and inspirational titles, which, according to the manager at Morehouse-Gorhman booksellers in New York, held special appeal "due, we believe, to the fact that many are beginners in religious reading."[11]

When asked to name specific titles, booksellers indicated Bibles, of course, and devotional books of the type familiar to Americans for generations. Booksellers had trouble keeping Bibles in stock, in fact, and introduced a variety of war-related specialty Bibles to capitalize on the demand; Link's research, not surprisingly, found the Bible the most frequent answer when interviewees were asked to name the most recent book they had read.[12] The single best-selling inspirational book of the war was a pocket-size volume of daily devotionals called *Strength for Service to God and Country: Daily Devotional Messages for Those in the Service*, mentioned repeatedly by booksellers across the country as perhaps their strongest seller other than the Bible. This little book, published in 1942, followed the popular format of a short reading per day, a format used with great success in the Scotsman Oswald Chambers's recent *My Utmost for His Highest* (1935). *Strength for Service* consisted of 369 short passages for contemplation, each based on a text from the Christian or Hebrew scriptures, accompanied by a short prayer. (The book contained devotionals for Good Friday, Mother's Day, Labor Day, and Thanksgiving, each a "floating" holiday, in addition to the standard one per day.) Prominent clergymen such as Daniel Poling of Philadelphia contributed entries, though most contributors were lesser-known clergymen or seminary professors. All were Protestants, mostly Methodist, Baptist, Presbyterian, Episcopalian, or Congregationalist. Conceived and edited by an army chaplain, Norman E. Nygaard, the book was shepherded into print by Pat Beaird at Abingdon-Cokesbury, its publisher. Appropriately for a wartime devotional, inside the front cover were pasted the words of the "Star-Spangled Banner," while the back pages made room for the Pledge of Allegiance, "America" ("My Country, 'Tis of Thee"), and "America the Beautiful." The book was an instant hit both at home and with the troops abroad, who undoubtedly appreciated its small size and sturdy vinyl cover. Soon the book's sales soared past one million and helped propel Abingdon-Cokesbury to the status of the world's largest publisher of religious books. By February 1943 the publisher still reported sales of over eighty thousand copies per month.[13]

A brief introduction, most likely written by Beaird himself, addressed the reader directly. It indicated clearly that the mission of this book was to socialize new readers into the practices of book culture and the values of reading religiously: "This book is for you. It is for you alone. Its purpose is to strengthen and sustain you in those troubled hours when you feel a Need that cannot be well put into words." Even those unfamiliar with reading need not fear this book, the introduction reassured, for "they are simple things, these messages.... There is no need for fine writing, for big words and labored sentences when hearts talk one with another." If readers required further assurance that this book would satisfy their unnamed needs, that those who produced it understood their struggles and fears, the publishers casually mentioned "that Dr. Norman E. Nygaard, who conceived the idea of this book and selected its contributors, has himself been called into active service."[14] Then, in the course of the next 369 pages, the devotionals themselves straightforwardly addressed the common struggles of those at war: fear of death, loneliness, grief, sexual temptation, clashes with authority, and loss of faith. To face these challenges, readers were urged to remember home and family, to pray, to read the Bible, and most of all to trust in God. As war disrupted ties of family and community and removed young men and women from regular church life and pastoral care, books offered comfort, inspiration, hope, distraction, and counsel. With its emphasis on service, self-sacrifice, duty, honor, and faith, *Strength for Service to God and Country* reaffirmed the core values of the traditional culture of character. And with its assurance that "there is no need for fine writing, for big words and labored sentences" it positioned this message in the safe and comfortable confines of middlebrow accessibility. In this way the most popular religious book of the war powerfully acculturated a new cohort of Americans to reading as a religious practice.

By stimulating reading, the war reinvigorated older cultural forms, represented by Bibles and devotionals. But the war also simultaneously facilitated processes of change. Reading during the war, as perhaps in all times, operated both as a technology of power, centralized and regulated by a "culture industry," and as a tool of individual agency.[15] Once a solider or sailor became a reader, vast new opportunities arose for indoctrination, but also for experimentation and innovation. The rapid growth in sales certainly delighted publishers, booksellers, and religious leaders, but none could be certain in just what directions these new readers would move. This reading revival occurred amid larger social dislocations, as the war destabilized community and family life and raised newly urgent religious and moral questions for soldiers confronting the hardships of war, civilians struggling with grief and loneliness, and each facing unprecedented threats and responsibilities. These wartime readers, grappling with such personal and societal strains, used religious reading both to rediscover familiar paths and to illuminate new ones.

Religious and political leaders knew that to defeat its fascist foes the nation would have to marshal all of its resources "both physical and spiritual," but few knew just what this meant.[16] Those who worked in religious publishing felt these anxieties with particular acuity, for the war challenged the very basis of their enterprise, both as a calling and as a business. Sales of religious books were growing, but doubts remained about the nation's spiritual and moral fitness. In such a fraught religious context, with so much riding on the faith of individual soldiers and civilians, books of religious inspiration became critical tools in the war effort. More than at any time in decades, readers, critics, authors, and publishers all agreed that religious books mattered in the 1940s— to civilians as well as those in the service. In response religious, governmental, and publishing leaders united in unprecedented ways to mobilize readers for the spiritual struggle of the age. Though deeply uncertain about the war's effect on faith, they were certain of their role: to create more and better readers, to comfort and inspire with a modern faith, and to aid the war effort through religious solidarity.

Pat Beaird and Religion at War

The publishing executive Pat Beaird understood these anxieties and responsibilities better than most. A Methodist from Tyler, Texas, Beaird had served in the navy and Marine Corps in World War I.[17] He fought at Belleau Wood and Soissons and spent fourteen months hospitalized due to a gassing. Upon recovery he enrolled at Southern Methodist University, and after graduation and a brief stint in newspaper advertising went to Nashville to work for the Publishing House of the Methodist Episcopal Church, South, in 1922. Two years later he became head of the book department, a position he held for over three decades. He managed the press through the Depression and World War II (and through a series of name changes; the press became Cokesbury in 1925 so as to expand its customer base beyond Methodism, and Abingdon-Cokesbury in 1940 after the merger of the northern and southern branches of the denomination). In addition to his position with Abingdon-Cokesbury, he chaired for many years the Religious Publishers' Group, a consortium of the major general-interest religious publishers organized under the auspices of the Book Publishers' Bureau (and previously under the National Association of Book Publishers, the former trade association). He also organized and chaired the Religious Books Committee of the Council on Books in Wartime and helped coordinate its collaboration with the National Conference of Christians and Jews. These roles positioned him at the center of the publishing industry's response to the spiritual demands of the war.

Beaird was therefore especially able to see the greatly expanded role of religious reading to minister across the miles to men and women facing hardship overseas and to those left working and worrying back home. He was a firm believer in the idea of a wartime religious revival and saw the invigorated interest in religious reading as part of the larger spiritual turn. "This sudden interest in spiritual things," he observed in a March 1943 *New York Times* essay, "is not confined to men in active combat."[18] The spiritual turn "extends all the way back through training camps to parents and friends and through them it touches in some manner almost every individual. In most communities churches are filled in spite of gasoline rationing; church budgets are comfortably met," and, of perhaps greatest interest to this bookman, "religious books are being bought and read in astounding numbers."[19] Other observers concurred. Willard Johnson of the National Conference of Christians and Jews discounted the claims of widespread religious revivalism among either the servicemen or in the civilian population, but agreed with Beaird that "one of the true signs of the return to religion" was the tremendous "increase in the sale of religious books."[20]

Beyond noting the sheer increase in sales, Beaird and others remarked even more tellingly on who the new readers of these religious books were, what kinds of books they were reading, and under what circumstances they turned to books for comfort and inspiration. Men and women in the service, of course, accounted for many of the new readers. "Sergeants kneel and pray under fire and testify that 'there are no atheists in foxholes,'" he wrote, borrowing Ernie Pyle's newly famous line. "Shipwrecked sailors and aviators float for weeks without food or water, reading testaments, and later thank God openly and unashamedly for a superior faith which sustained them."[21] But, Beaird was quick to note, "the demand for religious books on the home front is more significant perhaps because it receives little publicity, and its proportions are seldom recognized." Many of these home front readers, he conceded, were traditional churchgoers in traditionally faithful parts of the country, especially small towns in the South and Southwest. Yet in addition to these relatively stable audiences, Beaird observed new markets developing in response to war mobilization. "Larger cities in crowded war industry areas are having a healthy increased demand for religious books," he noted, "especially the devotional self-help type....Much of it comes from harassed workers, many of whom are separated from family and friends and normal church ties."[22] Farm boys from Oklahoma building airplanes in Los Angeles, a sergeant's wife in Detroit riveting armor plating on tanks, a Polish kid from Scranton unloading steel at the navy yards in South Philadelphia, a young mother in Texas raising children alone—these were the new readers Beaird saw for religious books.

Beaird believed that books had a unique role to play in the spiritual lives of these uprooted and anxious Americans. Many, torn from family and community, harried, tired, and afraid, "are seeking help from the fundamentals of personal religious faith as never before." Gerald Lawson, the librarian of Drew University and an active member of the ALA's Religious Books Round Table, conducted an informal study in 1943 that supported these claims. He polled publishers, booksellers, and librarians across the United States and based on their remarks concluded that "devotional literature, books which help in the interpretation of life...are the chief reading interests of people today."[23] Self-help and devotional books—especially, according to Beaird, books "designed to be read in small doses, usually in quiet moments at home, during the lunch hour, or while commuting"— offered reassurance, intimacy, and day-to-day and moment-to-moment spiritual guidance and companionship. Beaird the patriot and Beaird the businessman found hope in the expanding role for religious reading. As he commented on the various types of Americans now turning to reading, he solemnly predicted, "They will continue to do so in increasing numbers. Casualty lists will grow. The strain of long hours at high-speed production will affect us more and more. Worry about disrupted business and home life, shortages of necessities and lower living standards will take their toll in civilian morale. This is why religious books are becoming recognized as important to a sustained total war effort."[24]

Beaird saw religious books primarily as aids to morale, as sources of hope, comfort, inspiration, and consolation. Others stressed religion's civic functions.

Ellwood C. Nance, an army chaplain and an instructor at the Chaplain School at Harvard, compiled a widely read anthology, *Faith of Our Fighters* (1944), designed to unite Americans spiritually behind the national cause.[25] Nance's book contained essays from Protestant, Catholic, and Jewish chaplains; testimonials from servicemen and servicewomen; brief spiritual biographies of Generals Marshall, MacArthur, and Eisenhower; and reprints of letters home from men in combat. It concluded with a brief section, "Faith on the Home Front," highlighted by Vice President Henry Wallace's entry, "A Peace Worth Fighting For." Every item in the collection remarked on the righteousness of the Allied cause, the power of faith to aid that cause, and, most significantly, the need to overcome frivolous denominational squabbles so that Americans at war might present a united spiritual front. The long-standing liberal desire to transcend sect and creed, according to Nance, was now a national wartime imperative.

The linkage between heightened religious fervor and national spiritual unity was drawn not just by the glorifiers of war, but also by those careful observers more finely attuned to the cold reality of combat. Chaplain Richard Chase, decorated for courage under fire in North Africa and Sicily, wrote openly in *Faith of Our Fighters* of the spiritual pitfalls of war. He noted instances of petty coarsening, such as men becoming profane in speech or drinking to excess. More dramatically, he recounted the tale of one formerly humane soldier in Tunisia who now "had no pity, no redeeming quality in his heart. War to him was a sport. Killing men was like shooting ducks."[26] Yet, Chase was quick to observe, while "examples of the grinding effect of war are lamentable," they "are the exception rather than the rule." More commonly, because of the crucible of war, "soldiers become more sober-minded, more awake to the spiritual issues of life, more appreciative of their homeland and its unparalleled advantages."[27] "This," he concluded, in addition to the more mundane fact that his religious services were overflowing with soldiers, "is a convincing answer to those who want to know whether soldiers turn away from or to religion in wartime."[28] Like all the contributors to *Faith of Our Fighters*, Chase ultimately agreed that the war was leading to spiritual revitalization and that this revitalization was breaking down religious boundaries. *Faith of Our Fighters* was the product of a Disciples of Christ publishing house, yet it prominently featured Jewish and Catholic expressions of faith; in this way the anthology's very existence stands as a testimony to interfaith cooperation during the war.

Not all observers were as sanguine as those in *Faith of Our Fighters*, however. The national conversation about faith in wartime, in fact, featured deep divisions and profound concerns in addition to signs of hope. Lloyd C. Douglas, a former Congregational minister and author of the bestselling religious novel *The Robe* (1942), dismissed Ernie Pyle's oft-repeated claim about atheists in foxholes by noting rather dryly, "Preachers who quote it are well within their vocational rights. But too much should not be made of it, for there aren't so many atheists anyhow."[29] Douglas concluded that men would leave the service much as they had entered it. The senior chaplain at the Great Lakes Naval Training Station, the largest in the world, agreed, estimating professed atheists among his "raw recruits" to be one in a thousand.[30] Quite often critics with direct experience of combat remarked on the spiritual degradations of war. Indeed, contrary to the optimism of Beaird, Nance, Chase, and others, accounts from soldiers themselves often spoke of loss rather than gain. "The boys are not going to be angels when they get home. In fact, a good many of them are going the other way," wrote one soldier to Harry Emerson Fosdick in New York. "I just want to make plain that there is actually no great 'turning to God' movement going on."[31]

Fosdick, the nation's highest profile pacifist, was a natural correspondent for those with similar doubts. Years earlier he had jingoistically championed America's involvement in World War I, even writing a very successful little book, *The Challenge of the Present Crisis*, to whip up war fervor.[32] But his experiences as a chaplain with the U.S. Army in Europe in 1918 turned him from warmonger into unflinching pacifist. While overseas, Fosdick witnessed for himself the physical brutality of war, but just as powerfully saw how war so often debased psyche and spirit. Now, a quarter-century later, he was a leader of the Churchmen's Campaign for Peace through Mediation, a leading pacifist organization, and would not easily accept happy tales of the war's boost to faith. Thoughtful observers like Fosdick understood that war often ravaged not only body but also mind and spirit, through fear, grief, doubt, despair, and the dehumanizing brutality of mass violence. A chaplain serving in this second great war opened his heart to Fosdick, a chaplain from the first. "I believe the American press has given a false impression of the upswing of religion among the men in the armed forces," he wrote from aboard the USS *General J. H. McRae* in early 1945. "Being on a troop transport, I have seen the men 'coming and going.' I can't say that I know one person who has been made 'religious' by the war; but I do know a lot of otherwise 'religious' men who have let down their standards tremendously."[33] Fosdick concurred. "There is a lot of sentimental nonsense talked about the spiritual effects of war," he replied to the chaplain, "but the real effects are exactly as you have stated them. . . . It will not do to fool ourselves by any illusions about the religious consequences of war."[34] In his public pronouncements Fosdick was even more forthcoming, opening his collection of sermons on Christianity in wartime with the blunt declaration, "This certainly is a ghastly time to be alive."[35]

Fosdick and his correspondents in these exchanges expressed a special concern for the moral consequences of the war for individual soldiers, men "who have let down their standards" and therefore "are not going to be angels when they get home." But their concerns indicate more than mere priggishness. Rather the letters to Fosdick and the accounts in the popular press of heroic wartime religiosity reveal the complexity of the vibrant national conversations about war and faith. All sides understood the war as a testing time for the religious life of the nation, recognizing the critical role of religious faith in the winning of the war and, just as critically, the vast, unpredictable consequences of mobilization and combat for religion. Indeed the glowing testimonials from *Faith of Our Fighters* and the skepticism of Fosdick and his correspondents all stemmed from a shared set of deep anxieties about the course of the war, the toll it was exacting, and the spiritual resolve of those in combat. All participants in these debates— interventionists and pacifists, those who saw a wartime revival and those who did not—knew that petty squabbles about doctrine and denomination mattered little amid the global crisis. In this way the spiritual mobilization of the American people presented a great opportunity for the advancement of liberal religious sensibilities.

In recognition of these wartime responsibilities and opportunities, publishing leaders, including Pat Beaird, launched the greatest reading campaign in history. They did this, first and foremost, to aid the war effort, recognizing the importance of reading, including religious reading, as an aid to the cause, as a "weapon in the war of ideas." They also saw the tremendous possibilities the war presented to shape the habits of a generation of emerging readers. As the religious book business adapted to the cultural shifts brought about by mobilization for total war, publishing and religious leaders drew on the lessons learned in the previous two decades of religious book marketing, and now drafted the mechanisms of religious middlebrow culture for service in the wartime crusade. Americans in the 1940s already had a long history of using reading as a means of self-improvement, and since at least the 1920s, with the introduction of the Book-of-the-Month and other book clubs, the book industry had aggressively marketed reading and book buying to the middle class as a means of social ascent. Now, in the midst of the war, the cultural pressures to read books gained new and larger significance. Reading the right books became part of the war effort.

With the marketplace of reading expanding as never before, and with the personal networks of family, friends, and community that traditionally guided new readers increasingly strained, the role of professional cultural arbiters assumed even more importance as well. War mobilization greatly enhanced the role of centralized, expert planning in all phases of national life and offered previously inconceivable opportunities for publishing and religious leaders to coordinate with government at the highest levels. The wartime reading programs they created, including the Council on Books in Wartime and the Religious Book Week campaign of the National Conference of Christians and Jews, greatly energized and transformed the religious middlebrow project that had taken shaped over the previous two decades. These wartime reading programs helped America mobilize spiritually by creating new readers and new reading practices. Even more, wartime mobilization provided liberal religion with new, powerful allies, as the search for a common ground of faith became a national priority.

The Spiritual Crusade of the Council on Books in Wartime

By far the most important enterprise in wartime book promotion was the Council on Books in Wartime, a philanthropic organization founded by New York publishers.[36] Fearful of seeming opportunistic in a moment of crisis, the Council wisely settled on a policy of promoting reading in general rather than book buying in particular, and engaged in numerous activities to promote reading, including the production of radio and film programming and the distribution of recommended reading lists to booksellers and libraries across the country. Most impressively, through its subsidiary organization, Editions for the Armed Services, Inc., the Council coordinated the production and distribution of nearly 123 million copies of 1,322 titles in special Armed Services Editions (ASE), sent to American men and women in active service, in military hospitals, and held as prisoners of war.[37] These small paperbacks became "the greatest mass publishing enterprise of all history," according to one contemporary observer, and did more than any other program to introduce books "to GIs who had read little before the war."[38]

According to Council members, their plan to give away millions of books to service men and women would not only aid the war effort, but would also enhance their business prospects down the line by creating new readers and therefore new customers. Armed Services Editions, they noted, would contribute to "mass reading of books in the world to come."[39] The motivations and tactics of the Council during the war illuminate an increasingly influential orientation toward mass reading, a further democratization of the middlebrow emphasis on reading as a means of cultural betterment and self-improvement. The Council brought this expanded middlebrow orientation to its promotion of religious books, which it pursued through its own Religious Books Committee and its cooperation with the religious reading initiative of the National Conference of Christians and Jews.

The Council on Books in Wartime grew out of conversations among publishing executives in the months after the attack on Pearl Harbor. Originally conceived at a February 1942 lunch meeting of Clarence B. "Clip" Boutell of G. P. Putnam's Sons and George Oakes of the *New York Times*, the Council took shape quickly; by March its bureaucratic structure was sketched out. Publisher W. W. Norton and Frederic G. Melcher of *Publishers' Weekly* assumed leading roles, along with representatives from the American Booksellers Association and the Book Publishers Bureau. Dr. Henry Seidel Canby, editor of the *Saturday Review of Literature* and consultant to the Book Division of the Office of Facts and Figures (later the Office of War Information), was brought on as an advisor. Through Canby the Council also forged ties with Chester Kerr, chief of the Book Division of the Office of Facts and Figures. With this group of leaders in place, the Council was able from its inception to work at the highest levels to coordinate the military and federal government with private industry.

Following the book club model, the Council made its book selections in close consultation with a committee of cultural experts such as Canby. The publishers who ran the Council and, even more, the critics such as Canby brought in to advise it saw themselves as members of a cultural elite, as those with special knowledge and therefore unique responsibilities to use that knowledge for public good. As experts, they faced the same tensions that marked all facets of the professionalization of American life since the end of the nineteenth century, tensions felt with particular acuity in middlebrow literary culture. These men sought leadership of a public cultural endeavor in a society deeply committed to democratic values. How, then, to impart high standards to a reading public while respecting the autonomy of readers? This was the central challenge in all undertakings in the public promotion of reading, faced by organizers of the Religious Book Week of the 1920s and by the editorial committee of the Religious Book Club, and now faced again by the Council on Books in Wartime. Not coincidentally, then, given these challenges, the Council drew heavily on those men and women with experience navigating these tensions, men and women described by the historian John B. Hench as "of refined, if middlebrow, tastes, who had achieved a certain amount of celebrity through their own books, criticism, journalism, or public positions."[40] Canby, a former English professor with a Ph.D. from Yale, was the chairman of the selection committee of the Book-of-the-Month Club in addition to serving as editor of the *Saturday Review of Literature*. Also brought in to advise the Council at various points were the anthologist and poet Louis Untermeyer and the critic and Book-of-the-Month Club committee member Dorothy Canfield Fisher. These critics, with their experience as mediators between the worlds of high learning and mass culture, proved invaluable as the publishers on the Council struggled to define their roles as cultural authorities.

Members of the Council eventually came to realize that their contribution to the war effort must not simply be one of cultural enlightenment, as valuable as that might be. Rather they understood that books might play a larger role, one of spiritual sustenance, making the matter of expert guidance in reading all the more critical to the national cause. One of the most explicit articulations of the Council's spiritual role came from a statesman, Assistant Secretary of State Adolf Berle, who in May 1942 delivered an opening-night speech during the Council's inaugural meetings, held in Times Hall. In his address, "The Literature of Power," Berle boldly proclaimed the Council's spiritual mission. He asserted, as others had, that a central problem of the modern age was the overwhelming flood of new books and new knowledge. To combat the confusion and paralysis this profusion of books created, Berle proposed a clear guideline for selecting books amid the crisis of war. He implored Council leaders to endorse books that "move the spirit of men" and speak to "the deepest and most fundamental...riddles of human life." The American people, he told his audience, would surely face great hardships, both public and private, in the days and years ahead, and the leaders of the book business must be prepared to meet their needs. "Out of books which we are given there will largely be constructed those buildings in which all of us must dwell," he declared to his audience of book moguls. "In the greatest of our individual crises—the crisis of long parting, the crisis of bereavement, the crisis of fear, the crisis of death—in these we must live, in these mind-dwellings alone."[41] Berle here captured perfectly his audience's own sense of purpose. The spiritual undertone of the Council's mission reflected the liberal Protestant sensibilities of the Council leadership and pervaded the full range of the Council's undertakings throughout the war.

In March 1942 the Council adopted, on the suggestion of Norton, its famous slogan, "Books as Weapons in the War of Ideas." President Roosevelt himself soon became an enthusiastic supporter and explicitly endorsed the "books as weapons" theme. In a letter delivered to the annual banquet of the American Booksellers Association, meeting May 6, 1942,[42] in the Astor Hotel in New York, Roosevelt emphasized the contribution of books to the Allied cause. "We all know that books burn," he remarked, drawing an often-repeated contrast with the notorious Nazi book burning of May 10, 1933, when the works of Jews, Marxists, and other "un-German" authors were destroyed in a coordinated campaign. "Yet we have the greater knowledge that books cannot be killed by fire. People die, but books never die. No man and no force can abolish memory. No man and no force can put thought in a concentration camp forever. No man and no force can take from the world the books that embody man's eternal fight against tyranny of every kind. In this war, we know, books are weapons. And it is a part of your dedication always to make them weapons for man's freedom."[43] In this vision of the power of books, Roosevelt echoed ancient religious distinctions between the body and the soul, describing books at once as material objects that burn, yet also that embody greater, living spiritual forces that "cannot be killed" and "never die." More particularly, Roosevelt's language invoked the story from the Hebrew scriptures of Shadrach, Meshach, and Abednego, who were cast into a furnace for refusing to obey Nebuchadnezzar and yet, protected by an angel, emerged unscathed.[44] The spiritualization of reading, already endorsed by the assistant secretary of state, now received the full support of the commander in chief as critical to the war effort.

In a letter the following December to Norton, the chairman of the Council, Roosevelt repeated many of these themes, especially the central contention that books as spiritual entities constituted a kind of weapon. "In our country's first year of war," he wrote, "we have seen the growing power of books as weapons." A "war of ideas can no more be won without books," he continued, "than a naval war can be won without ships. . . . I hope that all who write and publish and sell and administer books will . . . rededicate themselves to the single task of arming the mind and spirit of the American people with the strongest and most enduring weapons."[45] American evangelists of religious reading had since the early nineteenth century championed the spiritual power of mass reading, an effort that gained renewed vitality in the 1920s. President Roosevelt, in advocating general reading with such spiritually charged language, drew on this deep cultural reservoir and anticipated the more explicit religious reading efforts to come.

The Council on Books in Wartime, the organization responsible for carrying out Roosevelt's grand vision, was remarkably small, staffed mostly with volunteer labor and operating on a total four-year budget, from February 1942 to February 1946, of only $98,000, $77,000 of which came from publishers.[46] The editorial advisory committee, composed of publishers, booksellers, librarians, and a representative of the Book-of-the-Month Club, chose the titles for the Council to publish in special Armed Services Editions, and from these lists the army and navy selected titles to purchase. Philip Van Doren Stern, a former editor with Pocket Books, oversaw the entire operation.[47] With the explicit endorsement of the president, careful coordination with military and government leaders, and financial support from publishers, this modest enterprise exerted a far-reaching influence on American reading during the war.

The Armed Services Editions proved the most lasting contribution of the Council. From the outset, W. W. Norton and others were aware of the profound cultural consequences of giving a vast array of reading material to millions of American fighting men and women. Critical to this contribution were the physical characteristics of the books themselves. Every effort was made to keep them small and cheap. The books measured either 5½" by 3⅞", half the size of a copy of *Reader's Digest* cut horizontally, or 6½" by 4½", the size of a standard magazine cut horizontally.[48] Each page contained two columns of text. Such an arrangement allowed unabridged editions, printed on presses and paper that were underutilized during the war, to be produced for only 6 cents and to fit in the pocket of a standard-issue uniform. At such a low price, the army and navy simply gave the books to soldiers and sailors; they did not have to be returned with other equipment upon discharge. This facilitated extensive, informal trading and the practice of leaving copies and taking others when passing through bases or other military facilities. Books that could be kept or traded also led to significant book-related conversation among army and navy readers, a practice Council officials knew would help create both more meaningful reading experiences and lifelong reading habits.[49]

Many in the industry were concerned that the production of massive numbers of cheap books would undercut domestic sales, and so precautions were taken to keep ASE copies out of civilian hands. But Norton did not share these fears. Since soldiers and sailors were free to keep their books, Norton knew the ASEs could mold an entire generation of readers. "The very fact that millions of men will have an opportunity to learn what a book is and what it can mean," he wrote in a memorandum to the Council's Executive Committee in March 1943, "is likely now and in the postwar years to exert a tremendous influence on the postwar course of the industry."[50] Like the tract and Bible societies of the nineteenth century, publishers working with the Council pursued a cause larger than the bottom line, yet astutely recognized that the success of that cause would also greatly expand their future customer base. A Random House survey of reading habits in army training camps found inductees had more time to read than civilians, a finding that surely made the Norton plan to use ASEs to cultivate new readers a promising proposition.[51] And according to historians of publishing, it worked; the ASEs were instrumental in stimulating the postwar boom of the fledgling paperback business.[52] Rather than merely flood the market with books, the Council on Books in Wartime flooded the market with readers.

Remarkably for an organization promoting books as weapons, the Armed Services Editions themselves remained relatively free of overtly nationalistic propaganda. This may be due, to a certain extent, to the ever-present desire to distinguish American practices from Nazi. Certainly the list of ASEs contained books describing the enemy, such as John F. Embree's *The Japanese Nation*, and a few titles about military life, such as Capt. Harry C. Butcher's *My Three Years with Eisenhower*, that one might consider propagandistic. But the vast majority of titles were chosen simply on their literary merits. The historian Trysh Travis describes the considerable anxiety Council members felt that their efforts would appear either self-promoting—using the war to make a buck—or beholden to the federal government in a way that could undermine their credibility: "The most persistent manifestations of the debate over how to promote their work without seeming self-promoting arose in discussions over how to publicize books directly related to the war effort." And so when actually faced with the task of producing books in ASEs, they skirted the issue by largely steering clear of such works.[53]

Rather than nationalistic propaganda, then, the Council engaged in literary propaganda. The Council used books as weapons with the remarkable notion that good books, in and of themselves, might make for better men and women, who would in turn become better soldiers and citizens. In this they adhered to the time-honored notion, rooted in the genteel tradition, that a healthy democracy demanded a literate public, a notion central to their self-understanding as public-minded experts. More typical than books about the Japanese or Eisenhower therefore were novels, biographies, and plays. Popular fiction dominated the list of ASEs, including 33 "adventure" titles such as *Call of the Wild* and *Tarzan of the Apes;* 160 "westerns" by Zane Grey, Ernest Haycox, and others; 122 "mysteries"; 113 "historical novels"; 23 "classics," ranging from *The Iliad* to the works of Mark Twain; and most of all, 246 titles of "contemporary fiction." That Sinclair Lewis's *Babbitt* and John Steinbeck's *Grapes of Wrath* might be considered "weapons in the war of ideas" testifies to the broad-minded and highly literary approach the Council took to its work.[54] The Council's willingness to produce books of mass appeal, such as westerns and mysteries, indicates its belief in the value, Travis notes, of "reading *qua* reading."[55] Books classified as "current affairs and the war," by contrast, numbered only twenty. The Council in fact lobbied successfully for the overturning of harsh censorship regulations in the army and navy, with the belief that open access to reading—no matter the specific literary merits—befit the fighting forces of a free people.[56]

Accounts from men in the service testify to the success of the Council's literary propaganda. Though anecdotal, letters from soldier-readers to the Council reveal some of the ways these texts were received and used. An army truck driver writing from New Guinea, for example, praised the Council for the ASEs' physical design, noting its many practical benefits. "Our modern 'bloomer-pocket' uniform makes it possible for us to conceal one of them perfectly from the watchful eye of a superior officer," he wrote. "They are easy to hide when you should be doing something else." In this regard the driver told the Council of a discovery he made when unloading a small landing boat. He found, he confided, "a small box with three or four [ASE books] in it fastened to the wall of [the] engine compartment." But more significantly, he concluded, "reading takes the mind away from the experiences we have that are so difficult."[57]

The use of reading by fighting men ranged from simple diversion to profound personal transformation. A *Saturday Evening Post* article from June 1945 about the Armed Services Editions, for example, told of men in combat, under constant shelling, laughing at passages from *A Tree Grows in Brooklyn* and, more commonly, of soldiers finding escape from boredom in an adventure story.[58] Indeed many of the soldiers who wrote directly to the Council mentioned this same sort of emotional uplift: reading as pleasure amid the misery of war. Yet a fuller accounting of the impact of these books must include uplift in a second sense, in the spiritual and intellectual sense, closer to the heart of Adolf Berle and the men and women who ran the Council. Ellwood Nance, the army chaplain who edited the *Faith of Our Fighters* anthology, also conducted an extensive survey of soldiers' reading habits, which he described in *Publishers' Weekly*: "Soldiers are seriously interested in religion, but in their religious reading they prefer a book that is written in non-technical language and that reaches its goal in less than 150 pages." But even if they stayed away from books written for the specialist, Nance noted, "many of them are seeking information as well as comfort in their religious reading."[59] Frequently letter writers confirmed his findings of these two related benefits of readily available reading material: books boosted morale and at the same time improved the spiritual well-being and intellectual sophistication of common fighting men.

Historians of reading often point to the perceived tension between reading for pleasure, which throughout the nineteenth century and into the twentieth was thought to be passive and feminine, and reading for intellectual development, which was seen as active and masculine. The experiences of readers of ASEs indicate a tremendous fluidity in these categories, a fluidity linked perhaps to the cultural turmoil brought about by the war. The double uplift of reading—both emotional and intellectual, both spiritual and cultural—crossed gender lines, coloring the reading experiences of men and women whether in uniform or on the home front. In the 1920s publishing and religious leaders regularly remarked on the masculine vigor and practicality of modern religious reading as part of their promotional campaigns aimed at disaffected young men. Soldiers in World War II regularly crossed these perceived barriers and embraced reading for all its joys, diversions, and uplifting and ennobling potential.

Again the soldiers themselves tell their tale best. "Reading material is more than scarce and more often than not your books are all that is available," wrote one soldier to Archibald Ogden, the Council's executive director. "Since these books are often the sole means of escape for G.I.'s, you are instilling in them, whether you are aware of it or not, a taste for good reading that will surely persist come victory."[60] A commanding officer shared the same observation. "It has been noticed that many men are acquiring the habit of reading for amusement and instruction who had previously viewed the printed word as a nuisance," he reported in stiff military prose. "It is believed that Editions for the Armed Services, Inc. has rendered a lasting service to both men and country, for this habit will endure."[61]

A sailor writing from Guam summarized clearly and personally the uplifting contribution of ASE books. "With six long tiresome days a-sea to look forward to and with only a small ship's crew library, we were far from happy," he recounted of his transit from Pearl Harbor across the Pacific. "But then the library produced a box of your books. We grabbed them," he continued, invoking a perfect image of innocent, bodily pleasure, "like children with a box of chocolates." This sailor reported finding a Quonset hut in Guam stocked with a complete collection of ASE titles, set aside for men in transit, since regular navy libraries would not lend books to men who could ship out at any minute. "So you can see your books have done several amazing things from the experience of one person. They have made a lot of sailors happy and entertained during the many days of travel asea," he remarked, highlighting the diversionary benefits of reading. Yet, according to this sailor, the books did more than distract; they ennobled. He noted, rather vividly, that because of ASE reading, "more fellows have gotten a real interest in books, who otherwise would not have gotten beyond the Superman stage." No longer children with a box of chocolates or a comic, through books they had matured. "I don't know who or what people I can thank for bringing these books to us, but we all thank them."[62] In his homespun way—not even knowing whom to thank—this sailor compellingly described the uplift provided by wartime reading.

The Council and Reading on the Home Front

In addition to the production of Armed Services Editions, the Council on Books in Wartime endeavored through a variety of channels to promote reading on the home front. It produced and distributed recommended reading lists to booksellers and libraries, lists mostly of books about Allied and enemy nations and other current affairs pertaining to the war. The Council also quickly seized on the popular media, including radio and film, to advertise its efforts and, more generally, promote reading and book buying. The Council's first radio project, suggested by Chester Kerr of the Office of War Information, was a reading of Stephen Vincent Benét's poem "They Burned the Books" on NBC in May 1942 (joining FDR in drawing attention to the Nazi book burning of May 1933). The success of this endeavor spurred the formation of a radio committee and the hiring of a radio director, Nan Taylor of WLB in Minneapolis. During the summer and fall of 1942 the Council arranged for authors to appear on popular women's radio shows and other news and chat programs. The Council soon moved to produce its own programming and eventually organized three recurring broadcasts, all interview shows: *Books Are Bullets*, hosted by Bennett Cerf of Random House, which ran on WQXR from October 1942 through December 1945 and included conversations with Louis Adamic, Pearl Buck, Norman Cousins, Dorothy Canfield Fisher, Margaret Mead, and Mark Van Doren, among many others; *Fighting Words*, which appeared on WMCA; and most important, *Words at War*, which in the late spring of 1943 gained a coveted network spot, 8:30 P.M. Thursdays, on NBC. Along the way, *Words at War* interviewed Ellwood Nance regarding *Faith of Our Fighters* and other social critics as politically diverse as Walter Lippmann, Ernie Pyle, and Friedrich Hayek.[63] In its radio programming the Council focused more on current affairs than fiction, yet, as with its Armed Services Editions and reading lists, it showed considerable editorial independence. Though hailed by *Variety* and the *New York Times* for its coverage of delicate issues such as racism and poverty, *Words at War* finally ran into trouble in the summer of 1945 after discussing a book advocating full employment, a notion associated with socialism. NBC, under pressure from business groups, began to add a disclaimer to the broadcast, and the Council decided to end the show rather than broadcast under such circumstances.

Figure 4.1 Victory Book Campaign posters. Courtesy of the Hennepin County Library, James K. Hosmer Special Collections Library, Kittleson World War II Collection, MPW00259, MPW00260.

The Council's brief foray into film grew out of the same desire to mingle educational current affairs programming with uplift. A committee of representatives from various publishers, the American Booksellers Association, and Warner Brothers secured an agreement with Newsreel Distributors, Inc., and Film Distributors, Inc., for the production and screening of a number of shorts based on interviews with authors. Due to film shortages, only six were produced. In each, newsreel footage from the war ran as the author and interviewer chatted about the book in question. These films were shown in theaters across the country and focused exclusively on books with direct relevance to the war, such as Eve Curie's *Journey among Warriors* and John Hersey's *A Bell for Adano*.

A more successful visual medium than film for spreading the Council's message was the poster. C. B. Falls's and Adolph Treidler's masterful Religious Book Week posters in the 1920s represented but two of the many antecedents of the Council's specifically book-themed posters. During World War II, the Office of War Information and a variety of private entities built on these earlier efforts, using the graphic arts for their own literary propaganda. For example, the Victory Book Campaign—a joint effort of the American Library Association, the Red Cross, and the USO—produced a series of posters to encourage Americans to donate books to men and women in the armed services (Figures 4.1, 4.2). The most simple of these posters—the two-color image of an eagle carrying a bundle of books—was often reproduced in magazine and newspaper advertising, while the other, more graphically sophisticated images were designed for greatest impact in full-size public display. C. B. Falls, creator of the bust-of-Lincoln poster from the 1920s Religious Book Week as well as a hugely successful "Books Wanted" poster from World War I, returned to this familiar theme with the "We Want Books" poster (and a nearly identical poster reading "Leave Books Here"). A third, even more evocative design with the caption "Give More Books—Give Good Books" featured a hand holding a book, open to a page depicting a soldier against a flag background. Each poster emphasized, as did the very name of the Victory Book Campaign itself, the contribution of book reading to the ultimate triumph of the Allied cause. The Victory Book Campaign, aided by such visually gripping posters, proved quite successful in securing donated books, but unfortunately many of the books were bulky hardcovers that were difficult to ship, and many others were of poor quality, limiting the number of soldiers who actually benefited from the campaign. But regardless of the success or failure of the campaign's stated goals, these posters nevertheless presented to the American public the notion of reading, and reading "good books," as critical to victory.[64]

The Council on Books in Wartime, in conjunction with the Office of War Information, produced its own posters for libraries, bookstores, and other public venues to support its much more productive undertakings. Almost all highlighted the contrast between American liberties and the Nazi book burning of May 1933, including one that depicted a book burning in the upper left of the poster and the Statute of Liberty, clutching a book in her left arm, in the lower right. Most famous and powerful of the Council's posters was a 1942 design, again featuring a Nazi book burning (Figure 4.3). Set against an ominous, glowing red sky, a giant book, seemingly made of stone, defies the diminutive book burners as it towers unscathed above their ghoulish, shadowy forms. Across the cover of this giant book runs an excerpt (slightly altered) from Roosevelt's May 1942 letter to the booksellers of America, beginning with the line, "Books cannot be killed by fire." The Council's slogan, "Books Are Weapons in the War of Ideas," frames the bottom of the image in equally bold red. When viewed with Roosevelt's highly spiritual language splashed in giant letters across the book, the scene becomes less a book burning than a burning at the stake, an unholy Inquisition in which a resolute martyr stands proudly, even as his body is tortured. The Council itself strove to make these religious meanings clear to the public, sending notices to 350 clergymen nationwide in May 1943,

Figure 4.2 Victory Book Campaign poster. Courtesy of the Hennepin County Library, James K. Hosmer Special Collections Library, Kittleson World War II Collection, MPW00262.

asking them to mention the tenth anniversary of the Nazi book burning in their weekly sermons.[65]

A final image from American wartime propaganda reveals most dramatically the deep spiritual meaning of books as weapons and the implicit but profound link between intellectual and religious freedom, both of which were understood to be at stake in the war against fascism. The Council, as noted, chose to focus its 1942 poster on the distinction between Nazi book burning and Roosevelt's vision of the eternal value of books, leaving the religious implications as subtext. By contrast, the following year the Office of War Information produced a poster that left no room for subtlety

Figure 4.3 Council on Books in Wartime poster, U.S. Government Printing Office, 1942. Courtesy of the Hennepin County Library, James K. Hosmer Special Collections Library, Kittleson World War II Collection, MPW00264.

(Figure 4.4). Produced in the same, stark black and red as the Council's poster, the image depicted the arm of a Nazi, replete with Swastika, thrusting a large dagger down through the center of a Bible. Beneath, the caption read simply, "This Is The Enemy." (This was just one of many posters bearing this slogan.) Here, most clearly, American spiritual, literary, and nationalistic propaganda efforts merged, as Nazi book burning morphed into a stabbing, a bloody and personal attempt to kill the book whose spirit cannot die. An attack on reading was an attack on faith itself, the Office of War Information was saying, with the Good Book a central symbol of all that Americans were fighting to preserve.

Figure 4.4 Office of War Information poster, U.S. Government Printing Office, 1943. Courtesy of the Hennepin County Library, James K. Hosmer Special Collections Library, Kittleson World War II Collection, MPW00520.

The Council and Religious Reading

Not surprisingly in such a climate, as reading assumed both patriotic and spiritual dimensions, the Council on Books in Wartime soon began to employ its extensive promotional apparatus for the advocacy of explicitly religious books. To many observers, the effort came none too soon. John E. Johnson, the senior chaplain of the Great Lakes Naval Station near Chicago, expressed a profound concern for the lack of high-quality religious reading, and therefore religious literacy, among the fresh recruits in the naval induction center where he served. In a commentary titled "The Faith and Practice of the Raw Recruit," Johnson noted that most new inductees read only joke books and cartoon books, with few dabbling in more edifying works. The result, he concluded, was that the typical new sailor "brings with him very little knowledge of the Bible and of religious literature, even though he may have attended Sunday School a good part of his life.... Words of the Christian Faith—sacrament, communion, grace, prayer, baptism, creed, commandments—convey very little meaning to the average raw recruit." As if pleading for the very effort the Council was poised to begin, Johnson remarked, "We take definite steps to prevent them from becoming intellectual morons. What steps are taken to prevent them from becoming moral and spiritual morons?"[66]

To such concerns the Council responded. In September 1942 W. W. Norton asked Pat Beaird, of Abingdon-Cokesbury and the Religious Publishers Group, for a meeting to discuss avenues for cooperation between religious publishers and the Council. The meeting, which took place October 6 over lunch at the Harvard Club in New York, proved immensely fruitful, and Beaird noted that the representatives of the religious book publishers were "thoroughly in accord with the purposes of the Council" and eager to support its work. In sentiments he would repeat the following spring in the *New York Times*, Beaird affirmed the essence of the Council's mission—to use books as weapons—and noted the special role that religious books were playing in that cause. "Religious books are making a very definite contribution to the war effort," he assured the Council, "in building and sustaining morale, in preparing for the peace to come, and the social problems to follow."[67] The Council's use of books as weapons and the culturally widespread recognition of the spiritual dimension of the war led to an easy and natural alliance between religious publishers and the Council.

With such an understanding of the scope and promise of their coordination, the meeting between Norton and the religious publishers produced two concrete proposals: the formation of a Religious Books Committee of the Council on Books in Wartime, "consisting of publishers representing the Catholic, Jewish and Protestant faiths," of which Beaird was named chair, and the recommendation that this committee work with the National Conference of Christians and Jews (NCCJ), assisting this prominent interfaith organization with its nationwide Religious Book Week, already planned for March 1943.[68] The Religious Books Committee oversaw the publication in Armed Services Editions of a small number of explicitly religious texts, including Bruce Barton's *The Man Nobody Knows* and *The Book Nobody Knows*, but the most significant work the Council performed in religious reading was its cooperation with the NCCJ. The idea of cooperation between the Council on Books in Wartime and the National Conference of Christians and Jews had first been proposed a few weeks earlier by Ellen O'Gorman Duffy, associate director of the NCCJ and head of its Religious Book Week campaign, in conversations with Clip Boutell of Putnam. Boutell excitedly forwarded the idea to Norton, announcing that "the promotion of this religious book week [is] directly in line with the aims of the Council."[69] Norton in turn recommended the idea to Beaird, and now the full weight of the Council and the Religious Publishers Group was behind the NCCJ book week proposal. The National Conference was poised to become the primary arbiter of "good" religious reading for the duration of the war.

*　*　*

World War II overshadowed American life as no event had since the Civil War eighty years earlier. As the nation mobilized for war, American religious and publishing leaders raced to enlist their own resources in the great battle at hand. Very quickly they came to see books as central to the war effort, envisioning the war as an ideological, and indeed spiritual struggle as well as a military one. The Council on Books in Wartime, the organization developed by publishers to coordinate their contribution to the national cause, cast their activities in decidedly spiritual language and imagery, and this patriotic spiritualization of reading influenced the entirety of middlebrow reading culture during the war years. It was also good for business. The sales of religious books soared during the war, most significantly because new readers sought out inspirational titles in this time of crisis.

The major religious book initiatives of the Council—its own Religious Books Committee and its support of the National Conference of Christians and Jews—soon developed into the most influential endeavor to promote religious books during the war. Significantly, each was an explicitly interfaith endeavor. As recently as 1931 the U.S. Supreme Court had self-assuredly declared the United States to be a "Christian nation," and, from a purely demographic (if not constitutional) point of view, they were largely right.[70] Within this "Christian nation," Roman Catholics and Jews faced considerable suspicion and exclusion from the politically and socially dominant Protestant majority. However, the demands of the war cut deeply into these long-standing prejudices and assumptions, greatly energizing interfaith efforts begun in the 1920s. So powerful were the forces calling for a united spiritual front in the war with fascism that the National Conference of Christians and Jews, a marginal group in the 1920s, was able by the early 1940s to assume a central position as the primary public arbiter of proper religious reading for the American people during the war and immediate postwar years. Old tensions did not disappear, especially between Protestants and Catholics and, within Protestantism, between liberals and conservatives. But with the backing of the Religious Publishers Group and the Council on Books in Wartime, this goodwill organization became the loudest advocate for religious reading in 1940s America. The reading agenda of the National Conference of Christians and Jews, then, came to stand alongside the Religious Book Club and the Religious Book Week of the 1920s as the major religious reading initiatives of the first half of the twentieth century and to exert an equally powerful influence on the course of popular religious thought and practice. The spiritual cosmopolitanism that for decades had been the privileged domain of elite seekers was poised to receive the full support of cultural and governmental leadership. What was once suspiciously radical was being quietly reframed as both a moral good and a national imperative.

5

Inventing Interfaith

The Wartime Reading Campaign of the National
Conference of Christians and Jews

The Council on Books in Wartime enlisted books as weapons in a war of ideas, but that ideological struggle raised a fundamental question: What were the American ideas—the American values—at stake in the battle with fascism? Government officials and civic leaders readily recognized the war as a contest between liberal democracy and fascist totalitarianism, and much of the official propaganda coordinated by the Office of War Information reinforced this basic message. The reading campaign of the Council aimed as well at bolstering liberal democratic values, such as freedom of thought and expression, through its high-minded literary propaganda, and contrasted its efforts most pointedly with the notorious Nazi book burnings. Yet many Americans saw the contest not simply as one of competing political philosophies. Rather they saw the war as a contest of competing religious systems, a struggle of American and Western religious values against the immorality and idolatry of fascism. The Council itself certainly cast the struggle in spiritual terms. And so the question remained: What, exactly, was the religious dimension of the American way of life?

Religious identity was a thorny problem for a diverse society, especially a society like the United States with no established church and with constitutionally guaranteed freedom of religion. Ultimately American policymakers seized upon a new cultural category—an invention of the 1930s—as the solution to this conundrum. The religion of American democracy was "Judeo-Christian." The notion of a shared Judeo-Christian national identity met with such widespread acceptance that it quickly became a defining feature of American public life in the war and postwar years. Yet the culture of Judeo-Christianity as it developed in the 1940s did more than foster a climate of intergroup civic cooperation. It also opened new avenues for explicitly religious interaction and exchange. Indeed the wartime effort to promote Judeo-Christianity—through lectures, radio, film, and most especially reading—became the single greatest force in popularizing the ethos of spiritual cosmopolitanism that had been slowly developing in religious middlebrow culture before the war.

The U.S. government called upon a private interfaith organization, the National Conference of Christians and Jews, to promote the Judeo-Christian concept to the American people. This required a considerable educational campaign, since the concept was largely unknown at the start of the war. The term *Judeo-Christian* only dated from the 1890s, when scholars first used it to refer to the common ancient heritage of Christians and Jews.[1] It remained obscure until intellectuals and activists, led by the NCCJ, revived and reframed the term in the 1930s in response to European fascist and American anti-Semitic appropriation of the word *Christian*. In contrast to earlier understandings of the concept, the NCCJ now maintained that Judeo-Christianity described not only an ancient reality but also a continuing cultural inheritance rooted in shared scriptures and common values. That heritage, they argued, had been essential to the historical development of American democracy and remained critical to its ongoing vitality. As the NCCJ wrote in its popular "Why We Fight" series of pamphlets, the meaning of World War II—the great test for liberal democracy—was best summarized as a "war of ideas between Totalitarian Dictatorship and the essentials in our Judeo-Christian tradition."[2]

The NCCJ utilized its close coordination with the military to remarkable effect, introducing millions in the service to the principles of Judeo-Christianity. The historian Deborah Dash Moore contends that military policy during the war "made possible the emergence of a civil religion for American democracy." "The Judeo-Christian tradition," she writes, describing that civil religion, "was largely a creation of the American military in World War II."[3] The military provided the NCCJ with such tremendous resources and access that by war's end "nearly every American soldier had touched a piece of NCCJ literature, watched an NCCJ film, or gone to an NCCJ Camp Program meeting" to hear a joint presentation from a minister, priest, and rabbi.[4] In this way the military facilitated the dissemination of the Judeo-Christian idea, but left the face-to-face, on-the-ground work to representatives of the interfaith movement. The National Conference of Christians and Jews, empowered by the American military, made Judeo-Christianity the widely acknowledged religion of American democracy. All told, the NCCJ distributed more than 8 million pieces of literature through military chaplains and made personal contact with nearly 9 million Americans during the war.[5]

The astonishing reach of the Judeo-Christian concept was not limited to men and women in the service. The war so moved the tectonic plates of American religious and political life that the previously dominant conception of the United States as a Christian nation—meaning, in practice, a Protestant nation—that tolerated the presence of religious minorities gave way to a new, more fully pluralistic society of Protestants, Catholics, and Jews that the historian Kevin

Schultz calls "tri-faith America." "Outside the service" as well as in, he writes, "the war brought almost all Americans into the fold of civic Judeo-Christianity."[6] The ultimate triumph of the Judeo-Christian concept stemmed from many factors: greater exposure to members of different religious traditions brought about by wartime relocation, both in the service and at home; the growing aware-ness of Nazi atrocities against the Jews of Europe; and official propaganda about the need for national unity and shared values. Whatever the reasons, the Judeo-Christian origin of American democracy was so commonly accepted by the early 1950s that references to it became a staple of American political discourse. Most famously, Dwight Eisenhower, the supreme Allied commander during the war, remarked shortly after winning the 1952 presidential election, "Our form of government has no sense unless it is founded in a deeply felt religious faith.... With us of course it is the Judeo-Christian concept."[7] An idea that had been invented little more than a decade earlier was now proclaimed by the pres-ident-elect to be, "of course," the very basis of American political life.

Despite the remarkable success of the Judeo-Christian concept, its acceptance was neither inevitable nor easy. Many obstacles blocked the way. Secular intel-lectuals such as Sidney Hook and John Dewey decried the heightened emphasis on religion during the war years as a liberal "failure of nerve," a disavowal of the scientific naturalism they felt represented a better path forward for a modern democracy.[8] Religious conservatives, especially fundamentalist Protestants and traditional Roman Catholics, likewise rejected liberal efforts to craft a common American religious heritage. They saw Judeo-Christianity as theologically vague at best, and as a threat to divinely revealed truth at worst. Catholics in particular were reluctant to support the interfaith movement. Pope Pius XI had issued an encyclical in 1928 opposing religious interaction with Protestants, and many American bishops in the 1930s and 1940s prohibited Catholics from joining the NCCJ and other ecumenical groups.[9] Leading Jewish intellectuals meanwhile feared that Judeo-Christianity might become, in the hands of the vast Christian majority, simply another name for assimilation and thereby "a syncretizing threat to the survival of Judaism"—a potent cultural threat even as Jews faced the far more dire threat of extermination in Europe.[10]

More problematic, however, than the reluctance of intellectuals or religious conservatives to join the Judeo-Christian cause were the deep religious divi-sions in American society. The Depression, first, and then the war itself greatly amplified religious tensions, even as the war also set in motion processes that ultimately reduced interreligious barriers. Jewish Americans, not surpris-ingly, bore the brunt of this intensified religious discrimination. "At no time in American history," noted the American Jewish *Congress Bulletin* in 1940, "has anti-Semitism been as strong as it is today."[11] On the rise since the revival of the Ku Klux Klan two decades earlier, hostility toward American Jews had accelerated with the Depression, as age-old canards about Jewish control of the money system combined with widespread economic hardship to form a combustible mix. Firebrands like the Catholic radio preacher Father Charles Coughlin, the aviator Charles Lindbergh, and the industrialist Henry Ford stoked the animosity with inflammatory speeches and pamphlets. A 1938 poll indicated that more than half of the American population "had negative impressions of Jews," and 35 percent thought the Jews of Europe somehow responsible for the Nazis' crimes against them.[12] Matters only worsened once the United States entered the war. Social antagonisms of all kinds increased, resulting notoriously in the internment of Japanese Americans beginning in 1942 and in racial violence in Detroit, Los Angeles, and elsewhere in 1943. Jews were not subjected to large-scale violence in America, but were singled out by fundamentalist Nazi sympathizers like William Dudley Pelley and Gerald L. K. Smith as particular threats to America's Christian identity. "For the first time in American history," writes the historian Leonard Dinnerstein, "Jews feared that their attackers might acquire the kind of political influence and respectability the antisemites had in Europe."[13]

Catholics too faced heightened discrimination in the 1930s and early 1940s. Whereas Jews were suspect in the eyes of many Protestants because of their leadership in promoting separation of church and state, Catholics were resented for opposite reasons, for aiming to entangle the state with religion by advocating state aid to parochial schools and the appointment of a U.S. ambassador to the Vatican. Likewise fears of Jewish sympathy for leftist politics in Europe were mirrored by fears of Catholic support for the authoritarian right, especially Franco's forces in the Spanish Civil War. Such charges built on long-standing concerns that Catholicism was inimical to democratic norms and institutions. The 1920s Klan had revived these long-held Protestant presuppositions, and anti-Catholic fear helped derail the 1928 presidential bid of New York's governor Al Smith. Though anti-Catholicism was not as virulent as anti-Semitism during the war years, Catholics as well as Jews faced renewed hostility from the Protestant majority.

The military and federal government collaborated with the National Conference of Christians and Jews precisely to combat these rising tensions and to define the aims of the war in religious as well as political terms. A common religious heritage, national leaders agreed, was necessary to unite the American people in the ideological struggle with fascism. But the ambitions of the NCCJ reached beyond the political; it worked to promote a theological as well as a political understanding of Judeo-Christianity, to demonstrate to Americans the spiritual kinship of Jews, Catholics, and Protestants. The NCCJ, Schultz writes, "wanted a new spiritual grounding for American life."[14] To this end, it produced a book, *The Religions of Democracy: Judaism, Catholicism, and Protestantism in Creed and Life* (1941), and the short "Declaration of Fundamental Religious Beliefs Held in Common by Catholics, Protestants, and Jews" (1942), each designed to underscore the religious as well as the political dimension of Judeo-Christianity.

Much more significant than its own literature, however, was the NCCJ's collaboration with the Council on Books in Wartime to promote a massive, nationwide reading campaign called Religious Book Week. With Religious Book Week the NCCJ leveraged the tremendous national political support for civic Judeo-Christianity to promote and legitimate an additional, more spiritual agenda. When combined with the Council's unprecedented promotional efforts and the great wartime boom in religious and inspirational reading, the reading campaign of the National Conference of Christians and Jews became a powerful force in the democratization of religious cosmopolitanism. The vast majority of Americans did not cease being Protestants, Catholics, or Jews, of course, nor did a new hybridized religion emerge. But for the first time, in the 1940s middle-class Americans began turning in significant numbers to other faith traditions for inspiration, wisdom, solace, and insight. For two decades religious middlebrow culture had served the liberal Protestant ambition to transcend creed and sect. During World War II it acquired a new, interfaith dimension.

The National Conference of Christians and Jews

The National Conference of Christians and Jews was founded in 1927 after nearly a decade of tentative outreach efforts between liberal Protestants and leaders in the Jewish community.[15] The heightened xenophobia in the late 1910s and 1920s, characterized most notoriously by the Red Scare, the resurgence of the Ku Klux Klan, and the passage of the National Origins Act in 1924, spurred these early interfaith gestures. Yet many Protestant denominations, while initiating unprecedented dialogue with Jewish groups, often clumsily contributed to the climate of suspicion. Though not typically acting from the same violently racist and nativist impulses that inspired the Klan, many in the mainline churches likewise feared the specter of unassimilated masses and soon after World War I established entities designed to help "Americanize" immigrants. These Protestant groups often associated Americanization rather explicitly with proselytization, and embarked on efforts to convert immigrants, mostly Jewish and Catholic, to their version of Protestantism. The aptly titled Department of Christian Americanization of the Protestant Episcopal Church, for example, announced in 1919 a drive to evangelize Jews in America.[16] Jewish groups protested, and out of the conversations that ensued over these and other similar protests, a variety of "goodwill" organizations formed, including the Central Conference of American Rabbis Committee on Goodwill, the American Good Will Union, and the Permanent Commission of Better Understanding between Christians and Jews. Foremost among these was the Federal Council of Churches of Christ Committee on Goodwill between Jews and Christians, formed in 1923, which eventually laid the groundwork for the NCCJ.[17] The International Order of B'nai B'rith was so pleased with the FCC's Committee on Goodwill it contributed $6,000 annually to the committee's budget.[18]

These early interfaith organizations faced considerable social and religious suspicion. The goodwill movement sought to overcome animosity and foster understanding, but initially participants approached each other from a cool distance, their outreach often tempered with skepticism. Evangelicals in the Federal Council, in fact, outright opposed the Committee on Goodwill, arguing that its presence might impede their obedience to Christ, as they understood it, and his command to make disciples of all people. Faced with such internal pressures, Samuel McCrea Cavert, general secretary of the Federal Council, and other leaders of the goodwill movement decided in the spring of 1927 to spin off a new, independent body, the National Conference of Jews and Christians. The group began formal operation in 1928. (It reversed the word order in its name in 1938, and in 1998 changed names again, to the National Conference for Community and Justice.)

Three cochairs—Judge Newton D. Baker, a Protestant and former secretary of war; Carlton J. H. Hayes, a Roman Catholic historian at Columbia University; and Roger Straus, a Jewish financier—assumed leadership of the organization, with the support of an executive committee composed of an assortment of eminent Americans, including Jane Addams, Justices Benjamin Cardozo and Charles Evans Hughes, Henry Sloane Coffin, Harry Emerson Fosdick, Mordecai Kaplan, Henry Morgenthau, Reinhold Niebuhr, the Jesuit Wilfred Parson, Father T. Lawrason Riggs (the first Catholic chaplain at Yale), Edward A. Filene, Theodore Roosevelt Jr., and Rabbi Stephen S. Wise.[19] The ideology of the group reflected new scientific and cultural thinking on the nature of racial and cultural difference, especially the ideas of the pioneering anthropologist Franz Boas, applied to the difficult problems of religious identity. S. Parkes Cadman of Brooklyn, the renowned Congregationalist preacher, radio personality, Religious Book Club editorial committee member, and president of the Federal Council of Churches (1924–28), articulated the vision of the NCCJ in an address at the National Vaudeville Artists' Club in New York, marking the NCCJ's founding. Speaking of the categories of race and religion, Cadman declared, "There is no dividing line, such as the arbitrary line established by teachers of expiring theological schools. We are upon an entirely new alignment at the present moment, which will eventually have to be respected, because it is on a more scientific basis." The struggle to spread this message, he assured his listeners, was "a common battle, a word war with bloodless weapons."[20] The NCCJ was born of the liberal faith in scientific progress, rational dialogue, and a common humanity.

The Presbyterian minister Everett R. Clinchy soon accepted the position as president of the NCCJ, a post he held for three decades. Clinchy vigorously carried out Cadman's call to battle the outmoded thinking of "expiring theological schools." In particular he decried all efforts to define the United States as a Christian or Protestant Nation. During a trip to Germany soon after the rise of Hitler, Clinchy witnessed firsthand both the pernicious effects of religious hatred and the dangers of linking religious and national identity. Back home, he feared, those who advocated a Christian America might send the United States down the same dark path as Hitler's Germany.[21] As president Clinchy guided the NCCJ firmly away from the earlier Americanization controversies and instead "popularized an ideology of cultural pluralism." "From the first goodwill initiatives," the historian Benny Kraut writes, "the Protestant goodwill movement of the 1920s culminated with the appearance of an organization that implicitly repudiated Protestant cultural authority in America."[22] Astoundingly the American military and the Council on Books in Wartime, when searching for ways to articulate the religious meaning of the struggle with fascism, called upon this organization, the National Conference of Christians and Jews, an organization that powerfully and deliberately sought to undermine Protestant hegemony. Many Jews, and even more notably many Catholics, continued to harbor doubts about the interfaith movement, at once suspecting the motives of Protestant leaders and fearing a loss of their own distinctiveness.[23] Nevertheless in meaningful ways the liberal Protestant establishment was turning over the keys to its own castle, and doing so in order to fulfill its own highest ideals and aspirations.

As it grew during the 1930s the National Conference developed a sophisticated range of promotional and educational programs. The highlight of the year was Brotherhood Day, held each February beginning in 1934, and expanded to Brotherhood Week in 1939. These events grew out of the hugely successful barnstorming tour of Rabbi Morris Lazaron, Father John Elliot Ross, and Everett Clinchy in 1933. Soon after this initial tour, which received national publicity, appearances from so-called Tolerance Trios became the organization's signature event. A team of clergy or lay people from the three faiths would arrive in town and lead local civic and religious groups—including schools, colleges, women's clubs, service clubs, labor unions, veteran's associations, youth groups, farm groups, churches, and synagogues—in what the NCCJ called "trialogues" to discuss religious stereotypes, obstacles to cooperation, and the need for unity in light of current affairs.[24] These appearances grew so popular that only six years later, in 1939, interfaith trios "appeared together at ten thousand meetings in two thousand communities in all forty-eight states."[25] The NCCJ also established a commission on education to promote its message in schools and colleges, the Religious News Service to provide information to newspapers and radio stations, direct radio programming on matters of religious interest, and operations to produce movies, books, and pamphlets.[26]

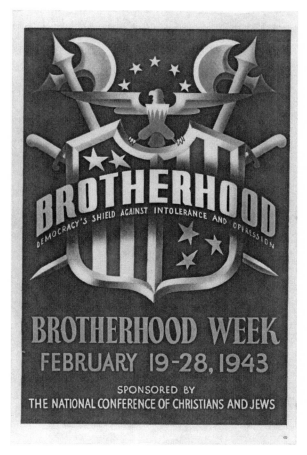

Figure 5.1 Brotherhood Week poster, 1943. National Conference of Christians and Jews. World War Poster Collection (MSS36), Literary Manuscripts Collection, University of Minnesota Libraries, Minneapolis.

The highly accomplished posters the NCCJ commissioned for Brotherhood Week captured the essence of the organization's message, especially during the war years. The 1943 poster featured a large central shield, emblazoned with the stars and stripes of the American flag (Figure 5.1). Upon the shield rested a modern, streamlined American eagle, and behind the shield stood two swords and two battle-axes. The message of the poster, "Brotherhood: America's Shield against Intolerance and Oppression," made explicit what the imagery portrayed: a united America was a stronger America. Nowhere did the poster depict any symbols of the various faiths; America at war was without division. The poster from 1945, as victory seemed inevitable, sought to combat the fracturing that many feared would occur once wartime pressures lifted (Figure 5.2).

Figure 5.2 Brotherhood Week poster, 1945. National Conference of Christians and Jews. World War Poster Collection (MSS36), Literary Manuscripts Collection, University of Minnesota Libraries, Minneapolis.

This poster represented Christians and Jews each as literal cogs in the machine of democratic teamwork, working together for the common good, as the tag line read, "In Peace As in War." With the National Conference of Christians and Jews, the liberal Protestant establishment worked not only to transcend creedal and sectarian divides, as it had for decades, but also to employ that liberal impulse in a grander project. The aim now was to transcend itself, to relinquish any claims of a uniquely Protestant right to define American identity.

That remarkable ambition toward self-transcendence guided Religious Book Week, the NCCJ's program to shape religious reading during the war. Many of the liberal Protestant leaders who supported the NCCJ in its early days—including Harry Emerson Fosdick, S. Parkes Cadman, and Samuel McCrea Cavert—were at the same time also founding the Religious Book Club. The club was a thoroughly liberal Protestant affair, though always with an openness to books from other traditions that might interest its readership. Only fifteen years later, however, the National Conference of Christians and Jews, which these same men helped found, began promoting a rather different model of religious reading. No longer a dominant group expressing occasional interest in other faiths—a model of tolerance—the new reading model reflected a growing sense of pluralism, with the three great American faiths, Protestantism, Catholicism, and Judaism, placed on equal footing, side by side, for American readers.

Religious Book Week (1943–1948)

The NCCJ's Religious Book Week campaign built on the practices of reading that had developed over two decades in religious middlebrow culture. Most basically it approached readers as consumers, recognizing their ultimate autonomy to pick and choose but also utilizing the authority inherent in cultural expertise to direct their buying and reading. The war generated a great boom in reading, and the Council on Books in Wartime exploited that boom to socialize millions of Americans into the practices of book culture. Religious reading in particular exploded during the war, making reading itself an increasingly important religious practice. The National Conference of Christians and Jews capitalized on these developments in Religious Book Week. Its central aim, of course, was to reinforce its political message about the Judeo-Christian foundation of American democracy. But aware of theological criticism about watered-down religion and sensitive to the concerns of Catholics and Jews about pressures to assimilate, Religious Book Week also aimed to educate readers in the distinctiveness of each of the traditions. In so doing it fostered for the first time a significant middle-class culture of reading across the boundaries of tradition. Religious cosmopolitanism, rooted in one tradition but open to illumination from others, had been an emerging aspect of religious middlebrow culture for decades. The NCCJ's Religious Book Week brought that cosmopolitan sensibility to a national audience.

The NCCJ borrowed the idea for Religious Book Week not only from the Religious Book Week of the 1920s, but also from a smaller event held in Boston in 1942, and adapted it for its own purposes. The 1942 book week had been organized by a Boston Unitarian minister and denominational leader, Albert C. Dieffenbach, in conjunction with Beacon Press (the Unitarian publishing house) and the leading Boston newspapers.[27] The NCCJ's book efforts, beginning with its first Religious Book Week, held March 28 to April 3, 1943, were much larger undertakings, both because of the NCCJ's decision to take the idea nationwide and because of the involvement of the Council on Books in Wartime. The centerpiece of each annual book week was a list of recommended reading crafted by a committee of literary and religious experts, a model of middlebrow instruction utilized by the American Library Association and countless other reading programs. The extensive marketing infrastructure of the Council disseminated the book lists across the nation, eventually enlisting schools, libraries, churches and synagogues, government agencies, unions, and book-sellers in its massive undertaking.

The leadership of the NCCJ worked easily and naturally with the Council on Books in Wartime. Each was a product of the New York social and cultural elite. As such they shared a broad-minded sense of obligation to use their influence on behalf of the national good, which generally meant working to shape the culture in their liberal image. The ties between these two enterprises were so close that Henry Seidel Canby, Frederic G. Melcher, Chester Kerr, and other leaders of the Council also served in leadership roles with the NCCJ's Religious Book Week. In a spring 1943 press release detailing its activities and cooperation with the Council, the NCCJ reflected its adherence to the spiritual and intellectual uplift goals at the heart of the Council's mission: "The Council on Books in Wartime is working with the National Conference on this important project, which is designed to further the reading of religious books by lay men and women." The announcement continued, "Religious Book Week has received the very hearty approval and endorsement of religious leaders of the three faiths. Wartime offers an opportunity to stress the importance of religion in our national life and to stimulate an intelligent understanding of it."[28] The experts assembled to craft the lists would decide for readers just what "intelligent" meant: socially tolerant, engaged with the latest teachings of science and history, concerned with literary standards, and spiritually open-minded.

No one embodied high literary standards, public-mindedness, and a liberal, tolerant spirituality more than Dr. Henry Seidel Canby. When the NCCJ orga-nized its gala event in March 1943 to mark the opening of its first Religious Book Week, it naturally turned to this elder statesman of American middlebrow culture to act as master of ceremonies. Canby, then in his midsixties, served as an advisor to the Council on Books in Wartime and the Office of War Information, in addition to his work as editor of the *Saturday Review of Literature* and chairman of the book selection committee of the Book-of-the-Month Club.[29] Though raised an Episcopalian and married in a Presbyterian church, he converted to the faith of his ancestors as an adult after coming to recognize his "essentially Quaker turn of mind." "The Quaker doctrine of an 'inner light,'" writes the literary historian Joan Shelley Rubin, "gave Canby . . . a model of the self—quiet, serene, radiant with spiritual integrity—that he retained throughout his career."[30] Son of a wealthy Wilmington banker, he completed his Ph.D. at Yale in 1905 and began to teach, but quickly became disillusioned with academic life. Canby's Quaker spiritual sensibilities and harsh criticisms of modern life—"the vulgar-ities of signboards, cries of cheap newspapers, noisy hustle of trivial commer-cialism, and the flatness of standardized living," as he put it in 1922—led him to pursue, with missionary zeal, the spiritual and intellectual uplift of the American public through books.[31] The opening gala for Religious Book Week, presented before an overflow crowd at the Times Hall on Forty-fourth Street (the same venue where the Council on Books in Wartime held its opening conference the preceding May), featured Canby presiding over a series of lectures from such notables as George N. Shuster, president of Hunter College and editor of *The World's Great Catholic Literature* (1942), and Rabbi Milton Steinberg, author of *The Making of the Modern Jew* (1943). In addition to hearing such presentations, attendees were encouraged to wander through an exhibit hall displaying copies of all two hundred of the first year's recommended books.[32]

The NCCJ printed its approved book list in a small booklet. The list was divided into four broad categories—Protestant, Catholic, Jewish, and Good-Will—each chosen by a distinct committee of representatives from the tradition, or in the case of the Good-Will list, representatives from each of the traditions. These lists were then subdivided into an adult list of forty titles and a young people's list of ten titles, for a total of eight distinct lists. These two hundred selections formed the official reading list for each Religious Book Week. In 1943 the reading list was sent to over six thousand public, university, and school libraries across the nation; libraries and booksellers were also offered an accompanying poster and bookmark. To further market the campaign, the NCCJ arranged for radio spots and for the lists to be published in major newspapers across the country. The *New York Times*, for example, ran the lists in their entirety across nearly four full pages on the first day of the event.[33]

The NCCJ's approach to book selection drew heavily on the conventions of religious middlebrow culture, especially the simultaneous focus on accessibility and enrichment. The 1944 pamphlet, which ran to twenty-eight pages, was typical, and the introductory commentary for each section of the list revealed the list makers' notion of the selections' intended audiences and uses. Overall the books were chosen almost exclusively from in-print titles available at bookstores, with "the aim . . . to select books of interest to the average layman."[34] The committee responsible for the Jewish Book List noted too that "the list was intended primarily for the intelligent layman and not for the specialist or the scholar."[35] The Protestant committee chose its list with "the busy reader" in mind, one who was "seeking . . . religious literature which will be clear, helpful, vital."[36] Only the Catholic committee dared stray from the narrow path of accessibility, advising potential readers, "Most of the books are not particularly easy reading. They are serious, thoughtful presentations of deep truths." Yet the Catholic committee was quick to add, in the spirit of expert guides, that the chosen books were nevertheless "worth the time and effort it will take to assimilate them."[37] The Catholic committee's willingness to impose tough demands on its readers reflected perhaps its strongly hierarchical control of instruction and doctrine. Nevertheless, as with the other selection committees, it hewed closely to the conventions of middlebrow reading, choosing books that would appeal to the average reader yet somehow improve that reader as well. In general each of the Religious Book Week selection committees strove to find the fine balance between expert guidance and respect for middle-class busyness and autonomy.

Religious Book Week, of course, was not simply a literary exercise aimed at intellectual or aesthetic refinement. Rather it clearly reflected both the social and the religious dimensions of the NCCJ's wartime agenda. Just as other religious reading campaigns, including the 1920s Religious Book Week and the Religious Book Club, promoted a modern, liberal religious outlook through their reading recommendations, so too the NCCJ's Religious Book Week aimed to transform readers through encounters with books. The social agenda of Religious Book Week was perhaps most evident. The 1943 press release announcing the first Religious Book Week stressed "the importance of religion in our national life" and drew particular attention to the sociological, historical, and political subjects addressed in the recommended books.[38] The lists for all six years of the campaign, in fact, covered these subjects extensively. The 1944 reading recommendations, for example, contained *The Jews in the Medieval World* (1938), *Economics and Society* (1939), Jacques Maritain's *Art and Scholasticism* (1930), Kenneth Scott Latourette's *The Unquenchable Light* (1941), and Reinhold Niebuhr's two-volume *The Nature and Destiny of Man* (1941–43). These were challenging books chosen in the best tradition of middlebrow culture: to make the "average layman" better than average.

Alongside books designed to feed the mind and expand one's sense of the world, each year the NCCJ committees also selected books meant to challenge, enlighten, and broaden readers spiritually. Here the list makers stressed the same psychological and mystical approaches to spirituality that had shaped liberal Protestantism for decades, finding in these discourses vocabularies of the spirit capacious enough to overcome sectarian divides. But as an explicitly interfaith enterprise, the NCCJ also selected readings that highlighted the particularities of the various faiths, recognizing the spiritual as well as political benefits of reading across the boundaries of tradition. In other words, central to the book week project was the clear understanding that a thriving pluralistic democracy required not just better *informed* citizens, but better *formed* citizens, citizens with spiritual and moral as well as intellectual maturity and sophistication. As Carleton Hayes, the Catholic cochair, remarked, the NCCJ rejected "the assumption that strife and prejudice would disappear if only you could teach people to hew through the jungle of their diverse beliefs and attitudes to a least common denominator." "On the contrary," he continued, the interfaith movement aimed to inculcate "esteem and appreciation for the highest reaches" of each tradition.[39] Remarkably, for the first time in history the most powerful sectors in American political and cultural life—government, military, civic organizations, religious organizations, and publishing—were now collaborating in a massive, nationwide campaign to get Americans reading about the "highest reaches" of religious traditions other than their own.

The religious dimension of Religious Book Week, then, combined the mystical and psychological discourses of liberal Protestantism with this new, "highest reaches" interfaith aim. The Protestant selection committee, not surprisingly, attended most especially to the psychological and the mystical. The 1943 committee, for example, composed of Halford Luccock of Yale Divinity School; P. W. Wilson, book reviewer for the *New York Times*; and Walter Russell Bowie of Union Theological Seminary in New York, developed a reading list divided nearly evenly between books in church history or current social problems, on the one hand, and personal inspirational works, on the other. *Abundant Living* (1942), from the acclaimed missionary and author E. Stanley Jones, and *Living Creatively* (1932), by the social activist Kirby Page, made the cut. More explicitly mystical were Rufus Jones's *Pathways to the Reality of God* (1931), Dean W. R. Inge's *Personal Religion and the Life of Devotion* (1924), Evelyn Underhill's *Worship* (1937), and Douglas Steere's *Prayer and Worship* (1938). The committee praised these books as "readable," "practical," and written "in a form the average reader can understand."[40] Also chosen were more narrowly psychological works, such as James Gordon Gilkey's *Solving Life's Everyday Problems* (1930), Carroll A. Wise's *Religion in Illness and Health* (1942), and Leslie Weatherhead's *Psychology in Service of the Soul* (1930). In 1944 Rufus Jones's *New Eyes for Invisibles* (1943), Harry Emerson Fosdick's *On Being a Real Person* (1943), and Henry C. Link's *The Return to Religion* (1936) were the most celebrated such texts similarly featured, but that year's list also included the less well known *The Self You Have to Live With* (1938), by Winfred Rhoades, described as an "informal discussion of the contribution of mental hygiene and religion to a satisfying personal life," and *What Is Religion Doing to Our Consciences?* (1943), the latest contribution from the psychologist George A. Coe.[41] Many of these selections, culled from the previous quarter century, had been at one time primary or alternate selections of the Religious Book Club and were now finding a new use in service to the country as aids to national spiritual strength and unity in a time of war.

In addition to works aimed at fostering psychological and mystical insight, the 1944 Protestant list also included popular works of inspirational fiction. Such books included Lloyd C. Douglas's *The Robe* (1942), about a Roman soldier who won Christ's garment after his crucifixion; Sholem Asch's *The Apostle* (1943), a telling of the life of St. Paul; and Franz Werfel's *The Song of Bernadette* (1942), which recounts the story of a French peasant girl's religious vision, later made into a popular feature film. (*The Robe* and *The Apostle* were also highly sought-after Armed Services Edition titles.) In addition to providing the basic pleasures of good storytelling, these works of fiction offered intimate accounts of direct religious experience. Alongside scholarly interpretations of mysticism or psychologically informed how-to guides, the suggested works of inspirational fiction offered readers emotional access to lives of faith.

The Jewish and Catholic lists in 1943 and in each of the subsequent years likewise promoted edifying texts for the betterment of their readers. But rather than highlight mystical and psychological forms of spirituality with their universal pretensions, which arose in the United States in the distinctive milieu of liberal Protestantism, these selection committees emphasized books designed to help clarify their own traditions, boundaries, and distinctiveness. The interfaith project had been inaugurated as a liberal Protestant endeavor on liberal Protestant terms, but from its inception the NCCJ made sure that its message eschewed any pressures to assimilate. While just as committed to the wartime goals of national spiritual unity as their liberal Protestant colleagues, Jewish and Catholic leaders therefore worked simultaneously to maintain the vitality of their own traditions. So the 1943 Jewish list, selected by a committee chaired by Louis Finkelstein of the Jewish Theological Seminary, focused almost exclusively on works of history, biography, contemporary social life, and classics of Jewish literature. History predominated. *The American Jew* (1942), *History and Destiny of the Jews* (1933), *History of the Jewish People* (1941), *Jewish Pioneers and Patriots* (1942), *The Odyssey of a Faith* (1942), *The Jews in Spain* (1942), *Jews in the Medieval World* (1938), *Social and Religious History of the Jews* (1937), and *History of the Jews* (1891–98) were all chosen in just the first year of the campaign, and subsequent years reflected a similar emphasis. As the Nazi program to slaughter the Jews of Europe proceeded on its awful course, the selection committee of the national Jewish reading list labored to make sure that American Jews would not lose the vital links to their ancient heritage.

The Catholic reading lists also featured heavy doses of history, including in 1943 and 1944 *Pageant of the Popes* (1942) and *The Story of American Catholicism* (1941) and numerous historical biographies of subjects such as St. Francis of Assisi, St. Teresa of Avila, Cardinal Richelieu, Bishop John England, Cardinal John Henry Newman, Thomas Moore, and G. K. Chesterton. The Catholic lists in addition plunged aggressively into philosophy and theology, with works such as Etienne Gilson's *Christianity and Philosophy* (1939), Jacques Maritain's *Freedom in the Modern World* (1936), and Walter Farrell's four-volume *Companion to the Summa* (1940–42). These works of history, biography, and theology, like the books on the Jewish reading list, all reinforced Catholic identity in the midst of wartime pressure toward unity. Finally, the Catholic lists placed a clear emphasis on social teaching, with titles like *Distributive Justice* (1941), a book about "the moral aspects of ownership, capital, profits, and wages in modern economics," *Reorganization of Social Economy* (1936), *The Race Question and the Negro* (1943), and *Morals and Marriage: The Catholic Background to Sex* (1936).[42] Books of Catholic social teaching were especially useful, as they simultaneously articulated aspects of Catholic distinctiveness and ethical imperatives to overcome intergroup tensions. In general, while the Protestant lists stressed ecumenism within Protestantism and the liberal Protestant search for spiritual essences, the

Jewish and Catholic list makers were more willing to choose books that under-scored the distinctiveness of their particular traditions of faith.

The centerpiece of the Religious Book Week endeavor, however, was the Good-Will list, the list compiled by representatives from the three faith tradi-tions and designed to be read by members of all. This was the reading list aimed not at furthering religious literacy or bolstering faith in each of the separate traditions—worthy causes, organizers felt, as seen in the three separate lists—but at crafting the religious unity among the traditions necessary for victory in war and peace at home. This list sought to advance interfaith understanding and to promote awareness of common spiritual ground, a common ground that would form the foundation for American postwar democracy. Nearly all Americans agreed that the American way of life was at stake in the battle with fascism, and Religious Book Week endeavored to educate the American people that interfaith dialogue, religious tolerance, and recognition of a shared spiritual heritage were essential to victory in that struggle. The Good-Will lists therefore featured heavy doses of social scientific investigations of racial and religious intolerance, histories chronicling the contributions of each group to Western civilization, especially American democracy, and polemics about religious free-dom, liberty, and democracy.

Most striking in the Good-Will list is the number of works of social science. *When Peoples Meet: A Study in Race and Culture Contacts* (1944), edited by Alain Locke and published by the Progressive Education Association, offered "768 pages of choice excerpts by experts," while *Race against Man* (1939), with an introduction by Franz Boas, presented "an authoritative and highly readable summary of the scientific findings on the subject of race which shows the error and absurdity of racial prejudice," according to the selection committee.[43] *Group Relations and Group Antagonisms* (1944), from the Institute of Religious Studies, provided a "scholarly and yet interesting" account of racial and religious interac-tion, and *Man's Most Dangerous Myth: The Fallacy of Race* (1942) outlined "a popular interpretation of modern scientific findings about race."[44] Other volumes of anthropology, sociology, and progressive education testify to the underlying assumption that sound scientific study, presented dispassionately to an eager reading public, could effect real social change. This agenda for progres-sive social science, which dated back to the late nineteenth century, had been championed by liberals in journalism, the churches, and higher education for half a century, and still clearly guided the work of the National Conference of Christians and Jews in the 1940s. Though the historian Kevin Schultz correctly notes the NCCJ's reluctance to support African American social equality and civil rights in the 1930s and 1940s, its reading lists nevertheless presented the social scientific basis for a modern understanding of race.

In addition to offering social scientific accounts of racial and religious equality, the Good-Will lists emphasized the contributions of the various traditions to

American civilization and recommended guidebooks for interfaith understanding. These texts all carried the same larger message: the three faith traditions of the West had each made distinct contributions to American democracy,
and interfaith understanding was critical to the preservation of that democracy.
So *Desert Democracy* (1939), from the Methodist publisher Abingdon-Cokesbury,
detailed "some principles of democracy as they derived from the Hebrew people,"
while *Religions of Democracy* (1940) featured contributions from William Adams
Brown, an eminent Protestant church historian, John Elliot Ross, a Paulist priest
and NCCJ leader, and Rabbi Louis Finkelstein, president of the Jewish Theological
Seminary.[45] *Religion and the Good Society* (1943), *Let's Talk It Over: A Manual on
Our American Way* (1942), *Get Together Americans* (1943), and *Common Ground*
(1938) each offered concrete calls for common understanding, again with the
idea that such understanding would strengthen the democratic life of the nation.
Common Ground aimed to advance not merely social tolerance but also deeper
religious interaction between Christians and Jews, and *Faith for Today* (1941)
featured five religious leaders, including Swami Nikhilananda, head of the
Ramakrishna-Vivekananda Center in New York, writing on contemporary social
problems. African Americans were occasionally included as a fourth American
religious group, with books such as *Brown Americans: The Story of a Tenth of the
Nation* (1943), which chronicled "their share in democracy, their mission and
public schools, their spiritual life and Christianity."[46] Whereas previous religious
reading campaigns had largely ignored African Americans—no accounts of the
first Religious Book Week, for example, appeared in the African American press—
the NCCJ now included black Americans in its understanding of religious diversity. The Good-Will book list, through these and similar texts, sought to reduce
intolerance while offering practical guides to those seeking deeper religious
interaction.

In all, the Good-Will lists, the centerpiece of Religious Book Week every year,
promoted a vision of religious life in the United States deeply rooted in core
liberal commitments. In particular the wartime reading campaign stressed both
the intellectual and spiritual formation of citizens as essential to a successful pluralistic democracy. Earlier religious reading endeavors had laid the foundation
for Religious Book Week by introducing middle-class readers to the universalistic
discourses of psychology and mysticism, thereby providing a common vocabulary of religious experience. Those earlier efforts had aimed to transcend
Protestant sectarianism, but now the same uniting impulses led outward, beyond
Protestantism. As the drive toward a common ground of faith assumed the
urgency of war, a clear identification of American democracy with Judeo-
Christian values displaced older notions of a narrowly Protestant America. Much
of the reading recommended by the NCCJ stressed the social, historical, and
political dimensions of Judeo-Christianity. But armed with liberal mystical and
psychological understandings of religious experience and riding a wave of readers

newly socialized into the practices of reading, Religious Book Week also contributed to a rising culture of spiritual cosmopolitanism. From the 1940s onward reading across the boundaries of tradition became an increasingly important practice for millions of ordinary Americans, whether Protestant, Catholic, or Jew.

Promoting Religious Book Week: Creating a National Audience for Spiritual Equality

As with the Council on Books in Wartime's own projects, the Council and the National Conference of Christians and Jews heavily promoted their joint Religious Book Week endeavor through a sophisticated, modern public relations campaign. The NCCJ used its regional offices throughout the country to distribute thousands of book lists, posters, and bookmarks to schools, colleges, libraries, and bookstores. Press releases were sent to major newspapers across the country, which willingly printed nearly verbatim stories describing book week events, and also to smaller regional and ethnic newspapers. In New England, for example, articles and reproductions of the annual poster were carried in French, Polish, Italian, Swedish, Finnish, Lithuanian, and Portuguese newspapers in addition to the English-language press.[47] In subsequent years accounts of Religious Book Week were carried in the African American press, including the *Pittsburgh Courier* and the *New York Amsterdam News*.[48] Book week promoters arranged for special displays in bookstores, and in San Francisco a number of bookstores reported sending promotional bookmarks to customers with their monthly bills. Museums and archives exhibited rare volumes of religious significance. Newspapers printed the reading lists and magazines highlighted reviews of selected titles. Pat Beaird got into the publicity act himself, using his high-profile "Religious Books and the War" essay from the *New York Times Book Review* to tout the NCCJ's book week.

The NCCJ used a small pamphlet of marketing suggestions to coordinate its public relations campaign with the vast array of local organizations that contributed to Religious Book Week across the country. Distributed by the thousands, the pamphlet contained recommendations for clergy, book editors, newspaper editors, booksellers, public librarians, school and college librarians, and clubs and societies, each group given a number of specific ideas for promoting the campaign. In addition to this host of cooperating institutions, the NCCJ also coordinated its efforts with government and labor unions. In 1944, for example, a member of the U.S. House of Representatives brought the campaign to the attention of the country in a speech on the floor, and in later years governors and mayors regularly issued official proclamations of support. By 1947, the fifth year of the book week, the Library of Congress produced an exhibit of "important rare books and manuscripts bearing on freedom of worship," and the chief of chaplains of the War Department arranged for dozens of sets of materials to be sent to chaplains in various theaters and departments around the world and to Veterans Administration hospitals and centers across the country.[49] The International Ladies' Garment Workers Union even supplied free kits of Religious Book Week materials to its chapters and libraries. Not since the Bible and tract societies of the early nineteenth century had a single organization acquired such an opportunity to shape American religious reading.

The NCCJ's publicity operation became increasingly sophisticated in the later years of Religious Book Week. For the 1948 campaign it developed a variety of short radio advertisements that ran on stations across the country. A Radio Committee for Religious Book Week organized these activities, chaired by Elinor Inman, director of Religious Broadcasting at CBS. The radio committee included as well the directors of religious broadcasting at NBC and ABC, the presidents and vice presidents of various Protestant, Catholic, and Jewish broadcasting associations, and even Red Barber, the famed sportscaster at CBS. Rather than taper off with the end of the war, calls for national spiritual unity only heightened with the start of cold war hostilities, as the nation now faced the menace of atheistic communism, and the radio spots reflected this renewed sense of urgency. "The perpetuation of American democracy," the committee wrote to radio stations across the country, "depends on adherence by our people to the principle of God-endowed inalienable rights," while religious ignorance, according to the NCCJ, threatened Americans' democratic rights.[50] In a one-minute radio spot for Religious Books Week the announcer observed, "Our country was founded on the principle that God created all men equal. Our rights are inalienable because God made them so. What a pity if Americans were to become religiously illiterate." Gaining religious knowledge might not be easy, this public service announcement told Americans, "but then nothing worthwhile is—Atomic energy, music, the UN, baseball." So pick up a good book, recommended by religious experts, and do your part. "This is a good time to start overcoming our religious illiteracy. This is Religious Book Week."[51] Radio spots of thirty, fifteen, ten, and five seconds made similar pitches, the last stating simply and urgently, "This is Religious Book Week. Read religious books for the answers to the only questions that count forever."[52]

For all the years of the campaign, however, the most significant ally of the NCCJ in promoting Religious Book Week was the thousands of public libraries across the country. By the early 1940s professional librarians had more than two decades of experience in the selection and promotion of religious reading through the Religious Books Round Table of the American Library Association. This entity, which originated in cooperative efforts among Protestant seminary librarians, had evolved in the 1920s to serve a new function, as the arbiter of appropriate religious reading for public libraries. By the late 1930s the Round Table selection committee had opened up to include Roman Catholic and Jewish members, including, during the war years, Louis Finkelstein, the renowned president of the Jewish Theological Seminary in New York. This long-standing involvement in the promotion of religious reading, and the recent foray into interfaith religious book selection, made the public libraries ready accomplices in the NCCJ's program. The public library branch in Queens, New York, for example, in 1943 simply shifted the basis for its annual spring display of religious books from the list of the Religious Books Round Table to the list from the National Conference of Christians and Jews.[53] And just as the reading lists and book clubs of previous decades had helped overwhelmed readers choose the best books, now also, according to Gerald Lawson, a leading librarian, "very few people come to the library with the purpose of reading along certain lines....There is a great need for a readers' advisor in every library, especially in the religious field."[54]

Reports from public libraries around the country indicate that Religious Book Week recommendations served just this role, often backed by significant community support. The NCCJ's promotional suggestions to public libraries encouraged them to "enlist all the forces of your community in this observance," "arrange a display," "purchase those volumes which are not on your shelves," "discuss...these books in your adult education classes," and otherwise get the word out to the community.[55] For decades public libraries had provided both access to reading—a particularly vital function in many small towns and rural communities without good bookstores—and gathering space for community and civic organizations. As such they were perfect partners for Religious Book Week. The library in Freeport, on Long Island, for example, actively supported the NCCJ program at the behest of the town's Inter-Faith Clergy Council and borrowed books for its display from local clergy in order to supplement those in the collection. The library held a special kick-off event attended by civic, cultural, and business leaders at which a local priest, rabbi, and minister spoke alongside the editor of the county newspaper and an area poet.[56] The public library in Montclair, New Jersey, organized volunteer church librarians to serve as liaisons between the library and the churches. Together with the public librarians, these church librarians organized an exhibit, offered an evening program to promote Religious Book Week, and distributed copies of the reading list. "The most thrilling thing about that first meeting," recounted one public librarian, Louise R. Miller, "was its uniqueness in bringing together Catholics, Protestants, Jews and Negroes—just another example of the public library's usefulness to all races and religions."[57]

Public libraries used suggestions and materials from the NCCJ to set up elaborate table and window displays. The Cleveland Public Library arranged special exhibits in each of its branches across the city, featuring the poster and book lists displayed in special cases (including a display in the main branch of Adolph Treidler's poster from the Religious Book Week of the 1920s). The main branch also displayed rare books of interest to Catholics, Protestants, and Jews and devoted its weekly radio program to the subject of religious reading. The Carnegie

Library in Atlanta, "as part of its program for promoting the religious tolerance characteristic of true Americanism," enthusiastically supported Religious Book Week from the start, buying all those titles from the reading list not in its regular collection.[58] The library mailed copies of the book list to 250 Protestant clergy across Atlanta as well as to Orthodox, Roman Catholic, and Jewish religious leaders, and even sent the list to the mayor, members of the City Council, county commissioners, officers of the city and county federations of teachers, and local labor leaders. A large display was erected in the main library, and posters and smaller displays were featured in each of Atlanta's branch libraries. More generally librarians from around the country, including the Enoch Pratt Free Library in Baltimore, the borough library of Queens, and the Public Library of Port Chester, New York, reported significant increases in the circulation of recommended books as a result of the promotional efforts. According to these reports, the increased demand often continued for months.[59]

Religious Book Week Posters and the Spiritualization of Reading

The National Conference of Christians and Jews annually commissioned a poster to serve as the focal point of its promotional efforts, just as the organizers of the 1920s Religious Book Week had done. These posters were the most visible component of the displays erected in libraries, bookstores, and churches across the country. The posters did not simply draw attention to the books on display, but, as with all forms of advertising, aimed to influence the customers' interaction with the product being advertised. In this case the Religious Book Week posters underscored the ideology of social, political, and spiritual equality that drove the NCCJ. The reading practices these posters encouraged therefore entailed more than a search for information; the reading agenda of Religious Book Week steered participants toward a quest for personal spiritual growth stimulated by reading across the boundaries of tradition.

The evolution of Religious Book Week marketing from year to year reveals an increasing emphasis on spiritual cosmopolitanism. The first book week, in 1943, for example, occurred during Lent, as had the Boston event in 1942 and the book trade's Religious Book Weeks of the 1920s. The decision to hold the event during Lent represented a vestige of the interfaith movement's origins in Protestant ecumenism. The poster that first year visually reinforced Christian cultural dominance as well (Figure 5.3). It depicted two books, standing upright, spines forward, bisected by a colored field containing the week's theme, "Tools for a Better World." The composition placed the books and message in the form of a cross, an impression reinforced by the shadow the books-as-cross cast. This shadow, cast without any apparent source of light, evoked traditional images of Christ's crucifixion as rendered in countless paintings and movies, an image fitting for the liturgical season but out of step with the NCCJ's larger purposes. The highly

Figure 5.3 Religious Book Week poster, 1943. National Conference of Christians and Jews. World War Poster Collection (MSS36), Literary Manuscripts Collection, University of Minnesota Libraries, Minneapolis.

instrumental message, books as "tools for a better world," squared nicely with the Council's theme of books as weapons, but it failed to obscure the essentially Christian symbolism of the 1943 Religious Book Week.

The imagery and timing in subsequent years departed significantly from this first effort and more effectively communicated the NCCJ's social and spiritual aspirations. Visually the posters became more ornate, with elaborate fonts and depictions of garlands, angels, candles, and Gothic windows; gone was the clean, modern aesthetic of the 1943 design. Gone also was the Christian symbolism of the books as a cross. Instead the visual rhetoric of the posters became inclusive. The 1945 and 1946 posters depicted symbols of the three traditions—the Star of David, the Keys of St. Peter (a symbol of the papacy, reproduced on the papal flag),

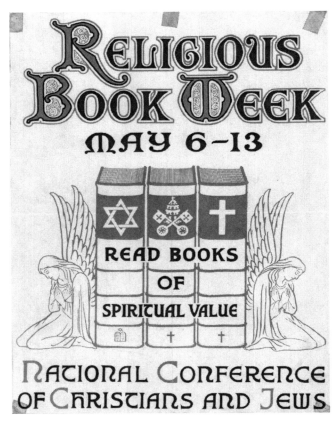

Figure 5.4 Religious Book Week poster, 1945 and 1946. (These posters were identical except for the dates.) National Conference of Christians and Jews. World War Poster Collection (MSS36), Literary Manuscripts Collection, University og Minnesota Libraries, Minneapolis.

and a simple cross—arrayed equally in height and size across the spines of three books (Figure 5.4). Also, beginning in 1944 the book week moved from Lent to the second week of May, a move aimed to coincide with the anniversary of the Nazi book burning of May 10, 1933. An NCCJ press release explained the date change, claiming, "It seems fitting that in the United States the week in which this anniversary falls should be dedicated to the reading of books with a spiritual background."[60] Newspapers publicized the changed rationale for the event, usually noting in their headlines the significance of the new dates. Now disassociated from the Christian calendar, the book week became more fully interfaith, designed to unite believers and strengthen spiritual resolve in support of the war effort.

Book week organizers altered the event's theme too, devising a new slogan, "Read Books of Spiritual Value." Rather than the more practical "Tools for a Better World," this slogan emphasized personal spiritual development over social scientific or historical knowledge as critical to both the interfaith movement and,

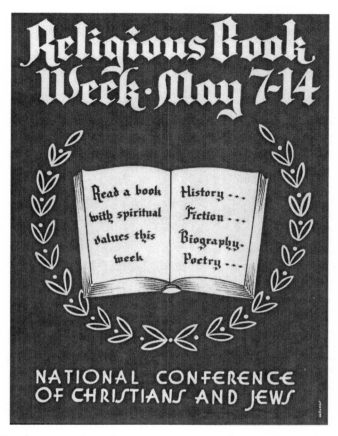

Figure 5.5 Religious Book Week poster, 1944. National Conference of Christians and Jews. World War Poster Collection (MSS36), Literary Manuscripts Collection, University of Minnesota Libraries, Minneapolis.

ultimately, a healthy American democracy. The first poster to incorporate the new slogan, the 1944 poster, was designed by a student at New York's School of Industrial Art (Figure 5.5). The more artistically accomplished posters from 1945 through 1948, which also bore the new slogan, were creations of Michael Gross, a commercial artist proclaimed by *Publishers' Weekly* as the "inventor of the book poster" in the 1910s, and the author of an influential 1948 treatise, "Book Windows That Sell."[61] Gross's two posters artfully foregrounded the Judeo-Christian common ground of the three traditions, while also suggesting a more modern, cosmopolitan approach to religious reading. In Gross's final poster, used in 1947 and 1948, an open book, apparently on the lectern of a house of worship, represented both the Bible—the common property and source of unity of the three traditions—and also the sacredness of all reading (Figure 5.6). The implication, shared with the Council on Books in Wartime and the entire culture of mid-dlebrow reading, was clear: enlightened individuals, ennobled by quality reading,

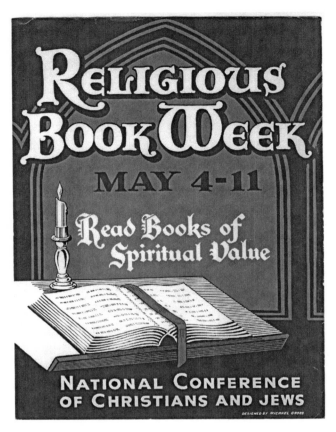

Figure 5.6 Religious Book Week poster, 1947 and 1948. (These posters were identical except for the dates.) National Conference of Christians and Jews. World War Poster Collection (MSS36), Literary Manuscripts Collection, University of Minnesota Libraries, Minneapolis.

formed the bulwark protecting American democratic values, and such reading transcended tradition. Spiritual cosmopolitanism, both in slogan and image, had become the central message of Religious Book Week publicity.

The contrast between the marketing of the Religious Book Weeks in the 1920s and that in the 1940s points to significant cultural and religious shifts in the intervening years, especially the religious implications of advancing consumerism. Those earlier endeavors were essentially commercial undertakings, launched by the book trade itself to stimulate sales. Though not without higher motives— many in the book business saw themselves as cultural ambassadors in the 1920s and shared with Henry Seidel Canby a disdain for naked entrepreneurial ambition—the men behind the earlier book weeks nevertheless devised their campaign as a response to changing economics in the book business, and only secondarily as a cultural or missionary endeavor. This was obviously not so with the wartime efforts of the National Conference of Christians and Jews, a group for whom books were not a business but rather "tools for a better world." Yet paradoxically the NCCJ's marketing campaign reveals just how thoroughly the ethos of consumerism had penetrated American cultural and religious life by the 1940s. Gone was the wistful longing for preconsumerist family and community values. In its place stood an unambiguous celebration of the book itself, a transportable, purchasable, religious commodity, perfectly suited for a transient population disrupted by war.

The clearest markers of these cultural shifts are the key words associated with each marketing campaign. The key word of the 1940s Religious Book Week, especially after 1943, was *spiritual*, as in the slogan "Read Books of Spiritual Value." During the book weeks of the 1920s the key word had been *character*, used in slogans such as "Religious Books Build Character" and "Good Books Build Character." This word, *character*, and the images in the 1920s posters—a Gothic cathedral, a bust of Lincoln, a Victorian family—demonstrated the ambivalence of the 1920s bookmen for the consumer culture they simultaneously inhabited. Tellingly the earlier book posters almost never featured images of a book itself, instead focusing on the context of book reading or its potential effects. The industry insiders behind the 1920s book campaign were reluctant to overtly hawk their wares, striving instead to maintain a sense of their work as a literary and spiritual calling precisely because of its obviously, and increasingly, commercial character. In the more urgent context of the 1940s, the NCCJ, itself not in the book business, showed no such reluctance and featured the image of a book in each of the five posters it commissioned. Character, the 1920s posters seem to say, must be found not just in books but in family, community, church, and nation, whereas the spiritual in the 1940s posters happens in the solitary encounter between reader and text.

The emphasis in the 1940s on the spiritual mirrored the wider cultural fascination with personality that appeared in the movies, magazines, and literature of the period, including Henry Link's *The Return to Religion*. Personality and spirituality represented related psychological and religious manifestations of consumerism, each a quality of the inner life amenable to market commodification and individual cultivation.[62] The term *spiritual value* clearly signifies such market logic, as each book, like any other commodity, is evaluated according to a cost-benefit analysis of *value*. By the 1940s, with the cultural ascendancy of consumerism complete, the new generation of religious book promoters focused more intensively on self-realization than on social or community life. Values associated with character—duty, honor, sacrifice, manhood—certainly remained central to wartime propaganda, yet the major religious book campaign of the period focused instead on the more individualistic and intimate notion of the spiritual. Even that aspect of the NCCJ's efforts that did invoke community values, its emphasis on brotherhood and goodwill, did not call on citizens to sacrifice for the common good, but rather asked individuals to develop themselves into the sort of thoughtful and sensitive persons who transcended petty prejudices.

Yet as the example of interreligious goodwill suggests, the shift from character to the spiritual did not entail a triumph of narcissism or a loss of social concern. The historian Leigh Schmidt's study of spirituality in America in fact reveals a rich tradition, dating back to Emerson, of American spirituality—individual, contemplative, and mystical as it may be—functioning simultaneously as a resource for progressive social and political engagement.[63] The historian Warren Susman's reading of beauty, health, and manners guides led him to conclude that the culture of personality "stressed items that could be best developed in leisure time" and that lacked the gravity of matters of character.[64] But Religious Book Week's focus on spiritual value indicates a greater seriousness than Susman's narrow focus on personality recognized. While the personality traits he describes might aid in self-oriented pursuits like career advancement or romance, reading books of spiritual value prepared the reader for much grander struggles: fighting fascism and communism and living successfully in an increasingly pluralistic democracy. And the right kind of concern with personality might even aid the cultivation of authentic spirituality. As William James and Rufus Jones had long since argued, the exploration of human personality through modern psychology opened a critical pathway to spiritual understanding, offering the potential both for enhanced human sympathy and for greater happiness, wholeness, and communion with God.

Personality and spirituality became defining aspects of the middle-class American sense of self in the middle decades of the twentieth century. Liberal Protestants had first advanced psychological and mystical approaches to religious experience in the nineteenth century in an effort to craft a faith suitable for modern living. Ethical and mystical liberals like James, Jones, and Fosdick, and positive thinkers like Glenn Clark, Emmet Fox, and Henry C. Link, all saw the cultivation and exploration of personality, in their own ways, as critical to spiritual development. Religious middlebrow culture, through the Religious Book Week of the 1920s and the Religious Book Club, tied personality and spirituality to consumer practices, implying that buying the right reading material was critical to self-development. In this way the advancement of consumer culture and the increasing importance of reading as a middle-class religious practice entrenched personality and spirituality into American religious culture. These processes were accelerated further by the social and cultural disruptions of the war. Not surprisingly the 1940s witnessed two of the most significant popular works on spirituality and personality in the twentieth century, Harry Emerson Fosdick's *On Being a Real Person* (1943) and Rabbi Joshua Loth Liebman's *Peace of Mind* (1946). Each was a Religious Book Week selection, and each reached a national, interreligious audience. These books, along with the Trappist monk Thomas Merton's *The Seven Storey Mountain* (1948), marked the arrival of a full-fledged, popular culture of spiritual cosmopolitanism in America.

*   *   *

World War II placed unprecedented spiritual demands on the American people. For the first time in history Americans were asked by governmental, religious, and cultural leaders to come together across religious lines for the good of the country. Previous wars, most notably and recently World War I, had heightened internal divisions, including the ethnic divisions so closely tied to religion; the NCCJ ultimately grew out of efforts to heal the social wounds of World War I. World War II also, of course, proved divisive in its way, not only and most shamefully in the internment of Japanese Americans, but also in the rank hypocrisy of racial segregation amid yet another war for democracy and in the pronounced shift away from the economic goals of the New Deal and toward the new focus on intergroup cooperation as the essence of Americanism.[65] Nevertheless World War II fostered a culture, if not always a reality, of national consensus, and reading campaigns, especially religious reading, played a key role in defining what this consensus might look like. Religious reading programs since the 1920s had advocated a new spiritual vocabulary, rooted in the liberal Protestant discourses of psychology and mysticism, as the means of overcoming narrow sectarianism. Now, in the crisis of war, goodwill between religious groups became the publicly advocated religious ideal, and so the search for spiritual common ground added a new interfaith dimension.

Leaders of the book business worked with allies in the liberal religious establishment to coordinate the massive effort to get Americans reading, and reading the right kinds of books. Men like Pat Beaird and Everett Clinchy and women like Ellen O'Gorman Duffy toiled diligently in the day-to-day struggle to bolster the spiritual defenses of the nation through religious reading. Standing at the apex of bookmen in the 1940s was Fredric G. Melcher, just as he had stood for nearly two decades. Long-time editor of *Publishers' Weekly* and the driving force behind the Religious Book Week of the 1920s, Melcher worked tirelessly throughout the war on behalf of both the Council on Books in Wartime and the National Conference of Christians and Jews. From long years of experience in these various capacities, Melcher held a unique stature to speak to—and speak for—the American book industry. As his business adapted to the demands of wartime, he drew the connections between the war, reading, and the growing cosmopolitan spirit.

Melcher saw clearly the emerging relationship between the goodwill efforts of the NCCJ and the modern literature of soul care that had been the main thrust of liberal Protestant book efforts since the early 1920s. In a March 1943 editorial titled "Religious Books for the Times," he commented, as did Beaird and others, on the rising tide of faith and religious reading. "So great are the issues of our time, so small does man feel in the midst of them, that it is inevitable he should seek for new strength and new faith," Melcher wrote. "Both those who face risks on foreign fronts and those who endure anxieties at home are finding a reason for turning to religious literature for inspiration and confidence." What kinds of books might these be? "Books of consolation," of course, as Americans confronted the tragedies of war, but also, more generally, "books on personal religion," for "though all these days are full of action and common endeavor, men can be lonelier than in the calmer years and far more earnest in the effort to think things out."[66] Ordinary readers, whether at home or abroad, earnestly seeking to "think things out"—this is what Melcher saw as the war's stimulus to faith, and these are the needs he implored his fellow bookmen to meet.

For Melcher to imagine that those facing crises of the spirit desired to "think things out" reflected the prevailing assumptions of liberal religion, the kind of faith that Melcher shared with most of his peers in the book world. Those who directed the Council on Books in Wartime and the National Conference of Christians and Jews all shared the notion that intellect and spirit worked together for human advancement. The erudition of Henry Seidel Canby was matched by his Quaker reliance on the leading of the "inner light," and Melcher turned to the fellowship of the Unitarian Church of Montclair, New Jersey, for his spiritual sustenance. At various times he served as superintendent of its Sunday school and chairman of its board of trustees. In earlier decades the liberal effort to think through one's faith entailed historical and literary study of the Bible, investigations of church history and theology, and especially the application of modern science to moral, social, and personal problems. This was the agenda of Melcher's first Religious Book Week, of the Religious Book Club, and of the American Library Association's Religious Books Round Table.

By the close of the war, however, Melcher saw that the winds had shifted and a new breeze was blowing. The new climate was interfaith: Jewish, Catholic, and Protestant. In a February 1945 editorial, "Religion on a Common Front," he articulated a broadened agenda for religious books in this rapidly changing world. Millions of Americans, at home and overseas, he noted, had faced great suffering, hardship, and death, and "have learned how one finds strength from his own faith." With this fresh evidence of the power of faith, Americans were ready to face the challenges to come. "No one can be satisfied with the world as we have built it," he claimed. "A better world of the future must be raised." In crafting this world, Melcher told his audience of industry insiders, "publishers and booksellers have a special opportunity," for "every church has a literature which throws light on 'the big problems of human life.'" To these books we must turn, he advised, as businessmen aware of the demands of the market, as patriots, and as those charged with the special responsibility of bringing books to people in need. "This literature of applied religion," he exhorted, "should be used as a common heritage just as sacred Scriptures have been used as a common source of spiritual strength."[67] The unity of "every church," an imperative now for building the peace just as surely as it had been an imperative of war, demanded a modern faith, rooted in a shared "literature of applied religion." The undertakings of the 1940s would be built on the success of the 1920s and 1930s. Religious unity would arise from this "common heritage" in the modern techniques of soul care.

Protestants, Catholics, and Jews, Melcher was well aware, in spite of their differences, had always found common ground at least in shared sacred texts. Now, as the war brought Americans of different faiths into closer contact than ever before, Melcher found a new common ground, a modern common ground, in the "literature of applied religion." In daring to speak of a "common front" and a "common heritage," he betrayed the assumptions he shared with many of his fellow liberal Protestants, especially those in positions of cultural authority—that their experiences, values, and desires represented those of the nation. Few African American Baptists, or southern Pentecostals, or Orthodox Jews—not to mention members of the still exotic faith traditions of Asia or of the myriad smaller traditions born in America—would find much application for the "literature of applied religion" Melcher proposed as the basis for a new common front. But the religious reading culture of the 1940s nevertheless transformed much of middle-class American religious life. The liberal ambition to find common religious ground flourished as never before, as mystical and psychological spirituality, consumer reading practices, and the political demands of war enabled a burgeoning religious cosmopolitanism. The book business in the 1940s witnessed the first fruits of this new religious culture. The decade's most significant books of religious inspiration spoke the familiar liberal Protestant languages of psychology and mysticism, now inflected with Jewish and Catholic voices.

6

Religious Reading in the Wake of War

American Spirituality in the 1940s

Elisha Atkins graduated from Harvard College magna cum laude in 1942 and immediately signed up with the marines. He served in the Pacific theater and returned wounded, having fought at Cape Gloucester in New Guinea, the only combat he saw in his few months of active duty. After his injury and return stateside, Atkins continued service in the Marine Corps Reserve. Brief as his tour overseas was, it lasted long enough for him to form a clear impression of the spiritual costs and consequences of war. In "A Soldier's Second Thoughts," published only months after the war's end, Atkins quickly dismissed the "false optimism" of those who saw the war as a boon to faith. "The too easy identification of a fox hole variety [of faith] with the principles of a real and creative faith," he remarked, "is a dangerous obstruction" to understanding the deeper basis of true religion. Yet "life in the service, despite the boredom, mud, and tragedy, has given something to those who shared it which perhaps no other human experience could have supplied"—a sense of shared endeavor, for goals both mundane and profound. While acknowledging that "war is a savage teacher," he granted nevertheless that "perhaps there is the slow and steady growth of a real religion in some of those brought face to face by personal tragedy with the compulsion and the necessity to believe."[1]

Conflicted as Atkins was about the war's impact on faith, he expressed no doubts about the spiritual needs of those returning from combat. "I believe that the only form of religion which will be able to permanently satisfy the minds and spirits of men who have seen this present struggle in all of its sordidness, confusion, and horror," he asserted, "is one which can find real answers through new and spiritually creative paths to the vital problems of life." He continued:

> War has brought millions of men face to face with personal tragedy too
> deep for any words to utter. It has brought men the realization that
> there is something brute and irrational in the world to which we have

given the name evil.... Many will come from this conflict less religious because the faith which religion demands is a constant struggle with the forces of doubt and disillusionment, and wisdom is not always born of suffering. Anything less than a belief which arises from man's most persistent questions as to the nature of life, which answers those deep-seated desires to make the world more meaningful, will not be enough.

Religion thus ceases to be metaphysical speculation and becomes a force in the lives of men for, in the final word, religion is not an affair of the head: the heart has reasons which the head does not know.[2]

Therefore, Atkins concluded, "the question which will be demanded of religion is, 'does it make a genuine difference in our lives?'"[3]

Atkins's observations showed keen insight. He recognized the complexities of the moment, both the spiritual depth of wartime experiences, of encounters with "the forces of doubt and disillusionment" and "something brute and irrational in the world," and the simultaneous desire of many to move beyond "metaphysical speculation" toward religion that "makes a genuine difference in our lives." These insights came from the crucible of war, but they applied broadly in the 1940s, as Americans turned in large numbers to "new and spiritually creative paths."

Another account of postwar religion, published a decade later, painted a dramatically different picture. Where Atkins saw a profound grappling with the nature of religion in a dramatically changed world, the theologian-sociologist Will Herberg saw a dangerous lapse of religious orthodoxy. In *Protestant-Catholic-Jew* (1955), a national bestseller, Herberg powerfully denounced the shallowness he thought had permeated American religion since the end of the war. His account has shaped perceptions to this day, though he was an unlikely person to exert such influence. A lifelong true believer, he was notoriously fickle about what to truly believe in. From Marxism in the 1920s and 1930s, he turned to the theological neo-orthodoxy and political realism of Reinhold Niebuhr in the 1940s and considered conversion to Christianity.[4] Niebuhr, however, persuaded Herberg to explore instead the theological possibilities of his own Jewish heritage. By the mid-1950s Herberg was on the move again, this time from the political left to the political right. Eventually he became a fellow traveler of William F. Buckley and the new conservatives, frequently contributing to the *National Review*, particularly on the need to weaken the separation of church and state, an unusual position for an American Jew of this era.[5] In *Protestant-Catholic-Jew* he presented an odd mixture of sociological analysis (subsequently discredited) and theological critique, decrying, most famously, the idolatry of the suburban middle class as it strayed from the "Jewish-Christian faith." Subsequent generations of critics and commentators have typically aped

Herberg's analysis, characterizing postwar popular religion as theologically unsound and probing no further, while ignoring the voices of Atkins and other ordinary Americans that speak to a much richer, more dynamic, and more complex cultural moment.[6] A look at religious middlebrow culture, especially as seen through the eyes of readers, offers a chance to recover those voices and tell that richer story of popular religion in the 1940s.

Whatever their religious point of view, all observers agreed that American religion was changing rapidly in the war and postwar years. Mostly obviously, congregations and denominations experienced tremendous growth, a surge some likened to the great awakenings of the eighteenth and nineteenth centuries. The numbers certainly are compelling. Southern Baptists, as just one example, added 300,000 members and 500 new churches from 1946 to 1949, while Methodists, Presbyterians, and other denominations showed equally astounding growth. By 1949 Protestant denominations were engaged in a billion dollars' worth of new construction, while Catholics were baptizing a million infants a year. Furthermore by 1950 enrollments in Protestant and Jewish seminaries reached nearly twice their prewar numbers, and Catholic vocations likewise soared.[7] In addition to these impressive measures of church growth, surveys revealed remarkable levels of religious belief and attendance: 94 percent of Americans believed in God, according to one study taken just after the war, while 90 percent engaged in regular prayer; 42 percent attended services at least weekly, and 66 percent at least monthly, both historically high rates.[8] All told, "from 1940 to 1954, Americans joined churches at three times the rate they had from 1928 to 1940."[9] The popular and religious press reported endlessly on these numbers and the apparent revival under way.

Postwar church growth was indeed a real and important phenomenon, but its significance can be easily overstated. The revival, after all, as the sociologist Robert Wuthnow and others have shown, was fueled largely by pent-up construction demand from the Depression and war years, the rapid growth of suburbs, the baby boom, and cold war politics. Suburbanization was particularly critical, as new suburbanites uprooted from small towns or urban-ethnic enclaves found in religious communities a sense of identity and belonging. By the early 1960s the suburb-fueled church boom had subsided, and the long decline of the mainline, dating from the 1930s, resumed. Certainly some of the trends in church life from the period held longer term significance. The crusades of Billy Graham that began in the late 1940s, for example, signaled the emergence of neo-evangelicalism out of a previously cloistered fundamentalism, portending the notable cultural and political influence of conservative evangelicals in the coming decades.[10] And traditional theological categories continued throughout the 1940s and 1950s to inform the way many "everyday Protestants," both evangelical and mainline, understood themselves and their world.[11] Nevertheless, like Will Herberg's later theological analysis, a narrow focus on church growth easily obscures the other, significant religious dynamics that Elisha Atkins observed.

Indeed, alongside and as part of the suburban and evangelical revivals, during the 1940s the psychological and mystical religious orientations that liberal Protestants had been championing for decades reached truly mass audiences. Three bestsellers from the 1940s provide the best window onto this popular religious phenomenon: Harry Emerson Fosdick's *On Being a Real Person* (1943), Joshua Loth Liebman's *Peace of Mind* (1946), and Thomas Merton's *The Seven Storey Mountain* (1948). In their content they were psychological and mystical; in their readership, interfaith. Despite their interfaith appeal, each book remained distinctively *of* its own tradition— Liebman and Merton in particular offered stark polemics for Judaism and Catholicism—a clear sign of an emerging popular cosmopolitanism rather than least-common-denominator universalism and a sharp rebuttal to Herberg's lament about lost religious distinctiveness. An examination of the content, print history, readership, and reception of these books, all number-one bestsellers, demonstrates how psychological and mystical approaches to religious experience enabled the practices of this emerging cosmopolitanism. The readers of these books in particular offer, alongside Elisha Atkins, critical accounts of the religious dynamics occurring beyond church life and theological debate.

The first two of these books, Fosdick's *On Being a Real Person* and *Peace of Mind* by Liebman, a Reform rabbi, helped bring depth psychology into the cultural mainstream. They did this by placing psychological concepts into a liberal religious framework, couched in a religious idiom. The third book, *The Seven Storey Mountain* by Thomas Merton, a Roman Catholic convert and Trappist monk, is "an autobiography of faith," unlike the other two books, which are how-to guides. Merton's story popularized and humanized matters of mystical experience and practice. Together these three books presented to the reading public ideas that had been germinating in liberal religious culture since the 1920s and now emerged after the war with renewed vigor and legitimacy. The dynamic interplay of modern psychology and ancient mysticism accelerated trends in American religious culture already moving toward an experience-based, instrumental, subject-focused spirituality.[12] Psychology and mysticism were hardly new in the 1940s, but their presentation in bestselling books, marketed with the techniques of modern middlebrow culture, proved especially potent in speaking to, and in turn shaping, the spiritual needs of millions of wartime and postwar American readers. That these books attained such tremendous commercial success while remaining distinctly Protestant, Jewish, and Catholic reveals the development, for an increasing number of American readers in the 1940s, of greater openness to spiritual enlightenment from other traditions of faith. It was the wide cultural acceptance of liberal Protestant values and sensibilities in the 1940s, in other words, that opened many Americans to religious insight from beyond Protestantism.

Herberg and like-minded critics failed to see how the extraordinary cultural success of mystical, psychological, and cosmopolitan spirituality stemmed from the wartime invigoration of long-standing liberal Protestant ambitions. Wartime reading programs socialized millions of Americans into the practices of book culture, both creating new readers and binding those reader's religious lives more closely than ever to the consumer marketplace. Furthermore the interfaith movement utilized the tremendous wartime resources of the military and government to promote the Judeo-Christian concept, a concept with spiritual as well as civic and political dimensions. The greater social interaction fostered by service in the military and defense industries and the ideological implications of conflict with fascism further extended the reach and impact of the interfaith message. Each of these developments helped make decades-old liberal Protestant priorities into mass cultural phenomena. Last, and of equal consequence, the war introduced psychological thinking to millions of Americans at home and in the service. This too realized a liberal Protestant ambition of long standing. Since Williams James's *The Varieties of Religious Experience* and Rufus Jones's *Social Law in the Spiritual World* at the dawn of the century, liberal Protestants had contended that psychological sophistication offered a pathway to greater spiritual understanding and fulfillment. After decades of efforts to promote psychological insight, the war ultimately brought modern psychology to the mainstream. In this moment of cultural ferment, Elisha Atkins's call for "new and spiritually creative paths" and Frederic Melcher's appeal for a "literature of applied religion" found a particularly receptive audience.

Psychology, Liberal Protestantism, and the War

Decades before the American military made psychology a mass endeavor in the 1940s, liberal Protestant clergy began working to introduce psychological concepts to ordinary Americans. The first sustained effort was the Emmanuel Movement of the early twentieth century, which "helped introduce the new psychology into the church at a time when it was barely understood within the hospital" and before long sophisticated ministers began to take note.[13] Fosdick, for example, first regularly employed psychology in his own pastoral counseling in the 1920s. The practice became professionalized through the pioneering work of Anton Boisen, Richard Cabot, Charles T. Holman, Seward Hiltner, and others who instituted clinical training as a routine component of liberal Protestant seminary education in the interwar years.[14] The liberal Protestant leaders who embraced psychology in the 1920s and 1930s were heirs to the Progressive faith in scientific expertise and the Social Gospel ambition to remake the world according to Christian ethics. Rather than a secularizing force, psychology in the hands of liberal Protestant clergy became a tool to fulfill more effectively their pastoral duties.

These spiritual pioneers revolutionized the practice of pastoral care, and their influence was eventually felt beyond the churches and seminaries, as a leading historian of the field notes. "The pastoral theologians of the 1930s did a considerable amount of stumbling around," E. Brooks Holifield remarks, "but they laid the foundations for a postwar renaissance that would have surprised even them."[15] During and after the war, through bestselling books, Fosdick and Liebman, two key religious figures of the 1940s psychological awakening, brought this new pastoral counseling to the nation.

For all the work of liberal Protestants in the pastoral counseling movement, however, it was the war that prepared Americans to accept a psychological message from their religious leaders. Without the experience of war, in fact, Fosdick and Liebman would most likely never have commanded the audiences they did. Depth psychology, especially in the psychoanalytic tradition of Freud, had been slowly gaining acceptance among cultural elites since just after the turn of the century, but not until midcentury did psychological conceptions of the self gain wide currency. Psychological analysis had been utilized in World War I, most notably for the 100,000 soldiers who were treated for "shell shock," but in World War II psychology truly became a mass endeavor.[16] During World War II army hospitals saw 1 million psychiatric admissions, yet the reach of the psychological and psychiatric professions extended far beyond the treatment of war trauma. Military officials used psychological assessment as a vital tool in the induction and training processes. By war's end 15 million draftees, more than 10 percent of the national population, had undergone some form of psychological testing, "most of them encountering psychological logic for the first time."[17] Throughout the war civilians back home read reports from the front thick with psychological analysis, such as a *Newsweek* story from the Pacific describing "Guadalcanal Neurosis." In a nation gripped by war and enamored of scientific expertise, the psychologist had ascended to an unprecedented cultural status by 1945. "It is hard to believe that a few hundred professionals could change the culture of a nation," notes the historian Andrew Heinze, "but that is what happened in the United States after the Second World War."[18]

The dramatic conclusions of the war in Europe and the Pacific further heightened its psychological impact. The advance of Allied forces into Nazi death camps in April and May 1945 forced the American public to confront unfathomable brutality in the heart of Western civilization. Stories of Nazi atrocities had circulated widely in the United States since 1942, but "the liberations made horrified believers out of the skeptics and brought a new and hideous sense of reality even to those who never doubted the worst."[19] Images from photographers such as Margaret Bourke-White, including those displayed by Joseph Pulitzer to throngs in St. Louis, and graphic newsreels shown nationwide made intimate to millions of Americans the worst in human nature. Though most Americans were intellectually able to grapple with these new realities—84 percent believed the reports about Nazi death camps, according to a Gallup poll in May 1945, up from 76 percent in November 1944—many experienced psychological and emotional strains.[20] "Like the soldiers at the camps," writes the historian Robert H. Abzug, "those who came upon Belsen and Buchenwald in a newsreel or picture magazine experienced a potent mixture of shock, anger, shame, guilt, and fear. And like the soldiers, they felt a great need for distance and disconnection."[21] Charles Clayton Morrison, the longtime editor of the liberal Protestant *Christian Century* and a prewar isolationist, had been a Holocaust skeptic until he visited the camps himself. In a May 9, 1945, essay in the *Century* entitled "Gazing into the Pit," Morrison reported that all that had been rumored was true, and more. "What can be said that will not seem like tossing little words up against a giant mountain of ineradicable evil?" he asked, knowing full well that no answer could be found for his shock and bewilderment.[22] When Elisha Atkins spoke of the "sordidness, confusion, and horror" of war, he captured a sentiment that Morrison and many others now knew well.

This shock, fear, and need for disconnection grew exponentially in August 1945, when the atomic bombings of Hiroshima and Nagasaki demonstrated a new means of mass extermination that might one day visit American soil. The threat of atomic annihilation meant "that no sentient man or woman can really find peace of mind or body," declared the psychiatrist Jules H. Masserman in an address delivered a year after Liebman's book made the phrase "peace of mind" famous, while the columnist Dorothy Thompson remarked in October 1945 that atomic terror was leading to "a world-wide nervous breakdown."[23] Though many Americans saw in atomic power the promise of a better future, all realized as well its potential for apocalyptic destruction. The wide use of professional psychology in the military and the myriad human tragedies of the war together created a receptive cultural environment for the psychologically sophisticated bestsellers of Fosdick and Liebman.

The war's effect on the public understanding of psychology was truly revolutionary. But the war also provided similar, if less dramatic opportunities for liberal Protestants to speak about the importance of personal religious experience. James's *The Varieties of Religious Experience*, of course, had provided the conceptual categories for a generation of American intellectuals to describe "the ineffable," and his ideas found their way to the wider reading public through fellow students of mysticism, foremost among them the Quaker Rufus Jones. In *Social Law in the Spiritual World*, Jones had placed psychological understanding at the center of mystical practice, recognizing that all experience of the divine is mediated through consciousness. Throughout his long and prolific career Jones argued in a steady stream of popular books and magazine articles that mystical experience is not the province of a spiritual elite, but open to all.[24] This populist understanding of mysticism animated his preaching and writing and drove his social activism as well. He was instrumental in founding the American Friends Service Committee in 1917, for example, and in the late 1930s traveled to Germany to negotiate aid for German Jewish refugees with the Gestapo. In 1942, toward the end of his life, Jones saw that from the horrors of war might come a revitalized concern for direct contact with the divine. "While I am writing this," he observed in a 1942 *Atlantic Monthly* essay on mystical experience, "the world seems to be collapsing into a primitive chaos of revolution and destruction."[25] Yet, he argued, "it is now if ever that we need the voice of those who, 'listening to the inner flow of things, speak to the age out of Eternity.'"[26] Jones concluded with one of his most stirring refrains, calling his readers to a higher life through intimacy with the Eternal. Mystics, Jones wrote, "are in every church and in no church at all. They are in towns and cities, on country farms, in CCC [Civilian Conservation Corps] camps and in the Army. They are laboratory professors and they are college students. They are rich and they are poor. They are good-livers and they are hardy ascetics. But they have, one and all, learned that they do not live by bread alone, but have resources from the World beyond the world of space and time, and their 'best moments of life' are times of spiritual fecundity, infused by contact with a Beyond."[27] The optimism of this passage reflects perhaps the will-to-hope of a lifelong mystic, activist, and pacifist when faced with a moment of such great violence and suffering. Yet Elisha Atkins sounded a similar note a few years later when he observed the widespread, "deep-seated desires to make the world more meaningful." The contemplative search for meaning in the wake of war assumed a newly practical dimension, and Thomas Merton's personal tale of reading and redemption made the mystical life into a mass cultural phenomenon.

The 1940s bestsellers of Fosdick, Liebman, and Merton drew on this wartime invigoration of psychology and mysticism. All three texts participated as well in the thriving middlebrow culture promoted by the Council on Books in Wartime and the National Conference of Christians and Jews. Fosdick and Liebman each deliberately crafted their texts to reach the same striving, busy, intelligent but average reader who constituted the imagined audience of these book campaigns. Fosdick and Liebman each, in addition, understood their role as expert guides into the challenging intellectual world of modern psychology. Merton too, though writing in a different literary genre, ultimately crafted a book of practical value as well, a guide by which ordinary men and women could learn the same hard-won lessons he had learned. In Frederic Melcher's terms, even Merton's book became, in the hands of its readers, part of the "literature of applied religion."

Religious leaders of the era encouraged the reading of religious books as a critical means of spiritual self-improvement. While leaders of the Council on

Books in Wartime and the National Conference of Christians and Jews surely acknowledged the benefits of reading for pleasure or diversion, reading for intellectual and spiritual betterment clearly lay at the heart of their efforts. The readers of Fosdick, Liebman, and Merton approached their texts with this same attitude of earnest, practical seeking, and the consequences of this burgeoning religious middlebrow culture were far-reaching. It provided millions of Americans with access to liberal theology, psychology, and mysticism and tied American religious culture ever more tightly to the consumer marketplace. These forms of psychological and mystical spirituality provided avenues for American readers to venture safely beyond the bounds of their own traditions of faith, creating for the first time in American life a culture of middle-class spiritual cosmopolitanism.

Reading Fosdick, Liebman, and Merton

Rabbi Joshua Loth Liebman's secretaries were very busy in 1947. His book, *Peace of Mind,* had burst onto the publishing scene in the spring of 1946 and would soon pass the 1 million mark in sales and become the best-selling nonfiction religious book of the twentieth century to that point.[28] Only thirty-nine years old when the book appeared, handsome, with a silky baritone voice, an engaging prose style, and an agile mind, Liebman was on his way to celebrity (Figure 6.1). His sudden death in 1948 at age forty-one is all that kept him from lasting fame. Before *Peace of Mind* he was already known across New England for his weekly radio sermons. Now, with the astonishing commercial success of this book, his office at Boston's Temple Israel was inundated with letters, mostly from women. Liebman would quickly scan each of the thousands of letters—many heartbreaking, others shockingly confessional—and scribble a brief but personal response in the margin. His staff carefully typed and mailed each of these responses, often with a relevant sermon enclosed.

A Jewish woman from Big Wells, Texas, wrote Rabbi Liebman for help. She was forty-two years old, a college-educated high school teacher, a wife and mother. She had been married for fifteen years to a man whom she "respected very much," but found, as she put it, "the sexual relation almost unbearable." Recently she had fallen in love with one of her students, a high school senior soon to join the marines. "I have tried to find something in religion to help me, and I have prayed for guidance and understanding thousands of times, but that has failed," she wrote. "If you cannot help me I do not know where to turn."[29] A man from Tampa, Florida, wrote to Rabbi Liebman of "an entity from another life or existence" that spoke with him. He had not yet finished reading *Peace of Mind,* but when he had, he assured the rabbi, he would write again to let Liebman know what the entity thought of the book.[30] One wonders indeed just what the entity made of this curious bestseller, the first religious book from a non-Christian

Figure 6.1 Rabbi Joshua Loth Liebman, 1946 or 1947. From the Joshua Loth Liebman Collection, Howard Gotlieb Archival Research Center at Boston University. Photo by Bachrach.

author to reach a mass audience in the United States.[31] For, despite its title, the book that inspired so many letter writers was no inspirational pabulum. Rather Liebman presented an account of human nature based on a sophisticated rendition of Freudian psychology. The insights of Freud, Liebman argued, when coupled with personal faith and the wisdom of the Jewish prophetic tradition, offered the best hope for survival and perhaps, one might dare hope, even happiness in the troubled modern world. And based on the flood of letters streaming into Liebman's office, it seems many troubled, modern souls in postwar America dared hope right along with him.

Simon and Schuster, Liebman's publisher, advertised *Peace of Mind* widely, but the book's sales, and Liebman's flood of fan mail, probably stemmed more from enthusiastic coverage in newspapers and popular magazines such as *Life*, *Look*, *Ladies' Home Journal*, and *Cosmopolitan*. These pieces cemented the book's status as *the* postwar spiritual guide. The *Look* piece focused on Liebman the man, his midwestern roots, his own experience with psychoanalysis, and his daily professional and personal routines. Carrying the subtitle "Joshua Loth Liebman's Best-seller Has Guided Thousands to Serenity," the article also included a digest of Liebman's chapter on grief, perhaps the most directly relevant portion to a postwar audience.[32] The *Boston Post* ran a story on Liebman under the banner headline "Writer of Clean Best-Seller Presents His Views," in which Liebman answered critics and offered his take on the success of his book. Naturally he pointed to the role of the war in opening American readers to a psychological message, but more personally he remarked on his place as a Jewish counselor to an overwhelmingly Christian nation. He told the *Post* reporter of the survivors of a deadly fire in Georgia who requested autographed copies of his book. The reporter recounted, "His eyes moistened, his shoulders sagged a little, as he told about it the other day. 'They are Christian men and women,' he stated softly. 'Here I am, a rabbi and a Jew.'"[33]

Liberal Protestants by 1946 were already open to psychological insight after decades of pastoral and popular interest, and now, in the wake of the Holocaust, American readers for the first time embraced the spiritual counsel of a rabbi. As early as 1942 book industry experts had noticed increased sales of Jewish books to both Jews and non-Jews, largely, according to one account, "because of the Nazi persecutions in Europe."[34] The war exposed the American public to modern psychology in massive numbers, and the horrors of Nazi crimes and atomic weapons made the promise of psychology seem all the more compelling. Psychology's emergence as liberal religion's lingua franca provided a vocabulary for a non-Christian to speak to the spiritual needs of Americans across religious lines. The historian Andrew Heinze in fact contends, "Psychology created a spiritual democracy. As a result, for the first time in nearly two millennia, a rabbi had a solid platform from which to preach spiritual answers to an interfaith audience."[35] The unique credibility bestowed on Liebman as a Jew in the postwar climate deepened his mass appeal. "By virtue of both his Jewishness and his Freudianism," continues Heinze, "Liebman was taken as an authority on wartime suffering and prejudice."[36] Liberal religious institutions in the United States had been moving toward a greater ecumenism for decades, as exemplified by the Federal Council of Churches and the National Conference of Christians and Jews. Even more compellingly war mobilization itself called on Americans to form a united front against common enemies. Now, in the wake of the war, the nation was ready for this ecumenism to bear fruit in Rabbi Liebman's literary ministry.

Liebman's work closely resembled Fosdick's *On Being a Real Person*, published three years earlier. Fosdick too had offered Americans an unusually learned mix of psychology and liberal religion and, like Liebman, was rewarded with a number-one spot on national bestseller lists. While Liebman was a fresh face on the scene of liberal religion in 1946, Fosdick was liberalism's best-known clergyman (Figure 6.2). Through his Sunday evening radio addresses (never called sermons), which ran until his retirement in 1946, and through his books, Fosdick brought theological modernism and modern psychology into the homes of millions of Americans. *Time* magazine estimated at Fosdick's retirement that his books and radio addresses brought him 125,000 letters a year, a number that would have surely overwhelmed Liebman's staff of two.[37]

Figure 6.2 Official portrait of Harry Emerson Fosdick, circa 1945, from the former Office of Public Information at Union Theological Seminary. Photographer unknown. Union Theological Seminary Records Series 18 in The Burke Library Archives at Union Theological Seminary, New York.

As soon as Liebman's book appeared in 1946, he and Fosdick were linked in the public mind. Liebman had been somewhat dismayed when Fosdick's book first appeared, fearing the eminent churchman's efforts would over-shadow his own planned work. Yet he delivered a very favorable sermon on *On Being a Real Person* in April 1943, in which he tied the main themes of Fosdick's work to those he was developing. "Now, if we are ever to be real persons, if we are ever to have genuine peace of mind," he declared, connecting the title of Fosdick's book and his own, yet to be published, "we must learn how to believe again—to believe in friendship and human love and social causes and an undergirding, universal mind."[38] He complimented Fosdick for renouncing Puritan notions of the body and original sin; even his criticisms of Fosdick, for failing to show his readers *how* to become the real persons he so ably described, were polite. Fosdick in turn warmly welcomed Liebman's publication, writing the young rabbi, "It is very gratifying and encouraging to know that a book like this is sustaining this preeminent position, and I congratulate you on behalf of the whole religious community."[39] Yet what most likely sealed the association between the two books in the public's mind was their simultaneous appearance in the 1948 hardbound volume *14 Reader's Digest Books*.[40] *Reader's Digest* offered the largest possible audience a chance to read critical portions of each book side by side.

In the fall of 1948, while *Reader's Digest* was promoting the psychological gospels of Fosdick and Liebman, Thomas Merton's autobiography hit the bestseller lists.[41] Merton, like Fosdick and Liebman, transcended the category "religious author" to become a national media phenomenon. Sydney Ahlstrom described Merton as "the American who brought the mystical tradition to full expression," and certainly to its widest American audience yet.[42] The success of Merton's autobiography, which shocked its publisher by remaining at or near the top of the *New York Times* bestseller list for the fall of 1948 and much of 1949, was due as well, no doubt, in large degree to World War II. Merton spoke, as few others did, to Americans' longing for security, meaning, and solace as they looked back on the horrors of war just concluded, and ahead to the potentially greater horrors of the atomic age.[43] Reviewers frequently referred to Merton in fact as an "atomic age Augustine," and in such troubled times what better symbol of security and serenity than the monastery? Merton's book reached soul-weary Americans with the story of his life transformed by a mystical faith. A *Life* magazine article on the *Seven Storey* phenomenon attested to Merton's broad appeal, noting that in many cities more Protestants than Catholics were reading the book.[44] This appeal across lines of tradition was true for Liebman's book as well, as indicated both by its huge sales and by the many letters from non-Jewish readers. Liberal Protestants such as Rufus Jones had been writing of mystical experience in popular books and magazines for decades, and Fosdick himself, influenced by Jones, often argued that for a liberal faith to remain living, it must make room for personal connection with the divine. Just as the welcome reception to Liebman's psychological bestseller stemmed from decades of cultural work by liberal Protestants, Merton's mysticism likewise found an audience primed by Jones, Fosdick, and similar Protestant forerunners.

Fosdick's *On Being a Real Person* (1943)

In chapters on "the principle of self-acceptance," "mastering depression," and "handling our mischievous consciences," *On Being a Real Person* presents the insights of a literate, compassionate, and insightful writer and pastor. Fosdick opened his book with an anecdote from twenty years earlier, when a young man in Fosdick's office for counseling threatened suicide. "Having received my education in pre-psychiatric days," Fosdick wrote, "when the academic study of psychology was a very dry and formal discipline, and such matters as mental therapy, so far as I can recall, were never mentioned in college or seminary, I was utterly untrained for personal counseling."[45] This case, he told his readers, propelled him on the twenty-year journey of study that resulted in this book. But more than simply explaining the genesis of the book, Fosdick's story cast himself of twenty years prior in the same position as the reader of today, as an unsophisticated but zealous seeker, scouring books and articles for practical guidance in matters of psyche and spirit. Through the ensuing chapters Fosdick became a virtual psychological tour guide, introducing his readers to the famous psychologists, theologians, poets, and novelists whose writings had formed his own thinking in this autodidactic quest. "Coming as it does out of personal experience, this book is necessarily as limited and partial as that experience has been," he warned. "Nevertheless, for what it may be worth, here is the story of what one minister has found out about people's 'insides' and what can be done with them."[46]

Fosdick was well known for his love of quotations, which he collected throughout his life in copious notebooks. In his celebrated sermons he freely shared the sayings of favorite writers, a practice he carried over into his popular books. In *On Being a Real Person* readers meet William James and Sören Kierkegaard, Josiah Royce and Ernest Hocking, Henry C. Link and Rufus Jones. Even more, one travels among poets, novelists, musicians, and playwrights, greeting Carlyle, Dostoyevsky, Chopin, and Shakespeare. Fosdick warned his readers, "Frequently I have turned to biography and autobiography, and to those novelists, poets, and dramatists who have been, as was said of Shakespeare, circumnavigators of the human soul." Fearing his serious readers would dismiss the quotations and allusions as "decorative," he reminded his audience that "nowhere are the common frustrating experiences of personal life more vividly described... and this rich storehouse of psychological self-revelation and insight has been too much neglected."[47] Fosdick's own story, in other words, which he invited his readers to share, exemplified the transformative power of the very same middlebrow reading culture in which it now participated.

As Fosdick's readers came to recognize, much of the advice he shared reflected nothing more than simple common sense, made authoritative with the vocabularies of science and faith. Stay rooted in the social networks of friends, family, and community; find happiness in serving ends outside oneself; get plenty of exercise (Fosdick himself was an avid walker). Never abstruse, arcane, or technical, his language stayed straightforward throughout; he employed his roster of guides and examples to verify the everyday wisdom his readers already knew. Even when introducing specialized terminology, such as *sublimation* or *projection*, he illustrated the term with an anecdote from common experience. When discussing the conscience, for example, which he sensibly noted suffers equally often from overdevelopment as from underdevelopment, he related psychological language to the everyday. "When God accused the woman [Eve, in the Garden of Eden, of eating the apple], she said, 'The serpent beguiled me, and I did eat.' What we call 'passing the buck' is an ancient process. Modern psychology has a word for this, 'projection.'"[48] At times he expressed overt hostility to the technical nature of psychology, even as he made use of it. In a chapter titled "Shouldering Responsibility for Ourselves," for example, he complained that "psychiatry weighs down our speech with half-understood, ponderous words describing the various *phobias* and *complexes*, so that, as Dr. Henry C. Link says, they become 'a vocabulary of defeat.' "[49] Here one authority is marshaled to combat the language of others, allowing Fosdick to both educate his readers and share in their frustration with excessive intellectualism.

A skillful rhetorician with years of practice in the raw arena of the pulpit, Fosdick deftly crafted this book to guide his readers while also respecting their autonomy, always the challenge when providing mass-market expertise in a democratic society. He had in fact honed the core ideas in the book in sermons and lectures to his Riverside congregation. Though Fosdick's church members were more prosperous and better educated in general than the average reader of his work, the Riverside congregation nevertheless provided direct contact with a live audience that almost certainly improved the style and substance of the book. As far back as 1939 Fosdick had conducted a lecture series at Riverside entitled "Being a Real Person" (also the original title of the book, maintained until "On" was added to the final draft in early 1943). The flyer announcing these lectures, held on successive Wednesday nights in October and November 1939, noted that with the recent start of war in Europe, "the World-Crisis confronts us with two problems: handling public policy and handling ourselves. With the second of these this series of lectures and questionnaires is concerned."[50] Anticipating the wartime push for religious reading, Fosdick early on drew the link between world events and personal spirituality. His sermons from the period also indicate a testing of the book's central themes. In a radio sermon from 1939 entitled "The Possibility of Transformed Personality," for example, he spoke to "anyone who wants to be a real person," and in "Achieving Personal Integrity" in 1941 he outlined for his listeners "what it means to be a real person."[51]

Fosdick's intention for *On Being a Real Person*, as the title so clearly indicates, was, quite simply, to help his readers lead happier, more productive, and more fulfilling lives. Regarding religion, he wrote, "I have tried not to be a special pleader. My main purpose in writing this book has not been to present an argument for religious faith."[52] At times he even seemed shockingly dismissive of the traditional language of faith, noting, "There is an understandable reason ... why in modern psychological parlance the word 'integration' has taken the place of the religious word 'salvation.' "[53] Fosdick here did not intend to undermine hope in life after death; he himself had written a devotional book called *The Assurance of Immortality* back in 1913, and his views on this matter remained unchanged. Rather he wished to demonstrate the essential unity of purpose between psychological pursuits and the spiritual. Though claiming that in writing he sought "to confront religion only when ... I ran headlong into it," nevertheless "one does run headlong into it."[54] This, he made clear, was because as science probed more deeply into the workings of mind, consciousness, and personality, and religion began to incorporate the advances of modern science, religion and the healing arts were regaining the unity they once held at the dawn of human civilization. The wisdom of the ages, Fosdick maintained, and the science of the moment were coming to speak with one voice.

And so when Fosdick did write of faith in *On Being a Real Person*, he wrote primarily of its usefulness in this world. The words *energy* and *power*, so often employed by mystics like Rufus Jones and New Thought writers like Emmet Fox and Glenn Clark, likewise occur throughout Fosdick's work. In a chapter entitled "The Principle of Released Power," he developed a connection between psychological integrity and spiritual life that affirmed the centrality of mystical experience. "That our spirits are continuous with a larger spiritual life," he wrote, in a passage clearly indebted to his mentor in these matters, Rufus Jones, "that in this realm also, as everywhere else, our power is not self-produced but assimilated, is the affirmation of all profound religious experience." Indeed, he continued, "in powerful personality on its deeper levels man's spirit does not seem like a self-contained, landlocked pool, but like a bay, open to the tides. In hours of receptivity man's reserves can be renewed."[55] Because of the power authentic religious experience makes available "faith has a therapeutic value beyond computation" and religion "has brought to those who genuinely have known it a transforming access of power."[56] Frequently this "therapeutic" and "transforming" power would find expression in a life-altering conversion experience, which Fosdick recognized in the traditional "coming to Christ" of evangelicalism and in its newer forms, such as the twelve steps of Alcoholics Anonymous.[57] "Conversion," he argued, "can now no longer be thought of as an ecclesiastical specialty. It is a profound human necessity, and far beyond the range of organized religion it is continually occurring as an indispensable prelude to the achievement of a healthy personality."[58] Scholars rightly consider Fosdick an evangelical as well as a liberal because of his continuing emphasis on transformation through encounters with a living Christ, and his evangelical sensibilities pervade even this highly psychologized text.[59]

Fosdick himself had firsthand knowledge of the intimate relationship between conversion and healthy personality and used his experiences to write his deeply compassionate and humane chapter "Mastering Depression." Both of his parents had suffered mental illness, and his most profound early religious experiences coincided with their breakdowns. His first conversion, at age seven, occurred when his mother suffered a depression, and a second "awakening," in 1896 at age nineteen, began as his father lay stricken. His spiritual resolve was soon put to the test when he too, after a trying year of early ministry in New York City, fell into a suicidal despair. Not a crisis of faith, according to Robert Moats Miller, his biographer, this depression instead actually reinvigorated Fosdick spiritually; in religious faith he found the resources to lead himself out of despair. "In his hour of need God came to him redemptively, and the experience was as profound as his conversion at age seven," Miller writes. "This mystical element in his nature later led him into close fellowship with the Quaker mystic, Rufus Jones.... The authority of personal experience was for Fosdick forever to be the primary authority."[60] In these formative years Fosdick developed not only a keen interest in the workings of the mind but also a hard-won empathy for those who suffered. "Find a task that dignifies [your] days," he counseled his readers, and no matter your state, whether naturally content or melancholic, "never despise your temperament."[61] Perhaps this was the same wisdom he shared with the young man threatening suicide in his office years earlier, a young man who must certainly have reminded him of himself.

"Revealed Psychology" for Modern America: Liebman's *Peace of Mind* (1946)

Liebman's *Peace of Mind* arose from many of the same autobiographical sources as had Fosdick's book. And Liebman too based his research on his own emotional needs and the needs of his congregation. *Peace of Mind*, then, like *On Being a Real Person*, was first and foremost a pastoral book, and though Liebman was not prone to despair or crisis in the same way the young Fosdick was, he nonetheless recognized a need for personal transformation in order to serve effectively as a spiritual guide to his flock. For Liebman, the path to spiritual maturity passed not through the gate of evangelical conversion, but through an extended period of intense Freudian psychoanalysis. Liebman in fact "was probably the first American preacher of national standing to undergo psychoanalysis," a process he began in the late 1930s while serving the congregation at KAM Temple in Chicago.[62] Liebman's own struggle for personal integrity and maturity shaped the contours of his literary ministry to come. With *Peace of Mind* he used the conventions of middlebrow print culture to offer war-weary Americans spiritual guidance based on Jewish wisdom, Freudian psychology, and a reinterpretation of the American pragmatic and transcendentalist spiritual traditions. In making the fruits of his own struggles accessible to all, Liebman made a lasting contribution to the Judeo-Christian spirituality newly emerging in the years after World War II.

Just what led Liebman into psychotherapy remains unclear. His parents divorced in 1909, when he was two years old, leaving him in the care of his paternal grandparents. A child prodigy, as a teenager he liked to quote, verbatim from memory, extended passages of Plato in Hebrew. He enrolled at the University of Cincinnati at age fifteen and raced through seminary and doctoral work in Jerusalem and at Hebrew Union in Cincinnati. In 1931 he returned to the United States and soon thereafter began to serve his first synagogue, in Lafayette, Indiana. He also married his first cousin, Fan Loth, who had been his student in Cincinnati. The couple married in Kentucky, since such a union was illegal in Ohio. Liebman's skeptical father forced him to produce textual support for the marriage from the Talmud before assenting to the union. He began his psychoanalysis around the age of thirty in Chicago with Dr. Roy Grinker and continued treatment with Dr. Erich Lindemann after moving to Boston in 1939 to serve as rabbi to Temple Israel. These two analysts specialized in the treatment of stress and grief, indicating perhaps that Liebman's analysis helped him cope with the early separation from his parents and his furious professional drive.[63]

Liebman's inner life in these years remains a matter for speculation. What is certain is that he emerged from his three years of psychoanalysis just as the nation was embarking on its own wartime encounter with psychology, perfectly positioning the young rabbi to apply his newfound insights to his various ministries. Though never overly confessional in his sermons or writings, during his years in the pulpit he nevertheless developed a masterly skill in applying the lessons of his own psychoanalytic journey to the lived experiences of his flock. Liebman was in constant demand on the lecture circuit across New England, and, like Fosdick, he broadcast many of his addresses in hugely successful radio appearances; by the mid-1940s he commanded audiences of between 1 and 2 million, 70 to 80 percent of whom were Christians.[64] In all these sermons and addresses, even as the war consumed the nation's attention, Liebman never strayed from his intense devotion to individual spiritual and psychological health. In a sermon called "The Road to Inner Serenity Today," for example, delivered in April 1943, he acknowledged "impersonal, economic factors at work and tremendous political frictions," yet, true to his psychological orientation, he averred, "But unless you're a mystic like the perverted followers of Hegel... you must agree that a diseased society begins at home, in sick human beings." As prime evidence he cited the sickest of all human beings. "You cannot tell me," claimed Liebman, "that Hitler is not corroded and eaten away by inner self-contempt."[65] In this sermon, and many others delivered during the war, Liebman presaged the themes of *Peace of Mind*. He eventually took his pastoral and homiletic skills and applied them directly to the war effort, serving as a member of the Committee on Army and Navy Religious Activities, a post that afforded him the chance to oversee the work of Jewish chaplains.

Liebman's oratorical gifts and psychological insight proved a winning formula in postwar America, yet he certainly benefited too from a bit of good old-fashioned luck. He was fortunate to begin his engagement with psychology in the years just before the nation as a whole encountered psychological thinking on a mass scale, and was fortunate as well to work personally with the leading authorities on the most pressing psychological issues of the day—those arising from the war itself. Indeed *Peace of Mind* arose directly from "his frustrations as a pulpit rabbi" at Temple Israel, where he experienced an early and deep immersion in the matters of greatest concern to a nation of readers grappling with the myriad traumas of war, especially stress, guilt, and grief.[66] Liebman's first analyst in Chicago, Dr. Roy Grinker, who was the head of psychiatry at Michael Reese Hospital and an analysand of Freud in Vienna in the 1930s, went on to become the nation's leading psychoanalytic expert in dealing with combat stress. After working with Liebman in the late 1930s, Grinker served with the U.S. Army in North Africa, where he developed pioneering treatments for the psychiatric wounds of war. Grinker commented while still in theater, "We have learned a great deal that is applicable to peace time psychiatry," and eventually authored the leading manual on the subject, the acclaimed and widely read *War Neuroses*.[67] Liebman's second analyst, the Boston psychiatrist Dr. Erich Lindemann, performed innovative research in the psychology of grief, studying the survivors of the Cocoanut Grove nightclub fire in 1942 in which hundreds died.[68] Liebman gratefully acknowledged the critical influence of these preeminent analysts in shaping his thinking in *Peace of Mind*. His own experience as an active preacher and pastor, his time spent training army chaplains, and his own two analysts and psychoanalytic mentors, Grinker and Lindemann, specialists in combat stress and grief, prepared Liebman well to write with deep insight into the religious and psychological needs of a war-wounded nation.

The postwar setting of *Peace of Mind* pervades the text. "It may seem strange," Liebman began the book, "for a man to write . . . about peace of mind in this age of fierce turmoil and harrowing doubts. It may seem doubly strange for a rabbi, a representative of a people that has known so little peace, to engage in such an enterprise."[69] Though he usually mentioned the war only indirectly—the terms *Second World War*, *Auschwitz*, *Hitler*, and *Hiroshima* never appear in the text, for example—he nevertheless made clear that his goal of providing Americans the intellectual tools for achieving spiritual maturity was now more important than ever in its wake. As a social scientifically literate liberal, Liebman recognized that "a more just social order will cure vast numbers of people of their present inner conflicts and maladjustments," and so, he continued, "we must battle for a decent and just economic social order as the matrix of personal sanity and balance."[70] Nevertheless he maintained that a "healthier society must be built by healthier human beings." For this reason *Peace of Mind* was first and foremost a pastoral, not a sociological or political, work.

Liebman's pastoral counsel came from a blend of psychoanalytic insight and the Jewish religious tradition. "I wrote 'Peace of Mind,'" he told an audience at the Woman's City Club in Boston, "to provide a kind of group-answer for many troubled minds and to show how this new science [psychoanalysis] and prophetic religion can become wonderful partners in a joint program of human health and happiness."[71] Psychoanalytic insights—which Liebman tellingly referred to as "revealed psychology" and "the sharpest tools that God has given men for the examination of the human mind"—formed the perfect complement to prophetic religion and together could provide "real help to perplexed moderns."[72] His chapter on grief, the book's most pastoral section, soon became its most talked-about as well. In the extensive advertising campaign promoting the book, images often showed it open to the first page of the grief chapter, and the

Reader's Digest excerpt featured this section extensively. The painful, unavoidable process of grieving was well understood by the mid-1940s thanks to modern psychology, Liebman thought, yet modern Americans still too often failed to experience grief in healthy ways. "The discoveries of psychiatry... remind us that the ancient teachers of Judaism often had an intuitive wisdom about human nature and its needs which our more sophisticated and liberal age has forgotten."[73] The Jewish practice of *shiva*, for example, with its careful ordering of time precisely for the expression of grief, had much to teach "liberal rabbis and liberal ministers alike," who "are continually committing psychological fallacies" in their desire to prevent awkward expressions of emotion. Such fear of basic human feeling revealed "the whole superficiality of modern civilization."[74]

In many instances throughout *Peace of Mind*, as in his chapter on grief, Liebman's advice took decidedly countercultural forms, as he used the discoveries of psychoanalysis to counter the prevailing assumptions of American liberalism.[75] Liebman's profound embrace of modern science marked him quite clearly as a religious liberal, and indeed *Peace of Mind* is replete with glowing passages about "the religion of the future" and other such tell-tale phrases. Yet as a Freudian and a Jew, Liebman also shared a deep skepticism about Western post-Enlightenment liberalism, especially the unblinking faith in rationalism he saw as the fatal flaw in Western culture. Such critiques resonated profoundly only a year after Hiroshima and the liberation of Auschwitz. "Modern liberal religion has shared the mood of the last several centuries—the mood of rationalism," he noted, and these reason-worshipping liberals have "built chilly meetinghouses upon the cold pillars of abstract reason."[76] The historian of psychology Nathan G. Hale Jr. notes that most Americans at midcentury—those who paid attention to Freudianism, anyway—downplayed Freud's emphasis on the darker side of human nature, but Liebman was not so quick to dismiss Freud's gloomier propositions.[77] "Man became half human while worshiping at the shrine of pure reason," he wrote. "The result was that the emotions were captured by perverts and tyrants."[78] Liebman's psychoanalytic insights here demonstrate, in dramatic fashion, the capacity of liberal religion for searching self-critique.

Despite its sharp criticisms of American culture, however, this book succeeded in large part because of Liebman's sensitivity to prevailing norms in American culture. Most obvious with regard to commercial success, *Peace of Mind* provided the kind of spiritual uplift and intellectual enrichment Americans had come to expect from religious middlebrow books. Like Fosdick and Jones, Liebman clearly understood his role as an intellectual tour guide, introducing his readers to the great thinkers, past and present, who had shaped his own psycho-spiritual development. He devoted numerous sermons and radio addresses to topics of intellectual and literary interest, speaking on WBZA radio about his "three favorite books of the year" and devoting sermons to the thought of Freud, Madame Curie, and John Dewey. In his sermon on his favorite books of 1945,

Liebman opened with a paean to the uplifting potential of reading: "The written page is the key by which we enter into many mansions—mansions of thought, of fantasy, of feeling.... It is the pen of the poet, of the novelist, the thinker that pushes back the confining walls of our daily routine—pushes them back until the room of our life becomes large and spacious, populated with interesting characters, challenging ideas, exotic scenes. Literature is the best interior decorator of all."[79] He brought this same sensibility to *Peace of Mind,* with obvious success. A bookseller from Nashville wrote to Liebman's publisher, Dick Simon of Simon and Schuster, praising the literary and intellectual merit of Liebman's work. "In nearly 25 years of bookselling I have at last encountered an 'inspirational' book that I am able to read," she wrote. "The flood of trash devoured under that name by the American public has always astounded and slightly disgusted me, although I have not been adverse to selling it—look how it made the cash register tinkle. This time your best seller will be a matter of pride—no need for a single inward blush."[80] This bookseller felt no need to blush because Liebman offered in *Peace of Mind* not just psychological and religious counsel, but encounters with Robert Frost and Thomas Mann, T. S. Eliot and Dante, John Dewey, Alfred North Whitehead, Lewis Mumford, and Bertrand Russell.

Yet central to Liebman's work, right alongside the psychoanalysts, prophets, philosophers, and poets, were those sunnier American giants who also reflected on matters of psyche and soul: Ralph Waldo Emerson and William James. Indeed for all the countercultural ambition of Liebman's critique of liberal rationalism, *Peace of Mind* nevertheless also exhibited a deep debt to the very American tradition of pragmatic and transcendental spirituality, foundational components of American liberalism. In his appropriation of Emerson and James, Liebman accomplished many things: he tempered the pessimism of unmitigated Freudianism, he spoke to the new reality of American global power and its attendant optimism, and he demonstrated that Jewish pastoral wisdom—which always remained central to this book—was also deeply and profoundly American.

Liebman's debt to American pragmatism was evident well before *Peace of Mind* appeared. In a March 1943 sermon broadcast from Temple Israel, called "How to Be Normal in Abnormal Times," Liebman turned to an American rather than a Viennese muse. William James, Liebman remarked, "taught himself to rise from sick-mindedness to healthy-mindedness.... This courageous liberal who suffered so profoundly himself and conquered his dark and wayward spirit can help us to take as the motto of our lives those words from the prophet Ezekiel, which he loved to quote, 'Son of man, stand upon thy feet and I will speak unto thee.'"[81] In *Peace of Mind* as well Liebman echoed James—"All men today need the healthy-mindedness of Judaism"[82]—and cited with great admiration the Seer of Concord's admonition to "give all to love ... nothing refuse."[83]

In ways even more profound than these occasional quotes from James and Emerson suggest, however, Liebman's *Peace of Mind* exhibits a Jamesian and

Emersonian ethos, including a pragmatic theology rooted in an expansive sense
of American possibilities. "I believe that the time is coming," Liebman rhapso-
dized, when "the age-old fears of want and poverty, illness and uselessness, will
be conquered by the collective conscience of democratic society."[84] Though Freud
and the Hebrew scriptures did indeed lead Liebman to acknowledge the inherent
evil in humanity, he nevertheless maintained that psychically and spiritually
healthy Americans, armed now with knowledge from the latest science and the
wisdom of the ages, would transform not only themselves but their own society
and indeed the whole of humanity. "The millions of Americans living far distant
from the scenes of carnage," he admonished, must "make the achievement of
moral resoluteness and courage in the presence of death a kind of ethical obligation—a determination to keep ourselves sane as the guarantors of the human
future."[85] Americans must find peace of mind not just for themselves, in other
words, but more critically as a kind of psychic and spiritual Marshall Plan for a
war-torn world.

On this foundation of postwar optimism and American exceptionalism
Liebman constructed a theological vision he grandiosely called "a new God idea
for America." America's new standing in the world required a new idea of God; as
Emerson had done in his day, Liebman called this new generation of Americans
to cast off the God of their parents and grandparents. "We must be brave enough
to declare that *every* culture must create its own God idea rather than rely on
outworn tradition."[86] And so, writing to an audience flush with victory, Liebman
saw in the power of American democracy a chance not only for a new world
order, but for a new divine order as well: "There is a chance here in America for
the creation of a new idea of God; a God reflected in the brave creations of self-re-
liant social pioneers; a religion based not upon surrender to submission, but on
a new birth of confidence in life and in the God of life."[87] Here, layered together
with Liebman's vigorous advocacy for the wisdom and healthfulness of Jewish
traditions, is an equally vigorous reinterpretation of the spiritual tradition of
American liberalism. At times the two strands run seamlessly together, and
Liebman in fact goes so far as to find in a Jamesian God and an Emersonian
democracy the very telos of Judaism itself. "God, according to Judaism, always
wanted His children to become His creative partners," he wrote, "but it is only in
this age, when democracy has at least a chance of triumphing around the globe,
that we human beings can grow truly aware of His eternal yearning for our
collaboration."[88]

In the years since *Peace of Mind* first appeared, scholars have often dismissed
it as yet another example of banal mind-cure philosophy, a claim tenable only to
those who have read no more of it than the title. Will Herberg certainly saw
Liebman's work in this light, declaring, "'Peace of mind' is today easily the most
popular gospel that goes under the name of religion," yet dismissing that
religion as "spiritual anodyne designed to allay the pains and vexations of

existence."[89] Andrew Heinze forcefully rebuts this line of criticism, emphasizing the surprisingly strident Jewish polemic that runs just beneath the surface of the text. As a commercially successful writer, Liebman surely understood the challenge of offering expert wisdom to a democratic readership. Though surely overheated at times, he challenged his readers with the latest scientific understanding of the human person while simultaneously empowering them to remake themselves, their society, and even their understanding of God. And as *Peace of Mind* soon demonstrated with its phenomenal commercial success— among Protestants and Catholics as well as Jews—Americans in the early postwar years were open to a spiritual engagement with another tradition of faith. Liebman's moral stature as a Jew in postwar America and his thoughtful presentation of a richly psychological spirituality allowed him both to critique and embrace American liberalism and to comfort his readers with peace of mind while simultaneously challenging them with the hard tasks of remaking themselves and their world.

Thomas Merton's *The Seven Storey Mountain* (1948): An Autobiography of Reading and Seeking

Thomas Merton's coming-of-age autobiography, *The Seven Storey Mountain*, first published in October 1948, is a very different book from Fosdick's and Liebman's inspirational bestsellers. Beyond the obvious and critical difference of genre, Merton's account of his youthful angst and eventual conversion revealed a deep alienation from Western modernity, whereas Fosdick and Liebman, though not without their criticisms, were fundamentally modern in sensibility and affirming of American life. Their embrace of psychology as a key aid to realizing spiritual maturity also rang hollow to Merton, who had once been enamored of Freud and Adler and Jung as a student at Cambridge, but finally rejected them completely. "Day after day I read Freud," Merton, the monk, recounted of his student days, "thinking myself to be very enlightened and scientific when, as a matter of fact, I was about as scientific as an old woman secretly poring over books about occultism, trying to tell her own fortune." This "psychoanalytical fortune-telling," he noted, "was to provide me with a kind of philosophy of life and even a sort of pseudo-religion," yet ultimately it was "nearly the end of me altogether."[90] Other Catholic writers of the period, most notably Bishop Fulton Sheen in his bestselling *Peace of Soul* (1949), shared Merton's disdain for modern psychology, especially psychoanalysis. (Catholic periodicals regularly "disapproved" of Liebman's *Peace of Mind* for similar reasons.)[91] And yet from the moment *The Seven Storey Mountain* first appeared, critics linked it with the other religious bestsellers of the decade, especially the works of Fosdick and Liebman, as evidence of the spiritual dynamism sparked by war.

Many Americans in the mid- and late 1940s in fact marveled at the resurgent popularity of inspirational books and at how this popularity crossed boundaries of tradition and genre. A newspaper reporter for a Boston paper asked both a prominent psychiatrist and a well-known preacher in 1949 to comment on the simultaneous mass appeal of Merton's *The Seven Storey Mountain*, Lloyd Douglas's novel *The Big Fisherman*, and Liebman's *Peace of Mind*. The psychiatrist, Gregory Zilboorg, stated flatly that the reason was simply a coincidence with no larger meaning; a number of good books just happened to appear at once. The preacher, however, himself a highly accomplished writer of religious middlebrow books, dug deeper. "There are two reasons," he replied. "First, a time of crisis raises the serious question about the meaning of life. People ask, what is your philosophy? People want a philosophy to put a meaning into the life ahead of them. Second, a time of crisis is a time of strain when people need an internal source of spiritual power that will give them what Liebman calls 'Peace of Mind.'"[92] To find meaning, to construct a philosophy, to nurture inner sources of spiritual power—for these reasons readers turned to Merton just as to Liebman. The preacher who understood this was none other than Harry Emerson Fosdick.

Merton's *The Seven Storey Mountain*, like Liebman's and Fosdick's bestsellers, became a fantastic commercial success because it offered coherence and hope, a trenchant critique of American shortcomings, and a personal story that was deeply American all the same. Though written from the often highly critical perspective of his new self—Father Louis, Trappist monk—Merton's story retained an overarching hopefulness, evident in the lyrical accounts of the joy he ultimately found in Catholic spiritual discipline. That it came from the pen of a Catholic—a monk nonetheless—and one offering a powerful critique, not just of American culture in general but of American Protestantism in particular, reveals all the more the cultural and religious ferment of the moment. For decades American liberal Protestant readers, through bestsellers and book week and book club offerings, had been told that mystical experience offered a bridge beyond sect or creed to the essence of the religious life. Now a Roman Catholic offered a joyful and liberating vision of the mystical life, and in the wake of war, with its horrors and sorrows and calls for unity, American readers, Protestants and Catholics, embraced it as they had the work of no Catholic writer before.

In his brief comments on *Peace of Mind* and *The Seven Storey Mountain*, Fosdick understood the critical role the war had played in shaping spirituality. Even more than sharing a broad cultural moment, however, these three bestsellers shared a common audience. In fact each book not only participated in this literary culture as a commodity, but also was a product of it. Fosdick and Liebman peppered their works with allusions and quotes that signaled their erudition. Much more fundamentally, however, Merton's autobiography revealed a life transformed by reading. His journey to devout Roman Catholic monasticism was a path very few of his readers would follow. But his account bore witness to a mystical awareness fueled by deep engagement with authors both living and dead. Indeed the remarkable power and commercial success of Merton's anticapitalist, frequently anti-American and anti-Protestant, world-renouncing, moralistic, long, dense, and highly literary account of a man's decision to become a monk resided precisely in his ability to evoke, with great poignancy and urgency, the despair and perseverance and ultimate triumph of a reader seeking spiritual fulfillment. The story of Merton, for all its potentially alienating differences, was the story of his own readers, striving for meaning and wholeness through their own encounters with books. By reading this account they too could participate both in his remarkable journey and in its dramatic resolution.

Merton's narrative deftly combines a deep dissatisfaction with American life, especially the emptiness of consumerism and popular culture, with a quintessentially American tale of the self-made man. He decried, at the very outset, "the spooky little prejudices that devour people who know nothing but automobiles and movies and what's in the ice-box and what's in the papers"—surely a rather pointed barb for his postwar audience, enjoying material abundance for the first time in two decades—and then recounted, in the first third of the book, his youthful fascination with precisely these things. Throughout the autobiography popular culture especially functions as a menacing seductive force. "My grandparents," he wrote, "were like most other Americans. They were Protestants, but you could never find out precisely what kind of Protestants they were." This was of no great consequence, however, because "the movies were really the family religion."[93] When the family lived in New York briefly in the 1920s, Merton's father, Owen, even played the piano at a small local movie theater, a role that Merton seemed to think nicely complemented his other musical outlet, as the organist at a nearby Episcopal church. Even years later, in college, the movies remained "a kind of hell" for Merton and his friends, who "were hypnotized by those yellow flickering lights." "The suffering of having to sit and look at such colossal stupidities," he added moralistically, "became so acute that we sometimes actually got physically sick."[94] Whether true or an instance of autobiographical embellishment, the notion of physical revulsion toward the movies clearly captured Merton's adult alienation from American cultural life.

Merton's youthful interests in literature and music faced the same condemnation from the adult Merton as his passion for the movies. He wrote of a childhood trip through Switzerland and France, noting, "By the time we reached Avignon, I had developed such a disgust for sightseeing that I would not leave the room to go and see the Palace of the Popes," which he later thought "probably the only really interesting thing we had struck in the whole miserable journey." Instead the young Merton "remained in the room and read *Tarzan of the Apes*."[95] Later still, in prep school at Oakham in England, Merton discovered jazz and the novels of Hemingway, Joyce, and D. H. Lawrence, but "I only discovered much later on" that aesthetic and moral modernism "were fused inseparably in a single order of taste."[96] Reading choices, for Merton, were moral choices, as reading had the power to shape one's mind and soul. Like nineteenth-century evangelicals and twentieth-century book club pioneers, Merton believed deeply in the power of reading and therefore in the moral imperative of right reading. Lacking the literary guidance available to his own readers, many of whom encountered *The Seven Storey Mountain* through one of the three book clubs that carried it, Merton as a young man read aimlessly and hedonistically and therefore lived, he thought, aimlessly and hedonistically.[97]

Merton's assessment of modern life, like his assessment of literary modernism, was a critique not simply of the mindlessness of popular culture, but of a much deeper and darker emptiness at the core of Western society. He portrayed European and American culture between the wars as fundamentally corrupt, and no one, he made clear, shared in that corruption more completely than he. He described his years at Oakham and then in college in the mid- and late 1930s at Cambridge University in England and Columbia University in New York as years of thoroughgoing immersion in modern intellectual, aesthetic, and moral currents, and therefore as spiritually deadening. These were the years of Freud and Adler and Jung, of Joyce and Lawrence, and of Marx. (Merton was briefly taken with communist teachings while at Columbia.) His narrative account of these years reveals the great inner turmoil he felt at the time and the conflicting pressures that shaped the retelling. His retelling turned not only on the vicissitudes of memory and emotion, but also on the didactic and evangelistic impulses that propelled him to write and the demands of his order, which exercised complete editorial control over the autobiography and which censored the most scandalous aspects of his previous life.

And Merton's early years did indeed contain scandal, scandal that ultimately became a source of deep guilt and shame. In addition to the drunken poetry jags and nights in smoky jazz clubs and flirtations with radical politics typical of an interwar bohemian, biographers have uncovered another facet of Merton's early life that, because of concerns from his Trappist superiors, he only obliquely referred to in *The Seven Storey Mountain:* while at Cambridge in the spring of 1934, when he was nineteen years old, one of the women he was seeing became pregnant.[98] That summer he left for New York. After receiving news of a poor showing on his exams, and in the wake of a hushed financial settlement with the young woman and her family, Merton decided to remain in New York and continue his education at Columbia, where he enrolled in January 1935. He never met his child and never had contact with the woman again.

In describing these years Merton the monk marshaled the full power of his newfound theological outlook to issue jeremiads against the social order, but even more to reflect on the grip of sin in his own life. Fosdick and Liebman were in many ways traditional moralists; Fosdick shared the adult Merton's disdain for popular culture, especially the movies, and Liebman shared his dark view of human nature, if not of the remedy for that darkness. But neither of these liberals articulated anything approaching the robust theology of corporate and individual sin that Merton related in his narrative. Just as neo-orthodox theologians such as Reinhold Niebuhr and popular evangelists such as Billy Graham were reviving the doctrine of original sin in Protestant circles as an antidote to liberalism's perceived inadequacies, Merton likewise preached to his postwar audience about the pervasiveness of evil. The autobiography in fact begins, in its very first lines, with a meditation on war, human nature, and sin: "On the last day of January 1915, under the sign of the Water Bearer, in a year of a great war... I came into the world. Free by nature, in the image of God, I was nevertheless the prisoner of my own violence and my own selfishness, in the image of the world into which I was born. That world was the picture of Hell, full of men like myself, loving God and yet hating Him; born to love Him, living instead in fear and hopeless self-contradictory hungers."[99] Merton returns to this theme of human depravity again and again. One of the great strengths of the book is his ability to capture his inner states at various points in his past. During his schooling in England, his years of movies and D. H. Lawrence and drinking and sex, Merton proclaimed, his "soul was simply dead. It was a blank, a nothingness. It was empty, it was a kind of spiritual vacuum.... The worst thing that ever happened to me was this consummation of my sins in abominable coldness and indifference."[100] For Merton, sin, meaning separation from God, always remained a central category of ordering and understanding both his own life and world affairs. In August 1939, with Europe on the brink of war, Merton thought, "I myself am responsible for this. My sins have done this. Hitler is not the only one who has started this war."[101] He saw himself as both creature and creator of a deeply fallen world, an outlook that gave the autobiography its occasionally heavy-handed sermonizing (and hubris), but also its searing honesty.

Merton ultimately found his liberation from sin in a spiritual conversion, first a conversion to the teachings and practices of Roman Catholicism, and soon thereafter to the contemplative life of the Cistercian Order of the Strict Observance, the Trappists. For all the foreignness of his tale, his European past and monastic Catholic future, Merton's path to this spiritual liberation, to the life of retreat he called "the four walls of my new freedom," was typically American.[102] He got saved by reading. Indeed despite the frequent and often apt comparisons critics made between Merton's autobiography and St. Augustine's *Confessions*, the central storyline of Merton's work is neither his focus on his own personal sinfulness nor the corruptions of Western culture, but on the power of reading—of earnest, anxious, probing reading—to lead one astray perhaps, but also to point one back to the true path. At every critical juncture along his journey, at each phase of his protracted and agonizing conversion, Merton read. From a childhood spent in study hall "with the others who did not go to Mass... reading the novels of Jules Verne or Rudyard Kipling" to his eventual discovery of romantic poetry, Eastern mystical literature, and Catholic philosophy, Merton just kept reading, until he read himself into conversion.[103]

His appetite for books and his habits of reading were formed early. His father had been a painter, his mother an intellectually demanding Quaker who trained her son to use reading as a means of self-improvement. His mother, Merton recalled, encountered the idea of progressive education in "one of those magazines" and "answered an advertisement that carried an oval portrait of some bearded scholar with pince-nez" from a company that offered books and school supplies. "The idea," he explained of this 1920s reading program, "was that the smart child was to be turned loose amid this apparatus, and allowed to develop spontaneously into a midget university before reaching the age of ten."[104] Merton the monk, steeped in the Catholic intellectual tradition, clearly valued the structure provided by church hierarchy and tradition, even approving of the imprimatur, though he recognized that it "is something that drives some people almost out of their minds with indignation."[105] But the adolescent and young man of *The Seven Storey Mountain* was not the monk of later years. The young Merton lived and read in a way remarkably in line with the idea of becoming a "midget university"—in the same way in fact, if perhaps a bit more intensely, as countless other Americans seeking meaning and inspiration through the marketplace of books.

The first critical encounter on Merton's path of reading was with the early nineteenth-century English prophetic and mystical poet William Blake, who, like Merton, was both a writer and a visual artist. "I think my love for William Blake had something in it of God's grace," Merton declared. "It is a love that has never died, and which has entered very deeply into the development of my life."[106] Merton was only sixteen when he discovered Blake, and later felt compelled to reassure his audience, and his superiors, that in extolling Blake he was not "recommending the study of William Blake to all minds as a perfect way to faith and to God" because, he readily admitted, "of all the almost infinite possibilities of error that underlie his weird and violent images."[107] Yet Merton nevertheless affirmed that Blake's "rebellion, for all its strange heterodoxies, was fundamentally the rebellion of the saints." Blake gave voice to Merton's sense of alienation from the modern world, both his unsatisfied inner longings and his deepening disgust with Western culture. Blake's longing for God, like the young Merton's, "was so intense and irresistible that it condemned, with all its might, all the hypocrisy and petty sensuality and skepticism and materialism which cold and trivial minds set up as unpassable barriers between God and the souls of men." Merton continued to live, for many years to come, this life of "petty sensuality and skepticism and materialism," yet he could later confidently declare, "The Providence of God was eventually to use Blake to awaken something of faith and love in my soul."[108] He eventually wrote his master's thesis at Columbia on Blake and, in the course of those studies, wrote, "As Blake worked himself into my system, I became more and more conscious of the necessity of a vital faith, and the total unreality of the dead, selfish rationalism which had been freezing my mind and will." Blake, for all his heterodoxy and eccentricity and abstruse mysticism, was the perfect spiritual guide for the restless, and similarly poetic and mystical, Merton. Once in the monastery, having found refuge in the dogma of the Church, Merton finally concluded, "I no longer need him. He has done his work for me: and he did it very thoroughly." But he still, even as a monk, refused to abandon his love for Blake, declaring, "I hope that I will see him in heaven."[109]

The Seven Storey Mountain expresses in many passages a vigorous, even zealous defense of Roman Catholic theology and ecclesiology, presented by an exuberant convert to pre–Vatican II teachings and practices. Nevertheless the Merton represented in this text still clearly prefigures the later Merton so famous for his dialogues with Buddhist contemplatives. Merton here, like the later Merton, was a restless seeker, a spiritual adventurer, and Blake was just the beginning. Soon thereafter came Dante—"The one great benefit I got out of Cambridge was this acquaintance with the lucid and powerful genius of the greatest Catholic poet," Merton wrote—and Etienne Gilson's *The Spirit of Medieval Philosophy*, a chance find in the window of Scribner's bookstore in New York. Gilson, a professor at the Sorbonne and a leading neo-Thomist historian and philosopher, was a serious scholar, and his works were promoted in religious middlebrow circles for their clarity of expression, recommended at times by the Religious Book Club, the Religious Book Week of the National Conference of Christians and Jews, and the Religious Books Round Table of the American Library Association. Though horrified at this stage in life to discover the imprimatur of the Church printed inside Gilson's work, Merton read anyway and "got out of its pages something that was to revolutionize my whole life": a new concept of God, "which showed me at once that the belief of Catholics was by no means the vague and rather superstitious hangover from an unscientific age."[110] Gilson's book, which Merton noted was one of the few he brought with him to the monastery, led to "a desire to go to church," but this desire soon faded, and Merton's quest continued for years afterward solely in the realm of books.[111] Indeed after Dante and Gilson, Merton turned not to other Catholic writers but to the mystical traditions of the East.

An Englishman, Aldous Huxley, first turned Merton toward the East, and an Indian, a man named Swami Bramachari, eventually steered him back, to the Catholic mystical writers. Merton first read Huxley's *Ends and Means* in November 1937 at the suggestion of his friend Bob Lax. As a teenager Merton had liked Huxley's fiction, and he was surprised to hear from Lax that Huxley now "was preaching mysticism" and that his mysticism, "far from being a mixture of dreams and magic and charlatanism, was very real and very serious." Just as Merton the monk felt compelled to apologize for the eclecticism and eccentricity of Blake, so too with Huxley he quickly averred that *Ends and Means* "was full, no doubt, of strange doctrines by reason of its very eclecticism"—the same kind of reservations expressed by the liberal Protestants who recommended this book as a December 1937 Religious Book Club selection.[112] But precisely this eclecticism, the fact that Huxley "had read widely and deeply and intelligently in all kinds of Christian and Oriental mystical literature," gave the book its potency for the liberal Protestants seekers of the 1930s and 1940s, for seekers like Eugene Exman, and for Merton the seeker as well. From Huxley, Merton learned about prayer and asceticism, that negation might "be freeing, a vindication of our real selves," and ultimately and most powerfully "of a supernatural, spiritual order, and the possibility of real, experimental contact with God." After reading Huxley, Merton ransacked the university library for books on Eastern mysticism, eventually reading "translations of hundreds of strange Oriental texts."[113]

While reading the mystical texts from the East, Merton befriended an actual Eastern mystic, a Hindu guru called Swami Bramachari who had come as a missionary to the United States, had earned a Ph.D. at the University of Chicago Divinity School, and was living with some of Merton's friends in New York. "We got along very well together," Merton wrote of Bramachari, "especially since he sensed that I was trying to feel my way into a settled religious conviction, and into some kind of a life that was centered, as his was, on God."[114] Bramachari shared Merton's growing revolt against "the noise and violence of American city life and all the obvious lunacies like radio-programs and billboard advertising" but never railed directly against these things or preached directly to Merton of his beliefs. Rather what impressed Merton was the guru's life of disciplined contemplative prayer and rigorous asceticism. *Ends and Means* had turned Merton to the Eastern mystics with the conviction that "Christianity was a less pure religion," but Bramachari, aware of Merton's inner turmoil and fascination with contemplative practices, finally told Merton pointedly, "There are many beautiful mystical books written by Christians. You should read St. Augustine's *Confessions*, and *The Imitation of Christ*."[115] Before long, as Merton recounted, he "added, as Bramachari had suggested, *The Imitation of Christ* to my books, and it was from there that I was eventually to be driven out by an almost physical push, to go and look for a priest."[116]

Merton's path to conversion, and from conversion to baptism, first Mass, sense of vocation for the priesthood, and ultimately the call to monastic life, unfolded with many more fits and starts. Jacques Maritain's *Art and Scholasticism*, a book, like those of Gilson and Huxley, heavily promoted by the book clubs and book weeks, proved critical as well, introducing Merton to the beauty and rigor of medieval scholastic thought. (Merton even mentions meeting Maritain at a Catholic Book Club event.)[117] After his first Mass his "reading became more and more Catholic," including a period of great interest in the poet Gerard Manley Hopkins, and after each meeting with a priest to discuss his conversion he would leave armed with even more books to read.[118] Merton, especially in these intense and spiritually fraught months before his entry into the monastery, was the near-perfect embodiment of the spiritual striving through reading that characterized the religious middlebrow culture of the day. Fosdick and Liebman had each revealed the fruits of their reading—reading born of personal struggle as well—in their own inspirational bestsellers. Merton likewise, through his autobiography, sought to educate and inspire his readers with his own story of a life transformed by reading.

Merton eventually decided to follow the path of mystical asceticism himself because of a final realization prompted by his reading. The insight was that "the conversion of the intellect is not enough." "Because of the profound and complete conversion of my intellect, I thought I was entirely converted," he confessed of the time just before choosing to enter the priesthood. "Because I believed in God, and in the teachings of the Church, and was prepared to sit up all night arguing about them with all comers, I imagined that I was even a zealous Christian."[119] But he finally came to see that he needed to mold his will, and not just his mind, to the will of God, and he determined that a life of monastic contemplation, disciplined by the rituals of the Church and nourished by its sacraments, would allow him the intimate rapport with the divine and the liberation from the burdens of his sinful self that he so ardently sought (Figure 6.3). He entered Gethsemani Abbey in Kentucky in December 1941.

Merton's story—an immigrant's story, a seeker's story, a reader's story—was fundamentally a very American story, a story of rebirth as a new man in the new world. His sharp critique of both Western civilization and human nature resonated with readers dispirited by the horrors of the war and bewildered at the material and cultural transformations of its aftermath. At Gethsemani he freed himself from the consumer striving and middle-class diversions that to many epitomized American life but that to him provided no peace. "I had managed to get myself free from all the habits and luxuries that people in the world think they need for their comfort and amusement," he wrote about his arrival in the monastery. "My mouth was at last clean of the yellow, parching salt of nicotine, and I had rinsed my eyes of the grey slop of movies so that now my taste and my vision were clean."[120] He had arrived, had found peace of mind and peace with God. But his tale resonated more for the journey than the destination. Merton relished the certainty the Church provided, but his continuing appeal for readers was that certainty for him did not mean the end of seeking. In later years he became one of the most influential figures in the dialogue between Zen Buddhist and Christian contemplatives that bore such fruit in the 1950s and 1960s, serving as an eloquent interpreter especially of the writings of D. T. Suzuki for American readers.[121] Merton died in 1968 in Thailand, having traveled to Asia to meet with the Dalai Lama and study Buddhist contemplative practices.

Figure 6.3 Thomas Merton's ordination, May 26, 1949, Abbey of Gethsemani. Photographer unknown. Used with permission of the Merton Legacy Trust and the Thomas Merton Center at Bellarmine University.

Reading the Readers of Fosdick, Liebman, and Merton

The 1940s bestsellers of Fosdick, Liebman, and Merton arrived during a critical moment in the history of American spirituality. Appearing after more than two decades of intensive marketing campaigns designed to encourage and shape religious reading habits, these books reflected the pervasiveness of religious middlebrow practices both in their own commercial success and in the representations of reading and seeking that constituted central themes of the books themselves. The war, of course, most particularly shaped the cultural moment in which these books arrived and to which they responded. The war simultaneously furthered the already strong culture of religious middlebrow reading and pointed that reading in significant new directions. In this way, in addition to serving as capstones to long-standing trends in religious middlebrow culture, the 1940s bestsellers of Fosdick, Liebman, and Merton also serve as harbingers of changes to come. For the first time, in the years after the war ordinary Americans looking for spiritual enlightenment in mass-market books turned, not reluctantly but eagerly, to authors from other traditions of faith.

Although the readership of these bestsellers was wide, it was nevertheless structured in significant ways by the social realities of American life, especially by race, class, and gender. The parameters of race and class are difficult to pin down, though the venues in which they were marketed and sold very likely limited the awareness, availability, and appeal of these books largely to the white middle class. The ways gender defined the reception of these texts, however, is more ambiguous, and possibly more significant. Attitudes about reading, especially religious reading, and notions of character and personality in American culture from the nineteenth century though the mid-twentieth century each carried powerful gendered valences. Women were the presumed audience for much of the literature of evangelical piety in the nineteenth century, a notion the liberal Protestant promoters of religious reading in the 1920s sought to overcome with their marketing blitzes that associated modern faith with masculinity. Nevertheless the historian Richard Fox observes that the "twentieth-century cultivation of personality," so critical to the formation and reception of each of these texts, "may finally have given women—generally excluded from the nineteenth-century quest for character—a means of pursuing a characterlike standard of social excellence."[122] The social democracy of the print culture marketplace, though bounded by race and class, and the spiritual turn toward the psychological and mystical may have ultimately proven liberating for women, so often excluded from the structures of power in institutional religion.[123]

Overall, circumstantial evidence indicates that more women than men read these books, though not overwhelmingly more. Most of the letters in the Liebman archive, for example, are from women, and while this hardly represents a scientific survey, it does provide one clue into the gender composition of his readership. Andrew Heinze likewise speculates that Liebman's book reached a largely female audience in part because "it spoke to a more 'feminine' interest in the psyche for its own sake" rather than preach a turn to inner power for material gain. One thinks, in contrast, of the popular positive thinkers Napoleon Hill and Norman Vincent Peale, each of whom applied his theories to success in the male-dominated business world.[124] Heinze's notion of the feminine draws on prevailing cultural notions, dating at least to the nineteenth century, which coded any deep examination of the inner life, whether emotional or spiritual, as feminine. Heinze also notes that Liebman's thoughtful and sensitive treatment of the subject of grief undoubtedly appealed to the women whose sons and fathers, husbands and lovers, had been lost in the war. Tellingly both the *Look* article and the *Reader's Digest* condensation of *Peace of Mind* chose to focus on Liebman's discussion of grief. The feature stories on him in women's magazines such as *Cosmopolitan* and *Ladies' Home Journal* further attest to the likelihood of a predominantly female readership.

Journalists and editors may have seen grieving as the emotional work of women in the year after the war's conclusion, but three years earlier, still in the midst of war, Fosdick's book entered a more ambiguously gendered cultural context. The Council on Books in Wartime chose *On Being a Real Person* for an Armed Services Edition. Thousands of copies were mailed to servicemen throughout the fall of 1943, straining limited resources, and the book was among those special editions selected for distribution to the men waiting to cross the English Channel into France on D-Day.[125] Demand, both military and civilian, remained so high that Fosdick's editor, Eugene Exman of Harper's, wrote repeatedly to the War Production Board to request increases in the book's paper allotment. Additional paper was warranted, Exman claimed, because the book was "speaking to the spiritual, mental, and morale needs of the American people."[126] In a later letter Exman further pleaded, "We respectfully request additional paper so that we may not be forced to curtail sales of Dr. Fosdick's book which is doing so much to add spiritual strength to people's lives today."[127] The War Production Board denied the request, and despite Harper's efforts at printing the book on lighter stock, ultimately the paper rationing necessitated reduced production. Some reviewers of Fosdick's book understood these wartime pressures and associated its call for "real personhood" with the wartime struggle against Nazism; these reviewers therefore gave the book a masculine spin. The review in the Champaign, Illinois, *News-Gazette,* for example, which appeared on Easter Sunday 1943, a day "when we pause to evaluate our religious—even our patriotic—faith," argued, "High on your reading list, if you would become a real person, a real American, [should be] Fosdick's 'On Being a Real Person.' "[128]

Men in the service were among the throngs who deluged Fosdick with correspondence. One soldier wrote in 1949, "On Being a Real Person was the set of ideas about religion and God that made sense to my somewhat skeptical mind. It was the key inspiration...the foundation that began a complete reorientation of my value system...and my life....I carried it for 22 months in the Pacific Theater of Operations. I'm certain that I've read it 15 times through while I was in the army."[129] Another wrote of reading the book in an internment camp in the Philippines.[130] A third, Capt. William Graber, wrote directly from the Pacific in November 1944: "After 1500 miles in the air our C-47 dropped in on Henderson Field, Guadalcanal. While having a quick cup of coffee at the Red Cross hut there on a reading table was a copy of *On Being a Real Person.* 'Stolen sweets are sweetest.' That's what I did. Now for the first time in ages a crime was committed and I'm not sorry. After that for another 1500 miles at an altitude of over 10,000 feet your book was greatly enjoyed."[131]

Yet this appeal to patriotic machismo does not by any means tell the whole story of Fosdick's readership. Women too served in World War II, and many encountered Fosdick's book in the military as well. A private, Janet Royce, from the Second Signal Company of Virginia, wrote Fosdick, "The book is making the rounds of the barracks and in our next all night session it will probably be torn to pieces and chewed back and forth between us."[132] Many more readers, of course, encountered the book as civilians than as military personnel, and it seems that, as with Liebman, the majority of Fosdick's stateside readers were women on the home front, who almost certainly turned to Fosdick's book for the same reasons they would read Liebman's a few years later. Fosdick, as noted earlier, had been a pioneer in the field of pastoral counseling, and in the introduction to On Being he wrote of his book's intended audience: "I have pictured its readers in terms of the many, diverse individuals who have come to me for help."[133] The Fosdick archive contains records of many hundreds of such counseling sessions, and from this evidence it seems the majority were white, middle-class women.

The marketing of the book provides further clues about its readership. It was excerpted in women's magazines such as Yours and advertised in venues likely to attract the notice of middle-class women. Marshall Field's, the large downtown Chicago department store, for example, took out a full-page advertisement in the Chicago Tribune to promote its sale of On Being a Real Person. "Out of his 20 years' experience as a personal counselor," the text of the ad ran, "Dr. Fosdick now writes to all those who need inner security in these trying times. Out of all he has learned…he has chosen the most important things to set down for you."[134] Alongside shoes for the kids and a tie for the husband, the ad seems to imply, you should come and get inner security for you. The likelihood of a female majority in both Fosdick's and Liebman's readership takes on added significance when one considers the central role that women, and feminism, played in the spiritual transformations of later decades. At a time when men dominated the leadership of church and synagogue, religious middlebrow reading—both the medium and the message—freed women to construct their own worlds of meaning from the raw materials provided by mass-market books.

At least as important as who read Fosdick's and Liebman's books are the questions of why readers turned to these books and how they read them. Each of these books was marketed heavily through the book clubs and book weeks that constituted the central organizational apparatus of religious middlebrow culture, and this provides the first set of clues. Fosdick, a long-term member of the editorial committee of the Religious Book Club, saw many of his titles appear as book club recommendations over the years, and On Being a Real Person too made the cut as an alternate selection in March 1943. "A graceful and persuasive style of writing," the committee noted of this book from one of its own, "will give the book a wide appeal to many who are not reached by ordinary preaching."[135] In addition to this designation and the book's selection for publication in an Armed Services Edition, *On Being a Real Person* was also a featured title in the National Conference of Christians and Jews' 1944 Religious Book Week campaign, recommended for its "expert guidance concerning the psychological and spiritual processes by which a well-organized life is achieved."[136]

The war, of course, shaped the actual reading practices of Fosdick's audience. As a perceptive reviewer noted, "The terrible pressures of the times are such that great numbers of people who have not manifested any interest in religion previously are now turning to spiritual sources for help in the time of their trouble." The anonymous reviewer noted, however, that "turning to religion does not mean, necessarily, a turning to Church," especially in a culture saturated with print. "Indeed, hundreds of thousands of people are reading religious books who will never darken the door of any house of worship."[137] Again, though, the servicemen and women who wrote to Fosdick offer the best direct testimony of religious middlebrow reading practices. In addition to the soldier who read *On Being* fifteen times and the private in the signal company who commented that her buddies would tear the book to pieces in an "all-night session," another Fosdick writer, a veteran recovering in a Miami hospital, wrote on Red Cross stationery, "[I am] now days deep in your book. The main fault with you is that it is too full of wisdom. I have read each chapter twice and then I am afraid I am missing something. Often I wonder why I hadn't thought of it before. What I like best about it is that it is all down right horse sense!"[138] This rereading of a book that is both "horse sense" and "too full of wisdom" perfectly describes a reader hoping to glean life lessons from a book that bridges the high and the low.

Rabbi Liebman's bestseller, like Fosdick's, was sold and marketed through the mechanisms of middlebrow culture. The Religious Book Club featured *Peace of Mind* as its main selection for May 1946, lavishly praising this title from "one of the most vigorous younger rabbis in America." Neither bland moralistic preaching nor technical treatise, Liebman's book, the editors proclaimed, "is a joining of hands, as it were, of the sanctuary and the laboratory. In style and manner, moreover, the treatment is so luminous that the reader is enabled to diagnose his own situation and to gain positive clues for dealing with it." The reviewers praised Liebman's discussions of love, fear, grief, and guilt, though they noted the potentially controversial nature of his account of sin for a Protestant audience. "His point of view," the review stated, "is always that of the 'once born'— not that of the 'twice born'—to use William James' famous classification."[139] *Peace of Mind* remained on the minds of the Religious Book Club editors in subsequent years. In their review of Swami Akhilananda's *Mental Health and Hindu Psychology*, an August 1952 alternate selection, the editorial committee noted, "What Rabbi Joshua Liebmann [sic] did for Liberal Protestantism ... this writer has tried to do for Hinduism."[140] *Peace of Mind* also appeared on the roster of Religious Book Week titles chosen for 1948, in a special subsection of the

Jewish list, called "Books of Lasting Value," introduced for the final year of the campaign.

The letters to Rabbi Liebman confirm the habits of religious middlebrow reading suggested by such marketing. The middle-aged high school teacher who wrote Liebman of her love for a student noted elsewhere in her letter, "I have read all of your book twice, and some parts of it several times. I found much help in it," but then added, "although some of it is too deep for me to understand."[141] Her relationship to the text—reading and rereading, probing despite its being "too deep"—sounds much like the veteran in Miami who read and reread Fosdick's book. An eighteen-year-old boy, a gentile, wrote to Liebman of his "searching, although rather confusedly, for some truths" as he found himself dangling "between utter confusion and complete and barren atheism." Liebman wrote in reply, rather optimistically, that the boy's confusion "will be straightened out by continued reading" and therefore not to lose hope.[142] Liebman's book was even reviewed in the San Quentin News, a newspaper written by the inmates of the notorious California prison, prompting the warden to write Liebman to see if inexpensive damaged copies could be secured for the "many, many" prisoners now requesting the book.[143]

"My husband works 18 hrs a day," wrote a woman named Lillian after reading Peace of Mind. With only four years of education, married at age twenty, now a housewife and mother, she confided to Rabbi Liebman, "Therefore, I am a very lonely woman, and since I have 2 children and have to do my own babysitting, I have resorted to reading. Dear Rabbi, words just couldn't express what reading has done for me. It has given me insight into the world around me." Contrary to stereotype, she then adds, "Of late it seems fiction doesn't seem to interest me. I can benefit from non-fiction so much more."[144] The word choices here, "resort to reading" and "benefit from non-fiction," testify to the potency of the religious middlebrow endeavor. Not reading for pleasure or escape, those motivations that Trysh Travis, Janice Radway, and other historians of reading tell us were so often considered the feminine manifestations of middlebrow uplift, this woman turns to Liebman's guidance for hard-earned spiritual and intellectual betterment.

Lillian's plight as a "lonely woman" trapped with small children perfectly mirrors the "problem that has no name" so famously described by Betty Friedan more than a decade later in The Feminine Mystique. Though Lillian was less well educated than Friedan's Smith College classmates, many of the other readers of postwar religious bestsellers were very likely college-educated women seeking to understand how to cope with the stifling demands of wartime, and later cold war, family life. As the nation shifted from fighting fascism to fighting communism, Congress passed the National Mental Health Act, which established in 1946 the National Institute of Mental Health in recognition of the need for a psychologically healthy population to win the long struggle to come. In this battle the family itself was on the front lines. Popular movies such as *The Snake Pit* (1948), the increasingly therapeutic-minded women's magazines, and even socially conservative authors such as Marynia Farnham all acknowledged the strains of cold war family life on American women.[145]

Though Friedan's assessment of postwar gender relations has become a commonplace, in the 1940s and 1950s, as the historian Elaine Tyler May notes, "critical observers of middle-class life considered homemakers to be emancipated and men to be oppressed."[146] Women such as those who wrote to Liebman and Fosdick were hard-pressed to find public advocates, especially among religious writers. By the mid-1950s a few women's voices, such as Anne Morrow Lindbergh's and Catherine Marshall's, were heard.[147] In a more elite cultural vein, Georgia Harkness published commercially successful books on prayer in the late 1940s.[148] Yet in spite of these few women writers, men dominated public religion—institutional leadership, broadcast media, and print—in 1940s and 1950s America as perhaps never before or since, producing a generation of what the historian Martin Marty has called "seething women." Their letters, written out of this silent suffering to distant, male authors, reveal layers of the social history of American religion obscured by polemics from critics like Will Herberg.

Indeed the Fosdick and Liebman reader letters, ripe with phrases such as "resort to reading" and "benefiting from non-fiction," demonstrate a complex interplay of reading practice and spirituality. More than anything, these readers' accounts indicate the practical utility of reading as a spiritual act and the felt need for religion itself to solve real-world problems. A member of the Riverside congregation who had served in the European theater wrote to Fosdick in August 1945, "I feel that one constructive result of the war will be a realization of the need for 'faith in belief' since we have put religion to work, and found that it worked!"[149] The missionary who wrote of reading *On Being* in an internment camp in the Philippines noted, "Even there I kept insisting that life in a camp is also life and an opportunity. What use would religion be if it could not help us in a situation like that?"[150] These voices echo the lonely housewife and the sexually conflicted schoolteacher who turned to Liebman's *Peace of Mind* for specific help.

Of course, Liebman's and Fosdick's books were how-to guides, and so an instrumental take on spirituality made sense for their readers. The readership of Merton's autobiography therefore provides an instructive comparison. While Merton's personal example in 1948 was as an apparently world-renouncing cloistered monk, his appeal for his readers was the same as Liebman's and Fosdick's: the book offered a faith of personal and social utility in everyday life. The October 11, 1948, issue of *Time* magazine carried a short article in the "Religion" section with the intriguing title "Mystics among Us" that profiled Merton, declaring, "The world still has millions of mystics, and the most mystical human beings are often among the most practical as well."[151] Bishop Fulton Sheen, in his comments about *The Seven Storey Mountain*, repeated the often-heard comparison of Merton's autobiography to St. Augustine's *Confessions*, but the British novelist Graham Greene, in his dust-jacket blurb, more closely captured the essence of Merton's tale. Greene indicated that Merton's book might inspire readers to follow Rufus Jones's book-reading advice from the 1920s: "*The Seven Storey Mountain* is a book one reads with a pencil so as to make it one's own." One can hardly conjure a better image of the middlebrow reader.

Indeed this long, dense, and demanding book achieved its success precisely because readers embraced it through the practices and expectations of middlebrow reading culture. "From the sedate lending libraries of New England to the bustling women's clubs of the West Coast," reported *Time* magazine in April 1949, "people are reading and talking about Poet Merton's sensitive, unhappy groping through the litter of modern civilization to find peace at last." Merton's account even generated the occasional conversion to Catholic monasticism, according to a *Life* magazine feature on the Trappists in America that appeared in response to his book. "Since the last war," *Life* reported, "the Trappists have gained young veterans who turned to them for the peace and quiet they thought they would find at a monastery. There are now 12 veterans of World War II at the Utah monastery alone."[152] The vast majority of readers, of course, did not seek to emulate Merton's path of retreat, but rather strove to learn from his story how to gain some measure of peace in their own very worldly lives.

Evidence from a range of sources indicates that Merton's book was read in these middlebrow ways not just by Catholics, but also by many others seeking their own paths to intimacy with God. Promotional material from Harcourt, Brace, the book's publisher, described it as an "autobiography that transcends all creeds"—certainly a sales pitch as much as a statement of fact—but Clifton Fadiman, an author, radio personality, and leading figure in middlebrow culture with no vested interest, declared, "It should hold the attention of Catholic and non-Catholic alike."[153] Reports from booksellers around the country showed that Merton's audience generally reflected regional variation. In heavily Catholic Boston, for example, booksellers estimated that 85 percent of buyers were Catholic, while in Atlanta, at least according to the manager of the book department in Rich's department store, more Protestants and Jews were buying the book than were Catholics. "Protestants and Catholics, businessmen and housewives," summed up the report *Time*, "in 26 weeks since its publication, have zoomed the *Mountain*'s sales."[154]

As *The Seven Storey Mountain* zoomed in sales, many of these readers took their pencils and wrote directly to Merton. Merton was so inundated with mail from readers, in fact, that, as he joked to a friend, "I have a secretary who mails out the 'Trappist-no-write-letters' card to the fans."[155] (Merton did, of course, maintain a lively correspondence with friends and colleagues.) Sadly, few of these fan letters remain, but Merton revealed much about who they were and how and why they read his book in letters to friends and colleagues. He confided to a friend, Sister Therese Lentfoehr, "Letters come in from everywhere, Park Avenue and San Quentin Prison, the sanctuary and the studio."[156] But he wrote elsewhere, "More of them are usually sensible married women who want to find out how you can lead the contemplative life and take care of the children at the same time."[157] This was the practical faith that Fosdick and Liebman had each advocated and that Merton's readers, those "sensible married women," evidently sought as well.

*   *   *

The surge in religious reading during World War II came after a quarter century of sustained promotional efforts, culminating in the reading campaigns of the Council on Books in Wartime and the National Conference of Christians and Jews. In the midst of these campaigns Harry Emerson Fosdick, Thomas Merton, and Joshua Loth Liebman—one Protestant, one Catholic, one Jew—produced widely successful texts, each read by large numbers of readers from other faiths. The commercial appeal of these texts, and the testimony of their readers, reveal the wide cultural embrace of psychological, mystical, and cosmopolitan forms of spirituality, a cultural development rooted in liberal Protestantism but expanding beyond. Conservative critics such as Will Herberg, of course, looked on in despair at this rapid cultural change. But his despair stemmed not only from a conservative's lament about the rise of liberal religion. More fundamentally, in *Protestant-Catholic-Jew* he presented an updated version of well-practiced Marxist critiques of bourgeois culture, now articulated as a failure of theological rather than radical political orthodoxy. It was the middlebrowing of religion as much as its liberalizing that so disturbed Herberg.

Certainly postwar America offered easy targets for one aiming to knock the middle class, especially the suburban revival in church life then under way. Examples of the kitschy, commercial, and simplistic abounded. Herberg's triple-melting-pot thesis—that "America today may be conceived...as one great community divided into three big sub-communities religiously defined, all equally American in their identification with the 'American Way of Life'"—was not borne out by subsequent history, as ethnic identity gained new salience among white Americans in the 1960s and 1970s.[158] But his observation that the "faith in faith" (rather than faith in God) of positive thinkers like Norman Vincent Peale functioned "to sustain the civic religion of 'laissez-faire capitalism'" certainly hit the mark.[159] Inasmuch as the letters to Fosdick, Liebman, and Merton reveal shared, pragmatic concerns for the everyday utility of spirituality while indicating very little interest in official theology or creeds, Herberg's fears about the lack (if not decline) of orthodoxy seem at least partially realized in the responses to these texts.

And yet even the case of Norman Vincent Peale, whose 1952 sensation *The Power of Positive Thinking* became the yardstick of mindlessness against which all subsequent inspirational literature was to be measured, reveals the way theological, cultural, and political concerns—about high versus low culture or orthodox versus heterodox theology—obscure the richer, more complex dimensions of popular religion and spirituality brewing among the postwar middle class.[160] Again readers tell their story best. "I have not read over 10 books in my entire life time," wrote a man from Missouri to Peale after reading *The Power of Positive Thinking*, "and I thank God that this was one of them. I intend to read it again and again until I get the full meaning. I needed this book desperately as I have wondered how and when I would ever find God."[161] Like Fosdick, Liebman, and Merton, Peale received thousands of letters like this, of faith, doubt, grief, temptation, loss, fear, love, and hope. "Dear Dr. Peale," another letter begins, from a woman in small-town Indiana in 1953. "For some time I have wanted to write to you and tell you how much your books have helped me. Without them and some other literature on the same order, I sometimes wonder how I would have gotten through the past two years."[162] She told Peale of her husband's death, her struggle to care for three children under the age of seven, all while juggling her own college education and the care of a grandmother. Still other writers reveal the increasingly eclectic nature of American spirituality in the postwar years. Peale received letters from Jews, as Liebman did from Christians, reflecting the emergence of a thriving popular cosmopolitanism in postwar religion. A writer from Los Angeles moved even farther afield. This letter writer recommended to Peale the popular *Autobiography of a Yogi* by Swami Paramhansa Yogananda, since its discussion of spirit visitation, the writer noted, closely paralleled Peale's own published account of a visitation from his deceased mother.[163]

These brief examples indicate once again the importance of reading as a middle-class religious practice in midcentury America and the slippery relationship between a text and the meaning readers make from that text. They also demonstrate how that reading, located in a consumer marketplace, facilitated religious boundary crossing. For Herberg, boundary crossing meant only a loss of theological and liturgical specificity. Protestantism, Catholicism, and Judaism, he contended, "have all tended to become 'Americanized' under the pervasive influence of the American environment."[164] Yet Liebman and Merton, each in his own way, were fiercely partisan, often criticizing Protestant religious culture, including core historic teachings. In his chapter in *Peace of Mind* on conscience, for example, Liebman criticized Paul, Augustine, Luther, and Calvin as unhealthily obsessed with human beings' natural wickedness—and with repression and atonement as responses—rather than advocating a more psychologically sound focus on growth. This was precisely the matter that gave the reviewers from the Religious Book Club, in an otherwise glowing recommendation, the most pause. In numerous instances throughout the book, in fact, such as in his reference to sitting *shiva* in his chapter on grief, Liebman used Jewish practices and teachings as the basis for a healthier approach to life than that offered by American Protestantism.[165] "Liebman thrilled to the idea that Judaism's insights into human nature matched those of dynamic psychology," writes Andrew Heinze. "That idea fueled the Jewish polemic in *Peace of Mind*."[166]

Merton likewise was not shy in his attacks on the prevailing values of Protestant America, a sharp contrast with many of his Catholic contemporaries who sought to downplay Catholic distinctiveness in an effort to further the social standing of Catholic Americans.[167] In a passage on virtue, for example, that echoes Liebman's on conscience, Merton declared that the term's enduring currency in Catholic countries "is a testimony to the fact that it suffered [in the United States and Protestant Europe] mostly from the mangling it underwent at the hands of Calvinists and Puritans."[168] Rising goodwill between faiths certainly contributed to the commercial success of *Peace of Mind* and *The Seven Storey Mountain*, but these were not thoroughly ecumenical books. Liebman and Merton shared with Fosdick a deep, modern distrust of traditional Protestant notions of sin, self, and emotional well-being. These books succeeded precisely because many Americans were eager, as Elisha Atkins noted, for "new and spiritually creative paths to the vital problems of life"—paths that emerged from psychological science, from mystical spirituality, and from other traditions of faith. For Herberg and many critics since, these changes indicated a regrettable secularization.

American mass culture did indeed bring changes to American religious life, but those changes are not best understood as secularization or decline. Religious middlebrow culture introduced millions of Americans to ways of understanding the self that blended modern psychology, mysticism, and interfaith religious exploration. The Judeo-Christian concept—and the broader culture of popular cosmopolitanism that emerged from it—gained widespread acceptance because of its ethical and spiritual vitality in addition to its political utility. Rather than an evisceration of faith, what Herberg called "the inner disintegration and enfeeblement of the historic religions," the emerging spirituality fostered by mass-marketed books marked the culmination of decades of liberal religious efforts to craft forms of spirituality adequate to meet the challenges of modern life.[169] Liberal religious culture moved first toward greater psychological sophistication beginning in the 1920s and accelerating after the war, then broadened even further in the second half of the century toward ever-greater openness to other traditions of faith. The increasingly central role of books as commodities in American religious life, and of the mystical and psychological spirituality advanced in so many of those books, facilitated genuine spiritual exchange among Protestants, Catholics, and Jews. These trends only continued in subsequent decades as psychological and mystical cosmopolitanism soon reached beyond the religions of the West to include Buddhist, Hindu, and other religious traditions. What critics have bemoaned as decline instead constituted a rising force in American religious life.

Conclusion

"This week a new and to me marvelous experience has come out of my loneliness," wrote the American missionary Frank Laubach to his father in the spring of 1930.[1] For months Laubach had been undergoing a spiritual upheaval, a process of heightened mystical awareness he called his "reconversion." "I am trying to be utterly free from everybody, free from my own self, but completely enslaved to the will of God," he explained.[2] When the spirit moved most powerfully, he wrote, "it was as though some deep artesian well had been struck in my soul and strength came forth."[3] Laubach recorded his experiences in long, gushing letters, often many each week, in which he told of despair and emptiness but also of new attentiveness to God's presence. "This afternoon," he recounted in a typical passage, "the possession of God has caught me up with such sheer joy that I thought I never had known anything like it. God was so close and so amazingly lovely that I felt like melting all over with a strange blissful contentment. . . . After an hour of close friendship with God my soul feels clean, as new fallen snow."[4] Laubach's father arranged the publication of these letters in their hometown newspaper, the Benton, Pennsylvania, *Argus*, and in 1937 they were edited and republished as *Letters by a Modern Mystic*. This slim volume has been regularly reprinted ever since, a minor classic of twentieth-century devotional literature.

Laubach's awakening arose out of deep despondency—he had come to regard his evangelization efforts a failure—but fifteen years earlier he had arrived in the Philippines full of hope. His path to the mission field typified the ambition of many liberal Protestants of his generation, abounding with optimism and self-assurance and riding the crest of America's new global power. Born in 1884 to devout Baptist parents, Laubach made a public confession of faith in the local Methodist church at age ten.[5] After college at Princeton he engaged in settlement house work in New York for two years before returning to school, studying first theology at Union Theological Seminary, and then sociology at Columbia, from which he received a Ph.D. in 1915. His doctoral research, a study of one hundred homeless men in New York published in 1916 as *Why There Are Vagrants*, blended Social Gospel ethics and social scientific analysis in a study of impressive gravity.[6] From New York he briefly ventured to the Bahamas, where he pastored a

Presbyterian church, before being commissioned in 1915 as a Congregational
missionary to the Islamic Moro people of the Philippines. During these years of
higher education, frequent denomination shifting, and Progressive social
reform, Laubach exchanged the fundamentalism of his father for a liberal theology more suited to a man of his training. He still burned with the evangelical
desire to bring Christianity to the far corners of the world, now only amplified
by the intellectual and imperial swagger of pre–Great War liberalism.

By 1930, however, the swagger was gone, and Laubach, like American
Protestantism itself, was in crisis. His efforts to teach the local people to read
had met with some success, but his religious message had fallen flat. This
failure, and the ensuing crisis of faith and purpose and identity, turned him
first to praying and ultimately to the insight that changed his life. "You feel
superior to them because you are white," he later recalled realizing, and
because he was American and Christian and educated too.[7] This sense of
superiority had ruined his missionary enterprise, he now felt, and only a
complete spiritual reorientation offered a path out of this moral morass. He
read furiously in the classics of Christian contemplative literature, but even
more radically asked a local religious leader if together they could study the
Qur'an. A letter home soon after this breakthrough shared the startling news:
"Mohammed is helping me," he told his father. "I have no more intention of
giving up Christianity and becoming a Mohammedan than I had twenty years
ago, but I find myself richer for the Islamic experience of God. Islam stresses
the *will* of God. . . . Submission is the first and last duty of man. This is exactly
what I have been needing in my Christian life."[8] The submission to God he
found in Islam undermined his racial and imperial pride and launched him on
the path to reconversion.

This initial account of Laubach's "Islamic experience of God" appeared in
Letters by a Modern Mystic, but other descriptions of his new religious sensibilities proved too provocative for publication. In an unpublished passage of a
letter he sent later that summer, he revealed the true extent of his indebtedness
to Islam:

> This entire philosophy of life which I have adopted in the past few
> months would have been impossible to acquire without the Moros, and
> the loneliness of my life here, and the fresh approach to God through
> the Moslem religion. Do not imagine that I am becoming a Moslem—
> dear no! But it challenges my religion splendidly, searchingly! Am I as
> earnest as Mohamad was? Do I know God as well as he did? One cannot
> ask these questions of Jesus so easily, just because we hold Jesus up so
> high that almost nobody tries to equal Him. . . . I am determined to try
> to be as sincere in my quest as Mohamad was, and as the best
> Mohamadans I find are.[9]

Laubach's awakening, sparked by his encounter with Islam, revolutionized his religious outlook. Gone was the hubris of his early missionary zeal, replaced by the humbler mystic's search for the presence of God. "They must see God in me, and I must see God in them," Laubach told his father. "Not to change the name of their religion, but to take their hand and say, 'Come, let us look for God.'"[10]

The life of Frank Laubach illustrates in many ways the history of liberal religion in the twentieth century. Most obviously Laubach's story provides a dramatic instance of mysticism facilitating spiritual cosmopolitanism. The historian Leigh Schmidt has observed that the mystical impulse arising from liberal Christianity in the late nineteenth century allowed adherents to "negotiate the intensification of religious diversity and to see it not as a threat to the solidity of Christian identity but as an opportunity for self-exploration and cross-cultural understanding." In this way, despite modern mystics' inarguable naïveté "about an underlying sameness and ecumenical harmony," Schmidt contends, mysticism for religious liberals nevertheless became a meaningful "means of interreligious engagement—a sympathetic meeting point in an increasingly global encounter of religions."[11] Laubach's mystical awakening made possible his sympathetic engagement with Islam, just as mysticism facilitated Eugene Exman's exploration of Hindu meditation and Thomas Merton's later dialogues with D. T. Suzuki, Thich Nhat Hanh, and other Buddhist contemplatives.[12]

Laubach's career evolved significantly after his mystical awakening, and its subsequent iterations provide additional illustrative moments. After publishing *Letters by a Modern Mystic* he wrote a number of inspirational works that drew on his developing mystical sensibilities. These books show how among religious liberals mystical religion, which had a lofty intellectual pedigree, often blended with more popular forms of psychological and mind-cure spirituality. With Exman at Harper's Laubach wrote *You Are My Friends* (1942), a spiritual meditation on friendship with Christ, and after the war published *Prayer: The Mightiest Force in the World* (1946), his one major commercial success. Like Henry C. Link and others, Laubach affirmed in *Prayer* that "modern psychology bears out every word Jesus said about thoughts, with sledge-hammer emphasis."[13] He called on readers to become prayer experimenters, to practice and evaluate various modes of prayer, and speculated that a scientific basis for intercessory prayer—prayer acting at a distance, rather than only internally—might be found one day through investigations of the "sixth sense" and "telepathy," possibly operating akin to radio waves.[14] "It is time to stop our 'conspiracy of silence' about intercessory prayer," he proclaimed. "Scientific investigation is hampered by the fear of being called a 'mystic.'"[15] Scientific prayer, Laubach argued, both drew one closer to God and opened God's power to act in the world, enabling possibilities for greater health, happiness, and peace. To support his claims, Laubach cited Rufus Jones, Walt Whitman, the seventeenth-century monk Brother Lawrence, and, most often, Glenn Clark.

Alongside this blend of mystical, psychological, and mind-cure spirituality—a blend that most resembled the teachings of Clark and Norman Vincent Peale—Laubach's popular writings also presented cosmopolitan and ethical concerns that more closely matched those of Rufus Jones, Harry Emerson Fosdick, and Thomas Merton. By bringing these strands of religious liberalism together, Laubach demonstrated a creative interweaving common to popular religious forms. His cosmopolitanism, so evident in his encounter with Islam in 1930, led him in *Prayer* to suggest Roman Catholic devotional practices to his readers. "Many of us, like the Roman Catholic," he counseled, "can pray better if we look at a shrine.... We can construct a little shrine for ourselves instantly at home or in a hotel room by placing a cross or the open Bible in front of our favorite picture of Christ." This made sense, Laubach told his presumably skeptical readers, because "the Catholics, with a cross around their neck to remind them of Christ, are using better psychology than those of us who use no helps."[16] Written in the midst of the National Conference of Christians and Jews' Religious Book Week, *Prayer* in this way promoted the spirituality of the emerging Judeo-Christianity.

Laubach's mystical cosmopolitanism reached beyond devotional life and became, more expansively, the basis for a global ethics of peace and justice for the poor. "V-Day did not mark the end of the war," he warned in the opening pages of *Prayer*. "The war is not won until we win the peace." He continued ominously, "The racial hatred in South Africa, and in our own South, has in it a possibility of bloodshed as hideous as the Nazi massacres of the Jews, as every wise person sees."[17] Most of the world in fact stood in poverty and ruin at war's end, and the United States must stand with the downtrodden or face ruin itself. "God has been with us in this last war," Laubach proclaimed, "but He would be on the side of the oppressed if we fought against them."[18] After *Prayer*, which sold steadily in revised editions through the 1960s, Laubach continued to write on the relationship of mysticism and intercessory prayer to peace, resulting in *Wake Up or Blow Up* (1951), *The World Is Learning Compassion* (1958), and *War of Amazing Love* (1965).

During these same years the interplay of mystical religion and social activism bore considerable fruit elsewhere in American religion. Eugene Exman, like many other liberal Protestants, directed his religious sympathies toward work with the United Nations and the antinuclear weapons movement. Much more significantly African Americans in the Congress on Racial Equality and other liberal Protestant pacifists in the Fellowship of Reconciliation brought together Christian and Gandhian forms of mystical practice to nourish and sustain the peace movement and the civil rights struggle.[19] The African American writer and clergyman Howard Thurman, for example, arrived at his form of Protestant mysticism in part through Rufus Jones, and Thurman's *Jesus and the Disinherited* (1949) became a midcentury classic that greatly influenced Martin Luther King Jr.[20]

Figure 7.1 Frank and Effa Laubach, center, behind umbrella. Farewell party in a schoolhouse in Dansalan (now Marawi), Philippines. Circa 1938. Photographer unknown. Frank C. Laubach Collection, Special Collections Research Center, Syracuse University, Box 430.

In one final way Laubach's tale usefully recapitulates the story of liberal Protestantism in the twentieth century. Like many others, as Laubach endeavored to live out the implications of his liberal theology, ethics, and mystical cosmopolitanism, he channeled his religious energies more and more into social and cultural work. In Laubach's case, this meant that the one-time missionary became the world's greatest evangelist of literacy (Figure 7.1). After working to perfect his teaching methods with the Moro, especially his signature "Each One Teach One" system, he traveled extensively in 1935 teaching other missionaries his techniques. This led to the establishment in 1935 of the World Literacy Committee, an organization that worked through religious bodies, including the Federal Council of Churches in the United States, to promote literacy. After the war governments and other secular entities began to express interest in Laubach's increasingly prolific literacy work, and in 1955, to facilitate this cooperation, he launched Laubach Literacy, Inc., a secular nonprofit organization. His literacy campaign, in this new incarnation, collaborated with UNESCO, USAID, and the Peace Corps, as well as national and local governments around the world. All told, from 1930 until his death in 1970, Laubach personally visited more than a hundred countries, aided in the development of reading primers for 312 languages, and, according to his *New York Times* obituary, directly or indirectly contributed to 100 million people learning to read.[21] Not surprisingly he chronicled his literacy work in a steady stream of books, including *Toward a Literate World* (1938), *The Silent Billion Speak* (1943), and *Thirty Years with the Silent Billion* (1959).

Laubach's transition from Congregational missionary to coordinator of secular literacy campaigns mirrored similar developments across midcentury Protestantism, as religious liberals increasingly devoted their energies to social and cultural endeavors. Religious middlebrow culture arose in the 1920s from just such liberal Protestant efforts to promote their values in the cultural marketplace. Aware of the psychic and spiritual dislocations wrought by mass culture, increasing consumerism, and the profusion of new scientific and theological knowledge, liberal Protestant cultural leaders sought to guide American moderns by offering their expertise in the field of religious reading. Through the Religious Book Week of the 1920s, the Religious Book Club, and the Religious Books Round Table of the American Library Association, liberal Protestants established a thriving religious middlebrow culture. The new religious publishing departments that emerged at the end of the 1920s, such as Exman's at Harper's, capitalized on this developing culture of religious reading to promote religious books, with increasing success, as one would any other commodity in a free marketplace. The mediation of middlebrow culture freed these new, commercially oriented religious publishers from the responsibilities of cultural stewardship that had regulated the engagement of previous generations of publishers with the market. The cultural work of the various book clubs and book lists in this way allowed liberal Protestants to more fully inhabit secular market culture.

The centrifugal forces of the marketplace and the ethical imperatives of liberal Protestantism itself ultimately undermined the cultural sway the Protestant elite once exercised. What emerged in the place of this waning establishment was a religious culture more strongly than ever dependent on the marketplace, especially the marketplace for books, and an enhanced emphasis on mystical and psychological spiritual forms. The structures, practices, habits, and content of middlebrow reading culture, built over two decades, made possible the changes of the World War II period. The reading program of the National Conference of Christians and Jews leveraged the mystical and psychological spirituality that had been promoted so heavily in the 1920s and 1930s to encourage and facilitate interfaith exchange as an important component of modern American spirituality. No longer the domain of cultural elites like Exman—or Laubach—spiritual cosmopolitanism after the war became a part of ordinary religious life for more and more middle-class Americans.

The historian David Hollinger helpfully connects the liberal embrace of social and cultural work, exemplified by middlebrow reading campaigns, to the rise of evangelicalism after World War II. The differences between liberal and evangelical Protestants, he writes, "hardened during the 1940s and after as a result of the discomfort felt especially by fundamentalists with how far the 'mainstream liberals' had pushed their program of cooperation across denominational lines and of alliances with non-Protestant, non-Christian, and eventually secular parties."[22] Billy Graham at age thirty-one launched his astonishingly successful career as an evangelist in 1949 with an eight-week crusade in Los Angeles that marked the resurgence of evangelicalism in American public life. Significantly his first book, *Peace with God* (1953), was a rejoinder to Joshua Liebman's *Peace of Mind*. But we must be careful not to assume, Hollinger asserts, that evangelicalism flourished in the postwar period because it won some imaginary head-to-head contest for American hearts and minds against liberal or ecumenical Protestantism. "Our narrative of modern American religious history," he writes, "will be deficient so long as we suppose that ecumenical Protestantism declined because it had less to offer the United States than did its evangelical rival. Much of what ecumenical Protestantism offered now lies beyond the churches, and hence we have been slow to see it."[23]

If we want to understand liberal religion "beyond the churches" in the twentieth century, we must look to the culture of books and reading that liberal Protestants built beginning in the 1920s. Doing this work adequately requires an expansion of our common understandings of both reading and religious practice. Middle-class Americans of the mid-twentieth century, after all, related to books not only as readers of texts, nor simply as consumers of a marketed commodity, but also, quite often, as religious actors acting religiously. The piety of reading—setting aside a designated time for disciplined attention; reading and rereading contemplatively; underlining and note taking; book talk with friends, family, or fellow book club members; and even the act of buying books itself— was for many Americans an embodied devotional practice as well as an intellectual engagement with words and ideas. A history of popular religion and spirituality that takes reading seriously must look therefore at reading as both a material and an intellectual endeavor, examining the way economic and political realities like advertising, book club promotion, and library collection practices shaped the meaning made of, and in, reading.

A religious and social history of reading, when conducted along these lines, mirrors the "lived religion" approaches now common in the study of American religion.[24] The ethnographic sensibility inherent in both lived religion and the social history of reading—the shared determination to see individual agency in the midst of overarching structures, narratives, and paradigms—asks scholars to look for religion where it happens, even if that happening occurs in embarrassingly ordinary, low, or uncouth places. The devotional reading of a subliterary inspirational bestseller—done with "pencil in hand," as Rufus Jones advised in 1921—in this way stands akin to the Catholic pilgrims who flocked to a replica of Lourdes in the Bronx, such as Robert Orsi has studied, or to the everyday Protestants, studied by the art historian David Morgan, who embraced Warner Sallman's famed *Head of Christ* painting as a twentieth-century icon.[25]

Religious middlebrow culture provides a critical analytical framework for investigating the mechanisms of popular religion and spirituality in the twentieth century. Most specifically, attention to middlebrow culture foregrounds the lives and experiences of middle-class women, highlighting both accommodation to the status quo and forms of dissent and resistance. Though the cultural apparatuses of middlebrow reading—the book weeks and book lists and book clubs—were largely founded and administered by men, and the books promoted through those venues were overwhelmingly authored by men through at least the 1940s, the majority of readers, according to the best available evidence, were women. The autonomy of the reader—the ability to make independent choices in the consumer marketplace and to craft individual meaning in the encounter with texts—provided critical religious agency for middle-class women in the postwar years, especially by opening cultural space for emerging feminist sensibilities and practices. Tellingly, when the Harper's religion department reinvented itself in San Francisco in 1977, much of its new output focused on feminist spirituality, both Christian feminism and the alternative feminisms emerging from New Age, recovery, Wicca, and ecospirituality, including Starhawk's groundbreaking *The Spiral Dance* (1979).[26] As many forms of institutional religion continue to resist feminist spirituality, books and book culture remain critical sites of women's religious agency and empowerment.

More broadly the framework of religious middlebrow culture helps historians account for the popularization of liberal religion in the twentieth century, filling a significant gap in current scholarship. Scholars in American religious history have thoroughly documented liberal religion as it flowered among an influential avant-garde in the late nineteenth century and early twentieth. This work has brought to life feminist sex reformers, disciples of Walt Whitman, converts and dilettantes of Baha'i and Buddhism, Theosophists, spiritualists, mystical psychologists, and psychological mystics, productively expanding our understanding of religious liberalism in this moment of ferment beyond Protestant theology alone.[27] In addition historians and sociologists of American religion have charted the pervasiveness of liberal religious sensibilities among the baby boomers and subsequent generations from the 1960s onward.[28] Christian Smith's work on the religious lives of teenagers and young adults carries that sociological work forward into the early twenty-first century. "Liberal Protestantism," Smith writes, "can afford to be losing its organizational battles now precisely because long ago it effectively won the bigger, more important struggle over culture."[29] The religious middlebrow culture of the 1920s, 1930s, and 1940s was, in large measure, the mechanism of that "long ago" victory and helps explain how the mystical, psychological, and cosmopolitan preoccupations of a fin de siècle cultural elite came to describe, half a century later, the spiritual outlook of so many ordinary, middle-class Americans.

All along the way, of course, critics labored to resist the tides of change, and not just evangelicals. For decades after the war loud voices from within liberal Protestantism continued to denounce the trends emerging from religious middlebrow culture. The *Christian Century*, the leading journal of ecumenical liberal Protestantism, published as a cover story in 1951 an essay with the foreboding title "Pluralism—National Menace," by which the writers specifically meant the newly assertive public presence of Roman Catholicism. Echoing Paul Blanshard's *American Freedom and Catholic Power* (1949), the editors of the *Century* decried the malevolent influence of "priests educated in Rome," especially the Catholic desire to operate parochial schools and thus resist the patriotic (and largely Protestant) indoctrination of the public schools. "As a result of this...propaganda among Roman Catholics," observed this editorial, "the United States is faced with the menace of a plural society based on religious differences." A plural society, the *Century* further warned, when stripped of the religious basis for its cohesion, "becomes particularly vulnerable to communist propaganda."[30] At the end of the decade notable liberal Protestants, including Norman Vincent Peale, worked to oppose, on religious grounds, the presidential candidacy of the Roman Catholic senator John F. Kennedy.[31]

Just as certain liberals resisted pluralism, so too the increasingly practical and psychological orientation of liberal Protestantism faced withering criticism. Paul Hutchinson, the editor of the *Century*, wrote a scathing attack in *Life* magazine in 1955 on the "cult of reassurance," by which he meant positive thinking and psychological spirituality in various guises, as a new religion undermining traditional Protestant Christianity. Hutchinson followed Russell Lynes's division of Americans into lowbrow, middlebrow, and highbrow and found that middlebrow Americans had turned in horrifyingly large numbers to preachers such as Peale, whose *The Power of Positive Thinking* (1952) had recently become the bestselling religious book of the century, surpassing Liebman's *Peace of Mind*.[32] "One reason why this cult makes such an appeal," Hutchinson wrote, "is that our middle-brows live in awe of the 'scientist'—especially the psychological scientist," a development he traced to "the sensational success of Rabbi Liebman's book."[33]

Though he saw some value in simple optimism, on the one hand, and psychological science, on the other, Hutchinson finally condemned the "new" religion as the ancient heresy of Pelagianism, which taught that humans were not inherently depraved but could overcome sin through an act of will. Reinhold Niebuhr and the history of the twentieth century, Hutchinson argued, should have put such teaching to rest, yet it had emerged with renewed vigor in the decade after the war. Niebuhr certainly articulated an important critique of liberalism in religion, and of positive-thinking religion in particular, with his insistence on human fallibility and limitation, but ultimately even his forceful, clear, and politically influential voice was unable to carry the day. Niebuhr's theology of paradox proved less viable in the decades after World War II than religious sensibilities like Peale's that championed the unlimited possibilities of America and Americans. Positive thinking continued to thrive through the latter half of the twentieth century in forms that crossed nearly all boundaries of faith, from New Agers channeling healing power to evangelicals proclaiming their own gospels of health and wealth. Positive thinking prospers in this country, in all its forms, because it is the ne plus ultra of American consumer capitalism in religious idiom, and consumer capitalism is the unrivaled bedrock of true Americanism.[34]

Hutchinson's and Niebuhr's critiques of positive-thinking religion failed to gain significant purchase despite their important insights. The lingering hostility in liberal Protestantism toward pluralism in general, and Roman Catholicism in particular, however, thankfully died a quick and quiet death. The election of John F. Kennedy in 1960 is often seen as the turning point in Protestant-Catholic relations in the United States, but at least as important was the Second Vatican Council (1962–65). Vatican II proved a watershed in the history of American Protestantism as surely as it did in Roman Catholicism, for Protestant identity had been forged as a movement of protest against Catholicism, and as Catholicism modernized, Protestants lost the point of origin of their axis of identity.

Alongside the revolution in Protestant-Catholic relations initiated by Vatican II, liberal religious Americans in the 1960s also turned with increasing attention toward the religions of Asia. The war in Vietnam and the repeal of racially exclusive immigration laws in 1965, which opened the doors to millions of Asian immigrants, stimulated an increased interest in Buddhism among American Christians and Jews.[35] Since the nineteenth century elite seekers and intellectuals had explored Buddhist teachings, a trend continued by the Beats and others in the 1950s, but by the late twentieth century the Dalai Lama had become a revered spiritual leader for countless ordinary Americans and a better selling author than all but a few Christian authorities. American popular interest in Hindu spiritual practices, such as yoga, followed a similar pattern from the cultural elite to the everyday, transformed all along by American consumerism.[36] A large majority of Americans in the postwar decades remained Christian, but many no longer saw appropriating practices and insights from other traditions of faith as a threat to their own integrity and identity.

"The religious beliefs and practices of Americans do not fit neatly into conventional categories," began, rather dryly, a 2009 Pew Forum report on religion in the United States. Entitled *Many Americans Mix Multiple Faiths: Eastern, New Age Beliefs Widespread*, the report, based on a representative survey of the American population, continued, "Large numbers of Americans engage in multiple religious practices, mixing elements of diverse traditions....Many also blend Christianity with Eastern or New Age beliefs such as reincarnation, astrology and the presence of spiritual energy in physical objects." The report further detailed that 24 percent of Americans believed in reincarnation, 24 percent regularly or occasionally attended religious services of other faiths, 23 percent engaged in yoga "as a spiritual practice," and fully 49 percent "have had a religious or mystical experience, defined as a 'moment of sudden religious insight or awakening.'" The findings shocked many in the news media, especially given that more than 75 percent of Americans in a similar survey identified as Christian.[37]

Yet Americans have always been a religiously restive people, and as the Protestant mainstream burst its banks in the middle decades of the twentieth century, new avenues for exploration emerged. The interplay of liberal religion and book culture in the 1920s, 1930s, and 1940s promoted the steady advancement in American culture of psychological and mystical vocabularies and practices of spiritual cosmopolitanism. From the broadening impulses of the Religious Book Club and Religious Book Week and the mass interfaith appeal of Liebman's *Peace of Mind* and Merton's *Seven Storey Mountain,* one can readily comprehend the move in postwar popular religious culture to Jack Kerouac and George Harrison and later to Deepak Chopra, the immense celebrity of the Dalai Lama, and the ubiquitous yoga centers, full of Jewish and Protestant and Catholic seekers, in strip malls across America.

During that tumultuous spring of 1930 Frank Laubach wrote once again to his father back home. "But why do I constantly harp upon this inner experience?" he asked. "Because I feel convinced that for me and for you who read there lie ahead undiscovered continents of spiritual living."[38] Across the twentieth century American readers indeed explored undiscovered continents of spiritual living, and in so doing charted the new religious world we still inhabit.

ACKNOWLEDGMENTS

Now comes the fun part: thanking the mentors, colleagues, librarians, archivists, funders, friends, and family who made this book possible. The years of labor on this project took me to five institutional homes—The University of Texas at Austin, Valparaiso University, Princeton University, Roger Williams University, and the University of Virginia—and to libraries, archives, seminars, conferences, hotel rooms, and friends' couches around the country. Along the way I piled up a mountain of debts and a treasure trove of memories, friendships, photocopies, and advice—too many to remember or recount in full. I am delighted now to acknowledge this abundance of kindness.

This book began in the Department of American Studies at the University of Texas. My first debt of gratitude is owed to Robert H. Abzug, who mentored me through this project's awkward early stages and never lost faith in its ultimate worth, or in me. The ideas for this project began in his graduate seminar on religion and psychology and were sustained and nourished through many memorable conversations. This book bears his imprint in ways large and small and is vastly better for it. Howard Miller of the History Department at Texas provided tremendous knowledge of American religious history, a firm commitment to intellectual excellence, keen editorial insight, and encouragement at once avuncular and professorial. Thank you, Howard, for your great generosity with this work and for your example as a teacher, mentor, and friend.

The next stops on my academic sojourn were postdocs in the happy environs of the Lilly Fellows Program at Valparaiso University and the Center for the Study of Religion (CSR) at Princeton University. My fellow fellows at Valparaiso, especially Franklin Harkins and Joanne Myers, offered stimulating lunchtime conversation and professional wisdom; even more, their friendship brought much warmth and levity to two long Indiana winters. Mark Schwehn read much of the manuscript in an early form and sharpened my thinking about mainline Protestantism in the twentieth century. My mentor at Valpo, David Morgan, not only steered a junior colleague through his first faculty appointment but also read much of this work and more generally inspired me with his intellectual range and vigor. I stumbled across David's work early in my graduate career and feel remarkably fortunate to have had the chance to work closely with him for two years at Valpo and to count him as a friend and mentor still. Thanks also to Dorothy Bass, Gretchen Buggeln, Joe Creech, Sara Danger, Andrew Finstuen, Margaret Franson, Stephanie Johnson, Elizabeth Lynn, Sandy and Hugh McGuigan, Andy Murphy, the late John Steven Paul, Mel Piehl, Jamie Skillen, Anne Spurgeon, Mary Streufert, and Kathy Sutherland for making Valpo and the Lilly Fellows Program an invigorating and happy home for two years.

At Princeton I was fortunate to work alongside friends and remarkable historians Darren Dochuk and Lauren Winner while participating in Leigh Schmidt's American religious history seminar. Darren, Lauren, and Leigh each generously read drafts. Leigh's *Restless Souls* appeared when this book was in its final stages as a dissertation; ever since, that book and Leigh's generous-minded approach to religious liberalism and American spirituality have shaped and energized my thinking profoundly. This book is indebted to *Restless Souls*, and Leigh's work, much more deeply than a few meager footnotes can adequately acknowledge. While at Princeton, I also benefited from workshops on aspects of this project in the CSR's Religion and Culture seminar and the History Department's Center for the Study of Books and Media. Thanks are also due to Robert Wuthnow, Dave Michelson, Anita Kline, and Barbara Bermel for so ably facilitating my stay in Princeton.

The Department of History and American Studies at Roger Williams University offered me my first tenure-track appointment and a warm welcome to full-time professorial life. Students and colleagues, especially Josh Stein, Jennifer Stevens, Mike Swanson, Joan Romano, and Jason Jacobs, made Rhode Island feel like home very quickly. I especially value the many long conversations, over lunch or baseball or conference planning, with Josh Stein on matters of religion and politics.

My new home in Virginia is really two homes, the Department of Religious Studies and the Program in American Studies at the University of Virginia. Maurie McInnis and Paul Groner brought me to UVa, while Kevin Hart and Sandhya Shukla have helped acclimate me to yet another university culture. Thanks are also due to colleagues and friends Ahmed al-Rahim, Hector Amaya, Daniel Chavez, Sylvia Chong, Valerie Cooper, Greg Goering, Jennifer Greeson, Grace Hale, Carmenita Higginbotham, Paul Jones, Eric Lott, Charles Marsh, Chuck Mathewes, Jennifer Petersen, Jalane Schmidt, Siva Vaidhyanathan, and Heather Warren for their advice, support, welcome, and friendship in Charlottesville. Chuck Mathewes generously read the manuscript in its penultimate form. His comments and mentoring somehow simultaneously pushed me toward greater clarity of thought and expression and the book toward the finish line. Thank you.

Various audiences and outside readers provided valuable feedback and leads over the years this project took shape: the late Paul Boyer, Charles Cohen, and others at the Center for the History of Print Culture in Modern America at the University of Wisconsin, Madison; Erin Smith, on many occasions; Trysh Travis; Phyllis Tickle; Wayne Wiegand; R. Laurence Moore; Charles Lippy; Judith Weisenfeld; Amanda Porterfield; Joan Rubin; David Hollinger; and audiences at the American Academy of Religion, the American Historical Association, the American Society of Church History, the American Studies Association, the Organization of American Historians, the Reception Studies Society, the Space Between, the Louisville Institute, the Research Colloquium of the Association for Religion and Intellectual Life at Union Theological Seminary in New York, Syracuse University, the University of Virginia, Yale Divinity School, and Duke Divinity School. Richard Wightman Fox gave the manuscript an especially careful and insightful reading at a critical early stage. Most important, this book and its arguments were refined in conversation with a marvelous collection of scholars gathered by Leigh Schmidt and Sally Promey as the Cultures of American Religious Liberalism symposium, meeting at Princeton in 2008 and Yale in 2009.

Scholarly work may be about ideas, but it also takes dollars, and I am pleased to recognize the sources of support that made this book possible: a Louisville Institute Dissertation Fellowship; a University Continuing Fellowship and a David Bruton Jr. Fellowship from the Graduate School at The University of Texas at Austin; the Louann Atkins Temple Endowed Presidential Scholarship in American Studies, and several Robert Morse Crunden Memorial Research Awards, from the Department of American Studies at the University of Texas; a Gest Fellowship from the Quaker Collection at Haverford College; a Coolidge Fellowship from the Association for Religion and Intellectual Life, which made possible a delightful month of work in New York City; and an Alexander N. Charters Research Grant from the Special Collections Research Center, Syracuse University Library. Though not a source of direct support for this book project, I would be remiss not to mention the Young Scholars program at the Center for the Study of Religion and American Culture, IUPUI, especially the 2010–12 cohort and our leaders Ann Braude and Mark Valeri. The Young Scholars program has exceeded its stellar reputation for collegiality, invigorating conversation, and smart, practical mentoring. I am deeply grateful to all of these institutions for their financial support.

Money for research would mean nothing without research to do, and as with all historical endeavors, mine is deeply indebted to the hard work of many archivists and librarians. Archivists and librarians at the Howard Gotlieb Archival Research Center at Boston University; the Rare Book and Manuscript Library at Columbia University; the Ecumenical Library of the Interchurch Center in New York; Haverford College Special Collections; the American Library Association Archive at the University of Illinois; the Library of Congress (especially the Prints and Photographs Division); the Riverside Church in New York; the Seeley

G. Mudd Manuscript Library, and the Firestone Library Department of Rare Books and Special Collections, at Princeton University; the Social Welfare History Archive at the University of Minnesota; the Hennepin County Public Library; the Burke Library at Union Theological Seminary in New York; the Wisconsin Historical Society; the Special Collections Research Center, Syracuse University; and the Yale Divinity School Library and the Beinecke Rare Book and Manuscript Library at Yale University all made contributions with their professional expertise. Gera Draijer and Sheila Winchester at the Perry-Castañeda Library at the University of Texas, and librarians at Valparaiso, Roger Williams, and Virginia, provided invaluable assistance as well.

I was tremendously fortunate to pass through graduate school with a band of students who quickly became colleagues, academic fellow travelers, and friends. Ole Bech-Petersen, Ed Donovan, Paul Erickson, Laura Hernandez-Ehrisman, Bill Fagelson, Lara Fischman, Steve Galpern, John Haddad, Kimberly Hamlin, Mark and Erica Metzler Sawin, Rebecca Montes, Sarah Mullen, Allison Perlman, Ray Sapirstein, Danielle Brune Sigler, Greg Tucker, Scott Blackwood and all the folks at the UWC, and the Sunday Morning Hoopsters (Troy Barber, Greg Barnhisel, Mike O'Connor, and Dean Rader) all made graduate school both intellectually transformative and just plain fun. Paul's genius for moving to the site of archives and generous hospitality on many occasions made much research possible on a grad student budget. I am also happy to acknowledge the American Studies faculty at Texas, especially the late Bob Crunden, Janet Davis, the late William Goetzmann, Jeff Meikle, Mark Smith, and Bill Stott, generous teachers and scholars all, and Michael White of the (now) Department of Religious Studies. Graduate school would not have been the same without all those happy hours.

I also want thank Oxford University Press, and my editor, Theo Calderara, for supporting and guiding this project as it lurched from dissertation to book. Though all those mentioned above, and many others, contributed to the intellectual work of this project in ways large and small, its inevitable mistakes, omissions, and errors are all my own.

Finally, and most especially, the love and support of my family and friends, especially my parents, Herb and Louise Hedstrom, have sustained me throughout this project. Mom and Dad showed me what it means to love learning, to work hard, and to find joy in what you do. But even more, they have simply loved me beyond measure. My in-laws, Jack and Judy Mullen, continue to astound and overwhelm me with their love, encouragement, and unwavering support. The rest of my family, especially my brother, sister, and siblings-in-law—Mark Brooks Hedstrom, Dar Brooks Hedstrom, Elizabeth Hedstrom, Scott Ward, Matt Mullen, and Elizabeth Mullen—and my nieces and nephews, Lucy, Nicholas, Caroline, Simon, Silas, and Henry, nurture me with the joys of family life. Doug and Kimi Gilbert, friends for more than two decades, remain cherished as ever.

These loved ones remind me what matters most and provide the good times along the way.

Sarah Mullen has walked every mile of this book with me, encouraging my faltering steps, sharing the triumphs and moments of quiet. She read every word, asked all the hard questions, debated when I needed debating, cooked when I needed cooking, laughed when I needed laughing. For all this, my words fail. Maybe Whitman comes close:

> Let the paper remain on the desk unwritten, and the book on the shelf unopen'd!
> Let the tools remain in the workshop! let the money remain unearn'd!
> Let the school stand! mind not the cry of the teacher!
> Let the preacher preach in his pulpit! let the lawyer plead in the court, and the judge expound the law.
> Camerado, I give you my hand!
> I give you my love more precious than money,
> I give you myself before preaching or law;
> Will you give me yourself? will you come travel with me?
> Shall we stick by each other as long as we live?

Happily, I know the answer, and dedicate this book to my companion on the open road.

ARCHIVAL COLLECTIONS

American Library Association Archive, University of Illinois Archive, University of Illinois at Urbana-Champaign

Bruce Barton Papers, Wisconsin Historical Society Archives

Council on Books in Wartime Collection, Seely G. Mudd Manuscript Library, Princeton University

Frank C. Laubach Collection, Special Collections Research Center, Syracuse University

Harper & Brothers Papers, Rare Book and Manuscript Library, Columbia University

Harry Emerson Fosdick Papers, Burke Library of Union Theological Seminary in the City of New York

Harry Emerson Fosdick Papers, Riverside Church Archive, Riverside Church, New York

Joshua Loth Liebman Collection, Howard Gotlieb Archival Research Center, Boston University

National Conference of Christians and Jews Records, Social Welfare History Archive, University of Minnesota

Norman Vincent Peale Papers, Special Collections Research Center, Syracuse University

Religious Book Club Bulletin, Library of Congress, Washington, D.C.

Rufus M. Jones Papers, Quaker Collection, Haverford College Library Special Collections, Haverford, PA

Thomas R. Kelly Papers, Quaker Collection, Haverford College Library Special Collections, Haverford, PA

Thomas Merton Papers, Rare Book and Manuscript Library, Columbia University

NOTES

Introduction

1. Rufus M. Jones, *Social Law in the Spiritual World: Studies in Human and Divine Inter-Relationship* (Philadelphia: John C. Winston, 1904), 15.
2. Jones, *Social Law in the Spiritual World*, 9–10.
3. Jones, *Social Law in the Spiritual World*, 15.
4. Harry Emerson Fosdick, ed., *Rufus Jones Speaks to Our Time: An Anthology* (New York: Macmillan, 1951), v.
5. Eva Illouz, *Saving the Modern Soul: Therapy, Emotions, and the Culture of Self-Help* (Berkeley: University of California Press, 2008), 4–5.
6. The use of the "spiritual marketplace" metaphor is a commonplace in the sociological and historical literature. For the postwar period, see especially Wade Clark Roof, *Spiritual Marketplace: Baby Boomers and the Remaking of American Religion* (Princeton, NJ: Princeton University Press, 2001). On religion and consumerism in American history, see especially Leigh Eric Schmidt, *Consumer Rites: The Buying and Selling of American Holidays* (Princeton, NJ: Princeton University Press, 1997); Laurence Moore, *Selling God: American Religion in the Marketplace of Culture* (New York: Oxford University Press, 1994).
7. Important exceptions to this inattention to the cultural importance of religious liberalism include Leigh Eric Schmidt, *Restless Souls: The Making of American Spirituality from Emerson to Oprah* (San Francisco: HarperSanFrancisco, 2005); Jeffrey J. Kripal, *Esalen: America and the Religion of No Religion* (Chicago: University of Chicago Press, 2007); Christopher G. White, *Unsettled Minds: Psychology and the American Search for Spiritual Assurance, 1830–1940* (Berkeley: University of California Press, 2009); Courtney Bender, *The New Metaphysicals: Spirituality and the American Religious Imagination* (Chicago: University of Chicago Press, 2010); Kathryn Lofton, *Oprah: Gospel of an Icon* (Berkeley: University of California Press, 2011); Leigh Eric Schmidt and Sally M. Promey, eds., *American Religious Liberalism* (Bloomington: Indiana University Press, 2012).
8. Christian Smith with Patricia Snell, *Souls in Transition: The Religious and Spiritual Lives of Emerging Adults* (New York: Oxford University Press, 2009), 287. Smith's argument here draws on N. Jay Demerath III, "Cultural Victory and Organizational Defeat in the Paradoxical Decline of Liberal Protestantism," *Journal for the Scientific Study of Religion* 34, no. 4 (1995): 458–69.
9. The literature on Protestant liberalism is vast. William R. Hutchison's *The Modernist Impulse in American Protestantism* (New York: Oxford University Press, 1976) served for a generation as the key American intellectual history, a history now greatly augmented by Gary Dorrien's encyclopedic three-volume *The Making of American Liberal Theology* (Louisville, KY: Westminster John Knox Press, 2001, 2003, 2006). Also of importance are two essay collections: William R. Hutchison, ed., *Between the Times: The Travail of the Protestant Establishment in America, 1900–1960* (New York: Cambridge University Press, 1989); Douglas Jacobsen and William

Vance Trollinger Jr., eds., *Re-Forming the Center: American Protestantism, 1900 to the Present* (Grand Rapids, MI: William B. Eerdmans, 1998). Alongside these titles stand shelves of books on the Social Gospel. Standout works include Susan Curtis, *A Consuming Faith: The Social Gospel and Modern American Culture* (Baltimore: Johns Hopkins University Press, 1991); Ralph E. Luker, *The Social Gospel in Black and White* (Chapel Hill: University of North Carolina Press, 1991).

10. What utility I do see in the secularization paradigm comes especially from the sociologist Christian Smith. Smith conceives of secularization as a "revolution" rather than as the inevitable outcome of modernization, and therefore as the accomplishment of specific human actors, not the telos of grand historical processes. Secularization, to the extent it has occurred, was, in his words, "the outcome of a struggle between contending groups with conflicting interests seeking to control social knowledge and institutions." Christian Smith, introduction to *The Secular Revolution: Power, Interests, and Conflict in the Secularization of American Public Life* (Berkeley: University of California Press, 2003), vii. Smith's focus on contingency, agency, interests, power, and conflict demands nuanced attention both to the vulnerabilities of the dominant religious culture in the period of its decline, specifically liberal Protestantism in the United States from the 1870s through the 1920s, and the motivations, resources, and grievances of the secular insurgents. Secularization in the late nineteenth century and early twentieth occurred most obviously at the institutional level, as many universities and publishing houses, for example, separated themselves from their religious roots. Understanding secularization or transformation on the level of the individual consciousness is a much trickier problem, one that the study of inspirational literature can help solve. Peter Berger, in *A Rumor of Angels: Modern Society and the Rediscovery of the Supernatural* (Garden City, NJ: Doubleday, 1969), though dated now by its appearance before the global resurgence of fundamentalism in the late twentieth century, offers what remains nevertheless a compelling account of secularization and of the possibilities for faith in a modern society. Along these lines, Christian Smith argues, "The secular revolution transformed the basic cultural understanding of the human self and its care, displacing the established spiritually and morally framed Protestant conception of the 'care of souls' (over which the church and its agencies held jurisdiction), and establishing instead a naturalistic, psychologized model of human personhood (over which therapists and psychologists are the authorities)" (3). This argument can be readily adapted as a neutral description of change rather than used, as is more commonly the case, to describe religious decline.

11. The most common New Testament references for the notion "*in* but not *of* the world" come from the Gospel of John, chapters 15 and 17.

12. As David Chappell demonstrates in *A Stone of Hope: Prophetic Religion and the Death of Jim Crow* (Chapel Hill: University of North Carolina Press, 2004), debates about progress and human nature remained central to Protestant liberalism well into the 1960s, long after Reinhold Niebuhr's *Moral Man and Immoral Society* (1932) so forcefully articulated the anthropological deficiencies of postmillennial liberalism. Jonathan Ebel's *Faith in the Fight: Religion and the American Soldier in the Great War* (Princeton, NJ: Princeton University Press, 2010), using a different body of evidence, also complicates conventional notions of mass disillusionment regarding progress after World War I. Nevertheless most scholars see the war as a critical tipping point in this long-standing theological conversation.

13. On religious experience, see especially Bender, *The New Metaphysicals*, 7–12; Wayne Proudfoot, *Religious Experience* (Berkeley: University of California Press, 1985). More broadly, see Martin Jay, *Songs of Experience: Modern American and European Variations on a Universal Theme* (Berkeley: University of California Press, 2005).

14. For an early sociological effort to analyze and classify the inspirational religious literature of this period, see Louis Schneider and Sanford M. Dornbusch, *Popular Religion: Inspirational Books in America* (Chicago: University of Chicago Press, 1958).

15. See T. J. Jackson Lears, *Fables of Abundance: A Cultural History of Advertising in America* (New York: Basic Books, 1994); Christopher Lasch, *The Culture of Narcissism: American Life in an Age of Diminishing Expectations* (New York: Norton, 1978); Robert Bellah et al., *Habits of the Heart: Individualism and Commitment in American Life* (Berkeley: University of California Press, 1985); Christian Smith and Melina Lundquist Denton, *Soul Searching: The Religious*

and Spiritual Lives of American Teenagers (New York: Oxford University Press, 2005); Philip Rieff, *The Triumph of the Therapeutic: Uses of Faith after Freud* (Chicago: University of Chicago Press, 1966).

16. An assessment of late twentieth-century criticism, as characterized by Beryl Satter in *Each Mind a Kingdom: American Women, Sexual Purity, and the New Thought Movement, 1875-1920* (Berkeley: University of California Press, 1999), 7.

17. See Michael Kammen, *American Culture, American Tastes: Social Change and the 20th Century* (New York: Basic Books, 1999); Lawrence Levine, *Highbrow/Lowbrow: The Emergence of Cultural Hierarchy in America* (Cambridge, MA: Harvard University Press, 1988); Janice Radway, *A Feeling for Books: The Book-of-the-Month Club, Literary Taste, and Middle-Class Desire* (Chapel Hill: University of North Carolina Press, 1997); Joan Shelley Rubin, *The Making of Middlebrow Culture* (Chapel Hill: University of North Carolina Press, 1992). On cultural hierarchy and middlebrow culture in America, see also Megan Benton, *Beauty and the Book: Fine Editions and Cultural Distinction in America* (New Haven, CT: Yale University Press, 2000); Lisa Botshon and Meredith Goldsmith, eds., *Middlebrow Moderns: Popular American Women Writers of the 1920s* (Boston: Northeastern University Press, 2003); Herbert Gans, *Popular Culture and High Culture: An Analysis and Evaluation of Taste* (New York: Basic Books, 1974); Andrew Ross, *No Respect: Intellectuals and Popular Culture* (New York: Routledge, 1989).

18. Quoted in Kwame Anthony Appiah, *Cosmopolitanism: Ethics in a World of Strangers* (New York: Norton, 2006), 111.

19. Appiah, *Cosmopolitanism*, 137–53.

20. This is quite similar to the argument about "cultural victory and organizational defeat" offered by Demerath in "Cultural Victory and Organizational Defeat in the Paradoxical Decline of Liberal Protestantism" and David A. Hollinger, "After Cloven Tongues of Fire: Ecumenical Protestantism and the Modern American Encounter with Diversity," *Journal of American History* 98, no. 1 (2011): 21–48.

21. R. Laurence Moore tells a similar tale of Protestant liberals and their ultimately futile efforts to control mass culture, first the movies and later radio. See *Selling God*, 220–35.

22. See Schmidt, *Restless Souls*; Eugene Taylor, *Shadow Culture: Psychology and Spirituality in America* (Washington, DC: Counterpoint, 1999); Robert C. Fuller, *Spiritual but Not Religious: Understanding Unchurched America* (New York: Oxford University Press, 2001). Charles Taylor's magisterial *Sources of the Self: The Making of Modern Identity* (Cambridge, MA: Harvard University Press, 1989) provides a highly useful intellectual history of the modern notion of "inwardness" so critical to the development of the kinds of spirituality these others describe. Taylor shares with Schmidt and Fuller an appreciation for these modern forms of the self so often derided by critics as mere narcissism. Also highly insightful by way of comparison is Jackson Lears's *Fables of Abundance*, in which he argues at length for the persistence of cultural traditions—in short, magic—that counter the hegemonies of Cartesian dualism and the Protestant Ethic.

23. The terms come from Taylor, *Shadow Culture*, and Thomas Luckmann, *The Invisible Religion: The Problem of Religion in Modern Times* (New York: Macmillan, 1967). Though by no means synonymous—Taylor is describing a particular cultural formation, while Luckmann theorizes more abstractly about the nature of religion and the individual in modernity—each of the terms does point to the hiddenness of extra-institutional religion in most scholarship and cultural criticism, at least through the late 1990s.

24. Rufus M. Jones, "The Habit of Reading," *Watchword* (Dayton, OH), March 13, 1921.

25. David Paul Nord and Candy Gunther Brown have produced the seminal works on religion and print in the nineteenth century: Nord, *Faith in Reading: Religious Publishing and the Birth of Mass Media in America* (New York: Oxford University Press, 2004); Brown, *The Word in the World: Evangelical Writing, Publishing, and Reading in America, 1789-1880* (Chapel Hill: University of North Carolina Press, 2004). In addition to Nord and Brown, see Peter J. Wosh, *Spreading the Word: The Bible Business in Nineteenth-Century America* (Ithaca, NY: Cornell University Press, 1994); Gregory S. Jackson, *The Word and Its Witness: The Spiritualization of American Realism* (Chicago: University of Chicago Press, 2009).

26. Brown, *Word in the World*, 47, 48.

27. Paul C. Gutjahr, "Diversification in American Religious Publishing," in Scott E. Casper, Jeffrey D. Groves, Stephen W. Nissenbaum, and Michael Winship, eds., *A History of the Book in America*, Vol. 3: *The Industrial Book* (Chapel Hill: University of North Carolina Press, 2007), 194.

28. Nord, *Faith in Reading*, 118.

29. Nord, *Faith in Reading*, 115.

30. Candy Gunther Brown's *The World in the World* led me to the following examples of evangelical reading guides.

31. Noah Porter, *Books and Reading: Or, What Books Shall I Read and How Shall I Read Them?* (New York: Charles Scribner, 1870), 8.

32. George Philip Philes, *How to Read a Book in the Best Way* (New York: G. P. Philes, 1873), 21.

33. Nord, *Faith in Reading*, 133.

34. Forms of this debate arise in numerous guises, including as one aspect of the argument over "great books" in higher education advanced by critics such as Allan Bloom in *Closing of the American Mind* (New York: Simon and Schuster, 1987). See also Mark Edmundson, *Why Read?* (New York: Bloomsbury, 2004); Mark Schwehn, *Exiles from Eden: Religion and the Academic Vocation in America* (New York: Oxford University Press, 1993). The most clearly articulated contemporary defense of religious reading comes from the Roman Catholic philosopher Paul J. Griffiths in *Religious Reading: The Place of Reading in the Practice of Religion* (New York: Oxford University Press, 1999). Griffiths proposes a discursive definition of religion, taking religion to be a particular kind of account of the way things are. Griffiths's religion as account resembles in many respects Richard Rorty's notion of "final vocabulary." See Rorty, *Contingency, Irony, Solidarity* (New York: Cambridge University Press, 1989). Reading, for Griffiths, is basic to the process of developing and maintaining a religious account: "Religious reading, like any other kind of reading, is done with a purpose: the acquisition or development of the skills and information necessary for offering a religious account" (40). The fierceness with which he defends reading religiously mirrors the polemics of a secular critic like Edmundson. On reading religiously, see also Alan Jacobs, *A Theology of Reading: The Hermeneutics of Love* (Boulder, CO: Westview Press, 2001).

35. Griffiths, *Religious Reading*, ix.

36. Griffiths, *Religious Reading*, 41.

37. Moore, *Selling God*.

38. A broadly framed example of concern about the takeover of American Protestantism by the culture of consumerism can be found in G. Jeffrey Macdonald, *Thieves in the Temple: The Christian Church and the Selling of the American Soul* (New York: Basic Books, 2010). For analyses of these same concerns over religion, consumer culture, and mass production, but in the realm of visual rather than print culture, see David Morgan, *Protestants and Pictures: Religion, Visual Culture, and the Age of American Mass Production* (New York: Oxford University Press, 1999); Sally M. Promey, "Interchangeable Art: Warner Sallman and the Critics of Mass Culture," in David Morgan, ed., *Icons of American Protestantism: The Art of Warner Sallman* (New Haven, CT: Yale University Press, 1996).

39. Paul C. Gutjahr, *An American Bible: A History of the Good Book in the United States, 1777–1880* (Stanford, CA: Stanford University Press, 1999), 175.

40. David D. Hall has articulated some of the most helpful methods for approaching the very difficult task of assessing what kind of meaning readers might have derived from texts. Hall helpfully suggests that scholars carefully comb texts for "reading as 'represented' in texts"—suggestions, in other words, that authors provided directly to readers about how to read their works—and augment these insights with primary evidence, from diaries or letters, for example, of how readers actually read, bearing in mind always that readers' accounts of reading "need to be understood in light of the rules... that inhere in genres. Otherwise, we may grant readers a misleading autonomy and particularity." David D. Hall, "Readers and Reading in America: Historical and Critical Perspectives," in David D. Hall, ed., *Cultures of Print: Essays in the History of the Book* (Amherst: University of Massachusetts Press, 1996), 180 n. 36. Ways of reading, in other words, are often so natural that readers may be unable to express their relationship to these rules.

41. I do not mean to suggest here that mysticism, mind cure, and psychology were solely creatures of print. Mind cure in particular was an embodied practice as well as a discourse or system of

thought. Bodily healing, after all, was a critical appeal of mind cure. But an alternate name for the movement, New Thought, reveals as well the centrality of philosophical insight to mind cure, and all three—mysticism, mind cure, and psychology—were much more dependent on the print marketplace for their success than traditional forms of Protestant or Roman Catholic Christianity.

42. Leigh Eric Schmidt, "The Making of Modern 'Mysticism,'" *Journal of the American Academy of Religion* 71, no. 2 (2003): 289.

43. The literature on mysticism in the Christian tradition is vast. The work of Bernard McGinn, published in many volumes, stands out from the scholarship of recent decades. See also Michel de Certeau, *The Mystic Fable*, Vol. 1: *The Sixteenth and Seventeenth Centuries* (Chicago: University of Chicago Press, 1992); Denys Turner, *The Darkness of God: Negativity in Christian Mysticism* (Cambridge: Cambridge University Press, 1995).

44. Schmidt, "Making of Modern 'Mysticism,'" 286. On the transcendentalist contributions to the discourse of mysticism, see Philip F. Gura, *American Transcendentalism: A History* (New York: Hill and Wang, 2007).

45. Schmidt, "Making of Modern 'Mysticism,'" 281.

46. T. J. Jackson Lears, *No Place of Grace: Antimodernism and the Transformation of American Culture, 1880–1920* (Chicago: University of Chicago Press, 1983), 142–81.

47. The best account of New Thought is Satter, *Each Mind a Kingdom*. See also Charles Braden, *Spirits in Rebellion: The Rise and Development of New Thought* (Dallas: Southern Methodist University Press, 1963); Gail Parker, *Mind Cure in New England: From the Civil War to World War I* (Hanover, NH: University Press of New England, 1973); Donald Meyer, *The Positive Thinkers: Religion as Pop Psychology from Mary Baker Eddy to Oral Roberts* (New York: Pantheon Books, 1980), 73–93.

48. See Heather D. Curtis, *Faith in the Great Physician: Suffering and Divine Healing in American Culture, 1860–1900* (Baltimore: Johns Hopkins University Press, 2007).

49. William Leach, *Land of Desire: Merchants, Power, and the Rise of a New American Culture* (New York: Vintage Books, 1993), 225.

50. Satter, *Each Mind a Kingdom*, 15.

51. The most useful historical accounts of religion and psychology in this period are Ann Taves, *Fits, Trances, and Visions: Experiencing Religion and Explaining Experience from Wesley to James* (Princeton, NJ: Princeton University Press, 1999); White, *Unsettled Minds*.

52. Christopher White notes as well the biographical similarities of many early psychologists, especially their personal connections to Protestant Christianity and the crisis of conversion. On the relationship of religious biography to the disciplinary history of psychology, see also the autobiographical essays by Coe, Leuba, and Starbuck collected in Vergilius Ferm, ed., *Religion in Transition* (New York: Macmillan, 1937), and the series, which began publication in 1930, *A History of Psychology in Autobiography* (Washington, DC: American Psychological Association, 1930–2007), now in nine volumes. See also Peter Homans, "A Personal Struggle with Religion: Significant Fact in the Lives and Work of the First Psychologists," *Journal of Religion* 62, no. 2 (1982): 128–44; Fuller, *Spiritual but Not Religious*, 123–51. Andrew Heinze contests this standard version of the origins of psychology in liberal Protestantism, noting that certain important early psychologists were Jewish. See Andrew Heinze, *Jews and the American Soul: Human Nature in the Twentieth Century* (Princeton, NJ: Princeton University Press, 2004). Nevertheless the roots of psychology in religious efforts to fathom the relationship of the self to metaphysical realities beyond the conscious self remain clear.

53. William James, *The Varieties of Religious Experience: A Study in Human Nature* (New York: Modern Library, 1999), 36.

54. James, *Varieties of Religious Experience*, 114.

55. Jones, *Social Law in the Spiritual World*, 66.

56. See Keith G. Meador, "'My Own Salvation': The *Christian Century* and Psychology's Secularizing of American Protestantism," in Smith, *The Secular Revolution*, 269–309.

57. Jones, *Social Law in the Spiritual World*, 152, 153.

58. Jones, *Social Law in the Spiritual World*, 198.

Chapter 1

1. Warren G. Harding to Religious Book Week Committee, February 27, 1922, published in *Publishers' Weekly*, April 1, 1922. Harding's note was often trumpeted in subsequent Religious Book Week publicity. For a discussion of the Harding letter and its use in pulpits and newspapers, see Marion Humble, "Religious Book Week," *Bulletin of the American Library Association* 16 no. 4 (1922): 296. For more on the ties between the American Library Association and Religious Book Week, see chapter 2.

2. On the related developments in social science in these years, especially the tensions between positivistic and moralistic conceptions of the field, see Mark C. Smith, *Social Science in the Crucible: The American Debate over Objectivity and Purpose, 1918-1941* (Durham, NC: Duke University Press, 1994); R. Laurence Moore, "Secularization: Religion and the Social Sciences," in William R. Hutchison, ed., *Between the Times: The Travail of the Protestant Establishment in America, 1900-1960* (New York: Cambridge University Press, 1989), 233-52.

3. Walter Lippmann, *A Preface to Morals* (New York: Macmillan, 1929), 6.

4. Lippmann, *A Preface to Morals*, 6.

5. Lippmann, *A Preface to Morals*, 6.

6. For an account of the interface of fundamentalism and the consumer culture of the period, written by a fundamentalist scholar, see Douglas Carl Abrams, *Selling the Old-Time Religion: American Fundamentalists and Mass Culture, 1920-1940* (Athens: University of Georgia Press, 2001). See also George M. Marsden, *Fundamentalism and American Culture: The Shaping of Twentieth-Century Evangelicalism, 1870-1925* (New York: Oxford University Press, 1980).

7. Lippmann, *A Preface to Morals*, 7.

8. Lynn Dumenil, *The Modern Temper: American Culture and Society in the 1920s* (New York: Hill and Wang, 1995), 9, 148.

9. Gail Bederman, *Manliness and Civilization: A Cultural History of Gender and Race in the United States, 1880-1917* (Chicago: University of Chicago Press, 1995), 184.

10. Christopher G. White, *Unsettled Minds: Psychology and the American Search for Spiritual Assurance, 1830-1940* (Berkeley: University of California Press, 2009), 91. On Hall, see also Amy Kaplan, *The Anarchy of Empire in the Making of U.S. Culture* (Cambridge, MA: Harvard University Press, 2002), 112-14; Bederman, *Manliness and Civilization*, 177.

11. Bederman, *Manliness and Civilization*, 77-78.

12. See Stephen Prothero, *American Jesus: How the Son of God Became a National Icon* (New York: Farrar, Straus and Giroux, 2003), 87-123; David Morgan, *Visual Piety: A History and Theory of Popular Religious Images* (Berkeley: University of California Press, 1998), 97-123; Clifford Putney, *Muscular Christianity: Manhood and Sports in Protestant America, 1880-1920* (Cambridge, MA: Harvard University Press, 2001).

13. Stephen Prothero reports on a 1910 survey conducted by the YMCA that determined that men accounted for only one-third of church attendance in the United States (*American Jesus*, 93).

14. Robert T. Handy, *A Christian America: Protestant Hopes and Historical Realities* (New York: Oxford University Press, 1971), 200-201, 205; Robert T. Handy, "The American Religious Depression, 1925-1935," *Church History* 29 (March 1960): 3-16.

15. Robert S. Lynd and Helen Merrell Lynd, *Middletown: A Study in Modern American Culture* (New York: Harcourt Brace Jovanovich, 1929), 350.

16. See Sydney Ahlstrom, *A Religious History of the American People* (New Haven, CT: Yale University Press, 1972), 895-917; Martin E. Marty, *Modern American Religion*, Vol. 2: *The Noise of Conflict, 1919-1941* (Chicago: University of Chicago Press, 1991), 15-58. One must be careful equating the term *liberal* with the term *Protestant establishment*, for while it is true that theological liberals predominated in leadership positions in seminaries, denominational bureaucracies, and various ecumenical enterprises, the denominations of the so-called mainline—Congregationalists, white Methodists and Baptists, Disciples of Christ, Presbyterians, Episcopalians, and Lutherans—contained many lay people in the first half of the twentieth century who rejected the tenets of theological liberalism. The efforts of the religious reading programs described in this chapter to bring theological liberalism to the public were aimed

just as strongly at members of their own denominations as at those in the wider culture. See William R. Hutchison, introduction to *Between the Times*, 13–16.

17. Gilbert Seldes, "Service," *The New Republic*, July 15, 1925, 207.

18. Richard M. Fried, *The Man Everybody Knew: Bruce Barton and the Making of Modern America* (Chicago: Ivan R. Dee, 2005), 13.

19. Fried, *The Man Everybody Knew*, 83.

20. Fried, *The Man Everybody Knew*, 84.

21. "'Religious Book Week' Is Now On," *San Jose Mercury News*, April 2, 1922.

22. Bruce Barton, *The Man Nobody Knows: A Discovery of the Real Jesus* (Indianapolis: Bobbs-Merrill, 1925), 9.

23. Forney Hutchinson to D. L. Chambers, April 6, 1925, Bruce Barton Papers, Wisconsin Historical Society Archives, Box 107, Folder "Man Nobody Knows—Readers—1924–1925, June."

24. Charles E. Adams to D. L. Chambers, April 14, 1925, Bruce Barton Papers, Wisconsin Historical Society Archives, Box 107, Folder "Man Nobody Knows—Readers—1924–1925, June."

25. Edward Grilley Jr. to Bruce Barton, July 30, 1926, Bruce Barton Papers, Wisconsin Historical Society Archives, Box 108, Folder "Man Nobody Knows—Readers—1926, July–October."

26. William R. Hutchison, preface to *Between the Times*, xii.

27. Ann Douglas, *Terrible Honesty: Mongrel Manhattan in the 1920s* (New York: Farrar, Straus and Giroux, 1995), 4.

28. Richard Wightman Fox, "Epitaph for Middletown: Robert S. Lynd and the Analysis of Consumer Culture," in Richard Wrightman Fox and T. J. Jackson Lears, eds., *The Culture of Consumption: Critical Essays in American History, 1880–1980* (New York: Pantheon Books, 1983), 103.

29. The most complete source of biographical information on Melcher is the obituary in *Publishers' Weekly*, March 18, 1963, 16–19, 36. See also *Frederic G. Melcher: Friendly Reminiscences of a Half Century among Books and Bookmen* (New York: Book Publishers Bureau, 1945), a compilation of tributes to Melcher; and Ellen D. Gilbert, "*Publishers' Weekly*, the Depression, and World War II," *Princeton University Library Chronicle* 59, no. 1 (1997): 59–82.

30. See especially Olivier Zunz, *Making America Corporate, 1870–1920* (Chicago: University of Chicago Press, 1990); Alan Trachtenberg, *The Incorporation of America: Culture and Society in the Gilded Age* (New York: Hill and Wang, 1982).

31. As Lynn Dumenil notes, the Census Bureau's definition of a city included any population center of more than 2,500, a very low number for any realistic understanding of urban life. This may diminish somewhat the importance of this watershed moment, yet the census findings did contribute to Americans' sense of their society as one in flux.

32. Joan Shelley Rubin, *Making of Middlebrow Culture* (Chapel Hill: University of North Carolina Press, 1992), 31.

33. Trysh Travis, "Reading Matters: Book Men, 'Serious' Readers, and the Rise of Mass Culture, 1930–1965" (Ph.D. diss., Yale University, 1998), 34.

34. Catherine Turner, *Marketing Modernism between the Two World Wars* (Amherst: University of Massachusetts Press, 2003), 31.

35. J. W. Clinger, "The Advertising of Religious Books," an address delivered to the Publishers' Group of the International Sunday School Council of Religious Education, meeting in Chicago, February 21, 1923, reprinted in *Publishers' Weekly*, March 24, 1923, 1007. On advertising, see Stuart Ewen, *Captains of Consciousness: Advertising and the Social Roots of Consumer Culture* (New York: McGraw-Hill, 1976); T. J. Jackson Lears, *Fables of Abundance: A Cultural History of Advertising in America* (New York: Basic Books, 1994); Roland Marchand, *Advertising the American Dream: Making Way for Modernity, 1920–1940* (Berkeley: University of California Press, 1985).

36. John Tebbel, *Between Covers: The Rise and Transformation of Book Publishing in America* (New York: Oxford University Press, 1987), 307–11.

37. Turner, *Marketing Modernism*, 87. See also Richard Minsky, *The Art of American Book Covers: 1875–1930* (New York: George Braziller, 2010).

38. Orion H. Cheney, *Economic Survey of the Book Industry, 1930–1931* (New York: National Association of Book Publishers, 1931), 68–69.

39. Cheney, *Economic Survey of the Book Industry*, 68.
40. *The Baptist*, the weekly magazine of the Northern Baptist Convention. March 5, 1921. (The Northern Baptist Convention, founded in 1907, changed its named to the American Baptist Convention in 1950 and American Baptist Churches in the USA in 1972.)
41. "Religious Book Week Finds Wide Support," *Publishers' Weekly*, March 12, 1921, 778.
42. Frederic G. Melcher, "Religious Books and Their Readers," *New York Times Book Review*, March 20, 1921, 8.
43. Gaius Glenn Atkins, "The Church and the Library," an abstract of remarks presented to the Libraries of Religion and Theology Round Table of the American Library Association, published in *Bulletin of the American Library Association* 16, no. 4 (1922): 298.
44. See "Libraries of Religion and Theology Round Table," *Bulletin of the American Library Association* 16, no. 4 (1922): 299.
45. *San Jose Mercury News*, March 17, 1921.
46. YMCA leaflet, quoted in "Religious Book Week Finds Wide Support," 778.
47. Quoted in "Religious Book Week," *Publishers' Weekly*, February 26, 1921, 620.
48. Melcher, "Religious Books and Their Readers," 8.
49. "Religious Books as Bestsellers," *Publishers' Weekly*, February 19, 1921, 513.
50. "Religious Book Week and After," *Publishers' Weekly*, April 2, 1921, 1048.
51. YMCA leaflet, quoted in "Religious Book Week Finds Wide Support," 778.
52. As quoted in "Religious Book Week Finds Wide Support," 778.
53. The literature here is extensive. See John M. Giggie and Diane Winston, eds., *Faith in the Market: Religion and the Rise of Urban Commercial Culture* (New Brunswick, NJ: Rutgers University Press, 2002); R. Laurence Moore, *Selling God: American Religion in the Marketplace of Culture* (New York: Oxford University Press, 1994); Penne Restad, *Christmas in America: A History* (New York: Oxford University Press, 1995); Leigh Eric Schmidt, *Consumer Rites: The Buying and Selling of American Holidays* (Princeton, NJ: Princeton University Press, 1995).
54. William H. Wooster, writing in *New Era Magazine*, March 1921, as quoted in "Religious Book Week Finds Wide Support," 778, italics original.
55. W. J. Smith, "A Progressive Religious Book Store," *Publishers' Weekly*, March 12, 1921, 777.
56. The book week publicists transcribed Bryan's rather staid proclamation, "The spiritual nature needs nourishment no less than the body, and religious books supplement the Bible, the Church, and the Sunday School," onto small cards for display in store windows and included Fosdick's call for "more who make it a duty to acquaint themselves with the great dynamic literature of spiritual life" in additional publicity materials. Quoted in Melcher, "Religious Books and Their Readers," 8.
57. Michael Kazin, Bryan's most recent biographer, makes a compelling case that Bryan himself was not a fundamentalist, strictly speaking. According to Kazin, he agreed in many respects with fundamentalist theology, but his primary concerns were pragmatic—the personal and social benefits of traditional Christianity—rather than narrowly theological. See Kazin, *A Godly Hero: The Life of William Jennings Bryan* (New York: Knopf, 2006), 262–95. Kazin makes no mention of Bryan's small role in Religious Book Week.
58. Robert Moats Miller, *Harry Emerson Fosdick: Preacher, Pastor, Prophet* (New York: Oxford University Press, 1985), 119.
59. Prothero, *American Jesus*, 93.
60. Harry Emerson Fosdick, "Shall the Fundamentalists Win?," *Christian Work*, June 10, 1922, 722. Also quoted, in shorter form, in Prothero, *American Jesus*, 111.
61. *Idaho Statesman*, March 9, 1921.
62. *San Jose Mercury News*, March 17, 1921.
63. "Second Annual Religious Book Week, April 2–8," *Publishers' Weekly*, March 18, 1922, 842.
64. Dr. Eliot had famously introduced his "Five-Foot Shelf of Books," also called the "Harvard Classics," in 1909 as perhaps the first middlebrow reading program in the nation. See Rubin, *Making of Middlebrow Culture*, 27–29.
65. "The Field of the Religious Book," *Publishers' Weekly*, February 23, 1924, 591.
66. Charles W. Eliot, "Books to Help Give Cheerful Beliefs," and Raymond Calkins, "Devotional Reading," reprinted in *Publishers' Weekly*, March 18, 1922, 848–49.

67. Maurice H. Harris, "Religious Literature for a Secular Age," reprinted in *Publishers' Weekly*, March 18, 1922, 849.

68. "What Is a Religious Book?," *Publishers' Weekly*, March 29, 1924, 1107.

69. "The Output of Religious Books," *Publishers' Weekly*, February 17, 1923, 501.

70. Henry F. Cope, "The Currency of Religious Books," *Publishers' Weekly*, February 19, 1921, 519.

71. Harold Hunting, "What is a Religious Book?," *Publishers' Weekly*, March 18, 1922, 843.

72. "What Is a Religious Book?," editorial, *Argus* (Rock Island, IL), April 1, 1922, reprinted in *Publishers' Weekly*, February 17, 1923, 512.

73. John Tebbel, *A History of Book Publishing in the United States*, Vol. 3: *The Golden Age between Two Wars, 1920–1940* (New York: R. R. Bowker, 1978), 331.

74. "Suggestions for Booksellers for Religious Book Week," *Publishers' Weekly*, February 17, 1923, 511.

75. The National Board of Review of Motion Pictures, founded in 1909 by a group of fourteen social workers, educators, and religious professionals, was originally called the New York Board of Censorship of Motion Pictures, later changing its name to the National Board of Censorship of Motion Pictures, and in 1916 to the National Board of Review of Motion Pictures. These changes reflected its growing national ambitions and its move away from censorship and toward viewer education as the best means for dealing with controversial material in film. The National Committee for Better Films was established as part of this shift away from censorship and toward the promotion of positive films.

76. "Motion Pictures for Religious Book Week," *Library Journal* 48, no. 4 (1923): 173.

77. "Suggestions for Booksellers for Religious Book Week," *Publishers' Weekly*, February 17, 1923, 511.

78. See Alain Weill, *The Poster: A Worldwide Survey and History* (Boston: G. K. Hall, 1985), 72–80; Michele H. Bogart, *Advertising, Artists, and the Borders of Art* (Chicago: University of Chicago Press, 1995), 79–124.

79. Bogart, *Advertising, Artists, and the Borders of Art*, 79.

80. Bogart, *Advertising, Artists, and the Borders of Art*, 82.

81. Bogart, *Advertising, Artists, and the Borders of Art*, 4.

82. Melcher was a champion of the graphic arts and, in his role with the National Association of Book Publishers and as chairman of Children's Book Week and Religious Book Week, acted as patron, commissioning posters for promotional purposes. The artist responsible for the introduction of the book poster in the 1910s, however, was Michael Gross, who would later design a poster for the 1940s version of Religious Book Week (discussed in chapter 5). Gross was widely acknowledged as the greatest innovator in book merchandising in the twentieth century. See "Take a Bow: Michael Gross," *Publishers' Weekly*, December 30, 1963, 23–28.

83. Turner, *Marketing Modernism*, 65.

84. Henry F. Cope, "The Currency of Religious Books," *Publishers' Weekly*, February 21, 1921, 519.

85. "What Is a Religious Book?," editorial, 512.

86. Cheney, *Economic Survey of the Book Industry*, 79.

87. On the role of libraries in World War I, see Wayne A. Wiegand, *"An Active Instrument for Propaganda": The American Public Library During World War I* (Westport, CT: Greenwood Press, 1989).

88. Norman Kent, "C. B. Falls, 1874–1960: A Career in Retrospect," *American Artist* 26 (February 1962): 41, 62.

89. The Treidler poster remained in use after the conclusion of Religious Book Week in 1927, which explains the lack of a "Religious Book Week" heading. With the phrase "Religious Book Week" gone, the publishers association opted to change the slogan "Good Books Build Character" to the more explicit "Religious Books Build Character."

90. Walt Reed and Roger Reed, *The Illustrator in America, 1880–1980* (New York: Madison Square Press, 1984), 110.

91. On Henry Adams and the vogue in medievalism in turn-of-the-century American culture, see T. J. Jackson Lears, *No Place of Grace: Antimodernism and the Transformation of American Culture, 1880–1920* (Chicago: University of Chicago Press, 1981), 142–81, 262–97.

92. Susman's framework built on earlier social criticism from David Riesman and Philip Rieff and has become the standard guide for decoding the significance of character and personality in American culture, though it has met with some criticism. Warren I. Susman, "'Personality' and the Making of Twentieth-Century Culture," in *Culture as History: The Transformation of American Society in the Twentieth Century* (Washington, DC: Smithsonian Books, 2003), 271–85.

93. "When Did You Buy a Book?," *The Baptist*, March 5, 1921, 133.

94. Richard Wightman Fox, "The Culture of Liberal Protestant Progressivism, 1875–1925," *Journal of Interdisciplinary History* 23, no. 3 (1993): 639–40.

95. "The Religious Book Season," *Publishers' Weekly*, February 18, 1928, 666.

96. William H. Leach, "Religious Books Do Move," *Publishers' Weekly*, February 16, 1929, 757.

97. Joan Shelley Rubin, "The Boundaries of American Religious Publishing in the Early Twentieth Century," *Book History* 2, no. 1 (1999): 211–12.

98. "The Religious Book Season," 666.

99. A useful introduction of Link is in James Hudnut-Beumler, *Looking for God in the Suburbs: The Religion of the American Dream and Its Critics, 1945–1965* (New Brunswick, NJ: Rutgers University Press, 1994), 55–60.

100. Henry C. Link, *The Return to Religion* (New York: Macmillan, 1936), 94.

101. Link, *The Return to Religion*, 7, 103.

102. Link, *The Return to Religion*, 19.

103. Link, *The Return to Religion*, 150.

104. Link, *The Return to Religion*, 152.

105. "About the Author," in Henry C. Link, *The Return to Religion* (New York: Pocket Books, 1941), 168–69.

106. The phrase comes from Christopher Lasch, *The Culture of Narcissism: American Life in an Age of Diminishing Expectations* (New York: Norton, 1978).

Chapter 2

1. *The Idaho Statesman*, March 9, 1921.

2. Warren I. Susman, "Culture and Civilization: The Nineteen-Twenties," in *Culture As History: The Transformation of American Society in the Twentieth Century* (Washington, DC: Smithsonian Institution Press, 2003), 107.

3. Susman, "Culture and Civilization," 108; Joan Shelley Rubin, *The Making of Middlebrow Culture* (Chapel Hill: University of North Carolina Press, 1992), 209.

4. Mortimer J. Adler and Charles Van Doren, *How to Read a Book* (New York: Simon and Schuster, 1972), 5.

5. John Heidenry, *Theirs Was the Kingdom: Lila and DeWitt Wallace and the Story of the Reader's Digest* (New York: Norton, 1993); Joanne P. Sharp, *Condensing the Cold War: Reader's Digest and American Identity* (Minneapolis: University of Minnesota Press, 2000); Janice Radway, *A Feeling for Books: The Book-of-the-Month Club, Literary Taste, and Middle-Class Desire* (Chapel Hill: University of North Carolina Press, 1997).

6. Catherine Turner, *Marketing Modernism between the Two World Wars* (Amherst: University of Massachusetts Press, 2003), 28–29.

7. Trysh Travis describes the middlebrow controversy at length in "Print and the Creation of Middlebrow," in Scott E. Casper, Joanne D. Chaison, and Jeffrey D. Groves, eds., *Perspectives on American Book History: Artifacts and Commentary* (Amherst: University of Massachusetts Press, 2002), 339–66. For another useful discussion of middlebrow, especially in popular magazines such as *Reader's Digest* and *Saturday Review of Literature*, see Christina Klein, *Cold War Orientalism: Asia in the Middlebrow Imagination, 1945–1961* (Berkeley: University of California Press, 2003), 61–99. For a discussion of interwar women's novels in terms of middlebrow, see Jaime Harker, *America the Middlebrow: Women's Novels, Progressivism, and Middlebrow Authorship between the Wars* (Amherst: University of Massachusetts Press, 2007).

8. Quoted in Rubin, *The Making of Middlebrow Culture*, xiii.

9. Dwight Macdonald, "Masscult and Midcult," in *Against the American Grain: Essays on the Effects of Mass Culture* (New York: Vintage Books, 1965), 3–75; Clement Greenberg, "Avant Garde and Kitsch," in *Clement Greenberg: The Collected Essays and Criticism*, Vol. 1: *Perceptions and Judgments 1939–1944* (Chicago: University of Chicago Press, 1986), 5–22; Max Horkheimer and Theodor W. Adorno, "The Culture Industry: Enlightenment as Mass Deception," in Gunzelin Schmid Noerr, ed., *Dialectic of Enlightenment: Philosophical Fragments* (Stanford: Stanford University Press, 2001), 94–136.

10. Rubin, *The Making of Middlebrow Culture*, xii–xiii.

11. Michael G. Kammen, *American Culture, American Tastes: Social Change and the 20th Century* (New York: Knopf, 1999), 95–100.

12. Lawrence W. Levine, *Highbrow/Lowbrow: The Emergence of Cultural Hierarchy in America* (Cambridge, MA: Harvard University Press, 1988), 225.

13. Hall defines a discursive formation as the "ideas, images, and practices" that "define what is and is not appropriate in our formulation of, and our practices in relation to, a particular subject or site of social activity; what knowledge is considered useful, relevant, and 'true' in that context; and what sort of persons or 'subjects' embody its characteristics." Stuart Hall, introduction to *Representation: Cultural Representations and Signifying Practices* (London: Sage Press, 1997), 6. For a useful discussion of Hall's notion of "discursive formation" in relation to media and popular religion in the twentieth-century United States, see Sean McCloud, *Making the American Religious Fringe: Exotics, Subversives, and Journalists, 1955–1993* (Chapel Hill: University of North Carolina Press, 2004), 26–27.

14. Stuart Hall, "The Rediscovery of Ideology: The Return of the Repressed in Media Studies," in Veronica Beechly and James Donald, eds., *Subjectivity and Social Relations* (Philadelphia: Open University Press, 1985), 34.

15. Rubin, *The Making of Middlebrow Culture*, xvi.

16. Radway, *A Feeling for Books*, 128. See also Jay Satterfield, *The World's Best Books: Taste, Culture, and the Modern Library* (Amherst: University of Massachusetts Press, 2002).

17. Quoted in R. L. Duffus, *Books: Their Place in a Democracy* (Boston: Houghton Mifflin, 1930), 87.

18. Rubin, *Making of Middlebrow Culture*, 31, 32.

19. David Brooks, "Joe Strauss to Joe Six-Pack," *New York Times*, June 16, 2005. Brooks's column presents a succinct and empathetic defense of midcentury middlebrow culture, when, in his words, "there was still a sense that culture is good for your character, and that a respectable person should spend time absorbing the best that has been thought and said." He fails to address, however, how and by whom and to what ends "best" is defined.

20. Rubin, *Making of Middlebrow Culture*, 27.

21. List reproduced in *Publishers' Weekly*, February 19, 1921, 515.

22. "Religious Book Lists," *Publishers' Weekly*, March 17, 1923, 942.

23. Frederick D. Kershner, "'A Book a Week': How a Worth-While Slogan Can Be Profitably Applied," *Publishers' Weekly*, February 17, 1923, 503.

24. The standard work in the history of the American public library in this period is Dee Garrison, *Apostles of Culture: The Public Librarian and American Society, 1876–1920* (Madison: University of Wisconsin Press, 2003). See Wayne Wiegand, *Main Street Public Library: Community Places and Reading Spaces in the Rural Heartland, 1876–1956* (Iowa City: University of Iowa Press, 2011), and the collection of essays in Thomas Augst and Wayne Wiegand, eds., *Libraries as Agencies of Culture* (Madison: University of Wisconsin Press, 2003). None of these addresses the matter of religious literature in public libraries.

25. The organization changed names frequently. In 1916 and 1917 it was known as the Theological Librarians' Round Table. From 1918 to 1923 it was the Round Table of the Librarians of Religion and Theology, and from 1924 through 1933 the Religious Books Round Table. The name changed again in 1934 to the Religious Books Section and in 1942 reverted to Religious Books Round Table. For the sake of clarity I simply refer to the body as the Religious Books Round Table or the Round Table.

26. "Theological Libraries' Round Table," *Bulletin of the American Library Association* 10, no. 4 (1916): 450.

27. "Round Table of the Libraries of Religion and Theology," *Bulletin of the American Library Association* 14, no. 4 (1920): 339.

28. Elima A. Foster, "Representations of Religious Thought in the Public Library," a paper presented to the Libraries of Religion and Theology Round Table of the American Library Association, June 24, 1921, reprinted in *Publishers' Weekly*, March 18, 1922, 845.

29. Frank Grant Lewis, "Selecting Religious Books for a Public Library," a paper presented to the Libraries of Religion and Theology Round Table of the American Library Association, June 29, 1922, reprinted in *Library Journal* 47, no. 14 (1922): 646.

30. Elizabeth Howard West, "Religious Books Are in Demand," *Publishers' Weekly*, February 17, 1923, 507.

31. "Libraries of Religion and Theology Round Table," *Bulletin of the American Library Association* 16, no. 4 (1922): 299.

32. "Librarians Pick 50 Religious Books," *New York Times*, May 18, 1929, 7.

33. Press release, June 25, 1935, Religious Books Round Table, American Library Association, American Library Association Archives, Record Series 51/2/2, University of Illinois Archive.

34. "Fifty Outstanding Religious Books, June 1, 1938–May 31, 1939," Religious Books Round Table, American Library Association, American Library Association Archives, Record Series 51/2/2, University of Illinois Archive.

35. "Important Religious Books, 1931–1932," Religious Books Round Table, American Library Association, American Library Association Archives, Record Series 51/2/2, University of Illinois Archive.

36. "Fifty Outstanding Religious Books, June 1, 1938–May 31, 1939."

37. Satterfield, *The World's Best Books*.

38. *New York Times*, January 15, 1938, 8.

39. *New York Times*, December 10, 1940, 22.

40. Very little has been written on the Hazen series. The best available source is Mark T. Edwards, "Bringing Our World Together: The Empire of Christian Realism, 1870–1940" (Ph.D. diss., Purdue University, 2006), 232–42.

41. Leon Whipple, "Books on the Belt," *The Nation*, February 13, 1929, 182.

42. Michael Winship, " 'The Tragedy of the Book Industry'? Bookstores and Book Distribution in the United States to 1950," *Studies in Bibliography* 58, no. 1 (2007): 152.

43. These statistics, originally from the Cheney report, are found in John Hench, *Books as Weapons: Propaganda, Publishing, and the Battle for Global Markets in the Era of World War II* (Ithaca, NY: Cornell University Press, 2010), 12.

44. Henry C. Link and Harry Arthur Hopf, *People and Books: A Study of Reading and Book-Buying Habits* (New York: Book Manufacturers' Institute, 1946), 79–83, 89–92. Also worth noting is the finding that book dealers generally thought book clubs increased sales through traditional outlets rather than siphoning away customers. See 150–51.

45. James D. Jeffry, "How a Pastor Introduces Books to His People," *Publishers' Weekly*, February 23, 1924, 594.

46. Hope Reynolds Myers, "Inter-Church Reading Program," *Publishers' Weekly*, February 20, 1926, 586.

47. Religious Book Club advertisement, publication information uncertain. From the context it clearly appeared in the fall of 1927 or the winter of 1927–28, soon after the club debuted in November 1927. Harry Emerson Fosdick Papers, Burke Library Archives at Union Theological Seminary in the City of New York.

48. On Cavert, an important and understudied figure in twentieth-century Protestantism, see William J. Schmidt, *Architect of Unity: A Biography of Samuel McCrea Cavert* (New York: Friendship Press, 1978); Heather Warren, *Theologians of a New World Order: Reinhold Niebuhr and the Christian Realists, 1920–1948* (New York: Oxford University Press, 1997). Cavert would later assume an active role in conceiving the Hazen Books in Religion series.

49. This account of the club's origin is from "Religious Books of the Month," *Publishers' Weekly*, October 29, 1927, 1641–42. A slightly different version, in which the idea originated with Cavert, is found in Schmidt, *Architect of Unity*, 306. The Schmidt account is based on a personal interview with Cavert conducted in 1971, more than forty years after the fact.

50. Schmidt, *Architect of Unity*, 75.

51. "Religious Books of the Month," 1641–42.

52. "Religious Books of the Month," 1641–42.

53. Letters to the editor, published in *Religious Book Club Bulletin*, June 1928, December 1927, and June 1928. Copies of the *Religious Book Club Bulletin* were examined in the Library of Congress, which holds the only extant collection.

54. J. F. Newton, "Religious Books," *Publishers' Weekly*, May 21, 1927, 2003.

55. Membership numbers come from the *Religious Book Club Bulletin*, July 1928. By contrast, the Book-of-the-Month Club counted just over 110,000 members in 1929, according to Rubin, *Making of Middlebrow Culture*, 96. The percentage of lay readers was reported in Whipple, "Books on the Belt," 183.

56. Karl Brown, "The Religious Book in the Library," *Publishers' Weekly*, February 20, 1932, 846–47.

57. "Sales Notes," *Publishers' Weekly*, February 20, 1932, 856.

58. *Religious Book Club Bulletin*, August 1928.

59. "Religious Books Round Table," *Bulletin of the American Library Association* 26, no. 8 (1932): 621.

60. *Catholic Book Club: Silver Jubilee, 1928–1953* (New York: Catholic Book Club, 1953). Pages 18–24 list each book offered as the main monthly selection in the first twenty-five years of the club. On the origins of Catholic reading clubs, see Thomas F. O'Connor, "American Catholic Reading Circles, 1886–1909," *Libraries and Culture* 26, no. 2 (1991): 334–47. On Catholic reading, particularly in regard to fiction and church censorship, see Una Mary Cadegan, "All Good Books Are Catholic Books: Literature, Censorship, and the Americanization of Catholics, 1920–1960" (Ph.D. diss., University of Pennsylvania, 1987). On Francis X. Talbot and Catholic literary culture in these years, see Arnold Sparr, *To Promote, Defend, and Redeem: The Catholic Literary Revival and the Cultural Transformation of American Catholicism, 1920–1960* (New York: Greenwood Press, 1990).

61. "Another Book Club," *Publishers' Weekly*, April 14, 1928, 1624.

62. Andrew C. Rieser, *The Chautauqua Moment: Protestants, Progressives, and the Culture of Modern Liberalism, 1874–1920* (New York: Columbia University Press, 2003), 121.

63. Mary Elizabeth Downey, "Making Religious Books Popular," address given before the Religious Books Round Table, American Library Association, April 27, 1932, published in *Bulletin of the American Library Association* 26, no. 8 (1932): 615–20.

64. Arthur H. Howland, *Joseph Lewis: Enemy of God* (Boston: Stratford, 1932), 122.

65. "Still They Come," *Publishers' Weekly*, April 14, 1928, 1624. Fifty clubs is the estimate of Eugene Exman, "Religious Book Publishing," in Chandler B. Grannis, ed., *What Happens in Book Publishing* (New York: Columbia University Press, 1957), 341. On the business of religious book clubs, see Judith S. Duke, *Religious Publishing and Communications* (White Plains, NY: Knowledge Industry Publications, 1981), 131–44. Duke's report indicates twenty religious book clubs in operation in the late 1970s. Duffus, *Books* also details the economics of book clubs in the 1920s.

66. Announced in the *Religious Book Club Bulletin*, October 1930.

67. Schmidt, *Architect of Unity*, 306.

68. Erin A. Smith points out the Mathews-Machen pairing in "The Religious Book Club: Print Culture, Consumerism, and the Spiritual Life of American Protestants between the Wars," in Paul S. Boyer and Charles L. Cohen, eds., *Religion and the Culture of Print in Modern America* (Madison: University of Wisconsin Press, 2008).

69. *Religious Book Club Bulletin*, February 1941. The "dubious position" was the classic mind-cure idea that all disease stems from wrong thinking.

70. Religious Book Club selections in November 1949 and August 1952.

71. Samuel McCrea Cavert, "What Religious Books Are Read," *Publishers' Weekly*, February 16, 1929, 752.

72. *Religious Book Club Bulletin*, April 1944.

73. *Religious Book Club Bulletin*, December 1933. Comments in end-of-year summaries.

74. Duffus, *Books*, 85.

75. Cavert, "What Books on Religion Do People Read?," *Publishers' Weekly*, February 22, 1930, 981.

76. *Religious Book Club Bulletin*, December 1929. Comment in end-of-year summary.

77. Christopher G. White, *Unsettled Minds: Psychology and the American Search for Spiritual Assurance, 1830–1940* (Berkeley: University of California Press, 2009). See also Philip Rieff,

The Triumph of the Therapeutic: Uses of Faith after Freud (New York: Harper and Row, 1966); Julius H. Rubin, *Religious Melancholy and Protestant Experience in America* (New York: Oxford University Press, 1994).

78. Kevin G. Meador, "'My Own Salvation': The *Christian Century* and Psychology's Secularizing of American Protestantism," in Christian Smith, ed., *The Secular Revolution: Power, Interests, and Conflict in the Secularization of American Public Life* (Berkeley: University of California Press, 2003), 272, 276.

79. H. Richard Niebuhr, "Theology and Psychology: A Sterile Union," *Christian Century*, January 13, 1927, 47.

80. Niebuhr, "Theology and Psychology," 47.

81. Niebuhr, "Theology and Psychology," 47.

82. Coué, a Frenchman, made a celebrated tour of the United States in 1922–23, promoting his system of autosuggestion summarized by the famous slogan "Every day in every way I am getting better and better."

83. From Michael Korda, *Making the List: A Cultural History of the American Bestseller, 1900–1999* (New York: Barnes & Noble Books, 2001).

84. For another contemporary assessment of these developments, see Grace Adams, "The Rise and Fall of Psychology," *Atlantic Monthly* 153 (January 1934): 82–92.

85. *Religious Book Club Bulletin*, November 1934.

86. *Religious Book Club Bulletin*, December 1937 and March 1939. The comments on the Luccock book appear in the end-of-year summary.

87 *Religious Book Club Bulletin*, July 1939.

88. E. Brooks Holifield, *A History of Pastoral Care in America: From Salvation to Self-Realization* (Nashville, TN: Abingdon Press 1983).

89. Holifield, *History of Pastoral Care in America*, 207.

90. On the history of pastoral counseling and liberal religious sensibilities, see Susan E. Myers-Shirk, *Helping the Good Shepherd: Pastoral Counselors in a Psychotherapeutic Culture, 1925–1975* (Baltimore: Johns Hopkins University Press, 2009). On psychoanalysis in particular, see Jon H. Roberts, "Psychoanalysis and American Christianity, 1900–1945," in David C. Lindberg and Ronald L. Numbers, eds., *When Science and Christianity Meet* (Chicago: University of Chicago Press, 2003), 225–44.

91. *Religious Book Club Bulletin*, March 1931.

92. Gary Dorrien, *The Making of American Liberal Theology: Idealism, Realism, and Modernity, 1900–1950* (Louisville, KY: Westminster John Knox Press, 2003), 540.

93. Ralph E. Luker provides the best account of the contributions theological personalism made to progressive thinking on race and to civil rights organizing. See Luker, *The Social Gospel in Black and White: American Racial Reform, 1885–1912* (Chapel Hill: University of North Carolina Press, 1991). David L. Chappell contends, in contrast, that the influence of Boston personalism on Martin Luther King Jr. in particular has been overstated, reflecting mostly his student writing at Boston rather than his mature, independent thought. Even if Chappell is correct—and the evidence Luker presents indicates strongly that King was indeed indebted to personalist theology—the larger matter of personalism's contributions to social Christianity, progressive race politics, and human rights doctrine remains clear. See Chappell, *A Stone of Hope: Prophetic Religion and the Death of Jim Crow* (Chapel Hill: University of North Carolina Press, 2004), 52–54. On personalism and civil rights, see also Gary Dorrien, *The Making of American Liberal Theology: Crisis, Irony, and Postmodernity, 1950–2005* (Louisville, KY: Westminster John Knox Press, 2006), 155–59.

94. Rufus M. Jones, *Social Law in the Spiritual World: Studies in Human and Divine Inter-Relationship* (Philadelphia: John C. Winston, 1904), 66.

95. *Religious Book Club Bulletin*, December 1929. Comment in end-of-year summary.

96. *Religious Book Club Bulletin*, March 1936.

97. *Religious Book Club Bulletin*, September 1931.

98. *Religious Book Club Bulletin*, April 1936.

99. *Religious Book Club Bulletin*, August 1935.

100. *Religious Book Club Bulletin*, February 1941 and April 1948.
101. "Religious Books?," *Time*, November 4, 1946, 72.
102. On the seeker culture built by Jones, Huxley, Heard, and others, see Leigh Eric Schmidt, *Restless Souls: The Making of American Spirituality from Emerson to Oprah* (San Francisco: HarperSanFrancisco, 2005), 227–68.
103. *Religious Book Club Bulletin*, April 1944.
104. Prior to the 1946 reorganization, committee members read advance copies of all books submitted by publishers for consideration as book club selections and voted to determine the final offerings. After the reorganization, a professional staff screened submissions, and committee members reviewed only final candidates in their fields of interest. This pattern continued with the 1959 reorganization.
105. Announced in the *Religious Book Club Bulletin*, October 1959.

Chapter 3

1. Mary Rose Himler, "Religious Books as Best Sellers," *Publishers' Weekly*, February 19, 1927, 691.
2. "The Religious Renaissance," *Publishers' Weekly*, February 19, 1927, 684.
3. In 1928, 1,135 new fiction titles and 776 new religion titles were published. Figures come from Dorothea Lawrance Mann, "Selling Religious Books," *Publishers' Weekly*, February 22, 1930, 973.
4. Eugene Exman, "Reading, Writing, and Religion," *Harper's* 206 (May 1953): 85. Exman's figures show religious books, narrowly construed, accounting for 6.1 percent of total book sales in 1925 and 8.2 percent in 1929.
5. For data on the "religious depression," see Robert Wuthnow, *The Restructuring of American Religion* (Princeton, NJ: Princeton University Press, 1988), 25–26.
6. The numbers come from Exman, "Reading, Writing, and Religion," 85. Religious books accounted for 8.5 percent of all books sold in 1931 and only 4.7 percent of those sold in 1935.
7. See Robert T. Handy, "The American Religious Depression, 1925–1935," *Church History* 29, no. 1 (1960): 3–16; Martin Marty, *Modern American Religion*, Vol. 2: *The Noise of Conflict, 1919–1941* (Chicago: University of Chicago Press, 1991), 250–302; Sydney Ahlstrom, *A Religious History of the American People* (New Haven, CT: Yale University Press, 1972), 918–32.
8. Robert S. Lynd and Helen Merrell Lynd, *Middletown in Transition: A Study in Cultural Conflicts* (New York: Harcourt, Brace, 1937), 297, 298.
9. Lynd and Lynd, *Middletown in Transition*, 301.
10. Frederick Lewis Allen, *The Big Change: America Transforms Itself* (New York: Harper & Brothers, 1952), 248–49.
11. Eugene Exman, *The House of Harper: One Hundred and Fifty Years of Publishing* (New York: Harper and Row, 1967), 288.
12. For an overview of Protestant religious publishing from 1880 to 1940 that briefly touches on these commercial developments, see William Vance Trollinger Jr., "An Outpouring of 'Faithful' Words: Protestant Publishing in the United States," in Carl F. Kaestle and Janice A. Radway, eds., *A History of the Book in America*, Vol. 4: *Print in Motion, The Expansion of Publishing and Reading in the United States, 1880–1940* (Chapel Hill: University of North Carolina Press, 2009), 359–75.
13. Charles W. Ferguson, "Selling God in Babylon," *Publishers' Weekly*, February 22, 1930, 969.
14. Ferguson, "Selling God in Babylon," 970.
15. Allan Fisher, *Fleming H. Revell Company: The First 125 Years, 1870–1995* (Grand Rapids, MI: Fleming H. Revell, 1995).
16. Paul C. Gutjahr, "Diversification in American Religious Publishing," in Scott E. Casper, Jeffrey D. Groves, Stephen W. Nissenbaum, and Michael Winship, eds., *A History of the Book in America*, Vol. 3: *The Industrial Book, 1840–1880* (Chapel Hill: University of North Carolina Press, 2007), 201.
17. As quoted in "The Religious Renaissance," *Publishers' Weekly*, February 19, 1927, 685.

18. Joseph Fort Newton, "Religious Books," *Publishers' Weekly*, May 21, 1927, 2004. *Publishers' Weekly* carried the transcript of lectures given to a gathering of English and American booksellers in London.

19. Gilbert Loveland, "The Laymen's Interest in Religious Books," *Publishers' Weekly*, February 16, 1929, 754.

20. Wilbur Hugh Davies, "Selling Religious Books," *Publishers' Weekly*, February 16, 1929, 749-51.

21. William L. Savage, "What about Religious Books?," *Publishers' Weekly*, February 21, 1931, 931-33.

22. Ferguson, "Selling God in Babylon," 970.

23. Ferguson, "Selling God in Babylon," 970.

24. Loveland, "The Laymen's Interest in Religious Books," 755.

25. Charles Francis Potter, "Spring—Religious—Books," *Publishers' Weekly*, February 19, 1927, 687. On the Straton debates, see Michael Lienesch, *In the Beginning: Fundamentalism, the Scopes Trial, and the Making of the Antievolution Movement* (Chapel Hill: University of North Carolina Press, 2007), 86.

26. Ferguson, "Selling God in Babylon," 970.

27. Potter, "Spring—Religious—Books," 688.

28. Davies, "Selling Religious Books," 749-51.

29. Savage, "What about Religious Books?," 931-33.

30. Charles Ferguson, "Religious Books and the Depression," *Publishers' Weekly*, February 20, 1932, 844-45.

31. "Why Harpers Have Entered the Field of Religious Books," *Publishers' Weekly*, February 19, 1927, 695.

32. Exman, *The House of Harper*, 235. After his retirement in 1965 Exman became the firm's historian and archivist. On these developments at Harper's, see also John Tebbel, *A History of Book Publishing in the United States*, Vol. 3: *The Golden Age between Two Wars, 1920-1940* (New York: R. R. Bowker, 1978), 240-41. Tebbel's account, it must be noted, contains a number of minor factual errors.

33. Eugene Exman, "Modern Religious Books," *Publishers' Weekly*, February 20, 1932, 841-42.

34. Biographical sources for Exman include *The National Cyclopaedia of American Biography* (New York: James T. White, 1984), 62:119; the obituary in *Publishers' Weekly*, October 20, 1975, 38; and the obituary in the *New York Times*, October 12, 1975, 73.

35. Eugene Exman, "Individual and Group Experiences," in *Proceedings of Two Conferences on Parapsychology and Pharmacology* (New York: Parapsychology Foundation, 1961), 10.

36. On the intellectual climate at the University of Chicago Divinity School in these years, see Gary Dorrien, *The Making of American Liberal Theology: Idealism, Realism, and Modernity, 1900-1950* (Louisville, KY: Westminster John Knox Press, 2003), 151-208.

37. Exman, "Individual and Group Experiences," 10.

38. Eugene Exman, "A Young People's Organization in a Citizenship Project" (M.A. thesis, University of Chicago, 1925), 31.

39. Exman, *House of Harper*, 287-88.

40. On Rockefeller's religious philanthropy, see Albert F. Schenkel, *The Rich Man and the Kingdom: John D. Rockefeller, Jr., and the Protestant Establishment* (Minneapolis: Fortress Press, 1995).

41 On Fosdick, see Robert Moats Miller, *Harry Emerson Fosdick: Pastor, Preacher, Prophet* (New York: Oxford University Press, 1985). For an early profile of Fosdick, see Lurton Blassingame, "A Twentieth Century Puritan," *New Yorker*, June 18, 1927, 18-20.

42. Harry Emerson Fosdick to Eugene Exman, March 6, 1947, Series 2b, Box 3, Folder 2, Harry Emerson Fosdick Papers, Burke Library Archives at Union Theological Seminary in the City of New York.

43. Harry Emerson Fosdick to Eugene Exman, March 25, 1947, Series 2a, Box 3, Folder 13, and Harry Emerson Fosdick to Fred C. Baker, March 19, 1953, Series 2a, Box 3, Folder 13, Harry Emerson Fosdick Papers, Burke Library Archives at Union Theological Seminary in the City of New York.

44. Harry Emerson Fosdick, *As I See Religion* (New York: Harper & Brothers, 1932), 1.

45. Louis Schneider and Sanford M. Dornbusch, *Popular Religion: Inspirational Books in America* (Chicago: University of Chicago Press, 1958), 26.

46. Fosdick, *As I See Religion*, 6.

47. Fosdick, *As I See Religion*, 2.

48. Fosdick, *As I See Religion*, 9, 17.

49 Fosdick, *As I See Religion*, 21.

50. Fosdick, *As I See Religion*, 100.

51. Fosdick, *As I See Religion*, 68, 75.

52. Fosdick, *As I See Religion*, 81, 92.

53. Fosdick, *As I See Religion*, 82.

54. For an important account of the connections between religious liberalism and aesthetic sensibilities in a later period, see Sally Promey, "Taste Cultures: The Visual Practice of Liberal Protestantism, 1940–1965," in Laurie F. Maffly-Kipp, Leigh E. Schmidt, and Mark Valeri, eds., *Practicing Protestants: Histories of Christian Life in America, 1630–1965* (Baltimore: Johns Hopkins University Press, 2006).

55. Fosdick, *As I See Religion*, 131.

56. Fosdick, *As I See Religion*, 139.

57. See Miller, *Harry Emerson Fosdick*, 435–40.

58. Fosdick, *As I See Religion*, 136.

59. Fosdick, *As I See Religion*, 150–51.

60. See especially Ralph Waldo Emerson, "Divinity School Address" (1838), in Brooks Atkinson, ed., *The Selected Writings of Ralph Waldo Emerson* (New York: Modern Library, 1992).

61. Fosdick, *As I See Religion*, 40.

62. Fosdick, *As I See Religion*, 49, 44.

63. Fosdick, *As I See Religion*, 51.

64. Fosdick's account of his early reading of Jones's *Social Law in the Spiritual World* is further discussed in the introduction. See also Matthew S. Hedstrom, "Rufus Jones and Mysticism for the Masses," *CrossCurrents* 54, no. 2 (2004): 31–44.

65. See Miller, *Harry Emerson Fosdick*, 393. As one small indication of Niebuhr's respect for Fosdick's ethical and political acuity, the neo-orthodox stalwart once declared, "No one in our generation could illuminate the ethical issues which modern man faced in our technical society with greater rigor and honest illumination than he." Quoted in Miller, *Harry Emerson Fosdick*, 479.

66. Quoted in Miller, *Harry Emerson Fosdick*, 484.

67. Quoted in Miller, *Harry Emerson Fosdick*, 485.

68 Miller, *Harry Emerson Fosdick*, 490–91.

69. In many other ways Fosdick's politics embodied the tensions inherent in the liberalism of his times. He was a strong backer of Planned Parenthood and liberalized divorce laws, for example, but defended Victorian sexual mores. He morally opposed alcohol but pragmatically opposed Prohibition. He denounced lynching, decried race prejudice from the pulpit, and raised money frequently on behalf of the NAACP—including for Thurgood Marshall's ultimately successful assault on the segregated schools of Topeka, Kansas, that resulted in the *Brown* decision of 1954—but early in his career occasionally used broad racial caricatures for humorous effect in his sermons. He always remained troubled by the practical difficulties posed by interracial marriage, though was pleased when a granddaughter chose to study at the African American Fisk University and cheered her on when she was arrested as part of a demonstration to desegregate the movie theaters of Nashville. On Fosdick's politics more generally, see Miller, *Harry Emerson Fosdick*, 449–547.

70. Rufus M. Jones, *Spiritual Energies in Daily Life* (New York: Macmillan, 1922), xi.

71. Rufus M. Jones, "The Mystic's Experience of God," *Atlantic Monthly*, November 1921, 638.

72. R. Townsend Seashaw, "Dr. Fosdick to His Critics," *New York Herald Tribune*, May 15, 1932.

73. "Religion Is an Art to Dr. Fosdick," *New York Time Book Review*, May 1, 1932, 2.

74. Review of *As I See Religion*, in "I've Been Reading" column, *News Journal* (Murfreesboro , TN), August 27, 1932.

75. *Religious Book Club Bulletin*, May 1932.

76. Justin Wroe Nixon, "Dr. Fosdick's Distinctive Service," *Christian Century*, June 22, 1932, 33–34.

77. H. E. L., "Religion through Fosdick's Eyes," *World Tomorrow*, October 19, 1932.

78. Frederick Lynch, untitled review, *Reformed Church Messenger*, May 5, 1932.

79. From summary of destroyed letters. Mrs. F. W. Norwood to Harry Emerson Fosdick, November 5, 1936, Harry Emerson Fosdick Papers, Riverside Church, New York.

80. Donald Meyer, *The Positive Thinkers: Religion as Pop Psychology from Mary Baker Eddy to Oral Roberts* (New York: Pantheon Books, 1980), 219.

81. Harry Gaze, *Emmet Fox: The Man and His Work* (New York: Harper & Brothers, 1952), 98; Steven Starker, *Oracle at the Supermarket: The American Preoccupation with Self-Help Books* (New Brunswick, NJ: Transaction, 1989), 51. On Fox, see also his obituary, "Dr. Emmet Fox," *New York Times*, August 18, 1951, 11; Robert Myron Coates, "Blue Flame on the Forehead," *New Yorker*, September 11, 1943, 58. Gaze was a New Thought preacher and friend of Fox.

82. Emmet Fox, *Power through Constructive Thinking* (New York: Harper & Brothers, 1932), 137.

83. Fox, *Power through Constructive Thinking*, 171.

84. Fox, *Power through Constructive Thinking*, 2.

85. Fox, *Power through Constructive Thinking*, 64.

86. Emmet Fox, *The Sermon on the Mount: A General Introduction to Scientific Christianity in the Form of a Spiritual Key to Matthew V, VI, and VII* (New York: Harper & Brothers, 1934); Emmet Fox, *The Ten Commandments: The Master Key to Life* (New York: Harper & Row, 1953).

87. Fox, *Power through Constructive Thinking*, 136.

88. Fox, *Power through Constructive Thinking*, 99.

89. Fox, *Power through Constructive Thinking*, 2, 113.

90. Untitled list of booksellers, Box 99, Harper & Brothers Papers, Rare Book and Manuscript Library, Columbia University.

91. The definitive history of Alcoholics Anonymous and the Big Book is Trysh Travis, *The Language of the Heart: A Cultural History of the Recovery Movement from Alcoholics Anonymous to Oprah Winfrey* (Chapel Hill: University of North Carolina Press, 2009).

92. Igor I. Sikorsky Jr., *AA's Godparents: Three Early Influences on Alcoholics Anonymous and Its Foundation: Carl Jung, Emmet Fox, Jack Alexander* (Minneapolis: CompCare, 1990), 19.

93. See Susan Cheever, *Bill Wilson: His Life and the Creation of Alcoholics Anonymous* (New York: Simon and Schuster, 2004), 149–53. See also "The Book," in Mitchell K., *How It Worked: The Story of Clarence H. Snyder and the Early Days of Alcoholics Anonymous in Cleveland, Ohio* (Washingtonville, NY: AA Big Book Study Group, 1999).

94. Travis, *Language of the Heart*, 120–21.

95. Exman, "Reading, Writing, and Religion," 87.

96. Glenn Clark, *I Will Lift Up Mine Eyes* (New York: Harper & Brothers, 1937) and *How to Find Health through Prayer* (New York: Harper & Brothers, 1940). The following citations are from a single-volume edition of these works published cooperatively between Harper's and Guideposts, 1937.

97. Rufus M. Jones to Eugene Exman, July 31, 1945, Box 85, Harper & Brothers Papers, Rare Book and Manuscript Library, Columbia University. Clark, Jones, and other well-known leaders in prayer and mystical spirituality, such as Frank Laubach, E. Stanley Jones, and Howard Thurman, collaborated on a series of prayer meetings during World War II, out of which they produced the collection of essays published as Rufus M. Jones, ed., *Together: A Book by Twelve Men* (New York: Abingdon-Cokesbury Press, 1946).

98. Glenn Clark, *A Man's Reach: The Autobiography of Glenn Clark* (New York: Harper & Brothers, 1949), 151–97.

99. Glenn Clark, *The Soul's Sincere Desire* (Boston: Little, Brown, 1925).

100. Clark, *How to Find Health through Prayer*, 2.

101. Clark, *How to Find Health through Prayer*, 32.

102. Clark, *How to Find Health through Prayer*, 52.

103. Clark, *How to Find Health through Prayer*, 36.

104. Clark, *How to Find Health through Prayer*, 39.

105. Clark, *How to Find Health through Prayer*, 45.

106. Clark, *How to Find Health through Prayer*, 72.

107. On Heard, see Alison Falby, *Between the Pigeonholes: Gerald Heard, 1889–1971* (Newcastle, UK: Cambridge Scholars, 2008).

108. Eugene Exman to Thomas R. Kelly, January 4, 194[1], Box 12, Thomas R. Kelly Papers, Mss. Collection 1135, Quaker Collection, Haverford College Library, Haverford, PA. Exman misdated this letter as 1940. Leigh Schmidt quotes this same excerpt from Exman's letter to Kelly in *Restless Souls: The Making of American Spirituality from Emerson to Oprah* (San Francisco: HarperSanFrancisco, 2005), 260. Schmidt develops in rich detail the interconnections among Kelly, Rufus Jones, Gerald Heard, Aldous Huxley, Douglas Steere, and Christopher Isherwood, a group of seekers with whom Exman felt great kinship and who were instrumental in his own spiritual explorations. See Schmidt, *Restless Souls*, 227–68.

109. Falby, *Between the Pigeonholes*, 106.

110. In addition to Falby, on Trabuco College see also Timothy Miller, "Notes on the Prehistory of the Human Potential Movement: The Vedanta Society and Gerald Heard's Trabuco College," in Jeffrey J. Kripal and Glenn W. Shuck, eds., *On the Edge of the Future: Esalen and the Evolution of American Culture* (Bloomington: Indiana University Press, 2005), 80–98.

111. Miller, "Notes on the Prehistory of the Human Potential Movement," 81–82.

112. The Toomer-Exman exchange can be found in the Jean Toomer Collection, Box 3, Folder 98, Beinecke Rare Books and Manuscript Library, Yale University.

113. Exman, "Reading, Writing, and Religion," 86.

114. Quoted in Falby, *Between the Pigeonholes*, 114.

115. Mary Luytens, *Krishnamurti: His Life and Death* (New York: St. Martin's Press, 1990). Luytens was a lifelong friend of Krishnamurti as well as his biographer.

116. "Harper to Go West with New Religion/Trade Unit," *Publishers' Weekly*, September 13, 1976, 47. Additional details on the Harper's move to San Francisco come from personal correspondence and conversations with Mark Tauber, Tom Grady, Stephen Hanselman, and Hugh Van Dusen.

117. Eugene Exman, "Researchers of the Spirit," in Wallace C. Speers, ed., *Laymen Speaking* (New York: Association Press, 1947), 42.

118. Exman, "Researchers of the Spirit," 41.

119. Exman, "Researchers of the Spirit," 41.

120. "Wainwright House Open," *New York Times*, May 21, 1951, 29. See also "Suburban Chateau Will Aid Religion," *New York Times*, June 13, 1951.

121. On LSD and American spirituality in this period, see Jay Stevens, *Storming Heaven: LSD and the American Dream* (New York: Atlantic Monthly Press, 1987); Don Lattin, *The Harvard Psychedelic Club: How Timothy Leary, Ram Dass, Huston Smith, and Andrew Weil Killed the Fifties and Ushered in a New Age for America* (San Francisco: HarperOne, 2010). See also Aldous Huxley, *The Doors of Perception* (New York: Harper & Brothers, 1954); Huston Smith, *Cleansing the Doors of Perception: The Religious Significance of Entheogenic Plants and Chemicals* (New York: Tarcher, 2000).

122. Falby, *Between the Pigeonholes*, 136.

123. Exman, "Individual and Group Experience," 11.

124. Exman, "Individual and Group Experience," 13, 12.

125. Exman, "Individual and Group Experience," 11.

126. Eugene Exman, "Search for Meaning," in Eugene Exman, Thomas E. Powers, and Douglas V. Steere, *Search for Meaning* (Rye, NY: Wainwright House, 1961), also published in *Hibbert Journal* 62, no. 239 (1962): 275–83.

127. See, for example, Eugene Exman, "Religious Book Publishing," in Chandler B. Grannis, ed., *What Happens in Book Publishing* (New York: Columbia University Press, 1957). Exman also served as chairman of the Religious Publishers' Group, a consortium of the major national religious publishers affiliated with the National Association of Book Publishers.

128. Exman, *House of Harper*, 287.

129. Eugene Exman and Erica Anderson, *The World of Albert Schweitzer: A Book of Photographs* (New York: Harper & Brothers, 1955); "Religious Services," *New York Times*, October 9, 1954, 10.

130. P. W. Wilson, "The Field for Religious Books," *Publishers' Weekly*, February 19, 1938.
131. Wilson, "The Field for Religious Books," 915.

Chapter 4

1   See Eugene Exman, "Reading, Writing, and Religion," *Harper's Magazine* 206, no. 1236 (1953): 85.
2. See Dan Lacy and Robert W. Frase, "Building on the 1940s, Section II: The American Book Publishers Council," in David Paul Nord, Joan Shelley Rubin, and Michael Schudson, eds., *A History of the Book in America*, Vol. 5: *The Enduring Book: Print Culture in Postwar America* (Chapel Hill: University of North Carolina Press, 2009), 195–209.
3. Paul C. Gutjahr, "The Perseverance of Print-Bound Saints: Protestant Book Publishing," in *A History of the Book in America*, Vol. 5: *The Enduring Book*, 376.
4. See, as examples, Wade Clark Roof, *A Generation of Seekers: The Spiritual Journeys of the Baby-Boom Generation* (San Francisco: HarperSanFrancisco, 1993), and *Spiritual Marketplace: Baby Boomers and the Remaking of American Religion* (Princeton, NJ: Princeton University Press, 1999); Robert Wuthnow, *After Heaven: Spirituality in America since the 1950s* (Berkeley: University of California Press, 1998).
5. Henry C. Link and Harry Arthur Hopf, *People and Books: A Study of Reading and Book-Buying Habits* (New York: Book Manufacturers' Institute, 1946), 23.
6. Link and Hopf, *People and Books*, 121, 24.
7. Link and Hopf, *People and Books*, 75. Paperback sales did vary by income level, accounting for 8 percent of books sold to upper-income readers and 23 percent of books sold to lower-income readers. On the so-called paperback revolution, see Kenneth C. Davis, *Two-Bit Culture: The Paperbacking of America* (Boston: Houghton Mifflin, 1984).
8. Quoted in Link and Hopf, *People and Books*, 132.
9. From "Current in the Trade," *Publishers' Weekly*, March 13, 1943, 1181–83, quote on 1182.
10. "Religious and Inspirational Books Continue Big Sales," *Publishers' Weekly*, April 10, 1943, 1502.
11. From "Current in the Trade," *Publishers' Weekly*, February 19, 1944, 861–63, quote on 863.
12. John B. Hench, *Books as Weapons: Propaganda, Publishing, and the Battle for Global Markets in the Era of World War II* (Ithaca, NY: Cornell University Press, 2010), 21; Link and Hopf, *People and Books*, 70.
13. Figures come from Nolan B. Harmon, ed., *The Encyclopedia of World Methodism* (Nashville, TN: United Methodist Publishing House, 1974), 1:241, and *Publishers' Weekly*, March 13, 1943, 1190.
14. Norman E. Nygaard, ed., *Strength for Service to God and Country: Daily Devotionals for Those in the Services* (New York: Abingdon-Cokesbury Press, 1942). The book went out of print in the 1950s and was returned to print in the 1990s. See http://www.strengthforservice. org/.
15. A useful discussion of the ways reading relates to social and cultural power can be found in Carl F. Kaestle and Janice A. Radway, "A Framework for the History of Publishing and Reading in the United States, 1880–1940," in Carl F. Kaestle and Janice A. Radway, eds., *A History of the Book in America*, Vol. 4: *Print in Motion: The Expansion of Publishing and Reading in the United States, 1880–1940* (Chapel Hill: University of North Carolina Press, 2009), 7–21.
16. Gerald L. Sittser, *A Cautious Patriotism: The American Churches and the Second World War* (Chapel Hill: University of North Carolina Press, 1997), 6.
17. Biographical material on Beaird is scant. See *National Cyclopaedia of American Biography* (New York: James T. White, 1968), 50:197; Nolan B. Harmon, ed., *The Encyclopedia of World Methodism* (Nashville, TN: United Methodist Publishing House, 1974), 1:241.
18. Pat Beaird, "Religious Books and the War," *New York Times Book Review*, March 28, 1943, 6.
19. Beaird, "Religious Books and the War," 6.
20 Willard Johnson, "Religious Books in Wartime," *Library Journal*, May 1, 1944, 379.
21. Beaird, "Religious Books and the War," 6.
22. Beaird, "Religious Books and the War," 6.

23 O. Gerald Lawson, "Religious Books in the Life of Today," *Library Journal*, June 1, 1943, 453.
24. Beaird, "Religious Books and the War," 6.
25. Ellwood C. Nance, ed., *Faith of Our Fighters* (St. Louis: Bethany Press, 1944).
26. Richard H. Chase, "What War Does to Spiritual Sensibilities," in Nance, *Faith of Our Fighters*, 33.
27. Chase, "What War Does to Spiritual Sensibilities," 39.
28. Chase, "What War Does to Spiritual Sensibilities," 29.
29. Lloyd C. Douglas, "War and Religion," *Publishers' Weekly*, February 19, 1944, 864.
30. John E. Johnson, "The Faith and Practice of the Raw Recruit," in William L. Sperry, ed., *Religion of Soldier and Sailor: One of a Series of Volumes on Religion in the Post-War World* (Cambridge, MA: Harvard University Press, 1945), 45. The estimate was given in the context of other, precise figures for Protestant, Catholic, and Jewish affiliation.
31. "Dave" to Harry Emerson Fosdick, December 7, 1944, Series 2b, Box 4, Folder 11, Harry Emerson Fosdick Papers, Burke Library Archives at Union Theological Seminary in the City of New York.
32. Harry Emerson Fosdick, *The Challenge of the Present Crisis* (New York: Association Press, 1918). Fosdick later said this was the only book he regretted writing; he tried in vain to withdraw it from circulation.
33. Chaplain Marvin Wilbur to Harry Emerson Fosdick, February 13, 1945, Series 2b, Box 4, Folder 12, Harry Emerson Fosdick Papers, Burke Library Archives at Union Theological Seminary in the City of New York.
34. Harry Emerson Fosdick to Chaplain Marvin Wilbur, March 2, 1945, Series 2b, Box 4, Folder 12, Harry Emerson Fosdick Papers, Burke Library Archives at Union Theological Seminary in the City of New York.
35. Harry Emerson Fosdick, *A Great Time to Be Alive: Sermons on Christianity in Wartime* (New York: Harper & Brothers, 1944), 1.
36. The best accounts of the Council are Hench, *Books as Weapons*; Trysh Travis, "Books as Weapons and 'The Smart Man's Peace': The Work of the Council on Books in Wartime," *Princeton University Library Chronicle* 60, no. 3 (1999): 353–99. For other histories of the Council and its work, see Robert O. Ballou, *A History of the Council on Books in Wartime* (New York: Country Life Press, 1946); John Alden Jamieson, *Editions for the Armed Services, Inc: A History* (New York: Editions for the Armed Services, 1948); John Y. Cole, ed., *Books in Action: The Armed Services Editions* (Washington, D.C.: Library of Congress, 1984).
37. Hench, *Books as Weapons*, 51. Slightly different figures are reported in Ballou, *A History of the Council on Books in Wartime*, 3.
38. Hench, *Books as Weapons*, 52, 54.
39. Hench, *Books as Weapons*, 54.
40. Hench, *Books as Weapons*, 14.
41. Quoted in Travis, "Books as Weapons and 'The Smart Man's Peace,'" 371–72.
42. May 6—perhaps coincidental to this meeting, perhaps not—was the feast day of St. John the Evangelist, who was the patron saint of the book trades in England in the medieval and early modern periods.
43. Franklin D. Roosevelt, "A Message to the Booksellers of America," May 6, 1942, published in *Publishers' Weekly*, May 9, 1942, 1740.
44. See Daniel 3:19–30.
45. Franklin D. Roosevelt to W. W. Norton, December 1, 1942, reprinted as an epigraph in Ballou, *A History of the Council on Books in Wartime*.
46. Ballou, *A History of the Council on Books in Wartime*, "Appendix A: Financial Summary," 95.
47. Jamieson, *Editions for the Armed Services, Inc.*, 15.
48. Hench, *Books as Weapons*, 52.
49. Hench, *Books as Weapons*, 47.
50. Reprinted in Ballou, *A History of the Council on Books in Wartime*, 66.
51. Hench, *Books as Weapons*, 21.
52. In this regard, see Davis, *Two-Bit Culture*.
53. Travis, "Books as Weapons and 'The Smart Man's Peace,'" 363.

54. These classifications come from the Council's own classification scheme, reproduced in Ja-mieson, *Editions for the Armed Services, Inc.*, 17. In contrast, Eric Johnson, the wartime head of the Motion Picture Producers' Association, told members of the Screen Writers Guild that when it came to making movies during the war, "we'll have no more *Grapes of Wrath*." Quoted in Lary May, "Making the American Consensus: The Narrative of Conversion and Subversion in World War II Films," in Lewis A. Erenberg and Susan E. Hirsch, eds., *The War in American Culture: Society and Consciousness during World War II* (Chicago: University of Chicago Press, 1996), 71.

55. Travis, "Books as Weapons and 'The Smart Man's Peace,'" 388.

56. See, in this regard, Ballou, *A History of the Council on Books in Wartime*, 20–26.

57. Elmer Pease to the Council on Books in Wartime, July 6, 1944, Council on Books in Wartime Collection, Box 32, 20th Century Public Policy Papers, Seeley G. Mudd Manuscript Library, Department of Rare Books and Special Collections, Princeton University. Used by permission of the Princeton University Library.

58. David G. Wittels, "What the G.I. Reads," *Saturday Evening Post*, June 23, 1945, 11.

59. Ellwood C. Nance, "Ours Is a Reading Army," *Publishers' Weekly*, February 17, 1945, 841.

60. Joe to Archibald G. Ogden, December 12, 1944, Council on Books in Wartime Collection, Box 31, 20th Century Public Policy Papers, Seeley G. Mudd Manuscript Library, Department of Rare Books and Special Collections, Princeton University. Used by permission of the Princeton University Library.

61. Lt. J. S. Arwine to the Council on Books in Wartime, December 1, 1944, Council on Books in Wartime Collection, Box 31, 20th Century Public Policy Papers, Seeley G. Mudd Manuscript Library, Department of Rare Books and Special Collections, Princeton University. Used by permission of the Princeton University Library.

62. John M. Cuddeback to the Council on Books in Wartime, n.d., Council on Books in Wartime Collection, Box 31, 20th Century Public Policy Papers, Seeley G. Mudd Manuscript Library, Department of Rare Books and Special Collections, Princeton University. Used by permission of the Princeton University Library.

63. For a list of all radio interviews, see "Appendix B: Radio Programs," in Ballou, *A History of the Council on Books in Wartime*, 96–100.

64. Patti Clayton Becker, *Books and Libraries During World War II: Weapons in the War of Ideas* (New York: Routledge, 2005), 127–48.

65. Travis, "Books as Weapons and 'The Smart Man's Peace,'" 376.

66. Johnson, "The Faith and Practice of the Raw Recruit," 47–48, 66.

67. Pat Beaird to Board of Directors, Council on Books in Wartime, October 15, 1942, Council on Books in Wartime Collection, Box 18, 20th Century Public Policy Papers, Seeley G. Mudd Manuscript Library, Department of Rare Books and Special Collections, Princeton University. Used by permission of the Princeton University Library.

68. Pat Beaird to Board of Directors, Council on Books in Wartime, October 15, 1942.

69. C. B. Boutell to W. W. Norton, October 2, 1942, Council on Books in Wartime Collection, Box 18, 20th Century Public Policy Papers, Seeley G. Mudd Manuscript Library, Department of Rare Books and Special Collections, Princeton University. Used by permission of the Princeton University Library.

70. Martin Marty, *Modern American Religion*, Vol. 3: *Under God, Indivisible, 1941–1960* (Chicago: University of Chicago Press, 1991), 54.

Chapter 5

1. The most thorough examination of *Judeo-Christian* as both formulation and formation is Mark Silk, "Notes on the Judeo-Christian Tradition in America," *American Quarterly* 36, no. 1 (1984): 65–85.

2. Quoted in Kevin M. Schultz, *Tri-Faith America: How Catholics and Jews Held America to Its Protestant Promise* (New York: Oxford University Press, 2011), 58.

3. Deborah Dash Moore, *GI Jews: How World War II Changed a Generation* (Cambridge, MA: Harvard University Press, 2004), xi.

4. Schultz, *Tri-Faith America*, 49.

5. Schultz, *Tri-Faith America*, 47, 43.

6. Schultz, *Tri-Faith America*, 63.

7. Patrick Henry, "'And I Don't Care What It Is': The Tradition-History of a Civil Religion Proof-Text," *Journal of the American Academy of Religion* 49, no. 1 (1981): 41. Henry's article is an indispensible investigation of the history of this famous, and often misquoted and misunderstood, line from Eisenhower.

8. Silk, "Notes on the Judeo-Christian Tradition in America," 68.

9. Schultz, *Tri-Faith America*, 33.

10. Silk, "Notes on the Judeo-Christian Tradition in America," 69.

11. Quoted in Leonard Dinnerstein, *Antisemitism in America* (New York: Oxford University Press, 1994), 123.

12. Dinnerstein, *Antisemitism in America*, 127.

13. Dinnerstein, *Antisemitism in America*, 126–27.

14. Schultz, *Tri-Faith America*, 59.

15. In addition to Schultz, *Tri-Faith America*, for the history of the National Conference of Christians and Jews see also James E. Pitt, *Adventures in Brotherhood* (New York: Farrar, Straus, 1955). Pitt was a long-serving official with the NCCJ.

16. Benny Kraut, "Towards the Establishment of the National Conference of Christians and Jews: The Tenuous Road to Religious Goodwill in the 1920s," *American Jewish History* 77, no. 3 (1988): 392.

17. Kraut, "Towards the Establishment of the National Conference of Christians and Jews," 390.

18. Kraut, "Towards the Establishment of the National Conference of Christians and Jews," 402.

19. The list is compiled from "Aims to Harmonize National Groups," *New York Times*, December 11, 1927, and Patrick J. Hayes, "J. Elliot Ross and the National Conference of Christians and Jews: A Catholic Contribution to Tolerance in America," *Journal of Ecumenical Studies* 37, nos. 3/4 (2000): 321–32.

20. "Aims to Harmonize National Groups."

21. Schultz, *Tri-Faith America*, 15.

22. Kraut, "Towards the Establishment of the National Conference of Christians and Jews," 412.

23. On tensions within the NCCJ, see Benny Kraut, "A Wary Collaboration: Jews, Catholics, and the Protestant Goodwill Movement," in William R. Hutchinson, ed., *Between the Times: The Travail of the Protestant Establishment in America, 1900–1960* (New York: Cambridge University Press, 1989).

24. Pitt, *Adventures in Brotherhood*, 88–107; Schultz, *Tri-Faith America*, 35–40.

25. Schultz, *Tri-Faith America*, 40.

26. See "The Purpose and Program of the National Conference of Christians and Jews," *Journal of Educational Sociology* 16, no. 6 (1943): 324–26.

27. A small collection of documents pertaining to Dieffenbach's involvement in the Religious Book Weeks of the 1940s is located in the Andover-Harvard Theological Library, Cambridge, MA.

28. "Religious Book Week" press release, 1943, Council on Books in Wartime Collection, Box 18, Seeley G. Mudd Manuscript Library, Princeton University. Used by permission of the Princeton University Library.

29. The historians Joan Shelley Rubin and Janice Radway describe Canby as the dominant force at the Book-of-the-Month Club for most of the years from the club's founding in 1926 to his retirement in 1956. See Joan Shelley Rubin, *The Making of Middlebrow Culture* (Chapel Hill: University of North Carolina Press, 1992); Janice Radway, *A Feeling for Books: The Book-of-the-Month Club, Literary Taste, and Middle-Class Desire* (Chapel Hill: University of North Carolina Press, 1997).

30. Rubin, *The Making of Middlebrow Culture*, 110, 111.

31. From Canby, *Definitions: Essays in Contemporary Criticism*, quoted in Rubin, *The Making of Middlebrow Culture*, 116.

32. "Meeting to Observe Religious Book Week," *New York Times*, March 30, 1943.
33. "Works of Permanent Value Selected for Religious Book Week," *New York Times Book Review*, March 28, 1943.
34. *Forward*, Religious Book Week pamphlet, National Conference of Christians and Jews, 1944, 3. The complete collection of Religious Book Week pamphlets is located in Box 6, Folder 21, National Conference of Christians and Jews Records, Social Welfare History Archive, University of Minnesota.
35. *Jewish Book List*, Religious Book Week pamphlet, National Conference of Christians and Jews, 1944, 5.
36. *Protestant Book List*, Religious Book Week pamphlet, National Conference of Christians and Jews, 1944, 15.
37. *Catholic Book List*, Religious Book Week pamphlet, National Conference of Christians and Jews, 1944, 10.
38. "Religious Book Week" press release, 1943.
39. Quoted in Schultz, *Tri-Faith America*, 33.
40. *Protestant Book List*, Religious Book Week pamphlet, National Conference of Christians and Jews, 1943, 12–13.
41. *Protestant Book List*, 1944, 17.
42. *Catholic Book List*, Religious Book Week pamphlet, National Conference of Christians and Jews, 1943, 9.
43. *Good-Will Book List*, Religious Book Week pamphlet, National Conference of Christians and Jews, 1944, 21.
44. *Good-Will Book List*, 1944, 20; *Good-Will Book List*, Religious Book Week pamphlet, National Conference of Christians and Jews, 1943, 16.
45. *Good-Will Book List*, 1944, 20.
46. *Good-Will Book List*, 1944, 20.
47. "Religious Book Week Activities 1944," *Library Journal*, April 1, 1945, 303.
48. "National Book Week Celebrated May 6–13," *Pittsburgh Courier*, May 12, 1945; "Printer's Ink," *New York Amsterdam News*, May 11, 1946.
49. "Religious Book Week Starts May 4," *Publishers' Weekly*, April 26, 1947, 2221–22.
50. "Factsheet: Religious Book Week, October 24–31, 1948," Box 6, Folder 21, National Conference of Christians and Jews Records, Social Welfare History Archive, University of Minnesota.
51. "Spot Announcements and Station Breaks for Religious Book Week, October 24–31, 1948," Box 6, Folder 21, National Conference of Christians and Jews Records, Social Welfare History Archive, University of Minnesota.
52. "Spot Announcements and Station Breaks for Religious Book Week, October 24–31, 1948."
53. "How Libraries Have Observed Religious Book Week," *Library Journal*, May 1, 1944, 395.
54. O. Gerald Lawson, "Religious Books in the Life of Today," *Library Journal*, June 1, 1943, 457.
55. Quotes from "Suggestions for the Sixth Annual Observance, Religious Book Week," Box 6, Folder 21, National Conference of Christians and Jews Records, Social Welfare History Archive, University of Minnesota.
56. "How Libraries Have Observed Religious Book Week," 392.
57. "How Libraries Have Observed Religious Book Week," 392.
58. "How Libraries Have Observed Religious Book Week," 394.
59. "How Libraries Have Observed Religious Book Week," 395.
60. "Religious Book Week" press release, January 10, 1945, Council on Books in Wartime Collection, Box 18, Seeley G. Mudd Manuscript Library, Princeton University. Used by permission of the Princeton University Library.
61 See "Take a Bow: Michael Gross," *Publishers' Weekly*, December 30, 1963, 23–28; Michael Gross, "The Principles of Good Window Display," *Publishers' Weekly*, November 6, 1948, 1962–67. Gross created other innovations in book promotion, including the giant book.
62. For two theologically critical and theoretically sophisticated accounts of spirituality and consumerism in a more contemporary context, see Jeremy Carrette and Richard King, *Selling Spirituality: The Silent Takeover of Religion* (New York: Routledge, 2005); Vincent Miller,

Consuming Religion: Christian Faith and Practice in a Consumer Culture (New York: Continuum, 2005).

63. Leigh Eric Schmidt, *Restless Souls: The Making of American Spirituality from Emerson to Oprah* (San Francisco: HarperSanFrancisco, 2005).

64. Warren I. Susman, "'Personality' and the Making of Twentieth-Century Culture," in *Culture as History: The Transformation of American Society in the Twentieth Century* (Washington, D.C.: Smithsonian Institution Press, 2003), 280.

65. In this last vein see especially Nelson Lichtenstein, *Labor's War at Home: The CIO in World War II* (New York: Cambridge University Press, 1982). See also Gary Gerstle's helpful overview essay, "The Working Class Goes to War," in Lewis A. Erenberg and Susan E. Hirsch, eds., *The War in American Culture: Society and Consciousness during World War II* (Chicago: University of Chicago Press, 1996).

66. Frederic G. Melcher, "Religious Books for the Times," *Publishers' Weekly*, March 13, 1943, 1179.

67. Frederic G. Melcher, "Religion on a Common Front," *Publishers' Weekly*, February 17, 1945, 827.

Chapter 6

1. Elisha Atkins, "A Soldier's Second Thoughts," in William L. Sperry, ed., *Religion of Soldier and Sailor: One of a Series of Volumes on Religion in the Post-War World* (Cambridge, MA: Harvard University Press, 1945), 101, 106, 110.

2. Atkins, "A Soldier's Second Thoughts," 114–15.

3. Atkins, "A Soldier's Second Thoughts," 115.

4. See Will Herberg, "Reinhold Niebuhr: Christian Apologist to the Secular World" (1956), reprinted in David G. Dalin, ed., *From Marxism to Judaism: The Collected Essays of Will Herberg* (New York: Markus Wiener, 1989).

5. See David G. Dalin, "Will Herberg in Retrospect," in Dalin, *From Marxism to Judaism*, xiii–xxvii.

6. See, for example, A. Roy Eckhardt, *The Surge of Piety in America* (New York: Association Press, 1958); Martin Marty, *The New Shape of American Religion* (New York: Harper, 1959); Gibson Winter, *The Suburban Captivity of the Churches: An Analysis of Protestant Responsibility in the Expanding Metropolis* (Garden City, NY: Doubleday, 1961); James Hudnut-Beumler, *Looking for God in the Suburbs: The Religion of the American Dream and Its Critics, 1945–1965* (New Brunswick, NJ: Rutgers University Press, 1994). On a later period, but with similar theological concerns and equally influential, see Robert Bellah et al., *Habits of the Heart: Individualism and Commitment in American Life* (Berkeley: University of California Press, 1985).

7. Robert Wuthnow, *The Restructuring of American Religion* (Princeton, NJ: Princeton University Press, 1988), 36–37.

8. Wuthnow, *The Restructuring of American Religion*, 15–17.

9. Andrew S. Finstuen, *Original Sin and Everyday Protestants: The Theology of Reinhold Niebuhr, Billy Graham, and Paul Tillich in an Age of Anxiety* (Chapel Hill: University of North Carolina Press, 2009), 14.

10. The literature on neo-evangelicalism is vast, but of particular note on its ties to conservative politics in the postwar period, see Darren Dochuk, *From Bible Belt to Sunbelt: Plain-Folk Religion, Grassroots Politics, and the Rise of Evangelical Conservatism* (New York: Norton, 2010).

11. Finstuen, *Original Sin and Everyday Protestants*.

12. See, for example, Harold Bloom, *The American Religion: The Emergence of the Post-Christian Nation* (New York: Simon and Schuster, 1992); Christopher Lasch, *The Culture of Narcissism: American Life in an Age of Diminishing Expectations* (New York: Norton, 1979); Philip Rieff, *The Triumph of the Therapeutic: Uses of Faith after Freud* (New York: Harper & Row, 1966).

13. E. Brooks Holifield, *A History of Pastoral Care in America: From Salvation to Self-Realization* (Nashville, TN: Abingdon Press, 1983), 207.

14. See Susan E. Myers-Shirk, *Helping the Good Shepherd: Pastoral Counselors in a Psychotherapeutic Culture, 1925–1975* (Baltimore: Johns Hopkins University Press, 2009).

15. Holifield, *A History of Pastoral Care in America*, 221.
16. The best account of the war's impact on psychology as a profession and as a force in American culture is Ellen Herman, *The Romance of American Psychology: Political Culture in the Age of Experts* (Berkeley: University of California Press, 1995), 48–123. Nathan G. Hale Jr. takes up the somewhat narrower matter of psychoanalysis in *The Rise and Crisis of Psychoanalysis in the United States: Freud and the Americans, 1917–1985* (New York: Oxford University Press, 1995), 187–210. See also James H. Capshew, *Psychologists on the March: Science, Practice, and Professional Identity in America, 1929–1969* (Cambridge, UK: Cambridge University Press, 1999).
17. Eva S. Moskowitz, *In Therapy We Trust: America's Obsession with Self-Fulfillment* (Baltimore: Johns Hopkins University Press, 2001), 102, 105.
18. Andrew R. Heinze, *Jews and the American Soul: Human Nature in the Twentieth Century* (Princeton, NJ: Princeton University Press, 2004), 202.
19. Robert H. Abzug, *Inside the Vicious Heart: Americans and the Liberations of Nazi Concentration Camps* (New York: Oxford University Press, 1985), 19.
20. Abzug, *Inside the Vicious Heart*, 10, 39.
21. Abzug, *Inside the Vicious Heart*, 170–71.
22. Quoted in Marty, *Modern American Religion*, 3:63.
23. Quoted in Paul Boyer, *By the Bomb's Early Light: American Thought and Culture at the Dawn of the Atomic Age* (Chapel Hill: University of North Carolina Press, 1994), 277, 281.
24 See Matthew S. Hedstrom, "Rufus Jones and Mysticism for the Masses," *CrossCurrents* 54, no. 2 (2004), 31–44.
25. Rufus M. Jones, "Mystical Experience," *Atlantic Monthly*, May 1942, 634.
26. Jones, "Mystical Experience," 635.
27. Jones, "Mystical Experience," 641.
28. The authority on Liebman is Heinze, *Jews and the American Soul*.
29. Many of the letters to Liebman and Fosdick contain personal information conveyed to a pastor in confidence. In order to protect the privacy of these correspondents, pseudonyms are used, in the text as well as the notes, when referring to individual readers. Edith Fischman to Joshua Loth Liebman, June 23, 1947, Joshua Loth Liebman Collection, Howard Gotlieb Archival Research Center, Boston University.
30. Charles Edmonds to Joshua Loth Liebman, August 22, 1947, Joshua Loth Liebman Collection, Howard Gotlieb Archival Research Center, Boston University.
31. Excluding, of course, the sacred texts of various traditions, most especially the Bible.
32. Harold B. Clemenko, "The Man behind 'Peace of Mind,'" *Look*, January 6, 1948, 15–17.
33. Mark Hatch, "Writer of Clean Best-Seller Presents His Views," *Boston Post*, June 22, 1947.
34. "Publishers of Jewish Books Find Increased Market," *Publishers' Weekly*, February 21, 1942, 859.
35. Heinze, *Jews and the American Soul*, 238.
36. Heinze, *Jews and the American Soul*, 215.
37. "Fosdick's Last Year," *Time*, June 18, 1946, 56. At the peak of his popularity, Liebman received about two thousand letters per week, not an insignificant number.
38. Joshua Loth Liebman, "On Being a Real Person: A Discussion of Harry Emerson Fosdick's New Book," sermon delivered Friday, April 2, 1943, typescript in the Joshua Loth Liebman Collection, Howard Gotlieb Archival Research Center, Boston University.
39. Harry Emerson Fosdick to Joshua Loth Liebman, April 9, 1947, Joshua Loth Liebman Collection, Howard Gotlieb Archival Research Center, Boston University.
40. *14 Reader's Digest Books* (Pleasantville, NY: Reader's Digest Association, 1948).
41. On Merton the biographical literature is extensive, but most comprehensive is Michael Mott, *The Seven Mountains of Thomas Merton* (Boston: Houghton Mifflin, 1984).
42 Sydney Ahlstrom, *A Religious History of the American People* (New Haven, CT: Yale University Press, 1972), 1035.
43. The cultural impact of the bomb was immediate. The historian Paul Boyer quotes a critic from the *New York Times* who wrote on August 8, 1945, that the dropping of the atomic bomb was "an explosion in men's minds" (*By the Bomb's Early Light*, xxi).

44. *Life*, May 23, 1949.
45. Harry Emerson Fosdick, *On Being a Real Person* (New York: Harper & Brothers, 1943), vii.
46. Fosdick, *On Being a Real Person*, xiv.
47. Fosdick, *On Being a Real Person*, xi.
48. Fosdick, *On Being a Real Person*, 139.
49. Fosdick, *On Being a Real Person*, 19, italics in the original.
50. "Seven Evenings with Dr. Fosdick on 'Being a Real Person,'" flyer, Riverside Church Archives, New York.
51. Harry Emerson Fosdick, "The Possibility of Transformed Personality," National Vespers sermon, May 14, 1939, typescript in Riverside Church Archives, New York; Harry Emerson Fosdick, "Achieving Personal Integrity," National Vespers sermon, November 23, 1941, typescript in Riverside Church Archives, New York.
52. Fosdick, *On Being a Real Person*, xii.
53. Fosdick, *On Being a Real Person*, 34.
54. Fosdick, *On Being a Real Person*, xii–xiii.
55. Fosdick, *On Being a Real Person*, 213.
56. Fosdick, *On Being a Real Person*, 131, 233.
57. Fosdick was an early and active supporter of AA, speaking often at AA events, writing reviews and essays for AA publications, using Riverside Church funds to support AA meetings, and maintaining some correspondence with AA's founder "Bill W." Among other things, the AA founders and Fosdick each shared a deep indebtedness to William James's notions of the psychology of conversion. See Robert Moats Miller, *Harry Emerson Fosdick: Preacher, Pastor, Prophet* (New York: Oxford University Press, 1985), 281–82.
58. Fosdick, *On Being a Real Person*, 232.
59. See Richard Wightman Fox, "The Culture of Liberal Protestant Progressivism, 1987–1925," *Journal of Interdisciplinary History* 23, no. 3 (1993): 639–60. Gary Dorrien's remarks on Fosdick as a liberal evangelical came at the Liberal Theologies Consultation session at the American Academy of Religion national meeting in Philadelphia, November 20, 2005.
60. Miller, *Harry Emerson Fosdick*, 48, 37.
61. Fosdick, *On Being a Real Person*, 207, 190.
62. Heinze, *Jews and the American Soul*, 204.
63. Heinze, *Jews and the American Soul*, 204. Other biographical details come from newspaper obituaries, especially from the Boston *Sunday Advertiser* and *Evening American*, located in the Joshua Loth Liebman Collection, Howard Gotlieb Archival Research Center, Boston University.
64 Heinze, *Jews and the American Soul*, 205.
65. Joshua Loth Liebman, "The Road to Inner Serenity Today," sermon delivered Friday, April 4, 1943, typescript in the Joshua Loth Liebman Collection, Howard Gotlieb Archival Research Center, Boston University.
66. Heinze, *Jews and the American Soul*, 205.
67. Nathan G. Hale Jr., *The Rise and Crisis of Psychoanalysis in the United States: Freud and the Americans, 1917–1985* (New York: Oxford University Press, 1995), 191. See Roy Grinker and John Spiegel, *War Neuroses* (Philadelphia: Blakiston, 1945). *War Neuroses* was first published in 1943 in a restricted edition for military medical personnel.
68. Heinze, *Jews and the American Soul*, 204.
69. Joshua Loth Liebman, *Peace of Mind* (New York: Simon and Schuster, 1946), xi.
70. Liebman, *Peace of Mind*, xii.
71. Joshua Loth Liebman, "Reconstructing the Individual for a New Society," address delivered before the Woman's City Club in Boston, May 14, 1946, typescript in the Joshua Loth Liebman Collection, Howard Gotlieb Archival Research Center, Boston University.
72. Liebman, *Peace of Mind*, 14, xiii.
73. Liebman, *Peace of Mind*, 122.
74. Liebman, *Peace of Mind*, 124.

75. Liebman, for example, often quoted with approval the French Catholic philosopher Jacques Maritain, whose own rejection of scientific positivism led him first to Henri Bergson and later, after his conversion to Roman Catholicism, to the writings St. Thomas Aquinas.

76. Liebman, *Peace of Mind*, 195.

77. Hale, *The Rise and Crisis of Psychoanalysis in the United States*; Andrew Heinze, "Jews and American Popular Psychology: Reconsidering the Protestant Paradigm of Popular Thought," *Journal of American History* 88, no. 3 (2001): 950–78.

78. Liebman, *Peace of Mind*, 196.

79. Joshua Loth Liebman, "My Three Favorite Books of the Year," sermon delivered January 20, 1946, typescript in the Joshua Loth Liebman Collection, Howard Gotlieb Archival Research Center, Boston University.

80. Elise Stokes to Dick Simon, February 15, 1946, Joshua Loth Liebman Collection, Howard Gotlieb Archival Research Center, Boston University.

81. Joshua Loth Liebman, "How to Be Normal in Abnormal Times," sermon delivered Friday, March 7, 1943, typescript in the Joshua Loth Liebman Collection, Howard Gotlieb Archival Research Center, Boston University.

82. Liebman, *Peace of Mind*, 143.

83. Liebman, *Peace of Mind*, 69.

84. Liebman, *Peace of Mind*, 102.

85. Liebman, *Peace of Mind*, 141.

86. Liebman, *Peace of Mind*, 174.

87. Liebman, *Peace of Mind*, 173.

88. Liebman, *Peace of Mind*, 174.

89. Will Herberg, *Protestant-Catholic-Jew* (New York: Doubleday, 1955), 267. Herberg mentions Liebman by name only in a footnote. For a more recent example of this common misreading of Liebman, see Patrick Allitt, *Religion in America since 1945: A History* (New York: Columbia University Press, 2003), 16–18.

90. Thomas Merton, *The Seven Storey Mountain* (1948; New York: Harcourt Brace, 1998), 137, 113. Merton's title refers to the mountain of purgatory in Dante's *Divine Comedy*.

91. See "Books of the Month Appraised," *Catholic News*, June 28, 1947.

92. "Religious Books Currently Bestsellers—But Why?," *Boston Traveler*, March 22, 1949.

93. Merton, *Seven Storey Mountain*, 27, 24.

94. Merton, *Seven Storey Mountain*, 165.

95. Merton, *Seven Storey Mountain*, 53.

96. Merton, *Seven Storey Mountain*, 88.

97. Robert Giroux, introduction to Merton, *Seven Storey Mountain*, xvi.

98. Mott, *The Seven Mountains of Thomas Merton*, 84.

99. Merton, *Seven Storey Mountain*, 3.

100. Merton, *Seven Storey Mountain*, 3.

101. Merton, *Seven Storey Mountain*, 272.

102. Merton, *Seven Storey Mountain*, 410.

103. Merton, *Seven Storey Mountain*, 58.

104. Merton, *Seven Storey Mountain*, 11.

105. Merton, *Seven Storey Mountain*, 187.

106. Merton, *Seven Storey Mountain*, 94.

107 Merton, *Seven Storey Mountain*, 96, 97.

108. Merton, *Seven Storey Mountain*, 96, 97.

109. Merton, *Seven Storey Mountain*, 208, 207.

110. Merton, *Seven Storey Mountain*, 189.

111. Merton, *Seven Storey Mountain*, 192.

112. Merton, *Seven Storey Mountain*, 203.

113. Merton, *Seven Storey Mountain*, 204, 205.

114. Merton, *Seven Storey Mountain*, 214.

115. Merton, *Seven Storey Mountain*, 216.

116. Merton, *Seven Storey Mountain*, 220.

117. Merton, *Seven Storey Mountain*, 240.

118. Merton, *Seven Storey Mountain*, 231.

119. Merton, *Seven Storey Mountain*, 253.

120. Merton, *Seven Storey Mountain*, 333.

121. Most influential of Merton's many writings on Zen was *Zen and the Birds of Appetite* (New York: New Directions, 1968).

122. Fox, "The Culture of Liberal Protestant Progressivism," 647.

123. The literature here is extensive, but see especially Anne Braude, "Women's History *Is* American Religious History," in Thomas A. Tweed, ed., *Retelling U.S. Religious History* (Berkeley: University of California Press, 1997).

124. Andrew R. Heinze, "*Peace of Mind* (1946): Judaism and the Therapeutic Polemic of Postwar America," *Religion and American Culture* 12, no. 1 (2002): 40. On Hill and Peale, see Napoleon Hill, *Think and Grow Rich* (Meriden, CT: Ralston Society, 1937); Norman Vincent Peale, *The Power of Positive Thinking* (New York: Prentice-Hall, 1952).

125. *On Being a Real Person* was issued as part of series D, and Eisenhower's staff ordered eight thousand sets of series C and D books set aside for the D-Day force. These books were distributed in late May 1944. John Alden Jamieson, *Editions for the Armed Services, Inc.: A History* (New York: Editions for the Armed Services, 1948), 26–27.

126. Eugene Exman to Harry West, July 30, 1943, Harper & Brothers Papers, Rare Book and Manuscript Library, Columbia University.

127. Eugene Exman to Harry West, August 4, 1943, Harper & Brothers Papers, Rare Book and Manuscript Library, Columbia University.

128. C. C. Burford, untitled review, *Champaign News-Gazette*, April 25, 1943.

129. Frederick Gorman to Harry Emerson Fosdick, April 29, 1949, Harry Emerson Fosdick Papers, Series 2b, Box 3, Folder 2. First two ellipses in the original. Used by courtesy of the Burke Library Archives at Union Theological Seminary in the City of New York.

130. Benjamin Berry to Harry Emerson Fosdick, April 26, 1945, Harry Emerson Fosdick Papers, Series 2b, Box 4, Folder 11. Used by courtesy of the Burke Library Archives of Union Theological Seminary in the City of New York.

131. Capt. William Graber to Harry Emerson Fosdick, November 28, 1944, Harry Emerson Fosdick Papers, Series 2b, Box 4, Folder 12. Used by courtesy of the Burke Library Archives of Union Theological Seminary in the City of New York.

132. Pvt. Janet Royce to Harry Emerson Fosdick, n.d., Harry Emerson Fosdick Papers, Series 2b, Box 3, Folder 2. Used by courtesy of the Burke Library Archives of Union Theological Seminary in the City of New York.

133. Fosdick, *On Being a Real Person*, ix.

134. *Chicago Tribune*, March 12, 1943.

135. *Religious Book Club Bulletin*, March 1943.

136. *Protestant Book List*, Religious Book Week pamphlet, National Conference of Christians and Jews, 1944, 16.

137. *Christian Advocate*, April 29, 1943.

138. Walter Blankenship to Harry Emerson Fosdick, April 10, 1943, Harry Emerson Fosdick Papers, Series 2b, Box 4, Folder 11. Used by courtesy of the Burke Library Archives of Union Theological Seminary in the City of New York.

139. *Religious Book Club Bulletin*, May 1946.

140. *Religious Book Club Bulletin*, August 1952.

141. Edith Fischman to Joshua Loth Liebman, June 23, 1947, Joshua Loth Liebman Collection, Howard Gotlieb Archival Research Center, Boston University.

142. James Carlson to Joshua Loth Liebman, February 2, 1948, Joshua Loth Liebman Collection, Howard Gotlieb Archival Research Center, Boston University; Joshua Loth Liebman to James Carlson, June 1, 1948, Joshua Loth Liebman Collection, Howard Gotlieb Archival Research Center, Boston University.

143. Clinton T. Duffy to Joshua Loth Liebman, April 28, 1948, Joshua Loth Liebman Collection, Howard Gotlieb Archival Research Center, Boston University.

144. Lillian to Joshua Loth Liebman, March 15, 1948, Joshua Loth Liebman Collection, Howard Gotlieb Archival Research Center, Boston University.

145. A point made by Moskowitz in *In Therapy We Trust*, 165. See Ferdinand Lundberg and Marynia F. Farnham, *The Modern Woman: The Lost Sex* (New York: Harper & Brothers, 1947). As Lundberg and Farnham wrote, "Women are the pivot around which much of the unhappiness of our day revolves, like a captive planet. To a significant extent they are responsible for it.... Women as a whole (with exceptions) are maladjusted, much more so than men. For men have appropriate means to social adjustment: economic and political power, scientific power and athletic prowess" (24).

146. Elaine Tyler May, *Homeward Bound: American Families in the Cold War Era* (New York: Basic Books, 1988), 20.

147. See Catherine Marshall, *A Man Called Peter* (New York: McGraw-Hill, 1951); Anne Morrow Lindbergh, *Gift from the Sea* (New York: Pantheon, 1955).

148. See, most notably, Georgia Harkness, *Prayer and the Common Life* (New York: Abingdon-Cokesbury, 1948).

149. Lt. Kenneth Booth to Harry Emerson Fosdick, August 31, 1945, Harry Emerson Fosdick Papers, Series 2b, Box 4, Folder 11. Used by courtesy of the Burke Library Archives of Union Theological Seminary in the City of New York.

150. Benjamin Berry to Harry Emerson Fosdick, April 26, 1945.

151. Religion section, *Time*, October 11, 1948, 87–89.

152. "Trappist Monastery," *Life*, May 23, 1949, 88.

153. Promotional clippings, Box 33, Thomas Merton Papers, Rare Books and Manuscript Library, Columbia University. Used by permission of the Merton Legacy Trust.

154. Religion section, *Time*, April 11, 1949, 63.

155. Thomas Merton to Sister Therese Lentfoehr, February 25, 1950, Thomas Merton Papers, Rare Books and Manuscript Library, Columbia University. Used by permission of the Merton Legacy Trust.

156. Thomas Merton to Sister Therese Lentfoehr, December 27, 1948, Thomas Merton Papers, Rare Books and Manuscript Library, Columbia University. Used by permission of the Merton Legacy Trust.

157. Thomas Merton to Robert Lax, November 24, 1948, Thomas Merton Papers, Rare Books and Manuscript Library, Columbia University. Used by permission of the Merton Legacy Trust.

158. Herberg, *Protestant-Catholic-Jew*, 38. On the ethnic revival of later decades, see Matthew Frye Jacobson, *Whiteness of a Different Color: European Immigrants and the Alchemy of Race* (Cambridge, MA: Harvard University Press, 1999).

159. Herberg, *Protestant-Catholic-Jew*, 263.

160. On Peale, see Carol V. R. George, *God's Salesman: Norman Vincent Peale and the Power of Positive Thinking* (New York: Oxford University Press, 1993); Donald Meyer, *The Positive Thinkers: Religion as Pop Psychology from Mary Baker Eddy to Oral Roberts* (New York: Pantheon Books, 1980).

161. As with the Liebman and Fosdick letter writers, the names of the Peale letter writers have been changed. Raymond Anderson to Norman Vincent Peale, January 15, 1960, Series IB, Box 122, Folder "Power of Positive Thinking Book Testimonials," Norman Vincent Peale Papers, Special Collections Research Center, Syracuse University.

162. Ruth Lattimore to Norman Vincent Peale, September 18, 1953, Series IIB, Box 8, Folder "Problem Correspondence, K-R, 1953," Norman Vincent Peale Papers, Special Collections Research Center, Syracuse University.

163. Martha Weidner to Norman Vincent Peale, November 24, 1953, Series IIB, Box 8, Folder "Problem Correspondence, S-Z, 1953," Norman Vincent Peale Papers, Special Collections Research Center, Syracuse University.

164. Herberg, *Protestant-Catholic-Jew*, 95.

165. Liebman, *Peace of Mind*, 24, 123.

166. Heinze, *Jews and the American Soul*, 220.

167. Merton's biographer, Michael Mott, writes rather simply, "His autobiography was neither ecumenical nor restrained." See Mott, *The Seven Mountains of Thomas Merton*, 247.

168. Merton, *Seven Storey Mountain*, 223.
169. Herberg, *Protestant-Catholic-Jew*, 104.

Conclusion

1. Frank C. Laubach, *Letters by a Modern Mystic* (New York: Student Volunteer Movement, 1937), 17.
2. Laubach, *Letters by a Modern Mystic*, 10–11.
3. Laubach, *Letters by a Modern Mystic*, 14.
4. Laubach, *Letters by a Modern Mystic*, 20.
5. The biographical material on Laubach is of mixed quality. See David E. Mason, *Frank C. Laubach, Teacher of Millions* (Minneapolis: T. S. Denison, 1967); David E. Mason, *Apostle to the Illiterates* (Grand Rapids, MI: Zondervan, 1966); Helen M. Roberts, *Champion of the Silent Billion: The Story of Frank C. Laubach, Apostle of Literacy* (St. Paul, MN: Macalaster Park, 1961); Marjorie Medary, *Each One Teach One: Frank Laubach, Friend to Millions* (New York: Longmans, Green, 1954).
6. Frank C. Laubach, *Why There Are Vagrants* (New York: Columbia University Press, 1916).
7. Mason, *Apostle to the Illiterates*, 33.
8. Laubach, *Letters by a Modern Mystic*, 9–10.
9. Frank C. Laubach to "My Dear Folks," June 15, 1930, Box 1, Folder "June–December 1930," Frank C. Laubach Collection, Special Collections Research Center, Syracuse University.
10. Laubach, *Letters by a Modern Mystic*, 14.
11. Leigh Eric Schmidt, "The Making of Modern 'Mysticism,'" *Journal of the American Academy of Religion* 71, no. 2 (2003): 289–90.
12. See Robert H. King, *Thomas Merton and Thich Nhat Hanh: Engaged Spirituality in an Age of Globalization* (New York: Continuum, 2001).
13. Frank C. Laubach, *Prayer: The Mightiest Force in the World* (New York: Fleming H. Revell, 1946), 70.
14. Laubach, *Prayer*, 44.
15. Laubach, *Prayer*, 60.
16. Laubach, *Prayer*, 75.
17. Laubach, *Prayer*, 11.
18. Laubach, *Prayer*, 25.
19. See Joseph Kip Kosek, *Acts of Conscience: Christian Nonviolence and Modern American Democracy* (New York: Columbia University Press, 2009).
20. On Jones and Thurman, see Matthew S. Hedstrom, "Rufus Jones and Mysticism for the Masses," *CrossCurrents* 54, no. 2 (2004): 31–44; Gary Dorrien, *The Making of American Liberal Theology: Idealism, Realism, and Modernity, 1900–1950* (Louisville, KY: Westminster John Knox Press, 2003), 559–66.
21. "Dr. Frank C. Laubach, Crusader against Illiteracy, Dead at 85," *New York Times*, June 12, 1970.
22. David A. Hollinger, "After Cloven Tongues of Fire: Ecumenical Protestantism and the Modern American Encounter with Diversity," *Journal of American History* 98, no. 1 (2011): 22.
23. Hollinger, "After Cloven Tongues of Fire," 48.
24. See David D. Hall, ed., *Lived Religion: Toward a History of Practice* (Princeton, NJ: Princeton University Press, 1997); Laurie M. Maffly-Kipp, Leigh Eric Schmidt, and Mark Valieri, eds., *Practicing Protestants: Histories of Christian Life in America, 1630–1965* (Baltimore: Johns Hopkins University Press, 2006).
25. The example of Bronx Lourdes comes from Robert Orsi, "Everyday Miracles," in Hall, *Lived Religion*, and that of Sallman's *Head of Christ* from David Morgan, ed., *Icons of American Protestantism: The Art of Warner Sallman* (New Haven, CT: Yale University Press, 1996).
26. See Patricia Holt, "Harper's Spiritual Quest," and "Pennies from Heaven," *San Francisco Chronicle Sunday Review*, June 2, 1991.
27. See Leigh Eric Schmidt, *Heaven's Bride: The Unprintable Life of Ida C. Craddock, American Mystic, Scholar, Sexologist, Martyr, and Madwoman* (New York: Basic Books, 2010); Christopher G.

White, *Unsettled Minds: Psychology and the American Search for Spiritual Assurance, 1830–1940* (Berkeley: University of California Press, 2009); Michael Robertson, *Worshipping Walt: The Whitman Disciples* (Princeton, NJ: Princeton University Press, 2008); Leigh Eric Schmidt, *Restless Souls: The Making of American Spirituality from Emerson to Oprah* (San Francisco: HarperSanFrancisco, 2005); Ann Braude, *Radical Spirits: Spiritualism and Women's Rights in Nineteenth-Century America*, 2nd ed. (Bloomington: Indiana University Press, 2001); Stephen R. Prothero, *The White Buddhist: The Asian Odyssey of Henry Steel Olcott* (Bloomington: Indiana University Press, 1996); Thomas A. Tweed, *The American Encounter with Buddhism, 1844–1912: Victorian Culture and the Limits of Dissent* (Bloomington: Indiana University Press, 1992). Also relevant is the vast literature on transcendentalism; see especially Phillip F. Gura, *American Transcendentalism: A History* (New York: Hill and Wang, 2008).

28. See Michele Dillon and Paul Wink, *In the Course of a Lifetime: Tracing Religious Belief, Practice, and Change* (Berkeley: University of California Press, 2007); Robert Wuthnow, *America and the Challenges of Religious Diversity* (Princeton, NJ: Princeton University Press, 2005); Amanda Porterfield, *The Transformation of American Religion: The Story of a Late-Twentieth-Century Awakening* (New York: Oxford University Press, 2001); Robert Wuthnow, *After Heaven: Spirituality in America Since the 1950s* (Berkeley: University of California Press, 1998); Wade Clark Roof, *A Generation of Seekers: The Spiritual Journeys of the Baby-Boom Generation* (San Francisco: HarperSanFrancisco, 1993); Robert S. Ellwood, *Sixties Spiritual Awakening: American Religion Moving from Modern to Postmodern* (New Brunswick, NJ: Rutgers University Press, 1994).

29. Christian Smith with Patricia Snell, *Souls in Transition: The Religious and Spiritual Lives of Emerging Adults* (New York: Oxford University Press, 2009), 289.

30. "Pluralism—National Menace," *Christian Century*, June 13, 1951, 702.

31. See Shaun Casey, *The Making of a Catholic President: Kennedy vs. Nixon 1960* (New York: Oxford University Press, 2009).

32. On Peale, see Carol V. R. George, *God's Salesman: Norman Vincent Peale and the Power of Positive Thinking* (New York: Oxford University Press, 1993); Donald Meyer, *The Positive Thinkers: Religion as Pop Psychology from Mary Baker Eddy to Oral Roberts* (New York: Pantheon Books, 1980).

33. Paul Hutchinson, "Have We a 'New' Religion?," *Life*, April 11, 1955, 143, 144.

34. For some time scholars have fruitfully applied economic models to early American religion, yet the insightfulness of these studies need not mitigate the argument that American religious life has become *even more* amenable to consumerist approaches with the psychological and positive-thinking turn of the twentieth century. See especially Roger Finke and Rodney Stark, *The Churching of America, 1776–1990: Winners and Losers in Our Religious Economy* (New Brunswick, NJ: Rutgers University Press, 1992); R. Laurence Moore, *Selling God: American Religion in the Marketplace of Culture* (New York: Oxford University Press, 1994).

35. See John Lardas, *Bop Apocalypse: The Religious Visions of Kerouac, Ginsberg, and Burroughs* (Urbana: University of Illinois Press, 2001); Porterfield, *The Transformation of American Religion*; Robert S. Ellwood, *Alternative Altars: Unconventional and Eastern Spirituality in America* (Chicago: University of Chicago Press, 1979).

36. See Stefanie Syman, *The Subtle Body: The Story of Yoga in America* (New York: Farrar, Straus and Giroux, 2010).

37. *Many Americans Mix Multiple Faiths* (Washington, D.C.: Pew Forum on Religion and Public Life, December 2009). See also *U.S. Religious Landscape Survey* (Washington, D.C.: Pew Forum on Religion and Public Life, June 2008); Robert D. Putnam and David E Campbell, *American Grace: How Religion Divides and Unites Us* (New York: Simon & Schuster, 2010).

38. Laubach, *Letters by a Modern Mystic*, 13.

INDEX

Page numbers written in *italics* denote illustrations.

See also Armed Services Editions (ASE)
Eisenhower, Dwight, 144
Eliot, Charles W.:
  Harvard Classics (Five-Foot Shelf), 56, 57,
    240n64
  on Religious Book Week, 36, 56
Eliot, T.S., 69
Elliott, Harrison Sacket, 73
Embree, John F., 130
Emerson, Ralph Waldo:
  emphasis on religious experience, 8, 16, 17, 91
  influence on other writers, 91, 96, 97, 192–93
Emmanuel Movement, 74, 176
Esalen Institute, 109
ethical and mystical liberalism. *See* mystical
    and ethical liberalism
evangelicalism, 6, 12–13, 15, 24–25, 34–35,
    36, 54, 83, 104, 147, 174, 187,
    219–220, 223
Exman, Eugene:
  childhood and education, 91–92
  friendship with Fosdick, 92, 93–94, 99,
    100, 104, 107
  on mind cure, 100
  nonsectarian philosophy, 82, 90, 92
  photo, *88*
  spiritual explorations, 82, 88, 90–92, 106,
    107–13, 117, 216, 251n108
  support for Alcoholics Anonymous, 103–04
  tenure at Harper's, 82, 88–92, 95, 99, 100,
    101, 103–04, 106, 107, 108, 109,
    112–13, 205, 248n32
  and Wainwright House, 90, 111, 112, 217
  See also Harper & Brothers

Fadiman, Clifton, 210
Faith of Our Fighters (anthology), 123, 125,
  131, 133
Falls, Charles Buckles "C.B.":
  Lincoln poster for Religious Book Week,
    44–46, *45*, 47, 48, 49, 134, 135
  World War I poster, 135
  World War II Victory Book Campaign, 135,
    136
Farnham, Marynia, 209, 262n145
Farrar, John, 30
Farrell, Walter, 156
Federal Council of Churches:
  and crisis of liberalism, 7
  ecumenism, 182
  founding, 146–47
  goodwill movement, 147, 148
  and Hazen Books in Religion series, 61
  leaders of, 63, 78

and Religious Book Club, 66, 67
and Religious Book Week, 27
and World Literacy Committee, 218
See also National Conference of Christians
  and Jews (NCCJ)
Ferguson, Charles, 83–84, 86, 87, 90
Filene, Edward A., 147
films:
  during World War II, 133–34, 254n54
  tie-ins with Religious Book Week, 38
Finkelstein, Louis, 156, 158, 161
First Presbyterian Church, 35
Fisher, Dorothy Canfield, 127, 133
Five-Foot Shelf (Harvard Classics), 56, 57, 240n64
Fleming H. Revell Co., 28, 34, 84, 85
Ford, Henry, 145
Fosdick, Harry Emerson:
  and Alcoholics Anonymous, 104, 259n57
  The Assurance of Immortality, 186
  and Bruce Barton, 26
  The Challenge of the Present Crisis, 124, 253n32
  clash with fundamentalism, 34–36, 92–93
  commercial success, 82, 86, 93, 98–99, 178, 182
  and crisis of liberalism, 6
  depression, 187–88
  as evangelical, 187
  friendship with Exman, 92, 93–94, 99, 100,
    107
  as head of Riverside Church, 35, 78, 92, 93,
    97–98, 100, 186
  interest in mysticism and religious experience,
    8–9, 49, 94–97, 98, 184, 195
  interest in personality, 96–97, 168
  interest in psychology, 74, 94, 176, 177,
    179, 180, 182
  James as influence on, 93, 94, 97, 100
  letters to, 124–125, 182, 205–207, 258n29
  "A Man and His Books," 32
  "A Man and His Reading," 36
  Manhood of the Master, 25, 93
  on mind cure, 100
  namesake, 96
  and NCCJ, 147
  pastoral counseling, 176, 177, 184, 206
  photo, *183*
  radio addresses, 93, 97, 182, 186
  and Religious Book Club, 63, 78, 93, 94, 95,
    99, 150
  and Religious Book Week, 34, 35, 36
  Rufus Jones as influence on, 3, 93, 94, 97,
    98, 100, 185, 187, 188
  "Shall the Fundamentalists Win?" sermon,
    34–36, 92–93
  social and political activism, 97–98,
    124–25, 249n65, 249n69

CPSIA information can be obtained at www.ICGtesting.com
Printed in the USA
BVOW01s1357060315

390605BV00001B/2/P